This book provides an introduction to the distinctive features of nineteenth-century English in England, from spelling to text-types. It examines a wide range of varieties, including political speeches, newspaper articles, advertisements, obituaries, Sunday-school poetry and culinary recipes, in order to illustrate the range of dialects and levels found in the language of that period. The first part of the book provides an overview of the subject, while the second part contains an extensive selection of texts. A hundred exercises spread throughout the book serve to introduce the student to the problems and methods involved in English historical linguistics.

MANFRED GÖRLACH is Professor and Chair of English linguistics and medieval studies at the University of Köln (Cologne). He has written and edited some twenty books, mainly in the fields of Middle English saints' legends, English historical linguistics and English as a world language. These include *Introduction to Early Modern English* (1991) and *An Annotated Bibliography of 19th-Century Grammars of English* (1998). He is also the author of over seventy papers and numerous review articles.

English in
Nineteenth-Century England

An introduction

MANFRED GÖRLACH

CAMBRIDGE
UNIVERSITY PRESS

PUBLISHED BY THE PRESS SYNDICATE OF THE UNIVERSITY OF CAMBRIDGE
The Pitt Building, Trumpington Street, Cambridge, United Kingdom

CAMBRIDGE UNIVERSITY PRESS
The Edinburgh Building, Cambridge CB2 2RU, UK
http://www.cup.cam.ac.uk
40 West 20th Street, New York NY 10011-4211, USA
http://www.cup.org
10 Stamford Road, Oakleigh, Melbourne 3166, Australia

First published 1999

Printed in the United Kingdom at the University Press, Cambridge

Typeset in Times [A U]

A catalogue record for this book is available from the British Library

Library of Congress cataloguing in publication data
Görlach, Manfred.
English in nineteenth-century England: an introduction / Manfred Görlach.
p.   cm.
Includes bibliographical references and indexes.
ISBN 0 521 47101 X (hardback). – ISBN 0 521 47684 4 (paperback)
1. English language – 19th century – Grammar, Historical.
2. English language – 19th century – Social aspects – England.
3. English language – 19th century – Variation – England.
4. English language – 19th century – Dialects – England.
I. Title.
PE1085.G67 1999
420'.9'034 – dc2   98-53642 CIP

ISBN 0 521 47101 X hardback
ISBN 0 521 47684 4 paperback

Contents

Abbreviations

ABib	*An Annotated Bibliography*, with no. (Görlach 1998c)
ALD	*Advanced Learner's Dictionary*
AmE	American English
AusE	Australian English
BrE	British English
CED	*Chronological English Dictionary* (Finkenstaedt *et al.* 1970)
cf.	compare
ch.	chapter
CHEL	*The Cambridge History of the English Language*
DNB	*Dictionary of National Biography*
EB	*Encyclopædia Britannica*
EDD	*English Dialect Dictionary* (= Wright 1898–1905)
EL	English Linguistics reprint series
EModE	Early Modern English
EngE	English English
ENL	English as a native language
ESL	English as a second language
Ex.	Exercise
fc.	forthcoming
HMI	Her Majesty's Inspector
IrE	Irish English
lModE	late Modern English
ME	Middle English
N	Northern
NED	*New English Dictionary*
NGI	Neo-Latin and Greek internationalism
OE	Old English
OED	*Oxford English Dictionary*
p.c.	political correctness
PDE	Present-Day English
RP	Received Pronunciation
S	Southern
SOED	*Shorter Oxford English Dictionary*
SPE	*Society for Pure English*
St E	Standard English
T	Text (quoted by numbers; figures following obliques refer to lines)

Preface

The present book has been in the making for a long time. Ever since I completed my handbook on Early Modern English (1978, English version 1991) I intended to supplement it with a survey of a more modern period, a project outlined in Görlach (1995b), the summary of which forms the basis of my introduction to this book. While collecting material (and being side-tracked by other projects) the study of the neglected English of the 19th century saw a new wave of interest: the books by Mugglestone (1995) and Bailey (1996) and the publication of Romaine (1998) have changed the scholarly landscape of the period. I hope that my manual will neatly complement the other books; in particular, it might well serve as a handy companion volume to the much more comprehensive (and expensive) volume edited by Romaine.

The methods used in the present volume to describe 19th-century English and the didactic considerations employed owe a great deal to the two books which I published in German in the 1970s; both are now available in English (Görlach 1991, 1997) and can be used to supplement this study. I have not consistently indicated where I have taken over arguments or other material from the two earlier books. One of the most successful features of the two is here repeated – the use of a great number of contemporary texts from various genres to illustrate the linguistic realities of 19th-century England as far as this is possible from printed (rarely written) sources. However, it has not proved possible to correlate the introduction and the textual specimens very closely as I tried to do in my book on EModE.

The restriction to England is intentional and has been kept almost consistently: I am convinced that the export of English English to Scotland, Ireland and to the colonies overseas, and the divergence of American English, can only be documented by a corpus of texts written in England. In particular, we need to know what input produced the Englishes of, say, India and New Zealand – so far as this can be done through printed sources.

The selection given here does not make for a 'representative' corpus as defined in modern corpus linguistics. However, for the didactic purposes followed, a judgement sample is the best way to illustrate the characteristic features of 19th-century English, especially where differences from the preceding and subsequent period are concerned (cf. Görlach 1990c).

Acknowledgements

Many people have been helpful in bringing this book to a happy conclusion. It is a pleasure to thank Janet Bately, R. W. Burchfield, John Davis, Ian Michael, Colin Milton, Leigh Mueller, Lynda Mugglestone and an anonymous reader for comment and corrections; the staff of the Bodleian Library and the British Library assisted me in finding many rare books; Christoph Stephan, Katja Lenz an Ruth Möhlig have produced an immaculate computer printout, and Katharine Brett and members of the publishing staff of Cambridge University Press have assisted me by giving me an early contract, supplying advance copies of the contributions to Romaine (1998) and providing invaluable formal and stylistic advice.

I would like to thank the following publishers and institutions for their ready consent to print copyright material:
Bodleian Library, John Johnson Collection (T73); Cambridge Record Office (T70, T71); Cambridge University Library (T36, T85, T93–95); Clarendon Press (T52, T57); Collins Educational (T79); Columbia University Press (T43, T65); Evans (T75, T82); Faber & Faber (T53); Leeds, Brotherton Library (T58) and Sheffield University Press (T48).

Figures

Texts

III   On literature and criticism (T38–T51)   215

IV   On history and culture (T52–T98)   230

1

Introduction

1.1 *Motivations for the present book*

Interest in the history of English[1] has recently focused on more modern periods than the traditionally favoured ones of OE and ME. However, whereas EModE is becoming a well-researched field, the investigation of the language after 1700 has been more patchy. The 18th century has, for various reasons,[2] received more attention than the period between 1800 and 1900.

No comprehensive description of 19th-century English – in particular that of England[3] – has ever been attempted. And yet such a study promises to yield important insights, for the following reasons:

(1)   The sociolinguistic foundations of PDE were laid in a period when the population expanded tremendously, especially in the industrial

---

[1] The present introduction is based on a chapter in Görlach (1995a), itself deriving from a contribution to a 1986 conference devoted to the historical foundations of present-day European languages (Görlach 1989); this focused on German, but colleagues from neighbouring disciplines were invited to contribute contrastive sketches of a few other European languages. I have since translated my paper and greatly expanded it by providing a much wider range of topics and by including more recent research. Some of my arguments and data have since also been re-used in my discussion of the emergence of St E (Görlach 1990b).

[2] Note the excellent bibliographic coverage by Alston (1965–73), also connected with a comprehensive programme of facsimile reprints (English Linguistics) and the analyses by scholars like Leonard (1929), Michael (1970) and Sundby *et al.* (1991), which have no equivalent for the 19th century. Since the period 1700–1900 was too large a topic to be covered in a single book, the greater need of a survey for the 19th century led me to decide for the chronological focus here adopted. A complementary volume devoted to 18th-century English is in preparation.

[3] My survey largely excludes Scotland, Ireland and overseas Englishes; however, it should not be overlooked that the Scots made a significant contribution to the defining and implementing of 'proper English' – efforts which had a notable impact on the English of England; many texts from Edinburgh are impeccable specimens of St E and the contribution of Irish writers, from the 18th century onwards, to the literary English of Britain is noteworthy. I have also included a few quotations from 'Censor' (c. 1880); although the author was an American, his book was published in London, illustrating trans-Atlantic concerns of propriety. (Otherwise American texts are strictly excluded.)

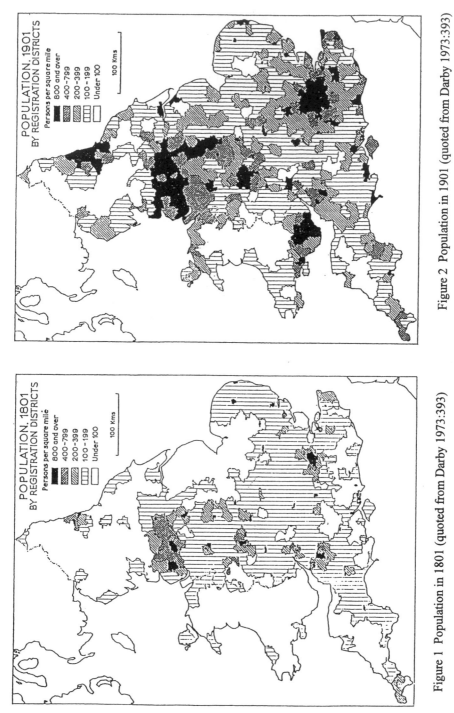

Figure 2 Population in 1901 (quoted from Darby 1973:393)

Figure 1 Population in 1801 (quoted from Darby 1973:393)

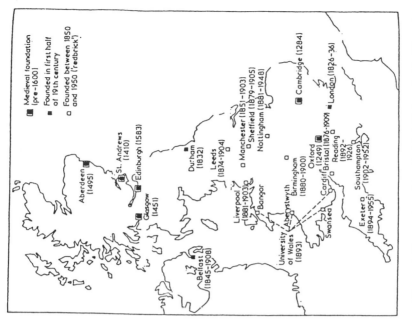

Figure 4 New universities (red-brick) founded in Victorian times (based on Bérida 1975:260, map 9)

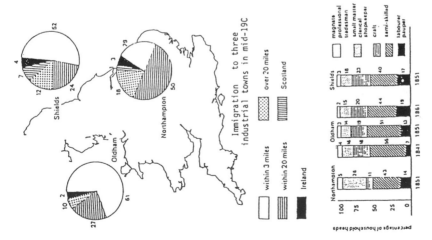

Figure 3 Social stratification in three towns (from Foster 1977)

urban centres (cf. figures 1–3), when the standard form of the language (St E) spread from the limited numbers of 'refined' speakers in the 18th century to a considerable section of the Victorian middle classes, and when general education began to level speech forms to an extent that is impossible to imagine for earlier periods.

Region/inhabitants	1821	1841	1861	1881	1901	increase %
England and Wales	12,000	15,914	20,066	25,974	32,528	+ 171%
Scotland	2,092	2,620	3,062	3,736	4,472	+ 114%
Ireland	6,802	8,175	5,799	5,175	4,459	– 34%
London	1,504	2,073	2,921	3,881	4,563	+ 203%
Urban England[a]	515	967	1,471	1,889	2,710	+ 426%
Urban Scotland[b]	360	567	787	1,127	1,628	+ 352%
Rural England[c]	544	705	781	801	822	+ 51%
Rural Scotland[d]	182	193	193	192	183	+ 0.5%

Figure 5 Population growth in the 18th and 19th centuries (rural vs urban, in different parts of Britain); figures, in thousands, are from Mitchell & Deane (1962). [a] = figures combined for Birmingham, Leeds, Liverpool, Manchester and Sheffield; [b] = Aberdeen, Dundee, Edinburgh and Glasgow; [c] = Cornwall and Lincolnshire; [d] = Argyll, Banff and Roxburgh

(2)   Comparisons between varieties of English in England and overseas are likely to provide evidence of the drifting apart of the colonial Englishes[4] in spite of the retarding influences of British administration, the schools, and the influence of the high prestige of London English on educated speakers world-wide. Moreover, a description of the BrE of the time is a necessary precondition for evaluating the British linguistic input in overseas Englishes – in regions where English is a native language (= ENL), like the American West, Upper Canada, Australia and New Zealand, the Cape and Natal, and in the great number of varieties of English used as a second language (= ESL) in Africa and Asia.

(3)   A comparison of English in England with standard languages on the continent may well permit interlinguistic insights into parallels and

---

[4] This divergence is widely attested for EngE vs AmE, where it also serves to confirm how 'British' the usage in the colonies was in the 19th century.

differences in development within the framework of an increasingly similar West European material culture. Such comparisons might also prompt new questions and the application of new methods in cases where it has proved fruitful to look at sociolinguistic conditions in one culture which have been neglected in another.

The aim of the present handbook is linguistic; my discussion and selection of texts was guided by the usefulness of passages for illustrating linguistic structures and attitudes to English. The final reduction from around 500 pages of excerpts to the 98 items or texts included in the book has resulted in the omission of many texts and authors that would have contributed to a more comprehensive, panoramic view of the times. Readers are requested to read longer texts by authors not represented, literary and expository, ranging from Byron to Browning, from Carlyle to Coleridge, from Darwin to Disraeli, from Eliot to Engels, from Gilbert to Gissing and from Macaulay to Müller. Coming from the present book they will be prepared to watch out not only for content and narrative, but also for linguistic structure and stylistic variation in these additional texts.

Ex. 1 Try to find evidence of 19th-century EngE features surviving ('as colonial lag') in exported varieties of English such as AmE or AusE.

1.2 *Historical foundations of nineteenth-century English*

1.2.1 *Periods*

There are no convincing landmarks in political history, the arts, economy or language development to demarcate a period within the boundaries of 1800 and 1900 as here accepted.[5] As the survey of events presented below suggests, the start of a new phase might have been marked by the social and economic reforms of the 1830s, a decade which also marked a watershed between the Romantic and Victorian eras, with the death of Coleridge (1834), Lamb (1834), Hazlitt (1830) and Scott (1832) and the first publications of Tennyson, Browning and Dickens. On the other hand, the beginning of the First World War saw a stable world going to pieces, a catastrophe also reflected in linguistic terms. It follows that there is no ideal

[5] DeKeyser (1975), when delimiting his time-frame to the 19th century, decided to look at the period roughly from one peak of prescriptivism, Murray's *Grammar* of 1795, to another, Fowler's *King's English* of 1906. If we wish to name the period between EModE and PDE (20th-century), the accepted term late Modern English (lModE) is to be preferred – but this would then, according to my classification, be divided into an earlier (18th-century) and a later (19th-century) subperiod.

decision and that many other solutions for the boundaries delimiting a period preceding the modern age are possible; for instance, 1832 to 1914 has many arguments to support it – or the period might be broken up into smaller units, such as

1776–1800	William Pitt's coalitions; the beginnings of the Industrial Revolution; the separation of the United States; the colonization of Australia and occupation of Ceylon and Malta; the start of the Romantic Movement; the end of Irish independence;
1800–1830	The final phase of the Hanoverian reign, predating the great reforms; Napoleonic wars and the Regency; Romantic poetry;
1830–1870	The great reforms; the Chartist movements; the heyday of capitalist industrialism; the expansion of literacy and printed matter; increased mobility as a consequence of railways;
1870–1914	Late Victorian imperialism and the last phase of global 'stability'; general education; modern communication.

These foundations form the basis of 19th-century English. It is obvious that the demographic basis of 'respectable' English expanded, but the details of this spread are still largely unexplored: the major histories of the English language from Brunner ([2]1960–2) to Leith (1983, [2]1997) pass over 19th-century conditions or provide inadequate information. Thus some of the major sociocultural developments of the 19th century can be enumerated as follows, starting from the beginning of an age of reform in the 1820s:

1824	the repeal of the Combination Acts;
1828	the emancipation of the Nonconformists;
1832	the First Reform Bill, which can be seen as a triumph of the middle class;
1833	the first important Factory Act restricting child work;
1834	the abolition of slavery;
1834	the Poor Law Amendment Act;
1838–48	the Chartist movement; publication of the People's Charter;
1846	the repeal of the Corn Laws;
1855	the final repeal of the Stamp Act of 1712 (making cheap newspapers available);
1867	the Second Reform Bill (1 million new voters) and Factory Acts;
1870	the Elementary Education Act (establishing compulsory education in the 1870s);
1884–5	the Third Reform Bill (2 million new voters)

1.2.2 *A survey of existing research*

Many of these facts are mentioned by Baugh & Cable ([4]1993:290), but they offer little in the way of correlation between social history and linguistic change:

The great reform measures – the reorganization of parliament, the revision of the penal code and the poor laws, the restrictions placed on child labor, and the other industrial reforms – were important factors in establishing English society on a more democratic basis. They lessened the distance between the upper and the lower classes and greatly increased the opportunities for the mass of the population to share in the economic and cultural advantages that became available in the course of the century. The establishment of the first cheap newspaper (1816) and of cheap postage (1840),[6] and the improved means of travel and communication brought about by the railroad, the steamboat, and the telegraph had the effect of uniting more closely the different parts of England and of spreading the influence of the standard speech.   ([4]1993:290)

Instead, their discussion (as in earlier chapters), is concentrated on the expansion of lexis as a consequence of scientific progress, with data drawn from the first edition of the *OED*:

> words, being but symbols by which a man expresses his ideas, are an accurate
> measure of the range of thought at any given time   ([4]1993:295)

– a sweeping claim which is not critically reflected on here or elsewhere in the book; in particular, it is evident that *social* reality cannot be captured by such an approach.[7] Note that two of the most important developments underpinning more widespread literacy are not even mentioned here – the abolition of the tax on newspapers (1855) and the introduction of general (basic) education, which brought the 'three Rs' within reach of all sections of society (1870).

The reasons for such neglect of the language of the period are not far to seek. traditional philology was not interested in the historical interpretation of recent states of languages – and even the major dialectological projects of the time (summarized in Ellis 1869–74, Wright 1898–1905) were 'historical' in that evidence from dialectal variation useful for the reconstruction of OE and ME was considered more important than contemporary conditions (cf. 2.5 below). Moreover, the masses of material available for the period

---

[6] For a few figures on the circulation of selected newspapers see p. 13 below; the number of letters trebled within three years (1.59 million per week in 1839 to 4.2 million in 1842, according to the *Newspaper*, 13 April, 1844) – but we would need to have a detailed analysis of the language used in them to see what the fact meant in sociolinguistic terms.

[7] There is nothing on the 19th century in Leith (1983, [2]1997), a book in which some treatment of the social and linguistic change in the period would be at least as urgently required as in Baugh & Cable. The authors necessarily depend for their lexical data on the first edition of the *OED*, which is notoriously weak on the period; the second edition of the *OED* was available for, but not used in, the fourth (1993) edition. The recent vol. IV of the *Cambridge History of the English Language* (Romaine 1998) is again somewhat disappointing in that the correlation of social, historical and educational developments with linguistic change in the 19th century is neglected.

are intimidating (no representative corpus of 19th-century texts has been attempted so far), and, finally, its distance from our own time has not been considered great enough for historical analysis.[8]

There is, admittedly, relevant research on the intellectual background and on the great research projects of the 19th century, especially the *OED* and dialectology. However, while Aarsleff (1967) and Crowley (1989) provide valuable insights into the abstract concepts underlying linguistic interest in the period, they do not cover the actual developments of the contemporary forms of English. Treatments of the history of lexicography and dialectology do not contribute substantially to the general topic of 19th-century English either – though for different reasons.

Two recent publications have begun to change the dreary picture sketched above. Mugglestone (1995) provided a detailed analysis of the interrelationship of social class, attitudes and linguistic correctness (almost exclusively related to pronunciation) based on statements found in grammars, dictionaries, conduct books and novels, a description which, however, suffers from the wealth of detail being arranged thematically, and is consequently not easy to follow in chronological development. Bailey's (1996) intention is much wider – his survey ranges from printing practices to sociolinguistic interpretations of pronunciation, from slang to changes in syntax; the failure to distinguish between data from Britain and the United States can, however, again lead to problems. In addition, the *CHEL* volume devoted to the period after 1776 (Romaine 1998) has set new standards; the difficulty with this collection is that it includes present-day conditions; thus, it is difficult to see the 19th century in its own right or in proper diachronic perspective.[9]

Ex. 2   How far do the authors of the books mentioned above distinguish between EngE, BrE (including Scotland and Ireland) and overseas varieties, esp. AmE?

---

[8] How difficult a proper evaluation of 19th-century niceties can be is illustrated by the insightful interpretations of stylistic variation and their social significance in Breen (1857) and Fowler (1926) – where the 'meaning' was obvious to language-conscious contemporaries, minimal stylistic distinctions can be lost on later readers who do not share the cultural and sociolinguistic background.

[9] The extensive collections by Harris (1993, 1995) make available major books and articles by 19th-century linguists and men of letters thus reflecting a helpful kaleidoscope of contemporary views of linguistic problems; however, Harris does not include any comment or interpretation – apart from his very short introductions. Also cf. Mugglestone (fc.) which is discussed under 'lexis' below.

Ex. 3   What is the relative value of different types of sources for socio-linguistic reconstruction? What is the danger of contemporary statements made by grammarians, schoolmasters and literary critics?

1.2.3 The seventeenth- and eighteenth-century background

Reflections on the state of EModE make it clear that the emergence of a linguistic standard came comparatively early in England, as a consequence of the early foundation of a nation state (which included Wales from the 16th century, and Scotland after 1603/1707), and the concentration of people, power and wealth in London (cf. Görlach 1990b); note in particular:

(1)   The homogeneity of 'educated' English as a written language (with the first signs of an incipient spoken norm) was largely settled by 1600; Puttenham (1589) limits the 'respectable' form of English to an area within sixty miles of London – a geographical boundary very similar to the regional basis of the standard in the 19th century.[10] This S BrE standard was described in detail by 18th-century grammarians and lexicographers, often with the explicit aim of ascertaining and fixing the norm, and after 1700 it began to become obligatory for spoken English, too – the public schools and the introduction of compulsory elementary education in the late 19th century made this norm available to much of the population. After 1700, the function of the court as an arbiter of correctness in linguistic matters came to be drastically reduced, the educated elites and schoolmasters taking over.

(2)   The classical period of English literature is that of Shakespeare's time; it includes the authorized version of the Bible, lyric poetry and scholarly prose, a corpus recognized by Johnson (1755) as the basis of standard lexis – with texts of the Augustan age in the early 18th century as a secondary peak.

(3)   The spread of the written standard in the 16th century (Görlach 1991) brought with it a stigmatization of regional dialects, which became

---

[10] Present-day concepts of 'northern English' are based mainly on the pronunciation of the vowels in *butter* and *castle*; although the regional split in the (ʌ) and (ɑː) variables is later than Puttenham, who must therefore have based his distinction on other features, the geographical basis for standard and prestigious norms has remained the same. In the 19th century this was reinforced by the prestige of Eton, Harrow and Oxbridge, all in southern England (cf. figure 4) – Lloyd's (1899) monograph which described N EngE as an independent norm was a scholarly treatment (published in Germany!) which was not intended to redress the balance. Note that even the area of 'Estuary English', a concept much discussed in the early 1990s, is largely consistent with Puttenham's demarcation.

restricted to literary niches such as pastoral poetry, satire and non-standard stage diction (in stereotypical form) before their scope was widened again in 18th-century Scotland and 19th-century England.

(4)   Latin had ceased to be used in textbooks and in university teaching by the late 17th century; in the school, curricula based on the teaching of the vernacular took over from the 18th century (Michael 1987). French was less influential in England in the 18th century than on the continent. Note that in the 19th century only small domains were left for either language, such as menus for French, or occasional epitaphs and university certificates for Latin.

1.2.4 *Population development, urbanization and the schools*

In what follows, I will try to summarize what is known about demographic developments, education and speakers' attitudes, and correlate these social facts with linguistic variation (dialects, sociolects and styles).

19th-century England provides a unique combination of philanthropic enlightened attitudes contrasting with the most appalling illustration of the excesses of early capitalism as reflected in child labour, excessive working hours, exploitation of employees, and living conditions with inadequate food, sanitary conditions, health care – and poor education. Much of this forms the basis of Marx's and Engels's sociological analysis (cf. Engels 1845); later in the century, 'British' industrial conditions spread with some delay and a certain amount of alleviation to other European countries. A pan-European view of the situation is therefore indispensable.

The upper and upper-middle classes in England (and in the major cities of Scotland and Ireland) had been affected by the standard language as defined by Johnson's *Dictionary* (1755) and the grammars of Priestley (1761), Lowth (1762) and L. Murray (1795), not to mention a host of smaller handbooks (cf. Alston 1965–72; Michael 1970, 1987, 1991, 1997), many of which were derivative, but very effective in spreading prescriptive norms among educated people throughout the country. However, Cobbett's example (1818) shows that this development had not yet reached the lower-middle classes: as an uneducated country lad himself, he learned English grammar from Lowth's work in order to pass this knowledge on 'for the use of schools and of young persons in general, but more especially for the use of soldiers, sailors, apprentices, and plough-boys', as the title-page of his own grammar informs us.[11]

---

[11] His intentions were expressed even more directly in a letter of 1817, when he justified the book 'with the ... agreeable view of instructing, in this foundation of all literary

Not all voices were in favour of education for all. Bailey (1996:29–30) refers to a parliamentary debate in which the scientist Davies Giddy (who was to become President of the Royal Society) opposed measures leading to widespread literacy, raising 'the specter of social discord':

> Giving education to the labouring classes of the poor ... would, in effect, be found to be prejudicial to their morals and happiness; it would teach them to despise their lot in life ... instead of teaching them subordination ... it would enable them to read seditious pamphlets, vicious books, and publications against Christianity.
>
> (Quoted from Bailey 1996:29–30)

The educational situation improved slowly but consistently in the course of the 19th century. Before compulsory elementary education was introduced in 1870, the responsibility for education was divided among many institutions. The £423,633 spent on educational support in 1856, according to the *Encyclopædia Britannica* (*EB*, 15, [8]1858:822) were divided as follows (in thousands of pounds, rounded):

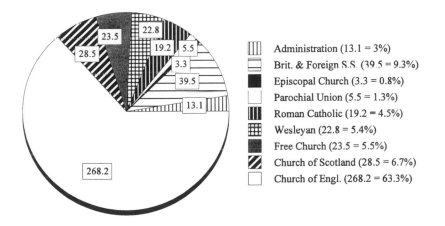

Figure 6 Educational support to individual types of schools, 1856

The money went into the following types of expenses:

knowledge, the great body of my ill-treated and unjustly condemned countrymen' (quoted from Cobbett 1823/1984:vii).

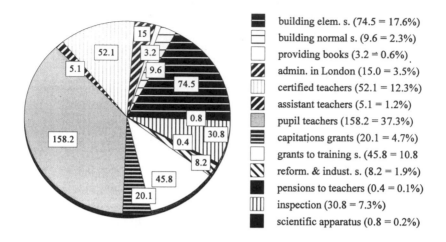

building elem. s. (74.5 = 17.6%)
building normal s. (9.6 = 2.3%)
providing books (3.2 = 0.6%)
admin. in London (15.0 = 3.5%)
certified teachers (52.1 = 12.3%)
assistant teachers (5.1 = 1.2%)
pupil teachers (158.2 = 37.3%)
capitations grants (20.1 = 4.7%)
grants to training s. (45.8 = 10.8
reform. & indust. s. (8.2 = 1.9%)
pensions to teachers (0.4 = 0.1%)
inspection (30.8 = 7.3%)
scientific apparatus (0.8 = 0.2%)

Figure 7 What the money was spent on in 1856

Seen from a modern perspective, these figures will come as a surprise on various counts. The Church of England schools (63.3%), with another 6.7% for the Church of Scotland, received more than two thirds of the money, leaving other ecclesiastical institutions far behind (Free Churches 5.5%, Wesleyan 5.4%, Roman Catholic 4.5%). As far as types of expenses are concerned, one is struck by the 37.3% paid out to pupil teachers; their number exceeded that of all other teachers: of the 14,843 teachers employed to teach 877,762 pupils in 7,454 schools, 69% were pupil teachers, but only 29.5% 'certificated teachers paid by government'. Pensions were almost unknown (0.1%) – and money paid for books, maps and scientific apparatus was less than 1%.

However, the statistics are misleading in so far as only the schools under inspection are taken into account. Many schools did not apply for grants, not wanting any interference. For March 1851, *EB* reports 43.8% of the population between the ages of five and fifteen attending schools (p. 823). Since attendance was still restricted, the Mechanics' Institutes continued to be important for the further education of workers who had not been able to attend school when young.

In the 1840s and 1850s, adult education is, then, as important for the expansion of literacy as is the teaching of the young. Hudson (1851, T77) provides a valuable survey of the extent of teaching offered through Mechanics' Institutes and similar institutions. There were in England 610 institutes, whose 102,050 members had access to 691,500 volumes; 16,020 persons attended evening classes and over 5,000 lectures were delivered in 1850. Many grammar books published in mid-century explicitly catered for self-teaching and adult education; thus Shelley's _The People's Grammar; or English Grammar without Difficulties for 'the Million'_ was intended as a 'manual in Infant Schools, the Nursery, and Day Schools, and especially in Night Schools and Mechanics Institutions' and aimed at 'simplicity, clearness and PRICE ... useful, especially to the mechanic and hard-working youth, in their solitary struggles for the acquirement of knowledge' ([2]1848: Preface).

However, historians of education agree that

> the most significant development in middle-class education, and the device that levered modern languages on to the secondary school curriculum, was the establishment in the 1850s of a system of public examinations controlled by the universities ... bringing some semblance of order into the chaos ... by setting and maintaining academic standards. There were schools of every conceivable type, private, endowed, denominational, and so on, and it was clear that some structure was required to distinguish the serious schools from the charlatans.
>
> (Howatt 1984:133)

What did the newly educated people read? They might be interested in the broadening of their factual knowledge, and the books read at Mechanics' Institutes were mainly technical in character, contrasting with the pious reading matter of Sunday schools. Chartists of the 1830s might prefer their unstamped papers, but most readers would be influenced by popular novels – and especially newspapers, whose number and distribution rapidly increased in the 19th century. The figures given by the _EB_ for 1854/57 can be summarized as follows: the total circulation of the leading _Times_ rose from 5,000 copies in 1815 to 10,000 in 1834, then doubled to reach 23,000 in 1844, and again to 40,000 in 1851; in 1854, an average of 51,648 copies were sold (1858:188). Although the circulation was exceeded by the _News of the World, Illustrated London News_ and _Lloyd's Weekly Newspaper_ (all just over 100,000), these were weeklies, so the number of individual copies sold (and stamped) was a third each compared to the _Times_ (cf. 1858:190). It is also worthy of note that the metropolitan papers had a great advantage over the provincial papers, until the invention of the telegraph made information universally and quickly available – and strengthened the position of papers published in Manchester, Leeds or Birmingham. (Of the 456 newspapers in England in 1857, the metropolitan–provincial ratio was 101–355: Liberal 40–134, Democratic 3–0, Conservative 20–90, Neutral 38–131.)

Books had become much cheaper from the 1830s/40s onward, but remained too expensive for many potential readers. Therefore the Public Libraries Act of 1850 gave a necessary foundation for the establishment of free rates-supported libraries, especially in the provincial towns. However, the reports we have of the situation in the 1850s are not always encouraging (Hudson 1851, T77 and T84 of 1862).

1.2.5 *Language teaching and grammar books*

How widespread the desire of the less educated layers of British society[12] was to improve their English (and to cater for the young) is shown by the great number of grammar books appearing at the time and may be illustrated by a selection of descriptive titles (taken from Michael 1987: 387–604, here chronologically arranged):

1800	Eves, Mrs. *The grammatical play-thing, or winter evening's recreation for young ladies from four to twelve years old.*
1802	Anon. *A grammatical game in rhyme. By a lady.*
1813	[Allan, Louisa]. *The decoy; or, an agreeable method of teaching children the elementary parts of English grammar by conversations and familiar examples.*
1815	Anon. *The adventures of Dame Winnifred, and her numerous family; or the infant's grammar.*
c.1820	Leinstein, Madame. *The rudiments of grammar; or, a party to the fair.*
1825	[Forrester, Alfred Henry]. *The holiday grammar, a Christmas present for the present Christmas, passing Murray, Dilworth, and all past grammarians in simplicity.*
c.1840	Corner, Julia. *The play grammar, or the elements of grammar explained in easy games.*
a.1845	Anon. *The Bible word-book; or, the rudiments of English grammar taught by the words of the Old and New Testament, classed according to the parts of speech, and arranged according to the number of syllables.*
[1854]	Guy, John. *The mother's own catechism of grammar.*
1854	Anon. *The heart's ease, or grammar in verse, for very young children.*
[1854]	Anon. *The rugged path made smooth; or, grammar illustrated in scriptural truths.*

Michael's (1987, 1997) statistics show that the increase in the number of books devoted to literary instruction was as marked as it was for grammar

---

[12] Phillipps (1984:67) quotes Kingsley's *Ravenshoe* (1861:ch. 50) to show that some sections of the upper classes might well not care so much about English grammar: 'When questioned by a lady about a point of grammar, Lord Ascot ... replied: "I can't say ... I was at Eton, and hadn't the advantage that you had of learning English grammar".' Hartley (1879:Preface) states his grammar was 'intended to explain and correct the common errors in speaking and writing, not only of the uneducated, but of those who have not looked into a Grammar since they left school'.

books – for both categories the rise in new titles was most spectacular in the mid 19th century (cf. p.17).[13] Books of this kind were adapted to the limited comprehension of the young and the educationally disadvantaged. Simple style was also required because, at least until 1850, the rules were usually expected to be learnt by heart (Michael 1987:347).

The writing of English grammars, already in full swing in the 18th century, continued. There is no exhaustive analysis of grammar books of English in the 19th century,[14] nor is there a reprint series such as we have for the earlier period (Alston 1967–70), but the sharply rising numbers in the last decades of the 18th century suggest that the production of grammar books continued unabated to cope with the demand from the growing reading public. Michael reports (1991) that there were at least 856 different grammars of English printed in the 19th century, as against 271 before 1800. The figures for the individual decades peak around the mid 19th century, but otherwise increase continuously – there appears to have been no saturation: 36 + 63 + 64 + 77 + 113 + 100 + 102 + 113 + 114 + 74. These figures are even more remarkable because reprints of 18th-century grammars, especially the classic works by Lowth and Murray, still largely dominated the field.[15] Michael's comparison with other types of textbooks (1993:6) shows that the numbers were almost identical for works devoted to literary study (but there was much more variation in the latter, whereas writers of grammars tended to copy from their predecessors). Michael (1993:5) summarizes the situation after 1830 as follows:

> The developments in society which had been taking place during the previous decades were now being reflected in the content of the books. National and church organizations were promoting textbooks in graded series; public examinations

[13] The figures given are still somewhat provisional, but Görlach (1998c) now provides an almost comprehensive bibliographical survey.

[14] The most comprehensive information available is found in Michael's works (1987, 1991, 1993). The microfiche collection of 19th-century books on linguistics collected by Alston and published by Chadwick-Healey (Alston 1992) concentrates on 'exotic' languages and does not aim at a comprehensive documentation of 19th-century writing on English grammar and usage.

[15] Scenes of grammar teaching are widespread in 19th-century novels (e.g. in *The Heart of Midlothian*); if a name is mentioned, it is likely to be Murray, as in *Middlemarch*, where much of ch. 26 is devoted to Mrs Garth's grammar lesson based on this author ('Mrs Garth, like more celebrated educators, had her favourite ancient paths, and in a general wreck of society would have tried to hold her "Lindley Murray" above the waves.'). Dickens has a playful discussion between Miss Peecher and Mary Anne on person, number and verb active in *Our Mutual Friend* (II, ch.1) and 'a parade of the jargon of a school grammar' in *Hard Times* (II, ch.3, both passages quoted in Brook 1970:84–5).

were beginning; education was a matter of wider, and more publicized concern than ever before.

More recent research (Michael 1997) has made us aware of the real extent of grammar writing in the period; Görlach (1998c) lists more than 1,900 such works dating from the period, not counting various textbooks which have some affinity with grammars. The surprisingly prolific production of grammar books in the period can best be visualized by the statistics in Michael (1997) which include some reconstructions of the dates of first editions which do not survive (figures 8 and 9).

However, proper research into the 19th-century tradition of grammar books has barely started.[16] With all their attempts at making English grammar teachable, not all writers of school grammars were convinced that their efforts were successful. Outis (1868:2) expressed such pessimism:

> In venturing to offer to the public some further remarks ... there may be but little hope of success, inasmuch as those who may feel themselves culpable will be numerically too strong a body to care about avowing their faults.

Others directed their efforts to readers outside the school, as William Lennie did: his grammar and key had the subtitle 'intended for ladies, junior teachers, private students, and others' or 'parents who assist their children at home'. Lennie's intention was

> not so much to rouse teachers of indolent habits from their lethargy, as to throw out a few hints which may perhaps be useful to those mothers who instruct their own daughters; to private students who wish to improve themselves, and particularly to young teachers who have not yet had time to acquire that experimental knowledge which is profitable to direct.   (Lennie [2]1816:Preface)

However, all these diverse considerations did not succeed in overcoming widespread concerns or prejudices:

(a)   Grammar was generally considered the dullest topic and greatly loathed. Attempts at making it more palatable by using rhyme (!) or

---

[16] A list of questions that future scholars ought to answer, now that the bibliographical data are more or less complete, is formulated in the introduction to Görlach (1998c). In particular, the enormous number of different grammar books remains a mystery (cf. Michael 1997). We should, however, keep in mind that although the number of new grammar books published each year is truly impressive, this should not be equated with their actual impact: Murray's *Grammar* and *Exercises* alone were more influential than dozens of grammars printed in very small numbers and used locally, some written for a single school.

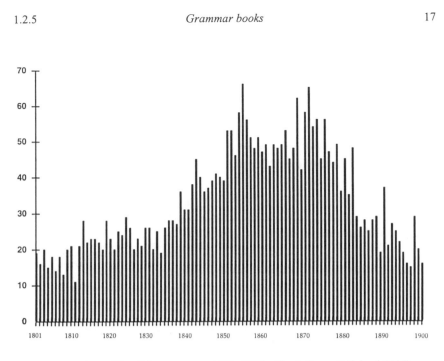

Figure 8 Number of English grammars, 1801–1900: all printings (Michael 1997)

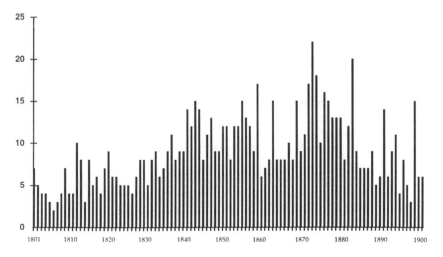

Figure 9 Number of English grammars 1801–1900: first printings (Michael 1997)

narrative form did not help much, nor did the conversational style, or the attempt to make memorization[17] easier through catechisms (which presented the matter in question and answer form). Mudie's grammar [1841] is a typical effort to overcome the tedium. A former editor of the *Sun* newspaper, he compiled a *Grammar of the English Language Truly Made Easy and Amusing, by the invention of three hundred moveable parts of speech* (with cards), justifying his innovation by harsh criticism of existing grammar books:

> Authors of 'School Grammars' by their utterly useless and contemptible exhibition of *frivolous* because already well known and well understood information, ... and by their ostentatious display of almost equally useless refinements and subtle distinctions ... – as the primary and ultimate objects of the Authors had been to terrify and subdue the spirit and to perplex and overwhelm the understanding of the Students, by the array of every thing likely to inspire them with the conviction of the impossibility of their ever comprehending a subject which has hitherto been rendered, by the mode of treating it, so abstract, and apparently both complicated and vast.   (Mudie [1841]:vi)

(b)   Authors continually complained that there was no accepted system, and doubted whether grammar would ever become a science. Introducing more 'scientific' topics such as comparative philology / history of English after 1850 served as a way of sidestepping an adequate description of grammatical structures.[18]

---

[17] Cf. the extreme form of rote learning advised by Henry Young:

> The rules of the grammar should be committed to memory, not in a superficial manner, but so as to be repeated without hesitation. In order to accomplish this, the pupil should go over them until he is perfect ... The mind, in its unexpanded state, cannot fully comprehend the nature of things; but if rules be indelibly imprinted on the memory, the learner will have in store a valuable quantity of raw materials for time and a matured judgment to digest.   (1832:xxiii, quoted from Michael 1987:347)

(A counter-movement came with the 'inductive' method offered in many grammars from the 1830s/40s onwards; cf. Michael 1987:364–8.)

[18] This distinction is made by Sweet (1891:4):

> But as the scientific study of language is more definitely expressed by 'philology', the term grammar is generally used to imply a mainly practical analysis of one special language, in which study general principles and theoretical explanations are subordinated to concise statements of facts, and definite rules.

An insightful summary still worth consulting is the anonymous assessment of six of the leading grammars published in 1870–3 in the *London Quarterly Review* of April 1874 (reprinted in Harris 1995:II, 154–81).

This uncertainty may explain why adequate (scholarly and really comprehensive) grammars of English were first written by continental authors – Mätzner, Koch, Jespersen, Poutsma and others.

The traditional division of grammar into orthography, etymology, syntax and prosody was obviously difficult to overcome. Grammarians might well question whether the first and last section should be included at all (etymology was still understood mainly as 'morphology'), but they would not break with tradition – Johnson had failed to do so in the grammar prefixed to his *Dictionary* (1755).[19] More damaging to a scholarly and adequate description of English was the dominance of 'parsing': here the definition of parts of speech had obviously become an end in itself, and it showed the continuing impact of Latin (however progressive the authors of the individual grammars might wish to appear). Moreover, a strong tradition still kept up the 18th-century quest for a 'universal' grammar, with arguments mainly based on the works of Harris or, alternatively, Horne Tooke – and since Latin and Greek were still considered more perfect than other languages, the pattern of the classical languages remained very influential – however indirectly – in this tradition too.

However, the following two new developments tended to call for qualitative changes (cf. Aarsleff 1967, Leitner 1986, Michael 1991):

(a) The 'invention' of the historical-comparative method in linguistics profoundly influenced the scholarly concept of grammar; it not only helped to focus descriptions more on genetic explanations, but also to create a new definition for etymology.[20]

[19] Hazlitt's excuse (1810:2) is quite typical of the more thoughtful writers of grammar books:

> In connection with grammar, Orthography, Punctuation, and Prosody have been usually treated of. The rules for pointing are indeed best explained by a reference to grammatical construction; those of spelling and pronunciation are quite independent of it. But as something of this kind is expected in grammar, and as our plan might seem defective without it, we shall consider them in the same order as they generally occur.

He accordingly expresses the marginality of the above topics by the number of pages devoted to them: Orthography (3–13), Etymology (14–99), Syntax (100–42), Prosody (143–4), Punctuation (145–7), Capitals (148) – a solution which is widespread in 19th-century grammars.

[20] Leitner (1986:1346–7) rightly points out that school grammars made little contribution to the advancement of syntax and etymology, but that there is much complexity in traditional grammars which shows that 'even the valuable distinction between "school" and "scholarly" grammars is an oversimplification' (1986:1347). Although the thinking of Max Müller was highly popular and influential among the educated, its impact on the teaching of English was quite marginal.

(b)   Advances in scientific phonetics raised hopes that the objective description and measurability of linguistic phenomena might become possible, yielding results as certain as those of the natural sciences.[21]

As the century progressed, grammatical correctness became even more important, and did so for a much larger section of the population than it had ever done before – for all the efforts of 18th-century prescriptive grammarians, whose advice had affected only a few people.

Cobbett's grammar documents a process of democratization taking place in popular attitudes,[22] the author (like Lowth before him) criticizing the language of people in authority, and claiming the right to append 'six lessons, intended to prevent statesmen from using false grammar, and from writing in an awkward manner' (1984:145–79). The interrelationship between correct language and power which was beginning to change around 1800 deserves special attention. Fairman (1986, following Smith 1984) describes the correlation between the success of petitions and the language they were couched in. Thomas Paine deliberately wrote *The Rights of Man* (1790) in a plain style in order to demonstrate that this does not preclude precision of thought and expression – a topic also of great concern for Cobbett.

The rapid growth of towns (cf. figures 1–3), and the deplorable condition of migrants, make it likely that literacy rates decreased in England in the early 19th century, in spite of attempts to raise the standard of (basic) education, especially through Sunday schools run by the churches (cf. Howatt 1984, Michael 1987). Gordon sees the later expansion of literacy as a consequence mainly of cheaper reading material and a much greater number of readers:

> The nineteenth century saw for the first time a concerted, and in the long term successful, effort to make readers of the labouring poor in the country and the industrial towns. The educational writings of the Edgeworths, the technique of class instruction associated with Bell and Lancaster, the growth from the late

[21] Linguistics, many would have claimed, has obvious parallels with biology: stemmas were used in similar ways to present the historical classification of both species and languages; language death (a consequence of the 'survival of the fittest'?) can be seen as similar to the extinction of animals, etc. (For the intellectual background of 19th-century linguistic thinking, cf. Aarsleff 1967.)

[22] His radical persuasions made the book suspect for many, however much they might praise Cobbett's breakaway from the Latin-based description (as Weldon did in his school grammar of 1848; cf. Bradley's *The Writer's and Student's Grammar of the English Language; After the Model of that by W. Cobbett, but Divested of all Political Illustrations and Offensive Personal Allusions* of 1838). Exercises using 'false English' were of course more widespread. Michael (1987:350) says that their popularity was 'immense during the 1790s, [and] continued until about 1820'.

eighteenth century of Sunday schools, the establishment in 1811 of the National
Society for Promoting the Education of the Poor, and in 1814 of its rival the
British and Foreign School Society led by 1833 to the first parliamentary grant for
elementary education and ultimately to the Act of 1870. By the end of the nineteenth century the printed word was open to all.   (Gordon 1966:153)

However, the first generation of urban dwellers, who came from neighbouring villages and, as the century progressed, from Scotland (as a consequence of the Highland Clearances) and Ireland (after the great famine of
1847), spoke forms of English quite distant from the norms observed in the
schools (cf. Altick 1957, Webb 1955). This situation started to change effectively only after the introduction of general education in 1870.

Various economic developments were essential for the explosive growth
of the printed media: the introduction of fast and cheap printing techniques
in the 1830s, the repeal of the stamp duty for newspapers in 1855 and the
abolition of tax on paper (widely seen as a 'tax on knowledge') in 1861.
(The production of paper in Britain rose from 11,000 tons in 1800 to
100,000 in 1860 and 652,000 in 1900; see Bailey 1996:40.) Finally, the fact
that prices for books remained quite high until the 1840s–50s caused a
noteworthy boom of the circulating libraries. The great expansion of literacy after 1840 had important effects on the spread of St E in written form –
and on a democratization (some might say, a vulgarization) of styles in
literature and especially in journalism (cf. 7.1.5). Outis (1868:2) is representative of such conservative criticism. He recommended the perusal of
pamphlets on the proper use of *shall* and *will* and on the difference between
adjectives and adverbs to:

> all contributors to penny publications, periodicals, newspaper reports, to many
> novelists, and even to some writers of what are called leading articles in the in-
> fluential daily journals. And, ... he begs leave to suggest to all those persons, who,
> having been denied the advantages of a complete education, were irresistably pro-
> pelled, from a sense of literary capability, to teach, or take up the pen, that they
> should procure themselves a copy.

1.2.6 *The rise of a standard*

The moves that led to a greater homogeneity of English are discussed in
detail under the individual levels below. In general, it is quite clear that the
radical changes in the structure of the English society had far-ranging effects on the sociolects of EngE. Wyld (1921/36:285) speaks of 'the new
English', 'new-fangled English' and 'improved English' – somewhat impressionistic categories which have since been refined by research by
Honey (1988) and Finegan (1998).

Alford, one of the most dedicated fighters for 'proper' linguistic norms summarized the standard under the label of the 'Queen's English' 'which the nation, in the secular unfolding of its will and habits, has agreed to speak and write' (T16/19–23). He goes on to elaborate on the metaphor in great detail.

Trench, one of the most important figures as far as the English language in the 19th century is concerned, even connected the maintaining of linguistic standards with proper morals and religion, fearing that a decline in language would also be reflected in the moral standards of the community (1851, T11). That such attitudes were widespread is suggested by Honey's analysis of reports by HMIs:

> A report that children who on leaving school for work 'become much worse in their language and manners' clearly means 'bad' language in the moral sense. Indeed, morality, character, discipline, punctuality, hygiene, 'general intelligence and moral tone', truthfulness, 'habits of industry' are the preoccupations of HMIs, *not* accent or dialect.   (1988:219)

The question of how the norms that formed the basis for the standard language were to be established remained undecided, although the adherents of 'analogy' (by which correctness was to be established by inner-language regularities) had lost ground since the 18th century. However, there were writers like Alexander ([4]1832, T5), who lashed out against the mistaken faith in custom, and Lambe in 1849 even spoke of the appeal to usage as the 'miserable doctrine of conventionality [which] has made our language the wilderness it is' (1849:38). Grammarians who believed in 'reason' were likely to insist on the normative power of Latin, whereas the more liberal writers might stress the independence of English structures. However, there were few as progressive as the contributor to the *EB* ([8]1857, 'Grammar'), who praised the *advantages* of English (T13).

Even though those who claimed that custom – the usage of the educated and powerful elite – determined what was right and wrong had the support of authorities ranging from Horace and Quintilian to Lowth and Murray, many paid only lipservice to the concept. Whenever linguistic change happened, the argument was likely to be that it was not sanctioned by usage.[23] Few writers were as enlightened as Sweet, who stated in 1891:

---

[23] The practice of including specimens of 'false grammar', with illustrations taken from 'the best writers' – a regular section of grammars between 1762 and the 1840s – cannot have strengthened trust in the reliability of custom, if the usage of texts ranging from the Authorized Version to Murray's *Grammar* was not good enough – even without Cobbett's iconoclastic intentions when he listed in Letter xxii 'Errors and nonsense in a king's speech' (1823, and cf. T3).

> In considering the use of grammar as a corrective of what are called 'ungrammatical' expressions, it must be borne in mind that the rules of grammar have no value except as statements of facts: whatever is in general use in a language is for that very reason grammatically correct. A vulgarism and the corresponding standard or polite expression are equally grammatical – each in its own sphere – if only they are in general use. But whenever usage is not fixed – whenever we hesitate between different ways of expression, or have to find a new way of expression – then grammar comes in, and helps us to decide which expression is most in accordance with the genius of the language, least ambiguous, most concise, or in any other way better fitted to express what is required. (1891:5)

Although the idea of an academy had more or less been given up as impossible to implement, there are occasional 19th-century references to how desirable such an institution would be to regulate usage – such as Heald's:

> It is to be regretted that in this country there exists no Philological Academy, with authority to decide on all matters connected with the English language, and from whose judgment there should be no appeal. Under present conditions erudite but irresponsible persons issue dictionaries and grammars, in many instances expressing views at variance with the result that frequently, on the particular points on which he desires instruction, the inquirer finds himself left in a state of uncertainty ... Were an Academy of Philology established, and granted a Royal charter, its first members being the various Professors of the English language and the leading men of letters of the day, it would speedily attain an unassailable position as the recognised literary authority and, in a short time, all ... would conform to its decisions. (²1898:7)

Likewise, the regional basis – the speech of educated Southerners – had been settled for centuries, and there were few disagreeing voices. Whereas Alford quotes Latham's statement that the best English was spoken between Huntingdon and Stamford, Lloyd, a partizan of N English went further:

> During the present century the criterion of good English has ceased to be metropolitan, and has become national. Its standard is no longer the practice of London, but the average practice of educated men throughout the kingdom. It is admitted by historians of the language that, if London tendencies had had their way, the letter *h* would have long ago become as silent in London as it has long been in Paris, and that the characteristic sound of *wh* and *ng* would ere now have vanished from the language. But these tendencies have been defeated by the resistance of the nation, and especially the North. At present London seems bent on deleting the letter *r*, but without much success outside her own immediate neighbourhood. Still, the influence of the metropolis is very great, and there is much fear lest thereby the English of these islands may be led into an insular course of development which would be fatal to its world-wide mission. (1897/1995, II:374)

1.2.7 *The makers of nineteenth-century English*

How far do individuals influence the language of their times? Little, we might expect looking at the impact that the schools and the media have – and have had from the 19th century onwards. However, there are a few authors whose works were so widespread that we must attribute some influence to their writings. This can range from individual phrases to particular styles and notions of what is correct and proper. Many English authors come to mind from earlier centuries such as in

(a)   literature: Chaucer (14th), Caxton (15th), Shakespeare (16th), Milton and Dryden (17th), Addison and Pope (18th)

(b)   religion: Tyndale (16th, also in his indirect impact through the Authorized Version), Bunyan (17th), Wesley (18th)

(c)   linguistics: Johnson, Lowth, Murray (18th)

There is nothing to compare for the 19th century, as Bradley found:

> It is not unlikely that the future historian of the English language may find that its development in the 19th century has been less powerfully affected by the really great writers of the period than by authors of inferior rank, both British and American, who have had a knack of inventing new turns of expression which commended themselves to general imitation. There never was a time when a clever novelty in combination of words, or an ingenious perversion of the accepted meaning of a word, had so good a chance of becoming a permanent possession of the language, as now ... we may easily be tempted to think that the future of literary English is in the hands of writers of defective culture and little seriousness of purpose, and that the language must suffer grave injury in the loss of its laboriously won capacities for precision, and in the debasement of words of noble import by unworthy use.   (1904:238–9)

We obviously have to distinguish (as Sweet does in 1891:v) between non-standard (dialect, vulgarisms), and literary and educated, English. While it is obvious that the 19th century did not contribute much to a homogeneous poetic diction, a number of writers broadened the scope of literary writing and became influential by covering new ground stylistically and by the great number of their readers (Dickens, and in a way Scott, and a vast range of other writers ranging from Jane Austen to Oscar Wilde).[24]

---

[24] No information on numbers of copies published is available (from which we could draw cautious conclusions on the number of readers and form hypotheses on the individual authors' impact as models of good style); although the methodological problems of such research are immense, even provisional findings might contribute a great deal to our understanding of how written standards developed in the crucial period between 1830 and 1870.

By contrast, many authors praised for their literary value or conspicuousness had little influence. A typical case is provided by Hopkins's work which has supplied a great number of *OED* entries, but whose work was largely published twenty-nine years after his death in 1889. A survey illustrating the life dates and periods of literary activity of 19th-century authors is therefore not to be equated with their contribution to 'the making of English'.

On a different level, the influence of grammarians and lexicographers is unique in the period. Some dictionaries (by Johnson 1755, and Walker 1791) continued to form the gauge of correctness, as did the grammars by Lowth (1762) and L. Murray (1795). 19th-century highlights in these areas were more elitist and had, therefore, less impact – the adoption of 'philology', the making of the *OED* (cf. 6.1.2) and scientific dialectology. The excellent survey of 19th-century linguistics by Aarsleff (1967) shows how little the discipline contributed to our understanding of the actual development of English.

1.2.8 *Languages spoken in England*

My discussion has concentrated exclusively on the English language so far. Other languages spoken natively had in fact become quite marginal in 19th-century England – nearly all speakers used English, although most did so in dialect form (cf. 2.3). There were no native speech communities of England's Celtic languages left, even though the neighbouring territories of Wales, the Isle of Man, Scotland and Ireland supplied England with a continuous stream of Celtic-speaking immigrants. French (and Anglo-Norman dialect) were much stronger on the Channel Islands than today.

The major non-English languages spoken in 19th-century England are then:

(1)   Immigrant Celtic, especially Irish in the urban centres of the west (Liverpool, Manchester, etc.) and London (cf. Mayhew 1851).

(2)   Immigrant Yiddish, mainly in London, from the 1880s onward, as a consequence of pogroms in Eastern Europe.

(3)   Romany, for many Gypsies still a full language in the 19th century – a fact of which many Englishmen became aware through G. H. Borrow's novels *Lavengro* (1851) and *Romany Rye* (1857).

Other immigrant languages are mainly a feature of 20th-century Britain (Caribbean, African, Asian, etc.).

Regional and social varieties

2.1   *Attitudes*

In spite of the documentation quoted above, there is an insufficiency of reliable data on what people thought about linguistic correctness and prestige (and how such opinions related to the same persons' actual usage); anecdotal evidence comes from private letters and similar documents, such as those quoted in Honey (1988, 1989), and from the prescriptive statements in grammar books and advice in books on etiquette. Attitudes can also be reconstructed from novels and plays, although these data need to be interpreted with particular caution. The authors' main objective, then as now, is unlikely to be the provision of a realistic account; rather, they tend to employ selected sociolinguistic features to characterize their protagonists in conversation or to make them comment on others' speech forms. Therefore, the title of Phillipps (1984) is somewhat misleading, since the book does not really treat 'Language and class in Victorian England', but deals with how writers of fiction described the situation, with particular focus on the 19th-century upper classes. Anyone using such literary evidence as a data base is in the position of a social historian writing on poverty, work relations and dependency in early Victorian society on the basis of *Hard Times*. Phillipps supplements his evidence from linguistic advice provided in books on etiquette, but largely reduces this to the very questionable contrast between 'U' and 'non-U'. Admittedly, this binary contrast may reflect much of the 19th-century upper-middle-class attitude towards correctness and good breeding, which is also mirrored in books like W. H. Savage's *The Vulgarisms and Improprieties of the English Language* (1833, T6).[25] Large numbers of 19th-century conduct books show how important etiquette was considered to be, especially by social climbers. Such conventions include much more than due attention to narrow linguistic norms.

Correct grammar and 'respectable' pronunciation were also main concerns of public-school teaching; these institutions saw an unprecedented expansion during the 19th century when upwardly mobile parents wanted to

---

[25] There is nothing in grammar books to compare with Savage's savage criticism of incorrect language, such as the statement placed right at the beginning of his book (T6).

give their children the type of education they had not been fortunate enough to have themselves (cf. 1.2.5).

Voices ranging from the writers of books on etiquette to intellectuals like Alford (T16) and Trench (T11) connected propriety and correctness in speech with moral excellence, and saw linguistic sloppiness reflected in careless dress and behaviour – a kind of linguistic relativity still very popular among people who feel called upon to preserve the wells of English undefiled. Alford was also one of many who saw the indiscriminate use of French words as a particular danger (cf. T16).

Ex. 4   Judging from Phillipps (1984) and T6, T20 and T25, can we establish the relative stigma of deviances in pronunciation, grammar and lexis?

2.2   Written and spoken English

As in all historical periods, a description of 19th-century English is necessarily biased towards the written medium, which is the only evidence that survives.[26] However, it is quite clear that the two varieties, reflecting different purposes and situational restrictions, diverged a great deal. This gulf was beginning to be reduced by the increase of literacy and the persuasion of both grammarians and the upwardly mobile learners that spoken English was the better the closer it was to the written medium. Such convictions were widely held in the 18th century but they now reached the majority of the population. The long-term effect was that written and spoken English came closer together, for the majority of Englishmen, than they had ever done before, even if differences in the channels made a complete merger impossible. Sweet, who believed in the written form as a gauge of correctness (1890:vi), recognized that there were major differences, e.g. in syntax:

> In the written language the fluctuation between the relatives is of course much greater, because of the greater variety of constructions, and the necessity of putting in relatives where they are omitted in natural speech, so that the writer has no linguistic instinct to guide him.

His meticulous description of S EngE pronunciation (cf. 3.2 and facsimile, p. 51) is the most reliable evidence we have on educated spoken English before the arrival of phonographic recordings (cf. 3.4).

---

[26] This limitation became less grievous in the late 19th century through the development of scientific phonetics and the rise of dialectology; both improved the description of speech a great deal, but they could not remove the principal imbalance between the two media.

Ex. 5 Explain why the homogenization of written English preceded that of the spoken forms by several hundred years.

2.3   *Dialect and dialectology*[27]

2.3.1 *Attitudes towards regional variation*

Among the variation recorded for 19th-century English, regional diversity was certainly the most important. Spoken dialect must have been the normal form of everyday communication in the 19th century, with the partial exception of the well-educated, but including some of the middle classes in the South of England.[28] (Local *accent* was, however, very common even among the upper crust, as Honey's analysis (1988, 1989) of leading politicians' speech has impressively shown.) On the other hand, it is significant that no dialect of BrE survived as a full linguistic system overseas, in America or Australia, and even dialect words were not retained in great numbers in individual areas or in the new national norms.[29] And this is so even though dialect was very commonly attested in English urban areas:

(1)   The dialectological research of Ellis (1869–74) and J. Wright (1898–1905) showed that dialect was common in towns, especially in the North.

(2)   The reports of school inspectors, very critical with regard to the 'ugly and debased' dialects spoken by the pupils countrywide, included urban areas.[30]

(3)   Dialect poetry (Hollingworth 1977) and prose almanacs (especially from Yorkshire), and the large numbers of such books sold,

---

[27] Dialect research reflects many of the attitudes also expressed in oral and written uses of dialect in 19th-century England, but is not treated here in detail; for the *EDD* and dialect items in the *OED*, cf. p.102 and Ihalainen (1994).

[28] There are of course differences in the broadness of dialect, a fact which was intentionally disregarded by early dialectologists in search of the 'pure dialect'. Such differences are carefully depicted by some novelists such as George Eliot (cf. Phillipps 1984: 84). For the West Country accent that remained even in an HMI, compare F.H. Spencer's self-characterization, quoted by Phillipps (1984:88).

[29] This loss of dialect is especially conspicuous in the case of Scots: the distinctiveness of Braid Scots, the great numbers of speakers among the emigrants and their concentration in certain regions (like the South Island of New Zealand) would have made survival likely. The situation is in contrast to most German-speaking emigrant communities: speakers in Pennsylvania, Brazil, Russia or Romania are normally dialect speakers (with competence in the biblical standard language).

[30] Honey (1988:219–21) rightly stresses the fact that such comments by Her Majesty's Inspectors became frequent only towards the end of the 19th century.

convincingly demonstrate that there was a large audience competent in local dialect and willing to take upon themselves the additional difficulty of reading 'irregular' spelling (see below).

A new self-assertive attitude towards dialects made itself felt from the early 19th century onwards – even though it was, of course, voiced by gentlemen and schoolmasters. The statement by 'a native of Craven' (1828, T27), which stresses the ancient status of the dialect and the threat of corruption by the outside world is a good example of this type of evaluation.[31]

The similarity to the statement made by Forby (1830, T28) on the dialects of East Anglia will be obvious. Note the value he ascribes to dialects for their preservation of old words – and the scathing criticism of cant and slang. Forty years later the attitude was much the same, though the desire to preserve dialect had become more urgent. The greatest threat to local dialect was, of course, still to come with the introduction of compulsory education in 1870. Huntley in his treatment of the Cotswold dialect points out the importance of the village schoolmaster (T31). The contrary opinion was held by the Hon. Samuel Best, who, obviously expressing a commonly accepted view, stated in the fourth edition of his *Elementary Grammar for the use of village schools* of 1857:

> The classically-educated man cannot, if it were desirable, so ignore his education as to address a congregation in the jargon and patois of the village ... We may and ought to raise them to our standard; we cannot, without profaneness in sacred things, descend to theirs. (quoted from Michael 1987:351)

The conclusion from these statements and from demographic evidence is that even in the major industrial centres (at least in the North) dialect remained stable because the vast majority of migrants came from the immediate neighbourhood. This meant that extreme forms of village dialects were given up in the new melting pots, but regional dialects in a somewhat levelled form were strengthened (cf. the figure in Foster [3]1977:76, where the difference in immigrant social stratification between Oldham/Shields and Northampton is probably significant, but where the similarity in the

---

[31] The point is made even more strongly in Richard Garnett's summary review 'English dialects' of 1836 (reprinted in Harris 1995:I, 45–77). Trench, referring to *leer* 'empty' and *lese* 'glean', also states that many old words 'have never dropped out of use among our humbler classes, so often the conservators of precious words and genuine idioms' (1851:120). The point is taken up by Müller, who states: 'We may select a small village in our neighbourhood to pick up dialectic varieties and to collect phrases, proverbs, and stories which will disclose fragments, almost ground to dust, it is true, yet undeniable fragments of the earliest formations of Saxon speech and Saxon thought' (1863:2).

overall social structure is clearly seen).[32]

There were obvious regional differences in the degree of deviation from the London-based standard, and in attitudes to rural speech. Batchelor's (1809) careful analysis of Bedfordshire dialect established only a few substantial differences from London speech (cf. Zettersten's introduction). Halliwell (1847, cf. T30) found Derbyshire dialect 'broad', but Buckingham close to standard, and Northern, Southwestern, East Anglian and London varieties best known (cf. Ihalainen's summary 1994:212). The degree to which regional dialects were accepted by their speakers as badges of identity is partly reflected by the number of publications the English Dialect Society could use as sources. Ihalainen's count of the pages devoted to each county in the 1877 bibliography (1994:273) gives the following proportions:

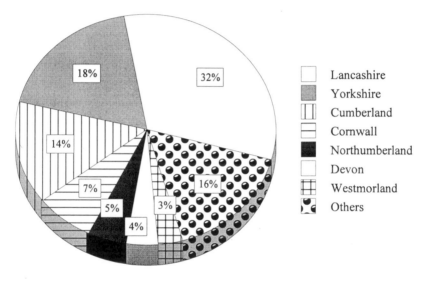

Figure 10 Provenance of dialect publications used for the *EDD*

Grievous concerns about the imminent loss of dialects began around 1870. When the English Dialect Society was founded in 1873, two motives were prominent:

---

[32] There is an obvious parallel in 20th-century urban German dialects; at least before 1945 newcomers to Cologne, Mannheim, Stuttgart and Munich, to name only a few centres, migrated from the surrounding countryside, which has made the regional urban dialects very stable to the present day.

(1)   The data collected from rural forms of speech were intended to
       broaden the basis for linguistic history and reconstruction, an objec-
       tive which was motivated by the comparative method in linguistics,
       now also dominant in Britain (though with some delay if compared
       with the continent).

(2)   Dialect lexis in particular was seen as rapidly disappearing under the
       influence of increasing mobility and the end of the relative isolation
       of many villages and entire regions – so data had to be collected
       quickly before it was too late. Hardy saw in retrospect what happened
       as a consequence of social stigmatization:

> education ... has gone on with its silent and inevitable effacements, reducing the
> speech of this country to uniformity, and obliterating every year a fine old local
> word. The process is always the same: the word is ridiculed by the newly taught;
> it gets into disgrace; it is heard in holes and corners only; it dies, and worst of all,
> it leaves no synonym.   (Hardy 1908:iii, quoted from Jacobs 1952:10)[33]

The continuation of traditional dialect in the North must have been interrupted at a later date. Recent investigations of the Yorkshire dialect (Petyt
1985; the research dates from the early 1970s) have shown that the old
dialect lexis has almost totally disappeared,[34] but so have broad dialect pronunciations like [nɪxt] for 'night' or [koɪl] for 'coal'. All this points to the
end of dialect speech as the dominant form of spoken communication in the
first two generations after general education became available, with a slight
delay in the countryside.

This scientific interest in dialect (as expressed by Ellis, T17) gave it a
new kind of prestige among linguists and certain sections of the middle
classes, but it did not stop its erosion and, finally, loss among those who
spoke it natively, mainly farmers and workers.

The expansion of the standard language, then, levelled out the major
regional differences. The process is symbolized (not the author's intention!)
in Hardy's account (1883, in Golby 1996:300–1) of Devon rural society. He
notes the disappearance of the old rural costume (~ dialect), replaced by
second-hand and ill-advised metropolitan dress, often in bad taste (~
modified standard). The mirror-image in the dress/language symbol in
Shakespeare's Edgar who adopts the dress and speech of a peasant (*King*

---

[33] Phillipps (1984:87) quotes Elworthy's 1886 account of how the Board Schools modified the speech of the rural working classes.

[34] The Survey of English Dialects cannot be used to draw conclusions about urban speech
since cities were almost completely bypassed; note that dialect features documented from
older speakers in villages in the 1950s and 1960s have largely disappeared from rural
areas, too, in the 1990s.

Lear iv. 6.232–52) is obvious. As a result, bidialectalism became more common than it had ever been in England (and lasted for two generations at least, until traditional dialect was lost). Hardy, again, remarked on the fact in 1891 in a much-quoted passage from *Tess*:

> Mrs Durbeyfield habitually spoke the dialect; her daughter, who had passed the Sixth Standard in the National School under a London-trained mistress, spoke two languages; the dialect at home, more or less; ordinary English abroad and to persons of quality.   (Ch.3, also quoted in Phillipps 1984:88)

Ex. 6   Summarize the assumptions and aims of 19th-century dialectology in England (from Ihalainen 1994).

Ex. 7   Summarize, on the basis of the sources quoted above, the impact of the schools on the erosion of dialect.

2.3.2 *Dialect literature*

The sociolinguistic change sketched above obviously affected the frequency and functions of dialect writing. In Hollingworth's (somewhat controversial) opinion, Lancashire dialect poetry developed in three stages:

(1)   A phase of predominantly oral poetry (of which a few famous specimens like 'Th' Owdham weyver' came to be written down after 1840).

(2)   The 'golden age' of Lancashire dialect poetry, 1856–70, represented by Waugh, Laycock and Ramsbottom: 'the amount of poetry produced, and its quality ... considering what came before and what came afterwards, are truly amazing' (1977:2). Hollingworth attributes much of the flowering of this tradition to the belated influence of Burns[35] and to 'the rapid and transient movement of dialect poetry at this time from an oral tradition in which it was already well established, though poorly recorded, into a written form where it became more permanent but quickly lost vitality' (1977:3).

(3)   A final phase, in which the tradition 'moved away from a living expression of the "songs of the people" to an antiquarian and rather

---

[35] 'Waugh in particular was often referred to as the Lancashire Burns, and he clearly relished the title. In his commonplace book he carefully preserved a letter from Spencer J. Hall of Burnley written in 1874. "You and your confreres [have] done for Lancashire what Burns and Hogg [have] done for the Lowlands of Scotland – you [have] immortalized a dialect and made it classical"' (1977:3). Similar cross-connections exist for prose and Anglo-Irish literature – Scott was stimulated by Maria Edgeworth's novels, and was in turn imitated by writers like the Banims (cf. Görlach 1992).

nostalgic attempt to conserve a dying culture and language' (1977:5), an interpretation used to explain why the three poets (who lived on until 1891, 1893 and 1901 respectively) had 'burnt themselves out' (1977:5).

There are various difficulties with Hollingworth's persuasive hypothesis, especially if we wish to look at his evidence from the viewpoint of the historical sociolinguist:

(1)   Since prose is much more difficult to read than (short) poems, how can we explain the fact that it lived on in the Yorkshire almanacs well into the 1920s?

(2)   Can we believe that the impact of compulsory education in 1870 was as immediate as here claimed? Potential readers of these poems who had gone through the new school system would not have read them as children, and therefore not before 1890 – when the tradition had been dead for some time.

Although the situation in Scotland was slightly different, especially with the much firmer hold Scottish dialects had on the countryside, it is interesting to see the parallels not just in the impact that Burns and Scott had on English writers, but also in what Scottish Kailyard poetry and newspaper prose (Donaldson 1986) had in common with Lancashire dialect poetry and the Yorkshire almanacs, namely dependence on dialect being dominant in everyday life.

Even 19th-century English novelists, who only made restricted use of dialect in their dialogue, depended on this vitality of spoken dialect when they wished to be moderately 'realistic' (cf. Dickens[36] and Thackeray for London and East Anglia, Mrs Gaskell for Lancashire,[37] George Eliot for Staffordshire/Derby and Hardy for 'Wessex'/Dorset). Emily Brontë's representation of Haworth dialect in the speech of Joseph is a much quoted example:

> 'Nelly', he said, 'we's hae a Crahnr's 'quest enah, at ahr folks. One on 'em's a'most getten his finger cut off wi' hauding t'other froo' sticking hisseln loike a cawlf. That's maister, yah knaw, ut's soa up uh going tuh t'grand 'sizes. He's

---

[36] Dickens's attempts at Lancashire dialect (e.g. Stephen Blackpool in *Hard Times*) are not very convincing – but it is likely that his readers did not care whether its representation was realistic or not. For the most recent summary of dialect in Victorian fiction, see Chapman 1994:50–66).

[37] There is a link with the poetry discussed above in that Mrs Gaskell's *Mary Barton* contains a (toned-down) version of 'Th' Owdham weyver' (Hollingworth 1977:128), apart from a good deal of dialect in the dialogues.

noan feared uh t'Bench uh judges, norther Paul, nur Peter, nur John, nor Mathew, nor noan on 'em, nut he! He fair likes, he langs tuh set his brazened face agean 'em! And yon bonny lad Heathcliffe, yah mind, he's a rare un! He can girn a laugh as weel's onybody at a raight divil's jest. Does he niver say nowt of his fine living amang us, when he goas tuh t'Grange?

(*Wuthering Heights*, ch.10, quoted from Blake 1981:149)

The authors saw the limitations on the use of dialect quite clearly, as, for instance, Hardy did in an 1878 paper:

> An author may be said to fairly convey the spirit of intelligent peasant talk if he retains the idiom, compass, and characteristic expressions, although he may not encumber the page with obsolete pronunciations of the purely English words, and with mispronunciations of those derived from Latin and Greek ... If a writer attempts to exhibit on paper the precise accents of a rustic speaker, he disturbs the proper balance of a true representation by unduly insisting upon the grotesque element.
>
> (quoted from Blake 1981:166)

This statement is apparently not quite true of the North. One of the most convincing uses of 19th-century literary dialect is found in Burnett's *That Lass o' Lowrie's* (1877, T33a), a story with a Lancashire industrial setting; the fact that her successful novel was part of a wider fashion for dialect prose is indicated by *Punch*'s immediate reaction (20 Oct. – 17 Nov. 1877, T33b) which made fun of such use of dialect. However, the low prestige of dialect restricted its use to non-formal prose and excluded religious writings. Foster & Foster stress how useful it might be for a better understanding of religious truths – but they exclude it for formal texts:

> There can be no question about the propriety of Ministers using provincial dialects in their stated ministrations; but there are some who think that when laymen, natives of the locality, stand up to address small companies, wholly of the humbler classes, it would be infinitely better to use the vernacular in the way of familiar exposition and exhortation, than to attempt a style of composition which they cannot manage without blundering. These good men might do much also as the teachers of the people even in the matter of language, bridging over the gulf we have alluded to, by translating the language of Scripture into their own, and explaining the words most commonly used by Ministers in the pulpit which happened to be unlike their vernacular modes of speech.   (1869/1995:I, 336)

Dialect poems are shorter and easier to read. Tennyson's Lincolnshire and Barnes's Dorset poems still have a claim to be authentic dialect. However, Barnes saw the danger of an artificial 'revivalist' type of poetry and compared writing in a dying dialect to writing in snow on a spring day (quoted in Görlach 1992), but he also saw the genuine, straightforward and honest character of local dialect. This attitude becomes apparent in his facetious 'translation' of stilted passages from the Queen's speech into plain Dorset dialect (cf. 7.1.9 and T35).

There is, then, a distinction to be made in dialect writing according to the audience aimed at: it can raise respect for the living dialect and give it a kind of prestige as long as it is an exclusively spoken, but common, form; however, it tends to become artificial and nostalgic when the basis of every-day use is gone – a development that has increasingly affected writing in English dialect in the 20th century and is becoming a danger to Scots (for the complete context see my discussion in Görlach 1992).

Ex. 8 What were the biographical qualifications of Mrs Gaskell and Emily Brontë for using Northern dialect? How far can we test whether their representations are reliable (cf. Blake 1981)?

Ex. 9 Find examples of the classificatory features listed by Ihalainen (1994:213–15) for 19th-century dialects in T26–T33.

Ex. 10 Why is dialect prose so rare in modern England, and what con-clusion allows the relative frequency of the genre in the 19th century (T29, T30, T33, etc.)?

2.3.3 *The question of Cockney*

The development which came to consider rural dialect as valuable (as re-presented by the 'best' speakers, usually NORMS (= 'non-mobile old rural males')) was a 19th-century innovation. The nostalgic reverence for dialect as a phenomenon of the lost golden age found its counterpart in the depre-ciation of urban lower-class speech – in Britain represented by London, since the other urban centres were still on their way to developing urban norms. Cockney received two quite different evaluations, both making it un-acceptable as 'the regional dialect of London' (cf. Mayhew T14).

(1) Seen from the perspective of a traditional dialectologist, the speech was unbearably mixed and discredited by its connection with poverty and crime, as Forby found as early as 1830 (T28). Later on, Halliwell was even more outspoken:

> The metropolitan county presents little in its dialect worthy of remark, being for the most part merely a coarse pronunciation of London slang and vulgarity.   (1847/80:xxiv, quoted from Ihalainen 1994:212; cf. T30)

(2) From the 18th century onwards, Cockney speech had been used for comic characters on the stage (Matthews 1938) and later on in dia-logue in narrative. The music-hall tradition and Dickens are probably the most typical representatives of this tradition – which became quickly stereotyped and fossilized. When Shaw looked back on the tradition (T37), he found it was already a matter of the past.

19th-century Cockney can, then, be regarded as a blend of regional dialect (being confined to London, and characterized by pronunciation, syntax and lexis (cf. slang 6.1.3) and sociolect (being restricted to informal uses of the lower classes).

Ex. 11 Has the negative attitude towards Cockney (vis-à-vis the positive evaluation of rural dialect) continued?

2.4 *Sociolect*

2.4.1 *Social varieties of English*

Sources for a realistic portrayal of class-related variation[38] are even fewer and less reliable than they are for dialect. All available data have to be interpreted with great caution:

(1) The writing of letters and diaries depends on literacy (which cuts out at least half of the population),[39] and less well-educated writers are likely to produce their 'best' English, often depending on, or modelling their language on, printed sources like Sunday-School readers, etc.

(2) Non-literary documents, like Mayhew's (T14, T83) accounts of the London poor, are of somewhat doubtful authenticity because they depend on what the gentleman collector overheard – and on his 'translation' of it into written form.

(3) Stereotypes are very likely to occur in literary representations of non-standard speech. However convincing the following Dickens text is, the density of lower-class features suggests that the author may have enriched his text to make his message more obvious – and the passage funnier for more educated readers (compare the function of malapropisms):

---

[38] Mugglestone (1995:73–4) has correctly pointed out that *class* as a sociological term was new in the 19th century. The fact possibly indicates a sharpened awareness of social distinctions which became even more important the more the stable boundaries of the 18th century became surmountable by social risers, making *rank* an outdated concept. Johnson had still found 'the fixed, invariable, external distinction of rank, which create no jealousy, since they are held to be accidental' (reported by Boswell, I:442, here quoted from Mugglestone 1995:73).

[39] Emigrants' letters provide a unique but largely unanalysed corpus for the study of semi-literacy since their writers needed to communicate with relatives and friends back home with whom they would normally have talked. (Their use for dialectology is much more limited than Garcia-Bermejo Giner & Montgomery, 1997, claim.)

'They're wot's left, Mr Snagsby,' says Jo, 'out of a sov'ring as wos give me by a lady in a wale as sed she wos a servant and as come to my crossin one night and asked to be showd this 'ere ouse and the ouse wot him as you giv the writin to died at, and the berrin-ground wot he's berrid in. She ses to me, she ses, 'are you the boy at the Inkwhich?' she ses. I ses, 'yes,' I ses. She ses to me, she ses, 'can you show me all them places?' I ses, 'yes, I can,' I ses. And she ses to me 'do it,' and I dun it, and she giv me a sov'ring and hooked it.' (Jo in *Bleak House*, ch.19, quoted from Brook 1970:94)

(4) Grammarians tended to warn against 'low' words and constructions. Michael (1987:351) summarizes 'Vulgarisms ... were a regular feature of all sorts of manuals'. Such prescriptive warnings do not, of course, add up to a coherent description of lower-class speech.

(5) Linguistic advice provided in books on etiquette, which tends to focus on shibboleths, is usually quite outspoken. While the evidence is highly selective, it often brings out the sociolinguistic stigmatization in a straightforward way.[40] A typical small book pontificating about correctness is *Don't* ('Censor', c. 1880). The (American) author advises against improprieties on all linguistic levels, such as careless pronunciations, the use of *don't* and *ain't*, incorrect preterites and *have got*, wrong concord, and slang, fashionable adjectives, Latinate words and Americanisms in general.

Class differences were also connected – more obviously than today – with religion. For instance, 'the language of Methodism and other Nonconformists was, by very definition, non-U'; thus Phillipps (1984:118),[41] who refers to *Adam Bede* and quotes from Disraeli's *Sybil*:

---

[40] Mugglestone (1995) has rightly placed a great deal of weight on titles such as the following (most of them published anonymously in London):

1833   W. H. Savage, *The Vulgarisms and Improprieties of the English Language*. (T6)
1855   Hon. Henry H., *P's and Q's. Grammatical Hints for the Million*.
1866   Hon. Henry H., *Poor Letter H. Its Use and Abuse*.
1868   *Vulgarisms and Other Errors of Speech*.
1869   *Good Society. A Complete Manual of Manners*.
[28]1872 *Live and Learn: A Guide for All Who Wish to Speak and Write Correctly*.
1879   *The Manners and Tone of Good Society by a Member of the Aristocracy*.
1880   *Society Small Talk. Or What to Say and When to Say it*. (T20)
1884   *Common Blunders in Speaking and How to Avoid Them*.
1897   C. Hartley, *Everyone's Handbook of Common Blunders in Speaking and Reading*.

[41] Phillipps adopts the distinction between upper-class and non-upper-class usage in his analysis of linguistic attitudes as expressed in 19th-century novels; the distinction was first suggested by Ross in 1954 and popularized through Nancy Mitford, but has since been given up as too vague.

Going to church was held more genteel than going to meeting. The principal tradesmen of the neighbouring great houses deemed it more 'aristocratic', using a favourite and hackneyed epithet, which only expressed their own servility.

(1845:ch. 11)

An analysis of the features criticized and the terms of reproof used ('barbarous', 'corrupt', 'improper', 'inelegant', 'low', 'uncouth' and 'vulgar', as well as instances of 'solecisms') shows the continuity passed on from the 18th century[42] – only the prescriptions are now directed towards a much wider section of the population.[43] Moreover, the linguistic insecurity of 19th-century readers leads one to expect that the objection to prescriptive guidance in grammar (and partly in pronunciation) would be even weaker than among their forefathers. 'Attitudes toward grammar', Bailey (1996: 215) rightly states, 'during the [19th] century hardened into ideology.'

Since the craze for correctness was a predominantly middle-class feature, it could lead to the seeming paradox that 'non-standard' features were retained in the lower and upper classes. Strang refers to /h/ and /ŋ/ in her comment:

the highest classes, in their self-assurance, remain traditional, and so do those untouched by education, but the new correctness catches on throughout a broad social spectrum between these extremes.   (1970:81)

Again, on the retention of /ɔ:/ before [s]: 'as usual, it persisted not only among the vulgar, but also among the most assured' (1970:85).

That the phenomenon was not restricted to pronunciation is shown by the use of *ain't* and *don't*:

For Thackeray and Trollope, the educated and upper classes could use *ain't* and (third-person singular) *don't* readily, but in familiar speech only.
(Denison 1998:197, referring to Phillipps 1978:121)

As far as lexis is concerned, at least five categories of usage are seen as indicators of the speaker's or (worse) the writer's lack of education and low social status (all discussed in ch. 6):

---

[42] The qualifying adjectives used to describe improper language are largely carried over from the 18th century (cf. Sundby *et al.* 1991). Only a close study concentrating on the form of such value judgements (leading up to Fowler's language of linguistic verdicts in 1926) could show how much change there really was.

[43] What all these attempts have in common is that authors believed in the educability of the masses – where Crombie in 1802 (T1) had flatly denied that 'the vulgar' were fit for remedial education. It has rightly been pointed out that there is a vital difference between an 18th-century 'conduct book' and Victorian publications on 'etiquette'. The former 'touches on manners and deportment, but in the main deals with religion, morality and self-control', whereas the latter are 'handbooks for social climbers' (Ousby [2]1992:198).

(1) malapropisms – garbled pronunciations and confusions of Latinate words, often exploited by writers for their comic potential;

(2) the lexical choice between synonyms misleadingly classified as 'U' and 'non-U';

(3) genteelisms – the inappropriate use of words thought to be more refined than the proper plain expression;

(4) the use and abuse of French and Latinate words;

(5) slang and cant characteristic of informality, in-group use and expressiveness.

Slang is certainly the most conspicuous marker of sociolinguistic distinctions. Attitudes towards 'low' words, from Johnson and before, were highly critical, and such 18th-century evaluation is evident in remarks like those of Forby (T28), who explicitly contrasted the treasures hidden in rural dialects and the debased lingo of the gutter. However, there were gentlemen collectors of such refuse from the 16th century onwards (cf. Harman's *Caveat*, Görlach 1991:231). Clarke, who based his collection on Grose (1785), rightly pointed out that:

> our young men of fashion would at no very distant period be as distinguished for the vulgarity of their jargon as the inhabitants of Newgate ... The propriety of introducing the *University slang* will be readily admitted; it is not less curious than that of the College in the Old Bailey, and is less generally understood.
>
> (1811:Preface, v–viii)

The fascination with the underworld continued into the later 19th century, as is documented by dictionaries like Hotten's (1874) and the comprehensive sociological description provided by Mayhew (1861). Since slang is, by definition, restricted to the vocabulary, the analysis is found in 6.1.2 below.

The social pressures to conform were, however, so great that the norms of 'proper' pronunciation came to be settled. The result was a standard which was defined as the speech of the best-educated persons with as little local flavour as possible and which came to be known as Received Pronunciation (= RP). Three contemporary statements (quoted from Mugglestone 1995:54, 30, 2) illustrate the acceptance of this ideal:

> (1) The common standard dialect is that in which all marks of a particular place and residence are lost, and nothing appears to indicate any other habits of intercourse than with the well-bred and well-informed, wherever they may be found.
>
> (B. H. Smart, 1836. *Walker Remodelled*, London, §178)

> (2) Purity of accent is the grand distinctive feature of an educated gentleman. It belongs to no city or district, and is acknowledged and accepted as current coin with all grades of society. (Anon., 1860. *How to Shine in Society*, Glasgow, p. 20)

(3) The best accent is undoubtedly that taught at Eton and Oxford. One may be as
    awkward with the mouth as with the arms and legs.

(Anon., 1870. *Mixing in Society: A Complete Manual of Manners*, p. 91)

It is quite a different matter whether such (intended) homogeneity in speech
can lead to a really unified community, as Newman who saw 'England in
terms of an alliance of national honour and linguistic reform' (Mugglestone
1995:46) believed it might. He stated that England was 'a nation which
desires to eliminate vulgar provincial pronunciation, to educate and refine
its people [and thus to] get rid of plebeianism, and fuse the orders of society
into harmony'. Nevertheless, all the institutional efforts to promote RP have
not fully succeeded, as only 3–5% of England's population are now claimed
to use it (at least in the pure form).

Linguistic insecurity could also lead to genteel, 'refayned' speech which
Ruskin considered as 'a great sign of vulgarity':

> In cases of over-studied pronunciation, etc., there is insensibility, first, in the
> person's thinking more of himself than of what he is saying; and, secondly, in his
> not having musical fineness of ear enough to feel that his talking is uneasy and
> strained. Vulgarity is indicated by coarseness of language or manners, only so far
> as this coarseness has been contracted under circumstances not necessarily pro-
> ducing it ... Provincial dialect is not vulgar; but cockney dialect, the corruption by
> blunted sense of a finer language continually heard, is so in a deep degree.

(Ruskin, 1888. *Modern Painters*, vol. V, p. 276)

Ex. 12   Discuss the use of the term 'vulgar' in 19th-century grammars and
     conduct books; what does the term mean with reference to the middle
     classes? (Cf. T54, T8, T15, T31)

2.4.2 *Modes of address*
(Phillipps 1984:143–73)

Since *thou* had receded to dialect in the 18th century, and even Quakers had
more or less given up the old singular pronoun, it no longer functioned as a
social marker (its use in biblical contexts, sermons and prayers is quite
distinct).[44] Social distinctions and degrees of intimacy were therefore expressed, in conversation and letter writing, by the selection from title + first
name + second name, each of which might be used by itself or in various

---

[44] One of the last to warn against the use of *thou* was Pearson (1865) – but since he wrote
for Yorkshire pupils there was reason to do so in order to ward off dialect interference.
He, too, mentioned that Quakers had largely given up the use of *thou/thee*. Compare the
earlier quote from Marshall (1788:41) in Ihalainen (1994:229) on *thou* as a Yorkshire
provincialism.

combinations; in the spoken form the intonation also played a part, but this variation is no longer recoverable.

The most formal kind of address was to use the title and second name, but more relaxed or informal uses differed from PDE a great deal:

(1) The use of Christian names was largely confined to the family; nicknames and hypocoristic forms were even more intimate. However, the use of 'Mr X' / 'Mrs X' to refer to one's spouse was quite common (more seldom: the surname only).

(2) The use of the bare surname was halfway between formal and informal (for men); it was universal in school but otherwise mainly found in addresses to servants.

(3) In appellatives outside the aristocracy (*my lord, my lady, your grace,* etc.) *sir, ma'am* and *miss* were used.

(4) In the family, children addressed their parents as *mama/ma/mammy/mother* and *papa/pa/dad/father*: the social rules about their use appear to have been complex and changing during the period.

(5) In written use, the choice of the proper form of address combines with adequate opening and closing formulas (and the address on the envelope). There was (and still is) a great variety of possibilities for blunders, including genteelisms. At the end of the century, Anon. (1898) has six pages of detailed advice relating to how to address members of individual classes of society. 19th-century innovations include the use of 'Esq.' to follow the name on the envelope being extended to all males, and the use of 'your affectionate/devoted/ dutiful daughter', etc., and the phrase 'Believe me' as in 'Awaiting your reply. Believe me, Dear Madam, Yours truly, NAME' at the end of letters (1898:61).

2.5   *Chronolects and the awareness of linguistic change*

The drastic changes that had happened to English society after the 18th century were felt by many observers, and formulated by some, as by the anonymous author in the *Westminster Review* of April 1849:

> The age of railways, art-unions, and 'Vanity Fair', is not that of post-chaises, literary patrons, and fulsome dedications: the age when we teach the people to be independent of that paternal charity which the middle-age gentry extended to their serfs, and to trust to themselves alone, is not that in which we can deny them facilities for intellectual culture. Past is the age of esoteric doctrines, the mystic cypher, and the cloistered learning: that of Polytechniques, Mechanics' Institutes, and the Edinburgh Chamberses is here.   (quoted from Harris 1995:I, 113)

These changes greatly affected the prestige attached to individual linguistic forms, and it would be strange if observers had not been aware of the linguistic change going on around them. However, most of this was interpreted (and criticized) as a social phenomenon – either in the form of nostalgic reflections on standards of earlier generations, or (less likely) a look forward by accepting innovative forms. Pronunciation is most often the focus of such observations – if older speakers are available for comparison. MacMahon (1998:374) quotes remarks by Ellis who, in 1874, interpreted the speech of octogenarians as representatives of a transitional phase of the 18th century; there are also the comments of the Arabist Francis Newman 'on the differences between educated English in the 1870s and in the earlier 19th century' made in 1878, and the British art critic Eastlake's recollections of earlier norms written down in 1902:

> Men of mature age can remember many words which in the conversation of old fellows forty years ago [i.e. of people born towards the end of the 18th century] would sound strangely to modern ears. They were generally much *obleeged* for a favour. They referred affectionately to their *darters*; talked of *goold* watches, or of recent visit to *Room*; mentioned that they had seen the *Dook* of Wellington in Hyde Park last *Toosday* and that he was in the habit of rising at *sivin* o'clock. They spoke of *Muntague* Square and St. *Tummus 'Ospital*. They would profess themselves to be their hostess's *'umble* servants, and to admire her collection of *chayney*, especially the vase of *Prooshian* blue.   (Eastlake 1902:992–3)

Finally, Honey's explanations of the rise of RP (1988) point to an awareness among a great number of educated speakers of social change and its reflection in linguistic change – including measures to retain social distance.

Changing vocabulary is also a frequent cause for comment; Outis's (1868:3) remarks are representative of more conservative attitudes:

> Custom will justify many alterations which have imperceptibly taken place. Those persons, whose recollections go back for half a century, will experience no difficulty in calling to mind many words which have crept into use since they were schoolboys; and no sensible man will refuse to concur in such alterations as etymology, taste, or even a well-grounded caprice, of society may call on him to acknowledge.
>
> But then new words or changes in old ones are surely not advisable or to be permitted except on the authority of speakers and writers of high repute and classical attainments; and when individuals, imperfectly educated or unsupported by legitimate pretensions, assume to themselves the right of leading their readers astray, it is time to endeavour to override their dictation, by shewing how misconceptions before these spread too widely.

In grammar, innovations tend to be regarded as mistakes and as indicators of corruption, and change is therefore often not recognized as such. How many observers correctly interpreted the change from *he is arrived* to *he has arrived* (5.3.1) and *the book is printing* to *the book is being printed* (5.3.6.2) as specimens of syntactical change in progress is now difficult to say. A liberal attitude such as White's (1882, T21) was needed to record (and not comment on) the grammatical changes that had taken place in the course of the century. Michael (1991:15) has pointed to the 'inertia' of both the grammatical system and the teachers:

> English grammar was a subject which they liked. Its content was fixed; it generally required the pupil to learn much by heart; in its earlier stages it could be marked right or wrong without hesitation; it was difficult for the pupil and easy for the teacher. There were powerful reasons why teachers should wish to preserve a system which eased some of their work, especially when any tinkering with it would expose them to the ambiguity, the relativity and the slipperiness of language in real use.

Awareness of linguistic change in other fields certainly played a part in the discussions about the loss of broad dialect and the change in Cockney (above); it is also evident from the complaints about the vulgarization of good style by journalists and literary writers from the midcentury onwards,[45] and by dialectologists about the vanishing rural dialects, which they rightly saw as threatened by mobility ('personalized' in the spread of the railway) and general education.

Ex. 13 Comment on the changes that White (T21) said had taken place in 19th-century EngE. Are all these innovations still found in PDE?

Ex. 14 How plausible is the assumption that speed of composition and reading (rather than an expanded audience) led to an alleged deterioration of prescriptive linguistic norms? Discuss the question with relation to recent developments and the causes adduced.

---

[45] Heald ([2]1898:1) summarizes these concerns at the end of the century:
> Whether the prevailing slovenly style of literary composition is due to neglect on the part of the instructors of youth, or to a feeling on the part of writers that grammar is of little consequence, so long as they make their meaning clear to their readers, or to the high pressure speed at which we move in this 19th century, it would serve no purpose to inquire; but that it exists is undeniable.

3

Spelling and pronunciation
(MacMahon 1998, Bailey 1996:23–138)

3.1 *Spelling*

Take care of the sense, and the sounds will take care of themselves.[46]

Spelling was the best-regulated part of the English linguistic system; at the turn of the century, an anonymous author could claim:

> Though it cannot be denied, that there is still some difference in our orthography, owing to the affectation of writers and caprice of printers; yet it is observable, that, since the publication of Dr Johnson's Dictionary, and particularly the last edition, less variation is found; and ... it is much for the credit of a language that its orthography should be fixed and immutable. (Anon. 1797:i)

However, certain options still remained even late in the 19th century (and many still remain, or are now classified as preferences of BrE as against AmE). James Murray (1888:x) notes variation in individual words like *aerie* (*aery, eyrie*, etc.) and 'whole series of words' ending in *-able* (*blam(e)able*), *-eer/-ier, -ize/-ise* 'and other endings, as to which current usage varies'. He adds:

> In making [a] choice, regard is had chiefly to the preponderance of modern usage, when this is distinctly marked; when usage is more or less equally divided, considerations of etymological or phonetic propriety, of general analogy with similar words, or of practical convenience are taken into account; but, in many cases, it is not implied that the form actually chosen is intrinsically better than others which are appended to it. (1888:x)

Although the correspondence between the spelling and the sounds it represented was highly ambiguous, comparatively few attempts were made in Britain to remedy the situation (cf. 3.2) – and they had hardly any lasting effect. (By contrast, Noah Webster at least tried to make the spelling of AmE more consistent, pointing to the opportunity to distance the American norm from BrE and make it more logical at the same time. He did not succeed, of course, apart from the changes in *theater, honor*, etc., which he promoted and which still distinguish American from British conventions.)

As far as orthographical correctness was concerned, there had been a

---

[46] The short quotations accompanying the subsections all come from Lewis Carroll.

radical change of attitude in the 18th century. From Chesterfield onwards, proper spelling was becoming a hallmark of good education, and in the 19th century it could be taken for granted that the upper and upper-middle classes knew their orthography. Being able to write, and to do so correctly, became a marker of social standing. That this change was a gradual process is illustrated by attitudes like those of Cobbett, who in 1823 could still say:

> *Orthography* means neither more nor less than the very humble business of putting *Letters* together properly, so that they shall form *Words*. This is so very childish a concern, that I will not appear to suppose it necessary for me to dwell upon it. (1823/1984:8)

Before the 1870s, when compulsory education brought the 'three Rs' within reach of every young person, spelling was one of the most important indicators of social acceptability. You might belong to one of three categories:

(a)   Those who spelt correctly, including those who had to for professional reasons, e.g. clerks;

(b)   those who could read, but spelt in a wayward manner, basing their homemade conventions more or less on the way they spoke; and

(c)   those who could neither read nor write, and signed with the proverbial cross when it came to marriage or registering the death of relatives, depositions and other formal occasions.

The (b) group is the most interesting as regards social history and regional variation, but the private letters and diaries written by such people have never been collected and properly analysed. The letters written by A. Layton in 1816 and by a Durham worker in 1831 (T26a and b) are such documents: Layton was a skilled worker who later became a self-employed craftsman and might well be classified as '(lower) middle-class' in modern terms. This document dates to a period before Sunday schools and secular establishments like the Mechanics' Institutes and the Society for the Diffusion of Useful Knowledge had begun to take effect. The latter

> published the *Penny Magazine* (1826–46), one of several efforts ... to provide reading matter to satisfy the curiosity of adult readers with little schooling. The *Penny Magazine* was directed to a mass audience of workers, and magazines like it anticipated the remarkable growth in literacy in the second half of the century.
> (Bailey 1996:36–7)

In fiction, deficiencies in spelling continue to serve to characterize the social status of its writer. 'A badly spelt letter by a semi-literate character had come to be almost a convention in comic novels, and Dickens tried his hand at it in Fanny Squeer's letter to Ralph Nickleby (*Nicholas Nickleby*, ch. 15)' (Brook 1970:107).

Special writing systems invented or at least popularized in the 19th century include hundreds of shorthand systems (cf. 3.2) widely used by court reporters and journalists (including Dickens); of these Isaac Pitman's became the most popular. There were also phonetic spellings invented by dialectologists (such as Ellis, cf. 3.2). These depended on handwriting, and their use in books was not possible before lithography had been invented (Bailey 1996:57).

The neat appearance, elegance and legibility of handwriting was a social grace rather than one of linguistic correctness; thus, hardly a book on etiquette is without advice on this point (cf. T22).

19th-century texts also became increasingly diversified as far as typography was concerned (Bailey 1996:42–62). The use of various typefaces in different forms and sizes on title-pages of books and in advertisements of various sorts (T96) brings out the important elements even where the text is syntactically complete; such strategies can be seen as precursors of block language (cf. 5.3.9) where the 'redundant' elements are omitted – both are developments of a period in which written information became too plentiful to take in, so that a quick selection was necessary (cleverly exploited in advertising).

Excessive use of italics to indicate emphasis was frequently criticized, as was underlining in private letters:

> Avoid underlining as much as possible. This is a bad habit, which belongs to women rather than men.
> (Anon 1898:23)

Ex. 15 Analyse individual cases of badly spelt letters fabricated to characterize the writers' lack of education in 19th-century novels (cf. Bailey 1996, Blake 1981, Phillipps 1984).

3.2   *Spelling reform*
(Scragg 1974:106–11; Zachrisson 1931/2)

Many linguists continued to see the need to reform the system of English orthography, but the movement (if it ever was one) had certainly lost some of its impetus by the early 19th century when the discussion in England was revived by Pitman. In contrast to the 20th century, when the leading promoters of a reform were foreigners, proposals before 1900 were at least put forward by native users – Americans like Franklin and Webster, Scotsmen like Elphinston and Bell or Englishmen like Latham, Pitman, Ellis and Sweet. Two major problems remained undecided: should a reform be strictly based on the phonemic principle or also allow for morphological and etymological considerations, and should the reformed spelling employ the twenty-six letters of the alphabet, and in addition allow digraphs like <th>, <ch> and <wh>, or should new letters be introduced to guarantee a straightforward 1:1 relationship between graphemes and phonemes?

The failure to agree on such points did not help solve the major difficulty – that of implementing a reformed spelling, however ingenious and didactically persuasive it might be. The failure of Webster's reform proposals which had ideal conditions for successful implementation, with the politically motivated breakaway from British norms and Webster's hold on the schoolbook market, did not promise well for similar efforts in the more conservative British society. Although schoolteachers, then as now, saw how much the complex orthography delayed literacy for most pupils, their influence was not strong enough. Early proposals include Batchelor's exemplary detailed proposal of 'a new orthoëpical alphabet, or universal character' (1809) which, he claimed on the title-page, '(with a few Additions) furnishes an easy Method of explaining every Diversity of Language and Dialect among civilized Nations', and which he 'Designed for the Use of Provincial Schools'. (It does not become quite clear whether Batchelor wanted his system to replace normal spelling; he does provide a coherent text on p. 80.) Later proposals range from Latham's of 1834 (T7) to the publications by Pitman and Ellis in the 1840s and those developed for the *Phonetic Journal* (1856),[47] followed by various attempts later in the century, such as those associated with the Philological Society.

A new development in the 19th century was the connection of spelling reform with shorthand writing. Isaac Pitman, who devised his first system in 1837, based it on phonemic principles – which kept him occupied with improvements of the alphabet until 1870, when he proposed a new alphabet of 38 symbols (Scragg 1974:107 reproduces the proposed new alphabet in facsimile). These letters were taken over from the conventional writing wherever possible, but modified from existing forms to create new graphemes – a method which very much reminds one of Hart's proposals in the 16th century (cf. Görlach 1991). Although many books and pamphlets were

---

[47] For some insightful remarks on three of Ellis's early publications of 1848, written in connection with Pitman, see the anonymous reviews of 1849 reprinted in Harris (1995:I, 101–28, 129–37). Trench was strictly against spelling reform which would destroy etymological information and, therefore, 'all the hoarded wit, wisdom, imagination, and history which it contains' (1851:180): 'In phonetic spelling is, in brief, the proposal that the educated should of free choice place themselves in the conditions and under the disadvantages of the ignorant and uneducated, instead of seeking to elevate these last to theirs' (1851:184). For a later period compare Müller's statements of 1876 (in Harris 1995:II, 205–37).

published in the new system, and there was, in 1876, support ranging from Max Müller[48] to the National Union of Elementary Teachers, the impetus flagged after Pitman's death.

A. M. Bell was the most prolific writer, from the 1840s to the 1890s, on universal principles of transcription; he claimed that his Visible Speech made 'Every language universally legible, exactly as spoken, accomplished by means of self-interpreting physiological symbols', as he put it in the title of a publication of 1864. Although the system was greeted with applause by journalists and scholars, its limitations for language learning were evident (Raudnitzky 1911:180), and Bell's ideas thus remained important mainly for the stimulus he gave to experimental phonetics and for the impact he had on Ellis and Sweet.

The major competitor of Pitman was, however, his early pupil and collaborator Ellis, whose Glossic (an improved version of the earlier Glossotype) was intended as a kind of initial teaching alphabet, 'a new system of spelling, intended to be used concurrently with the English orthography in order to remedy some of its defects, without changing its form, or detracting from its value'. This popular system contrasted with a much more intricate method, Palaeotype, developed for the representation of dialectal and historical texts.[49] Scragg rightly points out that 'The importance of Glossic is that it marked a change in direction of the movement; from the date of its introduction (1871) most reformers concentrated on a minimum disturbance reform confined to the letters of the Roman alphabet' (Scragg 1974:110). Zachrisson (1931/2:15) quotes the following specimen to illustrate that Ellis 'seems to have looked upon Glossic chiefly as a means of teaching children to read quickly'.

> Objjekts: Too fasil·itait Lerning too Reed,
> Too maik Lerning too Spel unnes·eseri,
> Too asim·ilait Reeding and Reiting too Heering and Speeking,

---

[48] Müller, who took pride in having invented an international spelling system for missionaries, was convinced of Pitman's success: 'and although Mr Pitman may not live to see the results of his persevering and disinterested exertions, it requires no prophetic power to perceive that what at present is pooh-poohed by the many will make its way in the end, unless met by arguments stronger than those hitherto levelled at the "Fonetic Nuz"' (1863:II, 100). His attitude in 1876 was still favourable, although he states that he was 'not an agitator for phonetic reform in England, [his] interest in the matter [being] purely theoretical and scientific' (1876:206).

[49] Raudnitzky (1911:177) points out that the description of the symbols used is unclear and the relation of the sounds not made sufficiently explicit; this makes Palaeotype impossible to use with precision even for linguists (for instance, in reconstructing late 19th-century pronunciation).

Too maik dhi Risee´vd Proanunsiai´shen
ov Ingglish akses´ibl too *aul* Reederz,
Proavin´shel and Foren.

Ellis raised the problem of what compromises are admissible between a consistent respelling and conventional orthography in a pamphlet of 1880 (here quoted from Zachrisson 1931/2:17). The conditions which have to be fulfilled include:

1. Tou hav a speling whitch coud bi iméedietly *yoozd* not *oa*nly for bóukwurk, but for awl keindz ov jobing printing, at eny printing pres throuowt the wurld thut pozésez a fownt ov Rohmun leterz. This condishun riqweirz that their shoud bee
    noh new leterz,
    noh turnd leterz,
    noh cut or méwtilaited leterz,
    noh mixtewr ov fowntz az Italic with Rohmun, or smawl capitulz with loher cais,
    noh deyacriticul seinz, whitch ar not leterz themsélvz, or poynts aulrédy egzi'sting in abúnduns,
    noh axénted leterz, excépt á, é, í, ó, ú, yoozd oanly tou i'ndicait stres and not tou diferénshiait sownd, and caipabl ov beeing supleyd, if not caast or not furnisht tou eny fownt, bey a comun poynt.

Another look at a selection of proposals for a 'scientific' representation of pronunciation printed by Ellis (1869–74:1206–7) in parallel columns shows how impracticable all the suggested solutions were – even for scholarly purposes. The International Phonetic Alphabet, developed in the late 19th century by A. E. Ellis, Paul Passy, Henry Sweet and Daniel Jones and based on ideas by Jespersen, was a notable improvement. It avoided the complications of a too narrow transcription, which makes it easy to learn, but it was of course never intended to replace the conventional orthography of any language.

Ellis was convinced that a homogenization of the pronunciation could only come about through a phonemic spelling – again an argument that could have come straight from John Hart's *Orthographie* of 1569 (cf. Görlach 1991:224). Ellis's reasoning comes of course from a time before phonographs were developed.

Finally, the British Spelling Reform Association, founded in 1879, had considerable intellectual support; at least five new schemes were proposed, but even those directed at the 'amendments of the worst anomalies in the traditional system' (Scragg 1974:111) were not successful, because the general public remained unconvinced. Sweet, and indeed various 19th-century authors before him, started with a respelling system which avoided the more glaring inconsistencies (Sweet 1884). A few years later in his

Elementarbuch of 1886 (and in Sweet 1890) he decided for a transcription which much more faithfully reflects the sounds of educated Southern English. This was based on his own pronunciation and (couched in dialogue form to match the colloquial register described) it took account of various degrees of stress, weak forms and allophonic distinctions (cf. the facsimile, p. 51). Developed for language teaching needs before phonographic materials became available, his documentation is invaluable evidence of S EngE at a time when RP was formed. Sweet rightly claims that it is the first scholarly representation of an educated idiolect – and only if a representative collection of such transcriptions were available would it be feasible to judge 'whether it is possible to reform our pronunciation, and take steps to preserve the unity of English speech all over the world' (1890/[3]1900:ix; cf. T24).

None of these well-meant proposals came to anything and the issue appears to have been decided quite early by the negative attitudes of the majority of the population – a rejection which is neatly summarized in Alford's comment:

> we became rather alarmed some years ago, when we used to see on our reading-room tables a journal published by the advocates of this change, called the 'Phonetic News', but from its way of spelling looking like *Frantic Nuts*. Time has now happily confirmed the conviction expressed in earlier editions of this work, that the system will never prevail in England.   ([3]1870:16)

A major reform of the English spelling still remains to be done, then. Ellis's sense of resignation in 1880 (quoted from Zachrisson (1931/2:18)) is probably typical of the frustration of generations of reformers:

> Revolewshun *may* bi the best solewshun, but ey doo not inténd tou wurk in that direcshun eny longger. Mey paast expeeriens, whitch haz been boatth grait and painfoul, wornz me tou trey anuther road. It iz not without egzurting grait fors ohver misélf thut ey-uv rinounst a pewrly fonetic alfabet. But Glosic woz mey furst step in the new direcshun, and Dimidiun or 'háafway speling' is mey secund.
>
> It iz thi owtcum ov thurty sevn yeerz ov consienshus wurk, coménst and carid on for edewcaishunul and filolodjicul purpusez.

:whot ə jŏ :vjuwz ŏn ðə :sabdʒĭkt əv edʒŭ·keiʃən ˋ?—əi ʃəd
bĭ glæd tə hiə ðəm.   welˋ, -ðɛə verĭ :suwn steitĭd : əi hæv nt
-enĭ ətɔl.   jŭ ʃuəlĭ doun mijn tə sei ðət jŭw v nevə gĭvn ə
moumĭnts þɔt tə ðə moust ĭmpɔtnt fæktər·ĭn ðə ʃjuwtʃə
dĭveləpmənt ə ðə hjuwmən reis?   sə:pouz jŭ -hæd tʃuldrən
əv jŏr ·oun ˋ—d jŭw mijn tə sei ðət -ðɛə fizĭkl, morəl ən
intĭ·lektʃŭəl dĭveləpmənt əd bĭj ə :mætər əv æbsəljŭwt ĭndifrəns
:tuw jŭ?   əv :kɔs əi wiʃ tə :sij məi :fɛlŏu krijtʃəz helþi ĭn bodĭ
ən maind :r̄aaðə ðən wijk ən viʃəs ˊ—:whot əi :mijn tə sei ĭz
ðət əi doun :þiŋk edʒŭ·keiʃən -æz :matʃ tə duw wĭð ĭt : ĭt s
nou juws tijtʃĭŋ mərælĭtĭ ən ðə lɔz əv helþ ət skuwl, if ðə
tʃuldrənz houmlaif s an·helþĭ ən viʃəs; ən nou ə:maunt əv
kræmĭŋ ðə maind l -meik ə stjuwpĭd :bɔi klevəˋ—ĭn :fækt ĭt i
-hæv ĭgzæktlĭ ðĭ ;opəzĭt ĭfekt.   mai faaðə wəz ə doktrĭˊnɛə
dʒes ləik juw—.   əi m ;not ə doktrĭˊnɛə.   wel ˋ; :enihəu hĭj
-æd strɔŋ vjuwz ŏn ðə :sabdʒĭkt əv edʒŭ·keiʃən.   ;hiz əi:diə
:woz ðət nou :hjuwmən :bijĭŋ z nætʃərəlĭ aidlˋ, ən ðət ĭf jŭ
wans :faind aut whŏt ijtʃ -wan -hæz ə speʃəl æptĭtjŭwd fŏə,
ən set ðəm tŭ ĭt, -ðei l -gou on ə ðəmselvz.   əi ;kwait əgrij
wĭð ĭm : ðĭ ounlĭ difĭkltĭ ĭz tə :faind aut ðijz speʃəl ætrĭbjŭwtsˋ
—əi :mijn æptĭtjŭwdz.   prĭsaislĭ sŏu ˋ—mai faaðə þot ĭj d
dĭskavəd ðət ;mai :speʃəl :æptĭtjŭwd wəz ðə :stadĭ əv ĭŋglĭʃ
litrətʃə əv ðə sevṅtijnþ senʃərĭ.

What are your views on the subject of education? – I should be glad to hear them. Well,
they're very soon stated: I haven't any at all. You surely don't mean to say that you've
never given a moment's thought to the most important factor in the future development
of the human race? Suppose you had children of your own – d'you mean to say that their
physical, moral and intellectual development'd be a matter of absolute indifference to
you? Of course I wish to see my fellow creatures healthy in body and mind rather than
weak and vicious – what I mean to say is that I don't think education has much to do with
it: it's no use teaching morality and the laws of health at school, if the children's homelife
is unhealthy and vicious; and no amount of cramming the mind'll make a stupid boy
clever – in fact it'll have exactly the opposite effect. My father was a doctrinaire just like
you. – I'm not a doctrinaire. Well, anyhow he had strong views on the subject of education. His idea was that no human being's naturally ideal, and that if you once find out
what each one has a special aptitude for, and set them to it, they'll go on themselves. I
quite agree with him: the only difficulty is to find out these special attributes – I mean
aptitudes. Precisely so – my father though I'd discovered that my special aptitude was the
study of English literature of the seventeenth century.

Figure 11 Facsimile illustrating Sweet's reformed spelling with transliteration

Ex. 16   Contrast the new spelling systems proposed by Latham (T6) and
Pitman (in Scragg 1974:107). Describe the underlying principles and
evaluate them for clearness and practicability.

Ex. 17   Transcribe the text provided by Sweet in 1890 (facs., p. 51) into
modern IPA. What are the improvements made in the present-day
system? Are there differences which are likely to be due to a change of
sounds in the past 100 years?

Ex. 18   Try to determine the principles of the (naive) respelling systems
used to render dialect texts in T30.

3.3   *Punctuation*

> Punctuation ought to be an *art*, but unfortunately no rules are observed. Every
> man does that which is right in his own eyes.   (Abbott [3]1879:70; T19)

Punctuation is to be seen in close connection with the syntactical structure
of sentences and paragraphs, which the author can help to make more transparent by judicious rhythmical or logical use of punctuation marks. 19th-
century sentences tending, at least in respectable prose, to be longer than
those used today, the frequency and interplay of commas and semicolons in
many texts is striking. In particular, commas can be found twice as often as
would be common today, one of the conspicuous positions being between
the verb and its (often overlong) complements.

However, there was still a great deal of choice left, as can be seen from
variation in the surviving texts. This was a consequence of rhythmical considerations as well as personal options, even mannerisms, especially in literary styles. Breen, when criticizing various 19th-century styles, discusses an
inscription in a style which

> has no time for colons or semicolons, and bestows but a passing notice on the
> commas. As to full stops, it admits of only one, and that it calls a *terminus*. Stops
> were well enough in the steady, stately, stage-coach phraseology of the Johnsons,
> but they are unsuited to our days of electricity and steam.   (1857:141)

Some individual authors punctuated in a great variety of ways for specific
purposes. For instance, Dickens used commas or stops to echo chords played, or the ticking of a clock (quoted in Brook 1970:41) – or no punctuation
at all, as in the long speeches of Flora Flinching in *Little Dorrit* to indicate
her breathlessness (pp. 41–2). Overpunctuation became much criticized by
the 1860s. Angus describes contemporary trends as follows:

> The tendency in modern English is to disperse with commas as far as a regard to
> the sense will allow. If very numerous, they distract the attention, without afford-
> ing proportionate help to the meaning.   (1862:330)

Looking back on the heritage of the 19th century, Fowler & Fowler (1906/ 30:234, 240, 243) spoke out against 19th-century excesses and advised writers to employ moderate punctuation:

> it is a sound principle that as few stops should be used as will do the work. There is a theory that scientific or philosophic matter should be punctuated very fully and exactly, whereas mere literary work can do with a much looser system ...
>
> Over-stopping ... is on the contrary old-fashioned; but it is equally compatible with correctness. Though old-fashioned, it still lingers obstinately enough to make some slight protest desirable; the superstition that every possible stop should be inserted in scientific and other such writing misleads compositors, and their example affects literary authors who have not much ear ... we make the general remark that ungrammatical insertion of stops is a high crime and misdemeanour, whereas ungrammatical omission of them is often venial, and in some cases even desirable. Nevertheless the over-stopping that offends against nothing but taste has its counterpart in under-stopping of the same sort.

Inverted commas were used to mark direct speech – but not as consistently as today; in consequence, indirect speech was occasionally thus indicated, or the marks were omitted in clear cases of direct speech, or in free indirect speech, a type developed by 19th-century novelists (cf. Denison 1998:262).

Special features of 19th century texts are asterisks, daggers and bars indicating the reference points for footnotes (which tend to be numbered in modern books) and the use of 'pointers' highlighting the most important facts, especially in advertising.

Ex. 19　Rewrite a passage exhibiting 19th-century 'over-stopping' (such as T1, T3, T5, T6) using modern punctuation, and formulate the different principles guiding the 19th-century author.

3.4　*Pronunciation*

As regards pronunciation, historical linguists depend entirely on descriptions and transcriptions by phoneticians, and various comments (often negative), on other people's speech habits. Hardly any recordings of *spontaneous* speech survive: the earliest tone document of EngE, the Irving cylinders of 1890, now in the BBC sound archives, do not appear to have been analysed phonetically.[50]

In the course of the 19th century, there was no radical change leading to a new phonemic system, but, rather, the spread of educated S BrE to

---

[50] Apart from Irving's recitation of the opening speech of Richard III, they include recordings of 'as many of [Irving's] distinguished friends as could be persuaded to talk into the revolutionary machine' (Argo record cover of 'Great actors of the past', 1977).

encompass a greater number of speakers.[51]

As far as the codification of pronunciation is concerned, a decisive step had been taken with Walker's *Critical Pronouncing Dictionary* of 1791, the first to record a norm for every single word.[52] However, its impact was confined to the restricted number of its readers (if they chose to conform), so that the claim in the Preface to the 1809 edition is certainly exaggerated. There it was stated that the late John Walker had fixed pronunciation and thereby given 'stability and permanence to the pronunciation of a language now spoken in most parts of the known world' – whereas it had been obvious at least since Johnson that a language could not be frozen (least of all in its pronunciation), and the differences between varieties of English around the world were becoming conspicuous. This is so, even though Ellis (1869–74:II, 625) admitted that 'Walker has undoubtedly materially influenced thousands of people, who, more ignorant than himself, looked upon him as an authority'. This quotation also indicates Walker's predominantly prescriptive intentions although he claimed: 'nor have I the least idea of deciding as a judge, in a matter of such much delicacy and importance as to the pronunciation of a whole people ' (1791:ix).

As far as the regional basis of a norm for correct pronunciation was concerned, the predominance of London was undoubted. However, Walker (1791) had pointed to the improprieties of London speech, and Smart (1812) made relevant remarks on class-related varieties of pronunciation current in the metropolis:

> Imitation of a Londoner, or of a person who pronounces like one, is the only method by which a just utterance can be acquired. Not that, as pronounced by a native of London, words and sentences are intrinsically more harmonious and euphonical than as they are heard in some of the provinces: very plausible assertions may be made to the contrary. But while it is necessary that there should be a standard pronunciation, and while the courtly and well-bred conform to it, that of the inhabitants of the metropolis will always claim the preference, and

---

[51] MacMahon (1998:380) rightly points out that statements before 1860 tend to be vague and prejudiced; the development of the science of phonetics changed the precision of the description, so that from Ellis onward we have much more reliable evidence available; other trustworthy 19th-century phoneticians, who greatly promoted the new discipline of experimental phonetics, include A. M. Bell and Henry Sweet. (The next step, that of recorded sounds preserved for analysis, is almost exclusively a 20th-century development.)

[52] Ellis (1869–74:624–5) strongly criticized Walker's method of employing 'constant references to the habits of a class of society to which he evidently did not belong [and] the most evident marks of insufficient knowledge, and of that kind of pedantic self-sufficiency which is the true growth of half-enlightened ignorance' (here quoted from MacMahon 1998:378). Similar criticism could of course have been uttered against Walker's predecessor Sheridan.

every deviation will be looked upon, if not as illiterate, at least as uncouth and inelegant.

But there are two pronunciations even in London, that of the well-bred and that of the vulgar. The well-bred speaker employs a definite number of sounds, which he utters with precision, distinctness, and in their proper places; the vulgar speaker misapplies the sounds, mars, or alters them ...

But while the vulgar commit errors through inattention, it not unfrequently happens, that the well-bred are guilty of similar faults through the affectation of correctness. That our language is chargeable with numerous anomalies of pronunciation must be allowed; and it is commendable to lend a little assistance towards reducing their number. But in attempting this, two things should be considered: first, that the speaker does not wrong himself by adopting peculiarities too glaring to escape invidious remark; and secondly, that he does not wrong the very cause he undertakes, by making changes without having sufficiently attended to the settled analogies of the language. (1812, quoted from Holmberg 1964:53–4)

By 1817, the desire for a uniform pronunciation had apparently penetrated to the level of children's education. Darton, Harvey & Darton of London, publishers of children's books, advertised Thomas West's *The English Pronouncing Spelling Book* 'on a Plan entirely new; calculated to correct Provincialisms, and promote a uniform Pronunciation, by exhibiting to the Eye the various Anomalies of the Language, along with the regular Sounds: accompanied by a great Variety of Easy and Progressive Reading Lessons. The whole intended as a First Book for Children'.

However, the wisdom of writers of grammar and conduct books may well be questioned when they include for pronunciation practice monstrosities like the following sentence from Savage, who has four pages of sentences which 'incorporate a great variety of words that are generally mispronounced and are brought together for orthoepical practice':

The belligerent parties were of Herculean force and sufficient to annihilate the allies whose supernumerary adherents gave an impetus to their actions which gave a poignant chagrin to the policy of the seraglio.   (1833:87)

By contrast, Cobbett still found that (proper) pronunciation 'ought not to occupy much of your attention; because (it) is learned as birds learn to chirp and sing'. There *are* dialect differences, but 'while all inquiries into the causes of these differences are useless, and all attempts to remove them are vain, the differences are of very little real consequence' (Cobbett 1823/ 1984:8–9). Apparently, the heyday of stigma attaching to 'wrong' pronunciation was still to come – an impression confirmed by the fact that educated men (such as leading politicians) were not ashamed to retain their accent in early 19th-century Britain.[53]

The tendency towards spelling pronunciation is obviously a consequence of many more people becoming literate, who regarded written English as the proper norm, adapting the sounds to the letters where the two diverged – an opinion sanctioned by the authority of Johnson and Murray.[54] Perhaps the most obvious case is the history of inflectional *-ing*. Walker had stated in 1791:

> Hitherto we have considered these letters as they are heard under the accent; but when they are unaccented in the participial termination *ing*, they are frequently a cause of embarrassment to speakers who desire to pronounce correctly. We are told, even by teachers of English, that *ing*, in the word *singing, bringing*, and *swinging*, must be pronounced with the ringing sound, which is heard when the accent is on these letters, in *king, sing* and *wing*, and not as if written without the g as *singin, bringin, swingin*. No one can be a greater advocate than I am for the strictest adherence to orthography, as long as the public pronunciation pays the least attention to it; but when I find letters given up by the Public, with respect to sound, I then consider them as cyphers; and, if my observation does not greatly fail me, I can assert, that our best speakers do not invariably pronounce the participial *ing*, so as to rhyme with *sing, king*, and *wing*.
>
> (Walker 1791:lxxxviii; quoted in Bailey 1996:87–8)

– but [-ɪŋ] was to win, based on the belief of middle-class speakers that a pronunciation based on spelling is best (cf. Bailey 1996:88–92).

Seven phonetic variables will bring out the changing norms of 19th-century pronunciation which were apparently not always determined by the persuasions of the upper classes and the guidance provided by the spelling:[55]

[53] Mugglestone (1995:89) rightly points out that Cobbett's son, when editing his father's grammar in 1866, commented on the regional pronunciations of *corn* adduced as specimens of variation in 1819: 'Many of these terms are of constant use, and the mispronouncing of some of them is particularly offensive' (cf. T15).

[54] Compare Buchmann (1940) and the lists of words in Strang (1970:81–4) in which pronunciations were (re-)modelled on spelling, mainly by restituting letters which had become mute. However, such advice was impracticable with polysyllabic words (cf. 3.5) and not without its risks elsewhere. As Holofernes was ridiculed by Shakespeare for his in-sisting on the insertion of [b] in *doubt*, etc. (cf. Görlach 1991:324), so Anon. warns against [l] in *balm, alms*, etc., 'though we often hear it sounded by the vulgar' (1797); *housewife* should be [hʊswɪf] – only 'some affected speakers pronounce it *House-wife*' (1797).

[55] The glottal stop, one of the most strongly stigmatized features in present-day Britain appears too late to influence 19th-century evaluations (cf. Bailey's summary 1996:76–8). First recorded in Scotland in the 1860s, it had spread (?) to non-standard London speech by the 1880s, but was not a regular feature. Its presence overseas is very irregular, another indication that it was a later development in Britain.

(a)   The *a* sound in *calf, glass, aunt, grant*. Modern pronunciation differs between America, the North of Britain and London/RP. Whereas the long /a:/ was accepted in *calf*, and there was not much objection to the same sound in *glass*, Walker (1791:11) found that the long pronunciation in '*after, answer, basket, plant, mast* ... borders very closely on vulgarity'. He did not object to this sound in *can't, han't, shan't*, pronunciations which were unacceptable to others.

(b)   The pronunciation of /u:/ vs /ju:/ in *due*, etc., now largely considered an American shibboleth, was criticized less frequently,[56] but Alford's strong words indicate it was a salient feature of correctness; he regarded it as:

> a very offensive vulgarism, most common in the midland counties ... it arises
> from defective education, or from gross carelessness.   ([3]1870:61)

(c)   Dropping your aitches[57] was not regarded as a grievous offence for centuries – and most dialects of England apparently lost /h/ at the beginning of words. However, from the late 18th century at least, a social stigma developed (which has remained to the present day).[58]

---

[56] Cf. MacMahon (1998:404-5); a full description would need to consider the various environments determining changes in progress and to specify which pronunciations were stigmatized and by whom.

[57] Compare the detailed documentation of attitudes towards /h/ in Mugglestone (1995:107–59), which she sees as one of the 'symbols of the social divide'. She quotes (1995.108) statements by Henry Sweet ('an almost infallible test of education and refinement', 1890) and Alexander Ellis ('at the present day great strictness in pronouncing *h* is demanded as a test of education and position in society', 1869). Even more outspoken are the authors of *The Laws and Bye-Laws of Good Society* of 1867 who state: 'The omission or importation of the aspirate in the wrong place is a sure sign of defective training. It grates on the ear with peculiar harshness, and is utterly out of keeping with pretensions to being considered *bien élevé*' (quoted from Mugglestone 1995:121–2). What seems particularly noteworthy is the consensus of all writers ranging from conduct book writers to the most eminent linguists of the period. The phonemes /h/ and /r/ even had complete books devoted to their correct use (cf. fn. 40 above).

[58] The history of *h*-dropping is partly elucidated by its presence in extraterritorial varieties. America has nothing of the sort, apparently because emigration was too early to export the feature. Australia has some instances, but not to any noteworthy degree; by contrast, there are many complaints relating to *h*-dropping from 19th-century New Zealand. The stigmatized feature was commented on at an early time in SAfE: 'The first thing that strikes an Englishman's ear is perhaps the utter disuse of the letter "H" among the educated English-speaking portion of the Dutch. On the other hand you seldom hear the Cockney abuse of the same letter. It is a social axiom that the dropping of the "H" is a sign at least of the want of good breeding; but in the Cape it would be a very fallacious mode of judging' (Legg 1890–1).

Walker (1791:xiii) warns Londoners in very explicit terms:

A still worse habit prevails, chiefly among the people of London, that of
sinking the *h* at the beginning of words where it ought to be sounded, and of
sounding it, either where it is not seen, or where it ought to be sunk.

The question was vital for 19th-century speakers, in particular for the
upwardly mobile. Mistakes were not forgiven, and one feature of
Dickens's character Uriah Heep that sticks in readers' minds is his
umbleness. Alford's verdict is harsh, but captures 19th-century
attitudes:

Nothing so surely stamps a man as below the mark in intelligence, self-
respect, and energy, as this unfortunate habit: in intelligence, because, if he
were but moderately keen in perception, he would see how it marks him; in
self-respect and energy, because if he had these, he would long ago have set
to work and cured it.   (^{3}1870:51)

Hypercorrection was a necessary consequence. Horn & Lehnert quote
from G. Hill's *The Aspirate* (1902):

In English an *h* is often put on by those among the uneducated who wish to
talk correctly ... It is not as a rule the very poor who introduce *h*'s, but the
small shopkeeper and the villager who reads at home in the evening instead of
going to the public house.   (1954:868–9)

(d)   As mentioned above, dropping your *g*'s in *-ing* was a different story.
       The increasing literacy apparently demanded a [-g] where it was
       spelt[59] – a tendency not affecting the lowest classes (who could not
       read or did not care) and the upper crust (who did not care) – so that
       a three-tier system lasted well into the 20th century, with the upper
       classes and workers having the uncorrected earlier forms – Wyld
       (1921/36:283) found that in his time [-n] was 'still widespread among
       large classes of the best speakers, no less than among the worst'.
       Bailey (1996:89) quotes a cartoon from *Punch* (6 Sept. 1873) which
       illustrates the principle with *-ing* and *ain't*.[60]

---

[59] This was most clearly stated by L. Murray in 1802 who thus objected to the [ɪn] pronunciation: 'As it is a good rule, with respect to pronunciation, to adhere to the written
words, unless custom has clearly decided otherwise, it does not seem proper to adopt this
innovation' (quoted from Horn & Lehnert 1954:842).

[60] 'Evil Communications', &c.: *Lord Reginald.* 'Ain't yer goin' to have some puddin',
Miss Richards? It's so jolly!' *The Governess.* 'There again, Reginald! "*Puddin'*" –
"*Goin'*"– "*Ain't yer*"!!! That's the way Jim Bates and Dolly Maple speak – and Jim's a
stable-boy, and Dolly's a *laundry-maid*!' *Lord Reginald.* 'Ah! But that's the way father
and mother speak, too – and father's a *duke*, and mother's a *duchess*!! So *there*!'

(e)   By contrast, little sociolinguistic evaluation, or comment, appears to
       be found on dropping your *r*'s: although non-rhotic pronunciation of
       car and *cart* is a minority choice in British and American dialects
       today, the loss of /r/ which was more generally criticized from the
       19th century onwards was accepted without resistance into educated
       BrE speech and, later on, into RP.[61] Note that frequent intrusive /r/
       which was more generally criticized from the 19th century onwards
       also conflicts with spelling.

(f)   The contrast between /ʍ/ and /w/ (<wh> vs <w>) was kept in edu-
       cated speech until after 1850; though supported by spelling it was
       finally given up due to pressure from 'vulgar' speech (according to
       Dobson [2]1968).

(g)   Finally, there is the well-known case of /v/:/w/ confusion. Its social
       history can here be summarized from one of the few linguistic his-
       tories that gave due weight to sociohistorical conditions, Horn &
       Lehnert (1954). In II:945 they trace the stigmatization of this feature
       from Elphinston (1786–7) to Walker (1791), who finds it frequent in
       'the inhabitants of London, and those not always of the lower order'.
       However, in the course of the next generation it somehow dis-
       appeared. Smart (1836) states:

> The diffusion of literature among even the lowest classes of the metropolis,
> renders it almost unnecessary to speak now of such extreme vulgarisms as the
> substitution of *v* for *w*, or *w* for *v*. Few persons under forty years of age, with
> such a predilection for literary nicety as will lead them to these pages, can be
> in much danger of saying, that they like '*weal and winegar wery vell*'.

---

[61] Although Mugglestone (1995:98) claims that 'dropped r ... exemplifies in many ways
the interactions of prescriptive ideology, literate speech, and those socio-symbolic virtues
which were never far from issues of phonemic propriety', objections to the sound changes
were few and far between. (Newman, in 1878, directed heavy censure towards the
'assimilating and trait-destroying tendencies of slovenly speech', and R. R. Rogers in
1855 made a plea for /r/ in his *Poor Letter R, Its Use and Abuse*.) Bailey (1996:102) adds
the statement (also interpreted in Horn & Lehnert 1954:916) by the Birmingham schoolmaster T. W. Hill, of 1821, who voiced 'the low esteem with which outsiders viewed the
innovative *r* of London' when he said: '*r* ... ought more carefully to be preserved for
posterity than can be hoped, if the provincialists of the Metropolis and their tasteless
imitators be to be tolerated in such rhymes as *fawn* and *morn*'. Bailey adds: 'Resistance
to the spreading London fashion was, however, not long sustained in Britain' – and how
could it be, the status of Northern and Scottish English being what it was? (Occasional
documentation of retained /r/ in Londoners' speech in the 19th century does not conflict
with the marked tendency towards loss.)

This statement is the clearest I have met with to explain a linguistic change (rightly or wrongly) by the growth of literacy, significantly in a decade which is likely to have seen the most rapid increase of literates. The later history of the feature is, then, one of an exclusively literary stereotype, first popularized by Dickens's Sam Weller – until even this stereotype was declared dead and buried by Shaw in 1900 in his epilogue to *Captain Brassbound's Conversion* (T37).

Honey (1988) claims that, as the social threat from the middle classes and graduates of the newly founded red-brick universities (notably concentrated in the industrial Midlands, see figure 4) came to be felt by the upper classes, new strategies were introduced to make the old class distinctions plain – the new function of Eton, Harrow and Oxbridge.

He has also drawn attention to the fact (1989:44–6) that in the 19th century many features, which were highly stigmatized in the speech of the common people, were nevertheless also used, or even cultivated, in the best society (46). Accordingly, *he don't, we ain't*[62] 'could be heard in the most aristocratic – even royal – households' (44); such apparent independence from middle-class propriety also included dropping *h*'s and *g*'s: 'the headmasters of Eton whose reigns spanned the years 1868 to 1905, Hornby and Warre, both used the *-in* form.[63] Warre thundered in the chapel pulpit against the evils of "bettin' and gamblin'" (45). By contrast, the proper pronunciation of *h* and *ng* was assiduously respected by the middle classes – not a single guide to correct English would be without explicit advice on these points.

Whereas this 'hyperlect' could only be learnt from educated speakers, the spread of the boarding-school system, and the emergence of prep schools, from 1860 onwards, led to the dominance of the public-school accent as the gauge of correctness, and this is responsible for the rise of

[62] Savage (1833:viii) alleges that public-school education did not guarantee high standards in correct pronunciation (without providing any detailed evidence): 'we know many who would feel ashamed of a false quantity in Greek or Latin that are absolutely incapable of reading with propriety an English newspaper' (There are also remarks relating to a similar neglect of English syntax).

[63] The forms are of course part of the larger problem of whether or *not* contractions are acceptable at all and, if so, whether they may be used in written or printed texts. Phillipps (1984:68–9) quotes a warning from the anonymous *Vulgarities of Speech Corrected* of 1826: 'Some of these are much less vulgar than others, but not one of them could be admitted into correct and elegant conversation.'

what became known as Received Pronunciation.[64] Honey states quite
explicitly:

> By the end of the nineteenth century a non-standard accent in a young Englishman
> signalled non-attendance at a public school, whereas if he spoke RP he was either
> a genuine member of the new caste of public school men or he had gone to some
> trouble to adjust his accent elsewhere, thus advertising the fact that he identified
> with that caste and its values.   (1989:29)

In the church, RP was considered a necessary qualification for Anglicans,
whereas 'a non-standard accent in a minister of religion would, until comparatively recently, be a fairly safe indicator that he belonged to a Non-
conformist denomination' (Honey 1989:34).

In modern dialectology and sociolinguistic investigations, pronunciation
is the most salient feature indicative of region and social class; it came to be
the touchstone of class distinctions in the course of the 19th century – as is
most clearly evident from the variables discussed under 2.4 'Sociolect',
above – and was accordingly much used for the characterization of personae
in both novels and plays from Dickens to Shaw's *Pygmalion* (the linguistic
value of such sources depending both on the good ear of the writer and on
his inclination to stereotype).

Words borrowed from French presented a special problem. From the
17th century on, those diverging from English pronunciation, or with an un-
English relationship between spelling and pronunciation, had not been consistently adapted (for example *machine*). However, it was not always easy
in 19th-century Britain to find a way between vulgar corruptions and a
genteel display of the speaker's competence in French or – as a writer stated
with regard to [a] – 'between vulgarity or affectation' (1866, in Mugglestone 1995:95). This problem was most obvious in the pronunciation of
non-English phonemes such as /y(:)/ and /œ(:)/ and nasal vowels, but there
were also choices to be made in individual words, such as *trait* pronounced
with or without final /t/. James Murray (1888:x) admits that there was variation 'with words from other modern languages, the pronunciation of which
depends largely upon the linguistic knowledge and taste of the person who
uses them'. Fowler (1926:193) still found that pronouncing French words
'as if you were one of the select few to whom French is second nature ... is
inconsiderate & rude', but such warnings were not always heeded.

---

[64] Ellis (1869:23; 1874:1216) was one of the first to define the term and to ascribe it to
'the metropolis, the court, the pulpit and the bar', to which he later added 'the stage, the
universities – and, in a minor degree, parliament, the lecture room, the hustings and
public meetings'. However, the emerging norm cannot be assumed to have been homogeneous.

Another difficulty is connected with the scientific vocabulary of physics, chemistry and biology. In so far as we would like to call some of the terms 'words' (and not, for instance, pronounceable formulas for chemical structures) they are found almost exclusively in written form. James Murray (1888) complains about the fact that even specialists did not agree about the pronunciation of a comparatively current word like *gaseous*.

Finally, proper pronunciation includes careful articulation. However, the extent of such statements was greatly reduced in comparison with the 18th century when there were still 'rhetorical grammars' (like Walker 1785) primarily intended for the orator. Enunciation in the 19th century came to be mainly a point mentioned in conduct books (as was handwriting). 'Censor' advises:

> Don't mangle your words, or smother them, or swallow them. Speak with a distinct enunciation. Don't talk in a high, shrill voice, and avoid nasal tones. Cultivate a chest-voice; learn to moderate your tones. Talk always in a low register, but not too low. (*c.* 1880:61–2)

Ex. 20 Discuss Honey's (1989) hypothesis of the rise of RP with reference to social-class differences in Victorian England, contrasting his views with Macaulay's (1997).

Ex. 21 Summarize the evidence on where the norm of pronunciation was permanently guided by the spelling and where it failed to be, and try to give reasons for these complex developments.

3.5 *Word stress, sentence stress and intonation*

The most careful description of stress, at the end of the period, is Sweet's (1890). He distinguishes between four degrees (and marks these in his transcribed passages): *weak* (–), *medium* (:), *strong* (ˈ) and *emphatic* (;), thus in :*kontrə'dikt*. He also has relevant remarks on level stress, as in *garden wall*, which he discusses under 'syntax' (p. 27). Strang (1970:87) points out that level stress in words such as *góld wátch* was 'first noted in the 17c, [and became] fully established and highly productive in the late 18th and 19th centuries; the relative newness of it is still shown by the marked fluctuation amongst speakers in [its] use'.

Stress in polysyllabic Latinate words had remained relatively free until the 18th century (see Lass fc.). An indication of how free it still was in 1797 is provided by Anon., who compared the advice given on word accentuation in the dictionaries by Ash, Bailey, Entick, Johnson, Sheridan and Walker and added his own preference (X). I here give a selection of seven problem words, with the stressed syllable preferred indicated by first letters of the compilers' names; the data from the first edition of the *OED* (= O)[65] can illustrate the development in the course of the 19th century:

	1st	2nd	3rd
acceptable	ESWX	**ABJO**	
advertisement	AE	**BO**	JSWX
caravan	**ASWXO**		JBE
centrifugal	W	ABESO	**JX**
compromise (n.)	**JSWXO**		ABE
contemplator	**SXO**	BW	AEJ
envelope (n.)	**O**	ABE	JSWX

Figure 12   Stress in polysyllabic words as suggested by various pronouncing dictionaries: A(sh), B(ailey), E(ntick), J(ohnson 1755), S(heridan), W(alker 1791); agreement with modern BrE usage is indicated by bold type

In the 19th century, usage was fixed – with solutions which often came to set BrE apart from AmE. Whereas a shift to the first syllable was accepted in BrE in words like *sécret(a)ry*, the American tradition – partly influenced by Webster's verdicts – insisted that all written syllables should be properly pronounced. By contrast, a stress opposition emerged and was later functionalized in EngE in nouns vs verbs like *progress* or *record*, whereas AmE has more instances of undistinguished pairs. Note that in the early 19th century some verbs had end-stress in contrast to PDE (*advertize, colleague*, etc., mentioned in Savage 1833:113). White (1882, T21) records a number of stress shifts within living memory.[66]

In sentence stress, Sweet lists six major functions (1890:18–29): emphatic, intensive, contrasting, modifying, grouping and distributed stress permit important distinctions, which cannot be easily rendered in written forms. (His statements do not allow us to see whether stress distinctions have

[65] The *OED* records varying usage for some of these: in *acceptable*, for instance, it includes stress on the first syllable as the original pronunciation, 'so in all poets to the present day'; for *advertisement*, the third syllable is recorded for the US; in *caravan*, end-stress is a second option.

[66] Scots pupils in particular had to be cautioned not to stress *súccess, áffiance, aliénat, alienable, difficult, démocracy, excéllency, embarráss, intelligible*, etc. (Buchanan 1757).

changed in the past 100 years.)

Sweet is, again, our most reliable source on late 19th-century intonation. He distinguishes level (̄), rising (´), falling (`) and the combinations (ˇ) and (^) – the latter 'as an expression of sarcasm' (p. 3). There are even sub-divisions, as '*ou* with a slight rise expresses slight curiosity or interest, with a more extensive rise astonishment'. Since punctuation marks are regularly correlated with intonation, no tone-mark is written, 'a comma or "?" im-plying a rising tone, a colon or semicolon a falling tone' (1890:3). There is, however, nothing period-specific in all this.

Ex. 22   Check in selected 19th-century dictionaries the stress given for polysyllabic Latinate words. If there are differences with PDE usage, does 19th-century EngE side with AmE norms (cf. Danielsson 1948)?

4

Inflection

'Curiouser and curiouser!' cried Alice (she was so much surprised that for the moment she quite forgot how to speak good English).

4.1   *Nouns*

The major problems of English inflectional morphology had long been settled – only a few questions in nominal inflection remained to be answered for grammarians of prescriptive grammars in the 19th century. A minor instance of unregulated usage was the genitive marker after stem-final *s*; there was still some variation, but the generalization of *'s* appears to be the rule (as in *Tess's, Dickens's*). Otherwise, case was (and still is) indicated only in pronouns (cf. 4.3). In plural formation, the distinction between countable and uncountable, i.e. whether a word could be pluralized (and whether a mass noun like *acquaintance* was to be constructed with a plural form of the verb), was a syntactical concern rather than one of morphology. However, the question of how a plural of a foreign word ought to be formed remained urgent (and is still unsolved), the speaker's competence in the classical languages competing with the tendency to integrate these words in pronunciation and morphology. Henry Fowler (1926, 'Latin plurals') decides in favour of a 'foreign' plural in the case of *nuclei, species, theses, opera, antennae*; zero plural in *forceps*; and allows both forms for *bacilli, lacunae, genera*, and, with semantic distinction, for *genii/geniuses*. In sum, 'when one is really in doubt the English form should be given the preference'.

Ex. 23   Has there been any development in the plurals of the above Latin/ Greek nouns in PDE, and how far can this be explained by receding competences in the classical languages? Check the practice of 19th- and 20th-century dictionaries for various 'problem' cases.

4.2   *Adjectives*

Adjectives had long been uninflected apart from comparison, and 18th-century grammarians had regulated where *-er, -est* inflection was to be used.[67] The rules were quite complex and often disregarded (as in the case of Alice above). However, Fowler (1926:145) warned that

> Neglect or violation of established usage with comparatives & superlatives sometimes betrays ignorance, but more often reveals the repellent assumption that the writer is superior to conventions binding on the common herd.

He goes on to admit that a certain degree of choice is left:

> The remarks that follow are not offered as precise rules, but as advice that, though generally sound, may on occasion be set aside.

He lists 'many others, e.g. *awkward, brazen, buxom, crooked, equal,* can take *-er* & *-est* without disagreeably challenging attention'.

Some of Fowler's remarks reflect 19th-century usage rather than modern conventions, especially when he talks about *-est*: 'Many adjectives ... are capable in ordinary use, i.e. without the stylistic taint ... of forming a superlative in *-est*, used with *the* & serving as an emphatic form simply, while no one would think of making a comparative in *-er* from them: *in the brutalest, civilest, timidest, winningest, cogentest, cheerfullest, cunningest, doggedest, drunkenest, candidest, damnablest, manner.*'[68]

He remarks, again on 19th-century mannerisms long out of date:

> As a stylistic device, based on *novelty-hunting,* & developing into disagreeable *mannerism,* the use of *-er* & *-est* is extended to many adjectives normally taking *more* & *most,* & the reader gets pulled up at intervals by *beautifuller, delicater, ancientest, diligentest, delectablest, dolefuller, devotedest, admirablest,* & the like. The trick served Carlyle's purpose, & has grown tiresome in his imitators.

Finally, he finds (in the collocation *deepest emotion* used without an article) 'the *vulgarization* of a use that is appropriate only to high-poetic contexts ... not unless he had been apostrophizing her in verse as "deepest emotion's Queen", or by whatever lyric phrase emotion (& not analysis) might have inspired, should he have dared to cut out his *the* & degrade the idiom sacred to the poets'.

4.3   *Pronouns*

From the 15th century on, pronouns were exceptional in the nominal system since they retained some categories of case apart from the genitive. The fact

---

[67] Double marking was considered vulgar from the 18th century onwards; Savage provides many examples like: *This is most hardest. You are more harsher* (1833:92).

[68] With derived adverbs, *-er* forms were still possible. Fowler & Fowler (1906/31:49) comment on uninflected adverbs in slang and continues: 'outside slang we have to choose between *stronglier* – poetical, exalted, or affected – and *more strongly*'.

created a great deal of insecurity which again reflected the contrasting trends of usage and prescriptive correctness. The problems discussed by 18th-century grammarians continued – but were not solved. They included:

(1)   object case following *it is (me)*: although subject case is required by logic, the position at the end of the sentence suggests object case;

(2)   uncertainty about *me*, etc., in subject position; the choice of the 'correct' case is also uncertain after prepositions, as in *between you and me/I*, and in answers: *Who is it? – Me!*;

(3)   the loss of *whom*: non-inflection in questions and relative clauses not only agrees with *which* and *that*, but is also suggested by the front position.

Otherwise the system is stable; loss of case distinctions in personal pronouns (apart from *you*) is a non-standard feature. See also the much-quoted gravestone inscription from 19th-century Wiltshire:

> Beneath this stane lyes our deare childe, who's gone from We,
> For evermore unto eternity;
> Where, us do hope, that we shall go to He,
> But Him can ne'er com back again to We.   (*Old Mortality*, p. 138; cf. T55)

Ex. 24 Summarize the treatment of any of the three problem areas above in available 19th-century grammars and the practice in texts, basing your arguments on DeKeyser (1975) and Denison (1998).

4.4   *Verbs*

Variation was still more conspicuous in verbal inflection, where the correct forms of irregular tense formation remained a problem. Johnson had despaired of finding general rules – but had spoken out against the participles *wrote* or *writ*:

> Concerning these double participles it is difficult to give any rule; but he shall seldom err who remembers, that when a verb has a participle distinct from its preterite, as *write, wrote, written*, that distinct participle is more proper and elegant.
> (1755, 'Grammar')

In fact, few 18th- or 19th-century grammars fail to provide lists of irregular verbs. These lists are largely identical; Cobbett stands out for his liberal attitude when he says:

I will here subjoin a list of those verbs which are, by some grammarians, reckoned irregular; and, then, I will show you, not only that they are not irregular, strictly speaking; but, that you ought, by all means, to use them in regular form.

(1823/1984:44)

He then goes on to list not only verbs with minor irregularities or mixed paradigms, but also verbs which have never been accepted as weak, such as *blow/draw/grow/throw*;   *cling/sling/slink/spring/sting/string/swing*;   and *freeze, swim*.

However, all other grammarians insist on correctness in this field; irregular verbs invariably form part of sections on 'false grammar', and advice is handed out in conduct books like Savage's (1833). He lists as vulgar the past tense forms *lit, druv, hot* ('hit'), *knowed, catched, see, begun* and *wringed*, and the participles *gave, drank, showed, fell, went, took, slew, riz* and *drove* – and insists on (archaic) *bare* for *bore*. Englishmen who may have modelled their speech on Cobbett's grammar would have been sure to feel the social consequences of their 'gross errors' and 'vulgar speech'.

Ex. 25   Can you find any evidence for a permanent shift of an irregular verb to regular inflection – or of rare and complicated verbs being avoided (i.e. replaced by synonyms)?

5

Syntax
(Denison 1993, 1998)

5.1 *Introduction*

[Alice] remembered having seen in her brother's Latin grammar, 'A mouse – of a mouse – to a mouse – a mouse – O mouse!'[69]

Rules prescribed by grammar books will have to be distinguished from actual usage in this chapter; although they are connected, there is no easy and obvious relationship between them. Statements by writers of grammar books tend to be the further away from actual usage the more prescriptive the authors are – recent and ongoing change is likely to be classified as 'mistake'. However, it is not always easy to describe with precision the clash between prescriptive correctness and linguistic reality; DeKeyser (1975) and Rydén & Brorström (1987) have shown for the areas they investigated how substantial the rift could be. Sometimes grammarians also focused their attention on rare items and artificial problems: *than who* was a combination invented by grammarians, and the existing *than whom* was too rare to merit much discussion (cf. 5.3.8 below). DeKeyser (1975:235) said he found only two instances in his 19th century corpus of three million words; he concludes '*than whom*, the target of much criticism in 19th century grammars, is an exceedingly rare construction'.

However, if we want to judge syntactical norms, it is important to realize what the school grammars taught. The continuing impact of a Latin-based concept of what 'grammar' was is seen in the short treatment of syntax (reduced to problems of concord and government) in many grammar books; as late as 1841, Latham could state in his *English Language* that:

Concord, Government, and Collocation are the heads to which the greater part of the English Syntax is reducible.   (1841:357)

In addition, right until the end of the 19th century, *parsing* was the catchword; this predominated to such an extent that the schoolbooks exclusively

---

[69] This 'paradigm' was invented by 16th-century grammarians who wanted to bring their descriptions of English grammar as close to the Latin pattern as possible, and resisted all attacks by common-sense and usage-based grammar books well into the late 19th century: Sir Winston Churchill, for example, remembered the paradigm from his schooldays.

devoted to these exercises were almost equal in number to comprehensive grammars, and no grammar book was without a proper treatment of the topic. Parsing was to train the student to identify both syntactic structures and parts of speech, often on the basis of (ultimately) Latin models. The exercise is best defined in the words of the 'classic' figure among late 19th-century grammarians, Nesfield:

> to parse a word is to show (1) to what part of speech it belongs; (2) to account for its inflections, if it has any; (3) to show in what relation it stands to any other word or words in the same sentence.   (Nesfield 1898:215)

Ex. 26 Summarize the 19th-century rift between prescriptive correctness and actual usage on the basis of DeKeyser (1975) and Rydén & Brorström (1987).

5.2   *A survey of syntactical change*

In view of this background, it may well come as a surprise to find that there *were* developments within English syntax, chiefly in areas which had not been fully regularized in the 18th century.[70] Other innovations, like the increasingly long strings of premodifying nouns and the increase in the use of the genitive in non-possessive functions, are not recorded with any conspicuous frequency in the 19th century and can thus probably be regarded as more recent changes, particularly in newspaper language. Developments in text structure are closely bound up with styles and text types. Their number and distinctive linguistic features are difficult to determine, but some remarks on 19th-century characteristics will be found in chapter 7 below.

An analysis of 19th-century texts clearly shows that most 'problems' discussed in 18th-century grammars (Sundby *et al.* 1991) were still very much in evidence a century later (and indeed today); descriptions of individual writers' (deviant) usage largely agree with the lists of complaints in grammar books (cf. Sørensen 1985:13, on Dickens).

Admittedly, most syntactical patterns of 19th-century St E adhere quite closely to present-day rules. Much of the difficulty in providing an overview like the one attempted here lies in the fact that – if frequencies and

---

[70] Denison's warning should, however, be kept in mind; he notes that 'there can be real difficulty in distinguishing between genuine changes in syntax and mere changes in conventions of decorum in written language' (1998:95). The choice of a corpus and genre-specific analysis is therefore of greatest importance (cf. his statements about the interrelationship between informal private letters and colloquial language, 1998:94, a point, of course, also made by other scholars).

preferences constitute the real differences from PDE usage – far too few statistical analyses are available for 19th-century texts, and where they exist, they are based on differing corpora and diverse methods, making reliable comparisons impossible.[71] However, there *is* remarkable internal variation according to medium, degree of education, social-class membership,[72] formality of situation and text type – a range that appears, impressionistically, somewhat wider than in modern texts.

A description of 19th-century syntax will, then, best

(a) start from those areas where the data deviate from those expected by modern users, and

(b) describe these features selectively and, where appropriate, attempt to point to the 19th-century conditions or causes of such deviances – whether social or stylistic.

5.3   *Individual problem areas*

The major fields in which 19th-century English syntax is different from the preceding period and from present-day usage were listed above; they are now described in greater detail. The analysis will focus on structures 'typical' of the 19th century and no attempt will be made to give a comprehensive account (as provided by Denison 1998).[73]

5.3.1   *The use of* be *to form the present perfect*

To be finally disappeared as a perfect auxiliary, where it had been dominant with verbs of motion (cf. the comprehensive investigation by Rydén & Brorström (1987) and 5.3.6.1 below, and note the parallels in French and German). It is interesting to see that AmE had been a forerunner in this development, as stated by Pickering (1816:37):

> To Arrive. It is remarked by Englishmen, that *we* in many cases employ the auxiliary verb *to have* with this and some other verbs of a similar nature, with

---

[71] Remarks by contemporary authors who notice change and comment on it often refer to individual features. This is the case with, e.g., White (1882, T21), and Bradley, who sees some positive features even in journalese (1904:239, cf. 7.2.5).

[72] Phillipps (1984:70–8) lists a number of 'miscellaneous points of syntax that seem ... characteristic of upper-class writers and speakers'. It is difficult to say whether we can generalize on his 'tentative suggestions' – these features are certainly much less distinctive than those of the lower class.

[73] Other problems which are not treated here include resumptive pronouns, special uses and frequencies of passives, deviant uses of articles, and functions of subjunctives in dependent clauses.

which the English more commonly use the auxiliary *to be*. We generally say, for example, the ship *has* arrived; when he *had* arrived, &c. The English would in such cases use *to be*, as in the following examples: 'We *are* now arrived at the end of a laborious task.'

Whether this change was a simplification of the tense formation, or motivated by the desire for a clearer distinction from the passive, is impossible to say. A graph from Rydén & Brorström (1987:200) demonstrates that the 19th century only completed a process that had been in progress for many centuries:

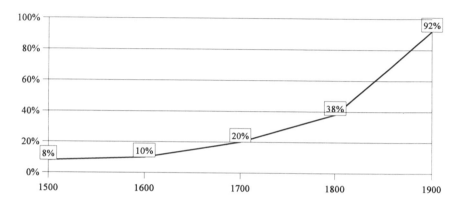

Figure 13 The increase of *have* with verbs of motion

5.3.2 *Negation*

Negation (unless expressed by word-formation) is indicated by negative adverbs (*not, never*) or pronouns (*nobody, nothing*). It presented problems of various kinds, some of which were still being solved in the 19th century.

Negation was to be expressed only once. At least from the 18th century onwards, multiple negation – previously frequent in all types of text – had become a grave impropriety. Its use is accordingly criticized in all grammars and is frequently found among specimens of false grammar, as it is among Savage's improprieties:

> *Not by no means*
> *There arn't none left*
> *They never takes no notice*
> *I don't never wear it*
> *She hasn't got none*
> *Never do so no more*

　　　　　　　　　　　　　　　　　　　　　　　　　　(1833:91–3)

For *not*-negated verbs which were not accompanied by an auxiliary, *do*-periphrasis had become standard in the 19th century. Exceptions are confined to a few frequent monosyllabic verbs (*wrote not, spoke not*, etc.) and these became disused in the course of the 19th century; the usage was confined to facetious, archaic, biblical and poetic contexts (cf. Denison 1998: 195). In *dare not, need not, ought not*, non-use of *do* indicates the auxiliary status of the verb. (Object negation did not, of course, require *do*; cf. *evidences not the true poet but...*, p.154 below).

Ex. 27   Collect data on *not* unaccompanied by *do* (where PDE would require its use) from early 19th-century texts and try to find out the writer's motivation for deviating from the expected pattern.

5.3.3 *Word order*

In word order, 19th-century English appears to have permitted somewhat more choice than modern English does, being open to considerations of rhythm (especially in long periods, supported by heavy punctuation, cf. 3.3) and emphasis.

However, some uses of inversion, i.e. the transposition of the subject and the (auxiliary or full) verb, strike one as particularly Victorian. Apart from cases where the use is standard (in questions and after sentence-initial *hardly*, etc.), inversion remained very much a question of stylistic choice, cf Earnshaw's extensive discussion:

> Perspicuity and Ornament
> Construction of Sentences
> ... The plain and grammatical order of a sentence, being that which corresponds to the usual mode of expression, may be deemed the most consistent with ease and simplicity. *Inversion* is a branch of ornament, combining an attention to sound, sense, and effect. The language that is addressed solely to the understanding, seldom admits much inversion. It is employed chiefly in works addressed to the passions, emotions, or imagination. It should not, however, be *indulged*, but to reach some beauty, or produce some effect, not attainable by the usual order. Nor should much inversion be employed in a long sentence, lest the mind become bewildered amidst the profusion and unusual order of the words.
>
> (1817:82)

The following categories can be distinguished; I here largely follow Fowler (1926) who again largely reflects late Victorian ideas of correctness:

(1)   In exclamations. 'One form of bad inversion arises from inability to distinguish between an exclamation & a mere statement';

(2)   In hypothetical clauses, where inversion is equivalent to *if* – more

frequent in the 19th century than today; *if*-less clauses had, however, seen a continuous decline from 1650 onwards (Denison 1998:300). If we combine the ratios of *had, were, should, could*..., their share in all conditional clauses drops as follows:

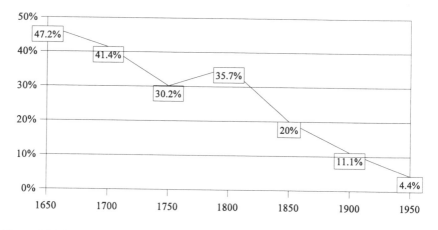

Figure 14 The proportion of *if*-less conditional clauses, adapted from Denison 1998:300

(3)   Inversion used for metrical or rhyming convenience (archaic and poetic);

(4)   Minor types justified by rhythm and text syntax ('balance inversion', 'link inversion', 'signpost inversion', according to Fowler).

Fowler goes on to criticize fashionable types of inversion among book reviewers; false exclamatory inversions ('adopted as an infallible enlivener; they aim at freshness & attain frigidity'); overused 'link inversion' following *yet, especially, rather*, etc. ('a curious habit'), wrong use in indirect questions ('how bold is his attack ...').

While misuses appear to illustrate attempts at genteel syntax in general, they seem to be especially characteristic of 19th-century society in which so many social climbers were aware of their deficits in correct grammar and good style, and this linguistic insecurity led them to use certain constructions they did not master fully.

The increase of sentence-initial dummy *there* in the 19th century (cf. Denison 1998:213–14) is likely to be connected with the problem since it permitted a grammatical form of inversion. Further general statements are problematic since it is difficult to establish to what extent the deviation found in texts of the period is a consequence of informal close-to-spoken style, or to idiosyncratic patterns used for specific effects, as in Dickens's:

Up went the steps, bang went the door, round whirled the wheels, and off they
rattled   (*Old Curiosity Shop*, ch. 41)

Out came the chaise – in went the horses – on sprung the boys – in got the
travellers   (*Pickwick Papers*, ch. 9, quoted from Brook 1970:30)

It is easier to interpret Mrs Chivery's inversions in *Little Dorrit* where
Dickens himself explained the 'linguistic eccentricities' of the persona he
created (Brook 1970:141).

Ex. 28   What evidence is there for unexpected (possibly idiosyncratic) inversion in the texts? Can you classify these uses according to Fowler's
categories?

Another minefield, largely uncleared in the 19th century is the position of
adverbs and adverbial phrases and clauses. Prescriptive grammar laid down
that adverbs ought not to 'split' infinitives and compound verbs, or separate
copulatives and their complements (or, worse, transitive verbs and their
objects). The fear of splitting infinitives (infrequent before 1830) is an exemplary case of a battle between usage, which might well allow the construction in certain contexts, and reason, which might object out of prescriptive concerns (cf. the extensive discussion still felt to be necessary in
Fowler 1926:446–50). The 'split infinitive' was one of the major concerns
of linguists. Surprisingly enough, Earle (1892/98:96) took it as a new phenomenon when he commented:

> But of late years a turn of fashion has placed the Adverb thus, 'to constantly
> maintain', as in the following quotation: 'Leafy huts made of the branches which
> the hill people know to deftly interweave' (W. Hunter). In the discussions which
> have been called forth by this innovation it has acquired a technical designation, ·
> and it is spoken of as 'The Split Infinitive'.
>   We note with pain that Mr Le Galliénne habitually and unblushingly splits his
> infinitives. On two consecutive pages of an Essay on Pater, we find him writing
> 'to merely hold' and 'to glibly review'.   (*Daily Chronicle*, 1 April 1896)

Ex. 29   Which authors of corpus texts split infinitives, and do they do so
regularly or occasionally? Can you find general tendencies and specific
motivations?

Denison (1998:239–43) points out other instances in which the placement
of light adverbials can differ from PDE usage.

   The question of whether a 'preposition' can be at the end of a sentence
was another problem inherited by 19th-century schoolmasters. From

Dryden onwards, writers who believed that the normative rules of Latin were also valid for English grammar objected to a construction they were not willing 'to put up with'. Fowler's (1926:458) is a very moderate statement:

> Those who lay down the universal principle that final prepositions are 'inelegant' are unconsciously trying to deprive the English language of a valuable idiomatic resource, which has been used freely by all our greatest writers except those whose instinct for English idiom has been overpowered by notions of correctness derived from Latin standards.

In fact, the 19th century, loosening the ties that bound English to Latin, arrived at a greater freedom in this respect, too.

Ex. 30   Collect instances of clause-final prepositions from the corpus. Are these diagnostic of period, formality and text type?

5.3.4   *Parts of speech*

5.3.4.1 *Introduction*

Most school grammars followed the traditional pattern of orthography, etymology, syntax and prosody; in this, 'etymology' was organized according to individual parts of speech, ideally categorized under formal (rather than syntactic) criteria, although the loss of inflections left little ground for such classifications. Traditionally, grammarians stuck to the 'classic' ten parts; deviations occurred mainly because the independent status of the article and the participle was questioned and the unity of the 'pronoun' class not accepted (cf. the succinct survey in Michael 1987:362–3). In consequence, various systems offering seven to nine classes were proposed, often with detailed and verbose justifications. A radical reduction to only two or three classes based on the tenets of universal grammar and proposed by Harris, Horne Tooke and Monboddo and their 19th-century followers found comparatively little support, at least not in school grammars. Many alternative systems suggested by frustrated grammarians, often using fanciful innovative terminologies, were apparently not taken up (for the 18th-century background cf. Michael, who lists 56 systems of classification (1970: 521–9)). A survey of systems used in 64 important 18th-/19th-century grammars is given by Martin (1824:207). After discussing the inadequacy of Tooke's and Monboddo's two classes, and the expansion to four categories in six other grammars, he comes down in favour of eight (omitting the article since it is a pronoun, and the participle which is an adjective). His statistics show that in the 64 grammars analysed the following solutions are favoured: 2 parts of speech (2 grammars), 3 (1), 4 (6), 6 (1), 8 (8), 9 (25), 10 (20) and 12 (1). He ends by quoting Crombie, who observed that:

> we have no definite or universally received principle, by which to determine what discriminative circumstances are sufficient to entitle any species of words to the distinction of a separate order. (Martin 1824:207)

The best contemporary survey appears to be that by Isbister (1865:8, fn.), who says 'Great diversity of opinion prevails with respect to the number of these classes or parts of speech ... The following table exhibits the principal systems of classification', listing the following categories for systems of *n* parts of speech:

3 – Noun, Verb, Particle
4 – Noun, Quality, Verb, Particle
6 – Noun, Pronoun, Verb, Adverb, Preposition, Conjunction
7 – adds: Adjective
8 – adds: Interjection
9 – adds: Article
10 – adds: Participle
12 – adds: Relative, Auxiliary

5.3.4.2 *Prescriptive concerns*

Among the features recommended by prescriptive grammarians in order to maintain a proper delimitation of classes were:

(1) marking derived adverbs by -*ly* not only where they qualified verbs, but also where they qualified adjectives;
(2) restricting the use of adjectives as nouns, esp. in the singular, by the increasing addition of prop words (*one, man, thing*) – which could regularly be marked for case and number;
(3) a distinction of gerund (with verbal properties) and verbal nouns, contrasting *the reading of books* (gives pleasure) with *reading books*, where the use of *him* vs *his* in 'agentive' position (*I hate him/his reading books*) remained undecided.

Other problems of classification were never properly tackled. One is the increase of nominal strings in block language (cf. 5.3.9) where the solution frequently adopted (and preferred in the *OED* tradition), namely to classify premodifying nouns as in *gold watch* as 'adjectives', is clearly unsatisfactory. Another type which 'developed rapidly from about 1800' (Strang 1970:101) and which has affected the classification of parts of speech is the *have a look/swim/walk* combination. This allows easy modification (*close look, long walk*, etc.) but is awkward or impossible with passives.

Note that there were also some changes in subclassification, especially of verbs. Many grammarians have noted an increase in at least the following patterns in the 19th century:

(1)   intransitives used transitively (*walk your dog*);
(2)   medio-passives (*sell, wash well*);
(3)   reflexives becoming intransitives (used absolutely: *dress, wash* [one-self]).

However, the importance of part-of-speech classification, for all the parsing exercises forced on to the pupils, seems to have slowly waned – there is less justification for classifying types of grammar on this principle as, Michael (1970) has so convincingly done for the time before 1800.

5.3.4.3 *Concord and government*

Concord was a problem carried over from 18th-century grammars (cf. the very full discussion in Sundby *et al.* (1991) and by DeKeyser (1975) for 19th-century conditions). Whereas some mistakes were marked as vulgar (*They goes, they was*) and *you was* for the singular was obsolescent,[74] other cases remained problematic (and still are in PDE). These can be illustrated from specimens listed as 'grammatical improprieties [which] may be accounted as part and parcel of the popular vulgarisms' by Savage (1833: 91–5):

> What signifies their opinions
> There is nine of us in the house
> Folly and ignorance is the evils of life
> The sheep was all sold
> The Parliament are assembled
> Neither/every one of them are dead

The choice of the correct number in the verb to follow words like *government* has remained a problem right into PDE. DeKeyser (1975:53) found that singular and plural forms were of similar frequency, but that the singular was on the increase – but that the plural continued to be preferred with words like *clergy, folk, people, mankind, majority, pack, rest, audience, couple* and *multitude* (as against *world, nation, society, cabinet, church* and *county* which have the singular almost exclusively).

---

[74] The contrast between *yourselves* and 'illogical' *yourself* remained well established; singular forms like *ourself* and *themself* were infrequent and never accepted (cf. Denison 1998:111–13).

Correct case remained a problem in four areas:

(a)   the subject of the gerund – most grammarians including Murray traditionally preferred the possessive in *the reason of this person's/
his/her dismissing his servant so hastily* (DeKeyser 1975:169–70),[75]
whereas Crombie and Grant point to the influence of Latin in constructions with the noun in the common case;

(b)   the use of the objective case in combinations like *you and me, it's me*,
and in an answer (*Who is it? – Me!*);

(c)   the use of the objective case after *than, as*, etc.; attitudes were split
between *than she*, etc., and *than whom* (where 18th-century grammarians' *than who* was generally rejected);

(d)   the use of *whom* in object position (as an interrogative and relative)
where usage preferred *who* and 'correct' *whom* came to be considered
bookish.

Ex. 31   How much variation and how many conflicting norms about concord are still found in PDE? (Cf. Sundby *et al.* 1991, DeKeyser 1975,
Denison 1998.)

Ex. 32   Formulate the criteria for distinguishing between individual categories of words ending in *-ing* (Jespersen 1909–49, Quirk *et al.* 1972).
Do authors of corpus texts make a distinction between gerund and verbal
noun? Are base forms or genitives used for the 'underlying subject' accompanying a gerund?

5.3.5 *The nominal phrase*

There were no major new developments in the 19th century, although the
frequency and style values of some constructions apparently changed, e.g.:

(1)   Combinations like *this our* came to be looked upon as archaic or unnecessarily formal; in Dickens the use can be 'playfully bombastic'
(Denison 1998:115).

(2)   Various elements, including syntactic strings became increasingly accepted in premodifying position (*his couldn't-care-less* attitude, *Britain's laissez-faire* policies), but the modest 19th-century beginnings

---

[75] The tendency is away from the genitive, as comparisons of the data of the first and
second halves of the century show. The decline is notable for nouns (from 77.7% to
54.1%) but minimal for possessive pronouns (from 97.4% to 93.3% according to
DeKeyser 1975:169).

of the pattern (cf. 5.3.7) were to develop fully only in the 20th century.[76]

(3)   This freedom continued to be expanded for genitives as well – although use remained restricted by acceptability, which made Jespersen's *the man I saw yesterday's hat* artificial or facetious, then as now. (The large-scale extension to non-possessives as in *the book's content* is predominantly a 20th-century development.)

In other ways, uses of the genitive exhibit contrary tendencies. On the one hand, the objective genitive (*God's love* for *the love of God*) is said to be last used by Jane Austen (Phillipps 1970), and on the other, various kinds of non-possessives were becoming possible from the late 19th century – though confined at first to American headline style; cf. Fowler's remarks (1925:39):

> It will be a surprise, and to some an agreeable one, if at this late stage in our change from an inflectional to an analytic language we revert to a free use of the case that we formerly tended more and more to restrict!

(4)   Developments among pronouns include a rise of *one(s)* as a head (also used by itself) and including objective and reflexive functions (cf. Jespersen 1909–49:II, 256–63; Strang 1970:96–7).[77]

Ex. 33   Collect instances of the four categories listed above. Is there deviation from PDE usage, and how are these cases to be interpreted? Is there any evidence of political correctness respecting gender?

5.3.6   *The verbal phrase*

The discussion in this section will concentrate first on the verb(al group) and then move on to look at patterns involving complements (objects, adverbials). A general tendency after 1800 appears to be to give the verbal

---

[76] There is an incidental remark by Earle (1892/98:95) on what he calls the 'expansion of the phrasal adverbs', an innovation which he puts down to German influence:

> 'Literature such as that is calculated to stir the passions and drown the reason of the too readily prejudiced masses.' (*The Saturday Review*, Aug. 15, 1896)
> This is a fashion which we have caught in the present century from our German lessons.

The fashion seems not to have left any permanent traces on English usage.

[77] For instance, *the one(s) I like best*; *the ones that*. Various patterns strike us as peculiarly 19th-century, such as those used by 'Censor', who takes up *one* by *he/his*: 'If one should lose his seat ... he would have ...', 'The first thing one encounters when he attempts to take a car ...' (c. 1880:57–8).

group more weight. This is evident not only from the increase in longer forms (aspect, passive) but through combinations:

> have a try, take a look, etc. develops rapidly from about 1800: ... Structures with what Jespersen (III, 383) calls 'quasi-predicatives', such as *fall flat, come in useful*, now very common, also appear from about 1800.   (Strang 1970:101;
>   cf. Denison's survey of the rise of the phrasal-prepositional verb, 1998:221–5)

5.3.6.1 *Tense*

Usage in the 19th century was nearly identical with that of PDE; the obligatory marking of 'future' was becoming common (cf. 5.3.6.4) and the distinction between past and present perfect permitted less room for personal choice.[78] The *form* of the latter was regularized in favour of *have* in the 19th century, the earlier use of *be* in verbs of motion (*he is arrived*) becoming rare by 1830 (cf. 5.3.1 above).

A peculiar 19th-century construction (not found after 1860?) is the use of 'pleonastic' *been*, apparently employed to stress the resultative character in, e.g., Jane Austen's *I have been returned since Saturday* (1816). Alternatives to the *will/shall* future slowly increased in frequency in the 19th century (BE + *-ing*, BE *about to*, BE *going to*, etc.).

A double use of *have* survives (recorded at least from the 16th century onwards and noted as non-standard in various 19th-century grammars) to express unrealized action in sentences such as *he would have wanted to have kissed her*, or, as a marker of lower-class speech in Dickens's:

> Well, I raly would not ha' believed it, unless it had ha' happened to ha' been here.
> (Mrs Saunders, in *Pickwick Papers* 1837)

Non-finite forms are generally tenseless, though anteriority can be indicated by perfective forms. However, tensing of gerunds and infinitives is often considered as hypercorrect (it may be partly based on Latin conventions). Thus *After going* is equivalent to *Having gone* and preferred to *After having gone*.

Ex. 34   Summarize the development of markers of future time in the 19th century (from Denison 1998:188–90).

Ex. 35   Early texts in the corpus can be expected to contain instances of *be* with verbs of motion; collect these and show whether there is any ambiguity about their use (e.g., whether passive interpretations are possible).

---

[78] A contrast between past tense (record) and present perfect (memory) occasionally served to express aspectual distinctions (cf. Adamson 1998:833).

5.3.6.2 Progressive[79]

Frequency of use, which had increased from the 17th century onwards, rose dramatically in the 19th. Arnaud (1983: 84) estimated that it increased three times between 1800 and 1900. Strang (1982) found that the explosive growth affected the use in non-subordinate clauses. The construction may have been a feature of spoken, non-formal English, which would explain some of the distributions according to text type (especially in some types of novels) and its specific rates of growth.[80] Even so, a 19th-century author's choice apparently included non-use of the progressive, which strikes a modern reader as strange (cf. instances quoted by Denison 1998:143–4). Also note that the 19th century also has first (infrequent) instances of progressives of state verbs, including *be* and *have*.

The 19th century saw the expansion of the progressive into the passive. The construction was among the most criticized innovations, being considered both unnecessary and ugly – the active form would not be misunderstood with intransitive verbs, or where the sentence meaning was impossible to misconstrue (*the house is building* *what; *the book is printing* *what). Fowler & Fowler (1906/31:117) comment on *the house is building*: 'older but still living and correct English for *the house is being built*'. Objections were even fiercer in the long forms of the perfect and future tenses where they resulted in a repetition of *be* (*he will be being married*).[81]

Denison points to the probably significant fact that early instances of progressive passives cluster around Southey, Coleridge, Mary Shelley, Shelley, Keats, Lamb, De Quincey and W. S. Landor, 'all friends or acquaintances ... Most early examples tend to come from the pens of young people writing informally.' Denison asks whether this is the product of 'a kind of social network whose group identity was reinforced by common syntactic usage?' (1998:153–4).

[79] Sweet (1890:37) apparently sees 'aspect' as a modification of 'tense', distinguishing between Present *I see* and definite Present *I am seeing* (explained 1890:40–1).

[80] How the pattern became more widely acceptable *and* was more frequently employed for expressive functions is illustrated by the progressive forms. Adamson (1998:666, based on Wright 1974) points out that while the form is next to absent in the works of Thomson and not found in Collins, its frequency significantly increased in Wordsworth, Coleridge, Keats and Shelley (although its form is awkward in metrical poetry).

[81] Denison (1998:155, referring to Visser 1963–73:§ 2158) quotes as typical verdicts 'uncouth English', 'an outrage upon English idiom, to be detested, abhorred, execrated', 'an awkward neologism [containing] an absurdity so palpable, so monstrous, so ridiculous that it should need only to be pointed out to be scouted'. Strang (1970:99) reminds us that 'Macaulay is said to have written "while brave men were cut to pieces" to avoid *were being* in a structure where *were cutting* could only confuse.'

5.3.6.3 *Subjunctive*

Formal correctness required the use of subjunctive forms after *although, unless* and *if*.[82] Phillipps (1984:75) finds that:

> In correct writing and even in speech, there was a tendency for the subjunctive to be used more frequently than today. *Had* in the sense of 'would have' and *were* in the sense of 'would be' were both more common, even in main clauses, where they are obsolescent today. The mood was especially likely where the speaker was not only well-connected but also bookish.

However, the scarcity of the forms made the category marginal. Sweet (1890) stated:

> The subj. hardly ever occurs except in combinations of 'were' with *if*, and in expressions of wish ... The pres. subj. only occurs in a few formal fossilized expressions of wish, such as 'God save the Queen!'

Obviously, PDE conditions had largely been reached by 1900; Denison's succinct summary (1998:160–4) confirms that there were hardly any developments in a category which had 'a tenuous existence' as a consequence of most of its forms having merged with the indicative. Even in the present subjunctive, for which 'many subtypes may be distinguished ... none of them are truly productive, and some are now entirely fossilized as set phrases' (1998:162).

5.3.6.4 *Modal verbs*
(Denison 1998:164–80)

The inventory of modal verbs was identical with that in PDE,[83] but there were a few differences in frequency and uses which are obsolete today, or only found in archaic and highly formal styles:

(1)   *may* is encroached upon by *can*; 19th-century attestations of *may* were still more frequent than in PDE, and *might* had more frequently past tense or tentative meaning than it has today;

(2)   *shall* and *will* (to indicate future tense) remained a problem for prescriptive grammarians, especially when 'correct' use (which prescribed *shall* for first person and questions with second person) was

---

[82] Savage (1833:94–5) was quite outspoken in considering *If it is so* and *Although he is there / does so* and *Would to God that it was so* as improprieties.

[83] Note that most grammars described modal verbs under the misleading category 'potential mood', with forms listed in the long sections on verbal inflection; the tradition went out of fashion in the 1860s.

to be taught to Scotsmen, Irishmen and Americans. Alford summarizes a wide-spread impression when he states:

> I never knew an Englishman who misplaced '*shall*' and '*will*': I hardly ever have known an Irishman or a Scotchman who did not misplace them sometimes.   (^{3}1870:207–8)[84]

Usage had apparently moved towards *will* (or undifferentiated '*ll*) far more than school-teachers were willing to admit. The rules endlessly given for correct use are not all logical and certainly not based on anybody's usage – although the Fowlers (1906/30:142) claim:

> It is unfortunate that the idiomatic use, while it comes by nature to southern Englishmen (who will find most of this section superfluous), is so complicated that those who are not to the manner born can hardly acquire it; and for them the section is in danger of being useless. In apology for the length of these remarks [i.e. twenty pages] it must be said that the short and simple directions are worse than useless. The observant reader soon loses faith in them from their constant failure to take him right; and the unobservant is the victim of false security.[85]

The expansion of the 'general' use of *will* weakened the earlier volitional meaning, and restricted the obligation meaning of *shall* to formal usage in the course of the 19th century (Denison 1998:168). The increase of 'future' *will* is also explained by a reduction of present tense for future reference, alternatives (even simple progressive) being still comparatively rare.

(3)   Other modal verbs include more frequent attestations with past reference uses (*must, need* and *durst*, today almost obsolete), as indeed all modals have continually lost the past tense function of their second forms.

(4)   The number of suppletive modals increased; they not only served to provide non-finite forms, but also started to expand their semantic distance to the core modals – *to have to/be forced to/must, be allowed to/may, be about to/will, shall*, etc. By contrast, *to be to* has been recessive from the early 19th century onwards.

Ex. 36   Summarize the conflict about *will, shall,* '*ll* (and *would, should*) from accessible 19th-century sources, including the corpus. Has there been any change in prescriptiveness?

---

[84] However, he says that the joke about an Irishman illustrating hypercorrect *shall* ('I will be drowned, no body shall save me') is a clumsy invention.

[85] Cf. the editorial comment in the *SPE Tract* 6 (1921:14): 'No grammar or dictionary can be held to have done its duty if it has not laid down the necessary rules.'

Ex. 37 What is meant by *might, could*, etc., losing their tense functions?
Are they becoming synonymous with *may, can*, etc.?

5.3.6.5 *The passive*

The frequency of passive forms has always depended on text types; they are
mainly found in formal, technical, scholarly expository prose where they
serve to avoid the naming of agents, and to fulfil syntactical functions of
topicalization.

The formality of many 19th-century texts favoured the use of passives;
this was also facilitated through two formal developments. They were not
introduced in the 19th century but became common only in this period:

(1)   the progressive passive (cf. 5.3.6.2 above),
(2)   the acceptance of the *get* passive – a colloquial by-form which be-
       came really widespread only in the 20th century (cf. Denison 1998:
       181–2).

Non-finite clauses are neutral to grammatical voice (*John is easy/eager to
please*), but the more explicit passive forms (*this was terrible to be borne*,
as Trollope wrote in 1860) were still a common option in the 19th century.
Variation is also found after *worth* (*worth repeating / being repeated*).

Ex. 38 Describe the functions of passive constructions in T59, T87, T89
and T95.

5.3.7 *Non-finite constructions*

The increase in non-finite constructions was notable, especially patterns like
it was easy for him to come replacing earlier *that ... should* clauses. A
proper distinction between verbal nouns and gerunds (with verbal government) remained unclear, but was ultimately settled in the 19th century:
whereas mixed constructions like *building of palaces* or *the building palaces* were common before, 19th-century grammarians insisted on the distinction between gerunds (*verbal*: *economically building houses*) and verbal
nouns (*nominal*: *the economic building of houses*, cf. Denison 1998:
268–72).

The frequent use of participles remained a specific feature of formal
(Latinate) diction: looser and more colloquial styles might prefer adverbial
and relative clauses. Correctness demanded participles not to be unattached
('a danger as insidious as notorious', Fowler 1926), rarely to be absolute,
and not to be fused (the term was 'invented for the purpose of labelling &

so making recognizable & avoidable a usage ... rapidly corrupting modern English style', Fowler 1926).

Ex. 39   Analyse the forms and functions of non-finite forms in Castle-reagh's note and the Queen's speech, and contrast Cobbett's and Barnes's rewritings of these texts (T3, T35).

5.3.8 *Dependent clauses*

Relative clauses: The major problems concerning a 'proper' use of relative clauses and their structure had been largely settled by grammarians of the 18th century, in particular:

(1)   The distinction between *who* and *which* (according to personal antecedent).
(2)   The distinction between defining clauses and non-defining (descriptive) ones – *that/which* and the use of commas.
(3)   Specific rules based on rhythmical and word-order considerations, such as the permitted distance from the antecedent, the opposition against the 'preposition-at-the-end' construction, etc.
(4)   The restriction which permitted zero relative only in objective use.

There are no statistics for the use of *who/which/that/Ø* in 19th-century texts. However, emancipation from Latin strengthened the 'native' choices: usage oriented to Latin is likely to prefer *who/which* because of the case and animate vs inanimate distinctions and prepositional uses (*to whom/to which*), whereas Ø especially conflicts with Latin patterns. Since *that* came to be used in restrictive clauses only, its frequency had dropped ever since the early 18th century. By contrast, *what* (for *who*) and *as* (for *who/which*) were clearly non-standard and are always included under 'improprieties', as by Savage, who warns against *That's the man as I saw, This is the stick as I had, Here's a man what's eighty* (1833:98). Note that Savage is out of step with his time when objecting to *the dog whose master* (for: *the master of which*).

On top of the unregulated choices, stylistic problems remained; these are not strictly to be judged according to norms of syntactic correctness but rather on rhythmical adequacy and logical perspicuity. One of the abuses of relative constructions was characterized by Breen as the 'railway' style (cf. p.52).

Since the grammatical principle is not violated, only aesthetic judgement is possible in constructions which stretch acceptability in sentences of the *The-house-that-Jack-built* type. Finally, differences between spoken English and the much greater explicitness of written texts must be taken into account, as Sweet pointed out (1890/1900:vi, cf. the quotation p.27).

We need to look at a stylistically marked construction if we wish to recognize the specific character of 19th-century English. From the Renaissance on, there was a largely formal/poetic clause introduced by *than whom/ which*, an obvious imitation of a Latin construction. The restricted use of this continued until 1900; it is now a very marginal option and is next to absent from 20th-century texts (Görlach 1998a). A statistical analysis shows it is a representative of some features of 19th-century style closely connected to the past, and that there has been radical change since 1914. Fowler & Fowler (1906, retained in ³1930:72–3), at a time when the construction was still very much alive, quote two sentences with *than whom* in which '*whom* is as manifestly wrong as *who* is manifestly intolerable' and concludes: 'The only correct solution is to recast the sentences', admitting 'But perhaps the convenience of *than whom* is so great that to rule it out amounts to saying that man is made for grammar and not grammar for man'.

By contrast, the EModE use of *which* for *this* (cf. Görlach 1991:126), most conspicuous in clause-initial *which when*, was still frequent in the 18th century but apparently rare in the 19th.

Adverbial clauses: The classes of these correspond to those of adverbials – clauses can be temporal, local, final, consecutive, causal, concessive, conditional, etc. Developments in the 19th century are not straightforward except that their high frequency contributes to the notable length of sentences in the period (cf. 5.3.10); for a succinct summary I can refer to Denison (1998:293–305).

Ex. 40   Is there evidence in the corpus that *whom/which* were preferred in formal texts, and *that/Ø* in informal ones?

5.3.9 *Block language*

In printing, reasons of space and the intention to inform quickly about the relevant facts led to the use of different typefaces (bold, large capitals for emphasis) and a reduction of the full syntax. The phenomenon is found especially in newspaper headlines, book titles, marginal summaries of chapters and advertisements and lists of contents in 'prospectuses' of books (T77) – in all these the tendency is towards explicitness in 1800, but for truncated sentences in 1900. This curtailment is achieved mainly through omissions (of articles, titles or the copula), and is supported by a special lexis of short words. Many of these features (but of course without the distinction of typefaces) are also found in note-taking and the new text type of

telegraphese (T93). The reductions introduced are of great linguistic interest
since they tend to go far beyond what is permitted by redundancy (of which
there is little left in PDE); as a result, the omissions create a great number of
ambiguities which can be resolved only by the reader's factual knowledge
– or by consulting the full syntax in the text beneath the headline. These
ambiguities can of course also be exploited in intentionally misleading
statements and puns fabricated as eye-catchers. The 19th century is the decisive period for the development of these structures, but comprehensive
documentation on the spread of the construction classified according to text
types appears to be lacking. My analysis of the fifty-two issues of the
Newspaper of 1844 showed that the use was restricted to two functions:
names of companies, etc. (*The Anti-State Church Conference, Anti-Corn-
Law League, Great Britain Mutual Life Assurance Society*), and sub-
headings in news reports (*Post Office Espionage, The Newfoundland
Church Ship* 'yacht to be used as a church in the remote settlements').

Ex. 41 Describe which elements are deleted in the telegraphese of T93. Is
the style identical with that in modern telegrams?

5.3.10 *Complex sentences and 'periods'*
(Cf. 'text syntax' 5.4)

One of the striking features of 19th-century syntax is the use of long involved sentences; these appear in text types in which a modern reader
would not expect periods built on the classical Latin pattern. The well-con-
structed period, illustrating the writer's logical arguments and ordered
scholarly discourse, was one of the achievements of 18th-century prose, at
least in respectable genres, and especially in expository texts. Earnshaw's
statement is a warning to less skilful readers, and true to 18th-century
ideals:

> Avoid long and intricate sentences. Errors are frequently committed in the extent
> of sentences. Sometimes they are too long; at other times too short and abrupt. A
> long period, perfectly clear, and well constructed, is always beautiful and pleas-
> ant, if it be not so prolonged as to exhaust the patience and attention of the reader.
> But it is extremely difficult to construct such periods; hence, long sentences are
> often feeble, ungraceful, and obscure.   (1817:82)

Such 18th-century periods include a great deal of hypotaxis, whether in the
form of finite or non-finite constructions (cf. 5.3.7). For 19th-century
writers this hypotactic style remained the normal option; paratactic style
was 'the marked option carry[ing] the connotations [of] powerful feeling,

intimate registers and/or uneducated varieties' (Adamson 1998:634–5).[86] Similar positions are reflected in statements against parentheses (Johnson) and for their use (Coleridge, cf. Adamson 1998:638). However, there are frequent contemporary complaints about the loss of the elegance found in 18th-century writing and about the incompetent handling of such structures – whether through lack of proper education (including competence in Latin) or through haste, as in the composition of newspaper articles. In retrospect, Fowler & Fowler (1906/30:235) comment:

> Now there is something to be said for the change, or the two changes: the old-fashioned period, or long complex sentence, carefully worked out with a view to symmetry, balance, and degrees of subordination, though it has a dignity of its own, is formal, stiff, and sometimes frigid; the modern newspaper vice of long sentences either rambling or involved (far commoner in newspapers than the spot-plague) is inexpressibly wearisome and exasperating. Simplification is therefore desirable. But journalists now and then, and writers with more literary ambition than ability generally, overdo the thing till it becomes an affectation; it is then little different from Victor Hugo's device of making every sentence a paragraph, and our last state is worse than our first. Patronizing archness, sham ingenuousness, spasmodic interruption, scrappy argument, dry monotony, are some of the resulting impressions.

Such long sentences provided ample opportunities for the writer to introduce what were seen as mistakes and infelicities, notably in:

(1) proper punctuation (including the use of dashes);
(2) concord;
(3) sequence of tenses and use of subjunctives;
(4) word order and ambiguous antecedents and anaphoric reference; incomplete syntactical patterns;
(5) rhythmic elegancies, brought out by reading the text aloud.

(5) includes the opposite vice of 'metrical prose' as illustrated by Fowler & Fowler (1906/30:304) from Dickens:

---

[86] Adamson (1998:634–5) goes on to explain:

> From the 1790s it also acquired political overtones when Romantic radicals, such as Godwin and Hazlitt, adopted the short sentence style as the medium for arguing the case for constitutional reform. In the aftermath of the French Revolution, what Hazlitt saw as a democratic style (the 'broken English' of 'common elliptical expressions' and 'popular modes of construction') struck others as dangerously subversive. It does not appear in the prose-writing of the more reactionary Romantics, such as Coleridge (who deplored 'the present anglo-gallican fashion of unconnected, epigrammatic periods') and its general diffusion was inhibited until well after the defeat of Napoleon in 1815.

Oh, moralists, who treat of happiness / and self-respect, innate in every sphere / of life, and shedding light on every grain / of dust in God's highway, so smooth below / your carriage-wheels, so rough beneath the tread / of naked feet, bethink yourselves / in looking on the swift descent / of men who *have* lived in their own esteem, / that there are scores of thousands breathing now, / and breathing thick with a painful toil, who in / that high respect have never lived at all, / nor had a chance of life! Go ye, who rest / so placidly upon the sacred Bard / who had been young, and when he strung his harp / was old, ... / go Teachers of content and honest pride, / into the mine, the mill, the forge, / the squalid depths of deepest ignorance, / and uttermost abyss of man's neglect, / and say can any hopeful plant spring up / in air so foul that it extinguishes / the soul's bright torch as fast as it is kindled!

Fowler & Fowler (1906/30:310–12) also point to the following imperfections frequent in excessively long 19th-century periods:

(1)   disproportionate insertions;
(2)   sentences of which the ends are allowed to trail on to unexpected length;
(3)   decapitable sentences (that keep on prolonging themselves by additional phrases, after each of which the reader hopes for a full stop).

Ex. 42   Analyse the syntactical changes made by Cobbett in Castlereagh's note (T3) and carefully read his annotations. How far did he succeed in making the complex structure of the original more intelligible? Did Barnes use the same principles in his dialect translation (T35)?

5.4   *Text syntax*

Conventions of how a 'sentence' is defined and how larger linguistic units are organized are language-specific; they also greatly depend on the functional range of the individual language and period-specific norms. This explains why the structure of texts in Latin, English and German is not identical, and why many English texts of the 16th or 19th century strike modern readers as unnecessarily complex, turgid or formal for the purpose.

Authors writing in English, from the 15th century onwards, had a great deal to learn about organizing longer texts, especially where abstract concepts and complex arguments were concerned. A history of how they learned to cope with structures larger than the sentence (a section of the history of the English language that remains to be written) would have to begin with the phase of Latin imitation (pre-1650) and then trace the process of increasing linguistic independence based on proper use of the structural possibilities inherent in the English language (from the Restoration onwards). Writers like Dryden, Addison and Swift showed that precision did not exclude smoothness and apparent ease, long sentences did not exclude perspicuity, and highly abstract reasoning did not exclude intelligibility. All this was achieved by a deliberate concentration on the coherence and cohesion of texts, affecting written compositions first, but then, with the model of proper English represented by the printed page, extended into formal spoken English in the 18th century. An analysis of 19th-century texts clearly shows a break around 1830–40, when carefully crafted prose which would have stood the test of 18th-century guardians of propriety and good style gave way to looser structures, a tendency which depended greatly on the individuality of the writer, the text type and intended function and expected readership.

According to the classic definition (cf. Beaugrande & Dressler 1981: 3–10), textuality is established by seven standards:

(1) *cohesion* (sequence in surface text),
(2) *coherence* (the configuration of concepts and relations; cause, time, etc.),
(3) *intentionality* (the producer's attitude),
(4) *acceptability* (the receiver's attitude),
(5) *informativity* (expected vs unexpected, known vs unknown),
(6) *situationality* (relevance to a situation or occurrence),
(7) *intertextuality* (dependence on textual traditions).

These standards can be divided into more narrowly linguistic (1, 2 and 7 in part; prominent in my analysis) and sociolinguistic ones (3, 4, 6 and, in part, 5 and 7). The relationship with text types and styles will also be evident (cf. ch. 7).

6

Lexis

6.1   Introduction

6.1.1   General considerations

'I move that the meeting adjourn, for the immediate adoption of more energetic
remedies – –' 'Speak English!' said the Eaglet.

It is very difficult to generalize about what characterizes the 19th-century
vocabulary of English. How different it was from PDE is easily demonstrated from a few everyday contexts. Consider what people drank when not
having ale, beer or wine, gin, tea, milk or water: Brook (1970:26) draws attention to the period-specific drinks *bishop, negus, porter, flip, dog's nose*
and *purl*. Vehicles then available included a *gig, stanhope, dog-cart, taxed-
cart, chaise-cart, cabriolet, rumble* and *barouche*, a selection to which the
first edition of Roget's *Thesaurus* (1852:64) adds *cariole, phaeton, curricle,
whisky, landau, droshki, désobligeant, diligence, cab, calash, brougham,
clarence* and various others, certainly not exhausting the range of terms
available.

The stylistic range of words found in print apparently increased in the
period. That the lexis available ranged from very formal and Latinate to
highly colloquial is illustrated by Roget's no. 584 (1852:134):

Loquacity, loquaciousness, talkativeness, garrulity, flow of words, *flux de bouche*,
prate, gab, gift of the gab, gabble, jabber, chatter, prattle, cackle, clack, twattle,
rattle, *caquet, caqueterie*, twaddle, bibble-babble, gibble-gabble.
Fluency, flippancy, volubility, *cacoëthes loquendi*, polylogy, perissology.

As far as statistics of the growth of the vocabulary are concerned, we still
largely rely on the figures of the *Chronological English Dictionary* based
on the 1933 *SOED* (Finkenstaedt *et al.* 1970).[87] In spite of the obvious limitations of the data-base, we can be confident that the number of new words
per year is at least illustrative of the increase until 1850 or so.

The details of why and how English lexis expanded in the 19th century,
as it clearly did, need careful investigation; the data are now available with

---

[87] For problems with the etymological classification of foreign words in the *CED* and
statistics based on this, cf. 6.3.2 below and Görlach (1998b).

the second edition of the *OED* which, completed in 1989, includes much more of the lexis of the period than the old *OED* did (for whose compilers the Victorian vocabulary was contemporary, or almost so).[88]

As far as conclusions can be drawn about trends in lexical expansion (and the acceptance of new words into a more central lexis as represented by the *ALD*) the table below will be helpful (figure 15, p. 94).

We still have insufficient answers to questions such as the following:

(1)   How often did individual authors add to the English lexis, not just by coining words, but also by having them accepted by the community to the extent that their provenance was quite often forgotten? Sir W. Scott (an *external* source) contributed words like *glamour* and *raid*, which became frequent only in the later course of the century, and Dickens is credited with hundreds of neologisms which 'have gone comparatively unnoticed, for in fact many – if not most – of the constructions, idioms, lexical items, and special uses of words that he introduced are current today, and hence unobtrusive' (Sørensen 1985: 12).[89] More experimental lexis, like coinages by Carlyle[90] and Hopkins, normally left fewer traces in general English.

(2)   How much of the new lexis was necessitated by the geographical expansion of the world (ranging from the Hebrides to the New Hebrides), how much by technological progress? How much of the latter is represented by neo-Greek and neo-Latin formations, and how many of these are actually loanwords from French (e.g. *eucalyptus*) and German (e.g. *biology*)?

(3)   Have there been noteworthy shifts in the word-formation patterns used? For instance, has the number of zero derivations increased particularly fast?

(4)   How did the social stigma attached to certain words affect their stylistic restriction, frequency of use and, ultimately, their meaning?

---

[88] Since the *SOED* editors no longer give the year of first attestations, recourse has to be had to the full evidence contained in the *OED*.

[89] Sørensen (1985:115–69) lists over 1,000 neologisms of very different status; they include '176 words and phrases that have been overlooked by the (first edition of) the OED, and ... 151 items not recorded in the Dictionary (115)'. Dickens's second important function was of course that he made Cockney/slang popular and acceptable to middle-class readers – far outside the London region (cf. p.99).

[90] Contemporaries coined 'Carlylism', 'De Quinceyism' and 'Gibbonism' for such idiosyncrasies; Marchand (1969:263) points out that Carlyle revived -*dom* derivations, modelled on German -*tum*; 'other writers followed'. Few of these new creations can be said to be 'alive' today.

	1801–		1811–		1821–		1831–		1841–	
1	119	39	138	28	126	20	172	27	151	28
2	<u>158</u>	<u>41</u>	133	41	194	40	204	35	304	35
3	115	24	118	32	220	<u>55</u>	195	32	155	33
4	108	24	102	18	124	26	236	<u>48</u>	159	27
5	127	21	106	21	199	46	<u>350</u>	46	200	31
6	95	27	181	34	254	31	295	35	276	33
7	99	29	129	<u>48</u>	140	26	265	47	<u>379</u>	36
8	118	23	192	39	<u>281</u>	41	238	40	196	35
9	105	30	<u>218</u>	31	127	32	295	<u>48</u>	225	27
10	105	25	122	32	271	41	231	31	246	<u>39</u>
Total	1149	283	1439	334	1936	358	2481	389	2291	324

	1851–		1861–		1871–		1881–		1891–	
1	204	33	210	<u>36</u>	108	19	213	<u>36</u>	<u>83</u>	16
2	164	30	156	21	163	18	<u>230</u>	27	64	<u>17</u>
3	171	27	204	20	110	17	172	21	42	12
4	241	25	<u>327</u>	<u>36</u>	150	20	157	24	49	14
5	192	17	199	30	252	15	106	13	59	12
6	158	34	250	20	190	23	111	16	50	12
7	<u>243</u>	33	129	17	198	13	121	18	45	10
8	208	34	200	21	166	21	91	17	41	14
9	217	<u>39</u>	127	18	<u>259</u>	19	125	25	50	14
10	186	24	195	21	257	<u>26</u>	105	20	39	15
Total	1984	296	1997	240	1853	191	1431	214	522	136

Figure 15　New words as recorded in the *CED/SOED* and the *ALD* (1967, second column): increase per year; total 17,083 (*CED*), of which 2,763 (= 16.2%) were also included in the 1967 *ALD*; the peaks in each decade are underlined

To what extent can social history be 'reconstructed' from such evidence?

Whatever the details of this expansion, it is obvious that 19th-century authors had available a larger range of stylistic choices than those of earlier periods. This is particularly noticeable in the amount of non-standard material found in 19th-century texts, such as dialect, archaic diction and slang in its various shades.[91]

Most authors made only restricted use of these possibilities, but there are writers like Doughty (cf. Watt Taylor 1939), who display a strange mixture of styles, in his case to suggest the difference between English and Arabic culture, and, by the use of loanwords, coinages and archaic words (together with archaic or idiosyncratic derivations in syntactical patterns), to indicate the primeval austerity of the Arabic way of life.

We will have to distinguish carefully between common vocabulary and poetic or otherwise idiosyncratic uses. Trench, who claimed that 'Language then is fossil poetry' and 'Many a single word also is itself a concentrated poem, having stores of poetical thought and imagery laid up in it' (1851:5), also conceded exceptional freedom in creating new words to poets:

> the all-fusing imagination, will at once suggest and justify audacities in speech, upon which in calmer moods he would not venture, or, if he ventured, would fail to carry others with him: for only the fluent metal runs easily into novel shapes and moulds. It is not merely that the old and the familiar will often become new in his hands; that he will give the stamp of allowance, as to him it will be free to do, to words, should he count them worthy, which hitherto have lived only on the lips of the multitude, or been confined to some single dialect and province; but he will enrich his native tongue with words unknown and non-existent before – non-existent, that is, save in their elements. (1851:110)

The two major sources of lexical innovation in the 19th century were, as in other periods, the borrowing of foreign words (cf. 6.3) and the coinage of items on the basis of productive patterns in word-formation (cf. 6.4). Minor sources tapped were the revival of old words, most conspicuous in the literary lan-guage of some writers (cf. 6.6), and innovation from internal resources, in-cluding regional and social subsystems.

These lexical changes were caused mainly by the tremendous techno-logical developments which make the 19th century the start of a new age.

---

[91] Note that the modern concept, until at least 1850, was expressed by the terms *flash* (*language*) or *cant*; *slang* denoting non-standard forms more generally. There was also a distinction between at least three sociolinguistic types of slang: *lingo* among the lower classes, *jargon* in the middle and upper classes, and *argot* among the cultured and pretentious speakers (according to Partridge 1940:176).

However, there were also important changes in attitudes, the structure of society, and educational-political and economic conditions, which had considerable influence on the vocabulary of English. The peak from 1820 to 1850 indicated in figure 15 is obvious, in both the *CED* and *ALD*, and this was no doubt prompted by technological developments. Murray reflects on *ph*-words (*NED*, 'Prefatory Notes' to vol. VII, 1905):

> The most extensive of these is the group of PHOTO-words, which ... number no fewer than 240, all except 3 being of the 19th century, and all except 6 consequent upon the introduction of photography in 1839.

A minor, but quite conspicuous, cause of lexical innovation was 19th-century prudery. Not only was *leg* often replaced by *limb* in all contexts, but other body parts and types of underwear came to be circumscribed by fanciful coinages (*trousers* were strictly to be avoided, *inexpressibles, indescribables, inexplicables* and *unmentionables* being suggested instead – however facetiously). Also note Dickens's unique paraphrases of 'damned' as *national participled* (*Christmas Stories*) and *somethin'-unpleasanted* (*Pickwick Papers*) – both quoted from Brook 1970:186, 188.

Dickens's 'Circumlocution Office' (*Little Dorrit*) reflects the dramatic increase in administrationese which saw its first peak in the 19th century and gave rise to numerous more or less necessary terms. (All these styles also had a notable impact on the English of the colonies, such as India.)

Ex. 43   Categorize Dickens's innovations according to types of word-formation and style (Brook 1970, Sørensen 1985).

6.1.2 *English lexicography in the nineteenth century*
(Simpson 1990)

The best documentation of the contemporary vocabulary comes of course from the dictionaries of the time. However, the value of lexicography in 19th-century England is restricted by various factors:[92]

(1)   The overwhelming influence of Johnson's prescriptive views continued well into the 19th century – one remembers Becky Sharp and her fellow graduates being given a copy of the dictionary as a prize at the end of their school career. Although Todd's edition of 1818 added quite a lot of lexis that would have seemed to Johnson inappropriate

---

[92] Contemporary reviews are still useful, although they tend to give excessive attention to the treatment of etymology, cf. those by Garnett in 1835, Fitch 1858, Baynes 1868 and Tylor 1873 (reprinted in Harris 1995, I:45–77, 245–80, II:59–88, 122–53).

for inclusion, the revision did not bring the book really up to date. As far as pronunciation was concerned, Walker's dictionary of 1791 (available in modernized editions) had a similar influence.

(2) Developments in America, most notably the publication of Webster's (1828) and Worcester's (1830) dictionaries stifled British alternatives, the books being exported in great numbers (Webster having repealed his linguistic declaration of independence in favour of a largely universal English language).

(3) The major dictionary published in England, Richardson's *New English Dictionary* of 1835–7, was misconceived because of its fanciful etymologies (which looked backward to the biblical 'Chaldee' tradition based on the Tower of Babel) and because of his failure to provide detailed definitions (he relied on his readers' capacity to gather the meanings from the lavish quotations provided).

(4) Minor lexicographers like John Boag (1848), Hyde Clark (1855), John Ogilvie (1850) and Charles Annandale (1882) for all their individual merits failed to supply really comprehensive and reliable dictionaries.

Such was the situation in the 1850s when a new start was made which ultimately resulted in the *New* (later: *Oxford*) *English Dictionary*.[93] The Philological Society of London spoke out for a new dictionary project; one member, Archbishop Trench, named the six major deficiencies of existing dictionaries (1851, here quoted from Simpson's summary, 1990:1961):

(a) the coverage of obsolete words was fundamentally relevant to lexicography;
(b) the analysis and presentation of distinct families or groupings of related words was imperfect;
(c) in many cases earlier examples of words and subsenses were clearly findable, which would make a revolutionary difference to the knowledge of the history of the vocabulary;
(d) lack of evidence had led to many important meanings of words being passed over through ignorance or incomplete analysis;
(e) synonyms were treated inconsistently; and
(f) dictionaries were often full of redundant information, because of editorial error or mistaken ideas of what a dictionary should contain.

In all this, Herbert Coleridge's 'Proposal', with reference to Trench, made it quite clear that only the standard lexis ought to be included; its point II reads as follows:

---

[93] A definitive account of the history of the project and the principles followed in the *OED* is expected in Mugglestone's forthcoming collection of papers.

> We admit as authorities all English books, except such as are devoted to purely
> scientific subjects, as treatises on electricity, mathematics, &c., and works written
> subsequently to the Reformation for the purpose of illustrating provincial dialects.
> As soon as a standard language has been formed, which in England was the case
> after the Reformation, the lexicographer is bound to deal with that alone; before
> that epoch, however, the English language was in reality another name for the
> sum of a number of local languages, all exhibiting an English type distinct from
> the Saxon, and therefore all equally entitled to notice as authorities in the for-
> mation of a Dictionary. At the same time we may reserve to ourselves a discretion
> of deciding, in doubtful cases, what shall or shall not be deemed a Dictionary au-
> thority, – a discretion which from special cases may often be required and use-
> fully exercised without at all infringing on the generality of the principles we have
> just laid down.   (1858, in Crowley 1991:154)

A huge reading programme with hundreds of helpers was initiated, and
since *printed* sources were to be quoted wherever possible, another vast project, that of the Early English Text Society was started. All words recorded
after 1066 were to be included in the dictionary and the intention was clearly historical – in line with the prevailing scholarly method of comparative
linguistics. The project was complemented by a new documentation of dialect lexis, finally published in Joseph Wright (1898–1905). The history of
the *OED* (retold by K. M. E. Murray 1977) combined the best in Victorian
dedication and scholarly sophistication.

James Murray could claim, with a great deal of satisfaction in 1900:

> The work thus done is done once for all; the structure now reared will have to be
> added to, continued, and extended with time, but it will remain, it is believed, the
> great body of fact on which all future work will be built ... In the Oxford Dic-
> tionary, permeated as it is through and through with the *scientific method of the
> century*, Lexicography has for the present *reached its supreme development*.
>
>   (1900:49, my emphasis)

Ex. 44   The *NED* was intended to correct and replace the new edition of
Johnson (by Todd, 1818) and Richardson's *Dictionary* (1835–7).
Summarize the *NED*'s achievement basing your judgement on a com-
parison of three to five selected entries.

6.1.3 *Social distinctions*

The use of the wrong word in a specific situation could amount to 'linguistic suicide' (Ellis 1869–1874), especially where it gave away the speaker or
writer as a member of the lower classes, a social climber and one affected
by 'genteel' diction.

Moreover, the 19th century saw an increase in interest in special languages like cant, slang and professional jargon. Clarke (1811) mentions *cant, flash, gibberish, patter, pedlar's French, slang lingo* and *St Giles' Greek* (which apparently shade into one another). More important than such special lexis, which is confined to certain groups of users, are developments which make words acceptable in neutral style, often rising from slang to colloquial/facetious diction and finally to the common core.

Such penetration was frequently seen as a danger. Graham (1869) is quite outspoken in his condemnation:

> Among the many signs of the corruption of the English language ... Is the prevalent use of slang words and phrases.

After discussing the modish adoptions of French terms in society, he continues with the slang of parliament, the universities, lawyers and merchants. Although there are individual cases of earlier slang words which became colloquial standard (*humbug, hoax, snob*) and

> though it may be allowed to use some of these terms in familiar discourse, no one of any sense or good taste will ever think of indulging in slang language either spoken or written. It is, no doubt, a bad sign of the times, and much to be deplored, that it is so common. Some writers have calculated that there are, at least, three thousand slang terms in common use. The above are but a few examples of this widespread corruption. We may regard it, as concerns our language, in the light of a pest to society. It takes a long time to clear the atmosphere from the baneful influences of certain epidemics. Now, the language of every-day conversation is suffering from the infectious disease, and it becomes the duty of every Englishman who has a proper feeling for his language, to refrain from this evil himself, and to throw in its way every possible discouragement.
>
> (1869/1991:166)

However, the popular tradition of novel writing represented by authors like Dickens and Thackeray greatly contributed not only to making slang palatable to the middle class, but also to spread slang terms across the country. Partridge (1933:88) rightly states:

> Usually less obtrusively and therefore more effectually, Dickens – the most read British author of the century – garnered a very large proportion of the slang current during the forty years ending in 1870, endowed much of it with a far longer life than it would otherwise have had, so popularized certain slang terms that they gained admittance to standard speech.

Such liberal attitudes left more conservative observers unconvinced. Mackay wrote in *Blackwood's Magazine* (May 1888):

> Slang ... has ... within the last half-century invaded the educated and semi-educated classes in England, America, and France, though it has not yet, to

anything like the same extent, permeated the literature and conversation of the European nations, other than the two named, where Liberty was more or less degenerated into Licence. Democracy ... is the real parent of vulgar slang. ... The slang of recent years, fashionable and unfashionable ..., is mostly ... derived from the common speech of illiterate people. ... [Words that, originating in the lower classes,] have obtained favour and currency among the imperfectly educated vulgar of the middle and upper classes, and have lately been raised to the distinction of print and publicity of newspapers and inferior novels ... are numerous and threaten to become still more fashionably and extensively employed.

(quoted from Partridge 1933/⁴1970:104–5)

Slang from the university, the army and the counting-house were a greater danger since they were less stigmatized and therefore more likely to be accepted into general speech. Phillipps (1984:98) quotes a relevant passage from an 1826 conduct book criticizing 'Some mercantile phrases (which) have become no less common than vulgar'. These include *ditto, per, via, sundries, concern* and *article*.

By contrast, Mayhew's (1861–2, cf. T14) interest was that of a sociologist. He possibly came as close to a realistic depiction of the London poor as was possible for a gentleman who had the observer's paradox very much against him. His detailed word-lists and background accounts of the individual groups of lower-class Londoners remain an invaluable document (cf. the analysis by Partridge 1933:92–6).

Almost all of the EngE slang recorded in the 19th century is from London; therefore there is a close affinity to the functions of Cockney (cf. Matthews 1938). Much of this lexis does not normally find its way into written texts and is therefore impossible to document; compare Trench's censure, who sees this vocabulary as an indication of human sinfulness:

And our dictionaries, while they tell us much, yet will not tell us all. How shamefully rich is the language of the vulgar everywhere in words which are not allowed to find their way into books, yet which live as a sinful oral tradition on the lips of men, to set forth that which is unholy and impure ... How much cleverness, how much wit, yea, how much imagination must have stood in the service of sin, before it could possess a nomenclature so rich, so varied, and often so heaven-defying as it has.   (1851:30)

Ex. 45   Which of the words criticized as 'low' (= slang) by Swift and Johnson in the 18th century had become unobjectionable in the 19th, and which Victorian slang expressions lost their disreputable character in the 20th? Consider, e.g., *coax, fun, mob, row, snob, swap, stingy, tiny* and *touchy.*

6.1.4 *Stylistic varieties*

In languages like English there is a large supply of words which can be chosen according to their appropriateness for the respective context (medium, topic, text type, formality, etc.); this choice can include options from regional lexis or words typical of a certain social class. These parameters are discussed in ch. 7 where special reference is also made to poetic diction, 'the language the poets use'.

6.1.5 *Etymology*

The investigation of word origins was becoming more scholarly (in the sense of being based on comparative philology) in the 19th century, but important lexicographers held on to the old tradition (cf. 6.1.2). They were also influenced by Horne Tooke's attempts to gain access to the true meaning by a proper analysis of the form of a word – for instance, he explained *heaven* and *head* as participles of *heave*.[94] However, there was a great deal of fancy left even in modern descriptions, e.g. in the assumed Celtic origin of opaque words. As late as 1870, Burton's statement represents the popular lore of the 19th century:

> The Keltic words left in English number only about fifty, and these being chiefly such as would be used by Slaves, – *basket, clout, darn, flannel, gruel, welt, gown, mesh, mop*, etc., – would seem to indicate that the Saxons destroyed the male portion of the Britons, but enslaved the women, who of course retained their own names for the utensils.   (1870:5)

As time progresses, the source of new words – coined according to various patterns of word-formation or borrowed from dialects or foreign languages – becomes increasingly clear. However, there are quite a few words first recorded in the 19th century which are classified as of 'unknown etymology'. Some of these, such as interjections (*chut, plunk, swish, tra-la, whisht* and *yah* are first attested 1800–25) and onomatopoeic words (*hee-haw, boo* vb.) obviously need no 'etymology', but the absence of any reliable information about *gully* (1800), *spree* (1804), *gag* 'joke' (1805), *rowdy* (AmE, 1808), *slum* (1812), *jibe* 'agree' (1813), *boast* (AmE, 1815), *bogie/bogey* (1817), *shindy* (1821), *trolley* (1823) is more disconcerting.

---

[94] Trench praised Richardson's (1835–7) etymologies and offered quite fanciful interpretations himself, as when he derived *shire, shore, share* and *sheard* from a common basis (1851:185–6); his views in these matters were, however, not carried over into the *New English Dictionary*. The closeness to folk etymology (*asparagus* 'vulgarly pronounced *Sparrowgrass*', as in Walker 1791) and malapropism is obvious.

Some of these may of course be blends or somehow imitative or onomatopoeic, but can rarely be pinned down, as *spoof* can, 'invented and named
by the British comedian Arthur Roberts' (Barnhart 1988), but more of such
words are likely to come from non-standard forms of speech, especially
dialects and slang.[95] James Murray (1888) pointed out the great contribution
that such unwritten layers have made to the English lexis – and discussed
the grievous problems that these words can present to the etymologist.

Ex. 46 Check in various modern etymological dictionaries whether they
have any provenance to suggest for the words named by Burton and the
others listed above and whether these assumed etymologies agree.

6.2   *Internal borrowing*

6.2.1   *Loanwords from BrE dialects*

The relative status of St E and dialects being what it was, the former had a
strong influence on the dialects (cf. 2.3.1) which were brought closer to the
standard language, or at least developed towards forms of regional speech
of wider communication, partly levelled out in the new industrial centres.
By contrast, their impact on the standard was minimal.[96] The *CED* does not
appear to list any 19th-century BrE dialect words that entered the standard
– there is not even an etymological category for this. Even Craigie (1937) in
his comprehensive account of northern words in St E admits that the impact
was minimal, being largely restricted to designations for the foreign culture
(*clan, collie, glen, plaid*), a few borrowings through northern writers and a
few relating to features of mainly northern countryside (*bracken, heather,
peat*).

6.2.2   *Borrowings from Scots*

Scots, and the development of Scottish English in Scotland, is not the
subject of this book (cf. McClure 1994, Jones 1997); the influence of Scots
on English *is*. This was effected mainly through two channels:

---

[95] AusE has quite a number of these, such as *dinkum, larrikin* and *tucker*, all said to be
from BrE dialects but without proper attestation.

[96] This statement does not refer to the individual writer's use of regionalisms: this can be
conspicuous, especially where an author's predilection for Saxonisms might suggest a
dialect word as a purer alternative to a Romance standard item (thus in various dialectal
words used by Hopkins, Barnes, Morris, Doughty, Blunden, etc.).

(1) Designations of Scottish *realia*; this section includes words from both Gaelic and Scots/Scottish English; many of these had been borrowed before 1800.
(2) Words occurring in the major Scottish poets. Even if these wrote in (a diluted, anglicized form of) Scots, they remained within the limits of an English national literature, which meant that their works were read in England and the rest of the anglophone world.

Borrowing from Scots literature had happened before 1800 (*eerie, gloaming* from Burns), but most loans date from the 19th century, coming mainly from the works of Sir Walter Scott. He gave to the English language possibly more English words than any author since Shakespeare. Although many of these items have remained marginal or were forgotten outside their specific literary source, a great number of words survived. These include *awesome, blackmail, brownie, cosy, eldritch, forbear, glamour* (n.), *glint, gruesome, guffaw, kale, kith, raid, warlock, winsome* and *wizened*; other words became at least better known than they had been before (*golf, bonny, dour*; cf. Tulloch 1980:232–7).

Note that Scots (and IrE) also handed on a few Celtic items, as happened to *sporran* and *colleen*; Scott made the earlier loans *slogan* and *claymore* popular.

6.2.3 *American English*

The US forms of English became relevant for 19th-century BrE in two ways – as sources of English neologisms and as transmitters of borrowings from other languages, whether from Native Indian or from immigrant languages. However, the status of AmE as a formerly colonial variety and BrE was not equal, and the 19th century (up to 1914) was the period of the greatest divergence between the two varieties. This explains why AmE words found in BrE texts are almost always foreignisms, referring to typically American objects and concepts. Although even Webster in his later years had stressed the unity of AmE and BrE, he had also pointed out the need for expanding the English language by coining words or adapting meanings of old words when he mentioned a few specimens in the introduction to his *American Dictionary of the English Language* (1828). However, for the few hundred cases where AmE diverged from BrE in the core vocabulary, these heteronyms were generally kept apart. Moreover, it was more likely for Americans to accept BrE words for formal or literary registers than for Englishmen to borrow from AmE. The widespread replacement of BrE items by their AmE equivalents (*wireless set* by *radio*) started only after 1945.

   This statement does not mean that the slow eastward movement of AmE lexis had not started in the 19th century. Strang (1970:35) refers to Craigie (1927) who had noted this trend particularly with regard to:

(1)   (former) foreignisms: *back-woods, blizzard, Indian-file*;
(2)   political terms: *carpet-bagger, gerrymander, lynch-law*;
(3)   business and trades: *snow-plow, to strike oil*;
(4)   miscellaneous: *at that, to take a back seat, to cave in, grave-yard, lengthy, loafer, law-abiding*.

Some of these expressions were criticized by 19th-century British writers, probably because they saw the entry of these words as a pollution of EngE. In fact, the criticism of British commentators was often scathing. Graham is one of many authors who could be quoted in this context; he admits that some Americanisms may become acceptable in due course, but he is quite certain that the stigma attached to most American expressions will make it very unlikely for them to be adopted into St BrE:

> The recklessness with which the Americans use the English language bids fair to flood it with many new and strange terms. It is very possible that some of these terms may some day take their places as forming part of the legitimate materials of our language ...
> The rapid communication established of late between England and the United States has brought the two nations into a much closer connection with each other. This, in a commercial or political view, may be of advantage to both countries. But every advantage has its drawback, and it is very doubtful whether this condition of things is likely to benefit the English language. The Americans are well known to set great store by liberty, and of course we have no right whatever to interfere with their opinions concerning principles or forms of political government. But it becomes a serious matter for us when they think proper to take liberties with our language. They set up for themselves, probably by way of showing their independence, new modes of spelling; and they are perpetually introducing all sorts of meanings, words and phrases, none of which have the remotest title to be called English ... These and all such must be looked upon as abortions and deformations of our language; and no English writer who has any respect for his own reputation should ever think of countenancing, far less adopting, such monstrosities.   (1869/1991:166, 169)

Dickens is a representative of a more popular (and more humorous) re-action; his American characters in *Martin Chuzzlewit* give us some insight into how AmE was perceived by non-linguist observers (for an analysis see Brook 1970:130–7).

   In sum, most 'Americanisms' discussed in 19th-century dictionaries or essays were not cases of internal borrowing in BrE; more often than not, British observers even doubted whether the Americans were entitled to use the language as they did, in particular to innovate in word-formation and meaning.

Ex. 47 Do you agree with Graham's evaluation? If the 'rapid communication' levelled the lexical differences between the US and Britain, how is it that the rift is particularly notable in the terminology of the newly invented motorcars?

6.2.4 *Purist neologisms*

Since borrowing and word-formation from Latin and Greek elements saw a peak in the 19th century (cf. 6.3.3), purist reactions were to be expected. However, whereas these were widespread and had official support in some 19th-century societies such as those of Germany and Iceland, they were confined to a few enthusiasts in Britain – as they had been in the 16th century (cf. Görlach 1991:163–6).

Scholars like Morris and Barnes argued that English, as a Germanic language with rich word-formation potentials, might well avoid some of the 'excesses' of NGI lexis by using native resources, in particular the revival of obsolete words (possibly surviving in dialect). Although not a purist, Trench was in favour of reviving words

> as are worthy to be revived; which yet through carelessness, or ill-placed fastidiousness, or a growing unacquaintance on the part of a later generation with the elder worthies of the language, or some other cause, have been suffered to drop.   (1851:119)

Barnes found that:

> In searching the word-stores of the provincial speech-forms of English, we cannot but behold what a wealth of stems we have overlooked at home, while we have drawn needful supplies of words from other tongues.   (1863:9)

Other methods used to avoid the import of 'unnecessary' foreign words were the employment of old words with new meanings (by extending their designation to new classes of referents, cf. 6.5) and coining compounds and derivations from native elements. Barnes's most consistent attempt at 'Saxonizing' was *An Outline of English Speech-Craft* (Barnes 1878) in which he made an effort to translate the entire linguistic terminology. However, the reactions of the general public to his purist innovations were far from encouraging. As early as 1863, Furnivall, the secretary of the Philological Society, had insisted on Barnes returning to terms like *synonyms* (and not *mate-words*) if he wanted his *Grammar* published, and the editors of the *OED* were not any more favourable. Jacobs (1952:78) points out that not 'even such attractive and valuable Barnesian neologisms as *bird-lore* (ornithology), ... *folkdom* (democracy), ... *heedsome* (attentive), *lawcraft* (jurisprudence), *linkword* (conjunction)', etc. were considered worthy of an entry. In fact, 19th-century purism has given the English language only a few permanent additions such as *folklore, folksong* and *foreword* (many coined on the pattern of German models). Whereas Barnes's purism was founded on his knowledge of SW dialect, that of Morris derived from his love of Old Norse literature combined with his dislike of the English he heard and saw around him. As with Barnes, critics were divided in their judgement of the quality of his experiments. An anonymous writer in the *Westminster Review* found:

> [he] has enriched our language by drawing upon the stores of our old and for-gotten words. Reading his poem is like reading a fresh and more vigorous style of English than that to which we are daily accustomed.
>
> (no. 155, April 1871, quoted from Gallasch 1979:44)

Negative remarks, however, predominated. A reviewer in the *Spectator* commented on the haphazard way in which the enrichment was undertaken, often conflicting with register restrictions, and added:

> nor will it ever do to 'Chaucerize' altogether, under pain of being unintelligible to by far the greater number of readers.
>
> (no. 43, 13 August 1870, quoted from Gallasch 1979:45)

Ex. 48   Check whether the absence of selected neologisms coined by Barnes and Morris (regretted by Jacobs 1952 and Gallasch 1979) has been rectified in the *OED* (^{2}1989).

Ex. 49   Compare Barnes's and Morris's innovations and revivals. Did they, in spite of their different backgrounds and motivations, arrive at the same methods and comparable results?

6.3   *Loanwords from foreign languages*

6.3.1 *Introduction*

Borrowing remained the most conspicuous source of new words. However, there were new developments that set off 19th-century English from earlier periods:

(1)   Although complaints about fashionable French lexis continued, the number of new words conspicuously French in form was beginning to decrease (cf. 6.3.2).

(2)   By contrast, there was an immense increase in international lexis –

combined forms using Greek and Latin stems, but with a certain preference for the Greek (NGI, cf. 6.3.3).

(3)   As a consequence of the colonial expansion in Africa, Asia and Australia, the English language began to import words from 'exotic' languages without the mediation of Spanish, Portuguese, Dutch or French.

(4)   The rise of English to the status of a proper world language meant that a time came when England exported more words than it imported (cf. p.111).[97]

There are no reliable statistics to measure the impact of loanwords, and their etymological classification is unreliable (so far) – for instance, more than half of the items classified as of French provenance in the Oxford dictionaries are in fact internationalisms coined from neo-Latin and neo-Greek roots.

It would of course be wrong to concentrate exclusively on new loanwords: many 19th-century styles are characterized by a high incidence of Latinate loanwords borrowed in earlier periods[98] – the entire anglophone world of the 19th century exhibits texts whose authors preferred Latinate diction at least for certain registers much more than would be usual today. Examples are found in authors as different as Poe and Sir W. Scott, Dickens and Carlyle.

Ex. 50   Assess the work of a number of 19th-century authors in relation to their use of Latinisms. Distinguish mannerisms from the use of Latinate diction for characterization, and from the expression of a period-specific kind of humour.

6.3.2 *French*
(Görlach 1998b)

French remained the most widely taught foreign language in Britain in the 19th century – a position it still holds. Although the French Revolution was

---

[97] Contrast the concern of Renaissance writers about England's 'trade deficit' in word borrowing as expressed, for instance, by Cheke (1557): 'our own tung shold be written cleane and pure, vnmixt and vnmangeled with borowing of other tunges, wherin if we take not heed by tijm, euer borowing and neuer payeng, she shall be fain to keep her house as bankrupt' (quoted from Görlach 1991:222).

[98] The 19th century still exhibited a large supply of learned alternatives; thus Roget (1852) lists under no. 606, 'Obstinacy': *pertinacity, pertinacy, pertinaciousness, pervicacy, pervicacity, pervicaciousness* and the adjectives *opinionative, opiniative, opinative, opinionate, opinioned.*

seen very critically by many politicians, and by writers such as Wordsworth and Sir Walter Scott, the general prestige of French as the language of refinement does not appear to have suffered greatly. Allison (1825:Preface) is probably representative of such attitudes:

> THE FRENCH LANGUAGE is now become not only a fashionable, but an almost indispensable, branch of a liberal education; and, if any Language might be ever expected to become universal, it is the French, which is already spoken in every court of Europe, and in all fashionable society.
>
> Hence many men of talents and of learning have devoted their attention to preparing easy and useful books, adapted to the different classes and ages of students ...
>
> Many young persons have given up the study of French, in despair of ever attaining to any degree of proficiency in the language, chiefly from disgust at having the rules of the grammar to commit to memory, and even when, having with great labour learned these rules, from their inability to apply them.

However, not all commentators praised French. One of the most caustic commentators combined criticism of the language with political arguments:

> With such a language as we now possess, with a hundred Grammars to assist in its cultivation, and with the classics lying open before us, what occasion have we for French literature? Will not the Englishman stagger with amazement, when he finds his countrymen recommending that language which has wrought the work of desolation in almost every European nation, and which has recently threatened to overthrow our own *a second time*?   (Martin 1824:276)

Martin also quotes in his support the similarly harsh criticism by Cobbett (1818). One might also add De Quincey's incisive verdict:

> The French itself, which in some weighty respects is amongst the poorest of languages ... amongst European languages this capital defect [the lack of fitness for poetic and imaginative purposes] is most noticeable in the French, which has no resources for elevating its diction when applied to cases and situations most lofty or the most affecting ... the very power of the French language, as a language for social intercourse, is built on its impotence for purposes of passion, grandeur, and native simplicity.   (1839/1995, I:85,88–9)

However, the majority of commentators appear to have seen the French language in a positive light, as Breen did in 1857:

> In recommending for imitation the example of the French, so far as it relates to grammatical propriety, I do not wish to be understood as recommending that we should sacrifice any of the advantages of our own mother-tongue to the attainment of that object. French is one of the poorest of modern languages; but its poverty does not arise from its method and propriety. This indeed is so little the case, that, if it were written with no greater attention to grammar than English commonly is, it would soon be reduced to an intolerable jargon. English, on the other hand, is one of the richest of living languages; but its copiousness and vigour would suffer

no diminution by being combined with a higher degree of method and propriety.
That these qualities are not unattainable is sufficiently shown by the examples of
such writers as Hazlitt, Southey, and Landor.   (1857:vi)

Critical voices continued to be heard right through the period. Bain (1872:
194) regarded French loans as 'barbarisms' if 'used without much necessity', quoting *sortie, dernier, resort, beaux arts* and *beaux lettres* (but accepting *ennui, prestige* and *naïveté*). Graham (1869) was outspoken in his
criticism of fashionable excesses in the use of French words in mid 19th-
century England:

> But slang is found in almost all classes of society. That of high life is drawn from
> various sources. One of its phases may be seen in the French words and forms
> which would-be fashionable people so delight in.   (1869/1991:164)

Such criticism appears only too justified when we look at texts like the
fashion report of 1851 (T76); one remembers that Mrs Beeton included a
glossary of French words in her cookery book of 1861.

At about the same time an anonymous correspondent complained about
Henry Alford dealing with 'the insubordinate little adverbs', but omitting
criticism of the greater danger of loanwords (T16/101–18).

Unsurprisingly, Morris was not in favour of the French influence. Taking
up Johnson's critical remark, he wrote in a letter to Fred Henderson:

> The great works of the English poets ever since Chaucer's time have had to be
> written in what is little more than a dialect of French, and I cannot help looking
> on that as a mishap.   (1885, quoted from Gallasch 1979:39)

On the other hand he had no qualms about reviving French words like
caitiff, devoir, faitour, gramercy and many terms for weapons and parts of
a suit of armour – apparently because they were attested in Chaucer and
other 'wells of English undefiled'.

Most British pupils must have felt that the French they were taught in the
schools was insufficient for conversing with native speakers on the continent, as Charlotte and Emily Brontë found when they arrived in Brussels in
1842:

> M. Héger's account is that they knew nothing of French. I suspect they knew as
> much (or as little), for all conversational purposes, as any English girls do, who
> have never been abroad, and have only learnt the idioms and pronunciation from
> an Englishwoman.   (Gaskell [1857] 1919:180)

The teaching of French continued to suffer from the fact that it was
considered as a 'soft option', and it was only from 1857/8 onwards that the
Oxford and Cambridge Local Examinations Boards gave English and
modern languages a legitimate position alongside Latin and Greek (cf.

Howatt 1984:133–5).

Attitudes towards French loanwords were a different matter. Although there were no widespread (or even institutional) purist tendencies in British society, excessive use of French words was criticized or ridiculed if it seemed to reflect the genteel pretensions of educated speech.[99] Breen (1857:40, 70) is again quite outspoken in his verdict.

Such attitudes are exactly parallelled in the Fowler brothers. Although the *Dictionary of Modern English Usage* was not published until 1926, the data were collected in 1903–6, and, considering the conservative nature of the enterprise, the judgements can be taken as representative of those prevalent in late 19th-century norms:

> Display of superior knowledge is as great a vulgarity as display of superior wealth – greater, indeed, inasmuch as knowledge should tend more definitely than wealth towards discretion & good manners. That is the guiding principle alike in the using & in the pronouncing of French words in English writing & talk. To use French words that your reader or hearer does not know or does not fully understand, to pronounce them as if you were one of the select few to whom French is second nature when he is not of those few (& it is ten thousand to one that neither you nor he will be so), is inconsiderate & rude.   (1926:193)

In spite of all this criticism, French loans retained their prestige value. Later on in the century, the number of French loanwords increased; Serjeantson (1935:165) found that they are concentrated in 'art and literature' and 'dress, textiles and furniture', and that the majority of the words belong to the period between 1830 and 1860.[100]

As in all borrowing, there might be changes of meaning and style affecting the loanword during the borrowing process, or after its integration. Any use of a French–English dictionary will show that, of the polysemic items *chassis, chauffeur, coup, cuisine, entente*, only one meaning was taken over. A comparison with French loanwords in German (such as *bureau, chef,*

---

[99] Occasionally, humorous distortions of French words were used to characterize lower-class speech. Phillipps (1984:91) quotes from Surtees's mid 19th-century *Jorrock's Jaunts and Jollities* malapropisms like *blankets of woe* for *blanquettes de veau* and *'orse douvers* for *hors d'œuvres*.

[100] Dictionary attestations do not tell us anything about currency, but the great number of French items (in particular, phrases) in Roget (1852) is striking – as is the number of Latin and Italian words and phrases. He explains: 'I have admitted a considerable number of words and phrases borrowed from other languages, chiefly the French and Latin, some of which may be considered as already naturalized; while others, though avowedly foreign, are frequently introduced in English composition, particularly in familiar style, on account of their being peculiarly expressive, and because we have no corresponding words of equal force in our language.'

menu) shows that the meanings selected can be different in individual languages. It is also common for a loanword to change its style value – the very fact that a general word will look *recherché* in the receiving language contributes to this.

English ceased to borrow to a conspicuous degree after 1900 when it became the great *exporter* of words (Görlach 1997). As far as the relation with French is concerned, the scales began to turn around 1880, with the international impact of British dominance in industry, and the prestige of British sports and fashions.

The only statistical evidence available for 19th-century neologisms is that provided by Finkenstaedt *et al.* (1970).[101] Apart from the limitations set by the somewhat outdated evidence on which conclusions are based, the etymological classification used leads to grievous misinterpretations. Of the 17,207 new words listed for the 19th century, 2,470 (14.35%) are said to be of French provenance. Of these, the majority is, however, Neo-Latin/Greek; only a small minority of the visibly French items consists of words that might be objected to by purists, 'proper' gallicisms ranging from *collaborateur* (1801), *débâcle* (1802), *parvenu, exposé* and *séance* (1803) to *chauffeur* and *questionnaire* (1899).

Ex. 51   How many terms in the fashion report of 1851 (T76) cannot be understood even with the help of the *OED*? Are these listed in *French* dictionaries?

Ex. 52   Is it true to say that 19th-century borrowings from French are not integrated, i.e. remain 'aliens'? (*CED*)

6.3.3 *Neo-Latin/Greek internationalisms (NGI)*

Technological progress necessitated the coinage of an immense number of new words; among them the increase of the English lexicon through NGI words is particularly noteworthy. Many of these come straight from Latin like the 19th-century borrowings *excursus, cognomen, opus, stet, ego, omnibus, sanatorium* and, in the second half of the century, *aquarium, consensus, referendum, bacillus*, or from Greek (*myth, pylon*), but others were

---

[101] Although the *OED* (^{2}1989) has been available for some time, no comprehensive statistical analysis of the growth of English lexis appears to have used this source. Finkenstaedt based his conclusions on the *SOED* of 1933; the new *SOED* is no use for a revision of his findings since it does not provide exact dates of first occurrences. No systematic search has been made to update or correct the *CED* data from ^{2}*OED*, but occasional checks show how provisional my figures are. The full data on which my arguments rest are found in Görlach (1998b).

fabricated from Latin and Greek elements.[102] These words can be derivatives and (quasi-)compounds (here restricted to Greek, which notably predominates in compounding):

prefix derivatives of *a-*, *apo-*, *dia-*, *syn-*
suffix derivatives of *-ia*, *-ism*, *-ize*;

or (quasi-)compounds made from adjectival and noun stems:

di-, *mono-*, *hetero-*, *auto-*, *poly-*; *neo-*, *archaeo-*, *palaeo-*; *tele-*;

(mainly as first elements): *anthropo-*, *bio-*, *chrono-*, *eco-*, *demo-*, *photo-*, *theo-*, *thermo-*, *xeno-* and the notably productive morphemes (occurring even in hybrid formations) *crypto-* and *pseudo-*;

(mainly as second elements): *-crat/cracy*, *-gamy*, *-glot*, *-gram(me)*, *-graph(y)*, *-logy*, *-meter*, *-morph(y)*, *-nomy*, *-pathy*, *-phily*, *-phoby*, *-phone*, *-scope*.

These elements can be freely combined to form technical terms and are largely transparent to those who have a modicum of Greek (some 200 word stems will be sufficient). The following facts should be born in mind:

(1)   The coining of such words increased from the Renaissance onwards and had its first peaks with the development of the new sciences in the 17th and 18th centuries; most of the better-known lexical items date in fact to this period (when international scholarship still largely used Latin as the medium of communication). Although the growth of NGI lexis is rapid in technical fields in the 19th century, the most notable growth was to come in the 20th century. However, counting is problematic, since so many items are ephemeral: Roget (1852:511) lists forty-two compounds on *-mancy* ('divination by') most of which are quite fanciful and can never have been current. Note the distribution of selected combinations (p. 113).

---

[102] Nouns greatly predominate in this process (and are therefore discussed below); however, new types of adjectives (commonly derived from NGI nouns) and of verbs were also coined. Thus, *de*-NGI-*ize/ate* verbs were coined from the late 18th century onwards (Marchand 1969:153–5).

NGI	19th-century coinages	attested in earlier centuries
anthropo-	*metry, morph*	*logy* 16, *pathy* 17, *phagy* 17
astro-	*metry*	*graphy* 18, *latry* 17, *loger/logy* ME, *nomy* ME
auto-	*crat, erotism, gamy, genous, scopy, tomy, type*	*biography* 18, *chthon* 16, *cracy* 17, *didact* 18, *graph* 17, *matic* 18, *nomy* 17, *psy* 17
bio-	*logy, scope, sphere*	*grapher* 18, *graphy* 17
chrono-		*graph* 17, *logy* 16, *meter* 18, *scope* 18
demo-	*graphy*	*cracy* 16
eco-	*logy*	*nomy* 15
geo-	*gony, morphy*	*desy* 15, *graphy* 15, *logy* 18, *many* ME, *metry* ME
micro-	*graph*	*graphy* 17, *logy* 17, *meter* 17, *phone* 17, *scope* 17
mono-	*geny, glot, graph, gyny, lith, mania, morphous, phony, type*	*cracy* 17, *crat* 18, *dy* 17, *gamy* 17, *gram* 17, *logue* 17, *machy* 16, *phthong* 17, *poly* 16, *theism* 17, *tony* 18
neo-	*lythic, plasm*	*logy* 18, *phyte* ME
photo-	*gen(ic), gram, graph, synthesis, tropic*	*meter* 18, *phobia* 18
poly-	*chrome, clinic, cyclic, ethylene, genesis, geny, mer, morph, phase, phony, ptych, semous, somatic, technic, type*	*andry* 17, *archy* 17, *gamy* 16, *glot* 17, *gon* 16, *math* 17, *phone* 17, *syllable* 16, *theism* 17
tele-	*gony, gram, meter, pathy, phone*	*graph* 18, *scope* 17
theo-	*morphic*	*cracy* 17, *dicy* 18, *gony* 17, *logy* ME, *machy* 16, *mancy* 17, *pathy* 18, *phany* OE, *sophy* 17
thermo-	*gram, graph, logy, phile, plastic, stat*	*meter* 17

Figure 16 Neo-Latin/Greek coinages (1)

(2)   The stock of these words is, then, international. Although they tend to be pronounced (and sometimes spelt) according to national conventions, they are intelligible across language boundaries. It is only where they are replaced by purist measures (most often calques) that international communication is disrupted – but Britain had very few such loan translations to replace NGIs. Only a few such words are not shared (such as German *Autogramm* 'signature').

(3)   Many of the neologisms hardly ever occur outside specialist contexts, and they are seldom spoken. There is no need, then, to adapt them to everyday usage (cf. the words starting with *phth-*).

(4)   NGI items largely resist integration; however, there are some tendencies away from 19th-century conventions of spelling (æ > *ae* > *e* and œ > *oe* > *e*) and inflection (in native plural formation: cf. p.65).

(5)   An increasing number of hybrid formations like *automobile, television, photoelectronic* and recently *eco-friendly* indicate a process by which these elements become available for national word-building. This means that complex NGI words are on their way to becoming analysed as proper compounds.

The ease with which combinations were made can be illustrated with a table indicating combinations documented for English (19th-century formations = X, others indicated by century, according to *SOED*):

	crat *cracy*	*gram*	*graphy*	*logy* *logue*	*meter* *metry*	*morph(y)*	*phone* *phony*	*scope* *scopy*
anthropo-				16	X	X		
auto-	17/X		17					X
bio-			17	X		X		
geo-			15	18	ME	X		
mono-	17	17	X	17		X	X	
photo-				18		X		
poly-	17					X	17/X	
tele-		X	18		X		X	17
theo-	17	X		ME		X		
thermo-		X		X	17			

Figure 17 Neo-Latin/Greek coinages (2)

The analysis of first occurrences is, however, only half of the story. Much of 19th-century English is equally characterized by the use of Latinisms in cases where a simple, short and native word would have been easily available. This tendency continues the tradition of Renaissance inkhornisms and 18th-century Johnsonese: apparently, voices warning against the use of more 'learned' words had not had any great effect. It is striking to find over-Latinate styles in various registers ranging from expository prose in newspapers or the *EB*[103] to literary writers from all parts of the anglophone world and with intellectual backgrounds as different as those of Poe and Scott, Dickens and Carlyle. And it is even more striking to find Cockeram's practice of reversing the hard word lists (1623, cf. Görlach 1991:151) and thus offering to the readers a choice of refined Latinisms repeated in the 19th century: in 1827 an anonymous *Writer's and Students' Assistant* (London: W. R. Goodluck) promises in the subtitle to produce a work:

> Rendering the more common Words and Phrases, in the English Language, into the more Elegant or Scholastic.

Although not all are as bad as those quoted below for the letter **B**, at least the items below very much smell of Cockeram:

> Babbling – loquacity, garrulity, talkativeness
> To go Backward – retrograde, retrocede, recede, retreat, retire
> A going Backward – retrogression, retrocession, recession, retreat, retirement

All this points to the fact that the 'language bar' that made it impossible for the lower classes to understand properly most printed texts was very much a problem for 19th-century teachers. One of the most telling statements is that quoted by Phillipps (1984:102) on the conditions around 1840:

> Those who have had close intercourse with the labouring classes well know with what difficulty they comprehended words not of a Saxon origin, and how frequently addresses to them are unintelligible from the continual use of terms of a Latin or Greek derivation; yet the daily language of the middle and upper classes abounds with such words ... hardly a sermon is preached which does not on every page contain numerous examples of their use. Phrases of this sort are so naturalized in the language of the educated classes, that entirely to omit them has the appearance of pedantry and baldness, and even disgusts people of taste and refinement ... It seems impossible to avoid using them, and the only mode of meeting the inconvenience alluded to is to instruct the humbler classes in their meaning.
> (Kay-Shuttleworth 1841:339)

---

[103] It is impossible to say how much the fact that the texts were written by Scotsmen may have contributed to a higher degree of Latinity in the *EB* and in Scott's and Carlyle's prose: it is plausible to claim that a Latinate style is easier to handle, not being so easily tested for idiomaticity.

Although many writers state that the 19th century had overcome the Latinate style of Johnson, complaints about contemporary excesses did not cease; Alford summarizes:[104]

> The language ... is undergoing a sad and rapid process of deterioration. Its fine manly Saxon is getting diluted into long Latin words not carrying half the meaning. This is mainly owing to the vitiated and pretentious style which passes current in our newspapers ... The greatest offenders are the country journals, and, as might be expected, just in proportion to their want of ability.   (³1870:301)

Unsurprisingly, a purist like Barnes could not help seeing these connections quite clearly:

> The Latinish and Greekish wording is a hindrance to the teaching of the homely poor, or at least the landfolk. It is not clear to them, and some of them say of a clergyman that his Latinized preaching is too high for them, and seldom seek the church.   (1878:88)

Although people might see the justification for such views in principle, Barnes's practice was rather to put them off. Compare his description of 'expansion':

> Expansion: Outbroadening of wild or overwrought fullness readily becomes a bad kind of wordiness: 'Farmer Stubbs drank beer', 'The votary of Demeter, who rejoiced in the name of Stubbs, indulged in potations of the cereal liquor.'   (1878:60)

Ex. 53   Explain why certain formations cluster in specific periods (*photo-, thermo-; mono-, poly-*); how many of these are 'English' (rather than imported from France or Germany)? (*OED*)

6.3.4   *Other European languages*
(Serjeantson 1935)

Borrowings from Italian, Spanish, German, etc. in the 19th century reflect the increasing international communication in trade, science and technology, the arts and topics relating to food, drink, dress and sports. However, no coherent pattern emerges – every word has its own history; whatever type of lexis is counted, all the sources outside French and Neo-Latin/Greek are numerically unimportant. A few specimens will serve for illustration:

---

[104] His anger was roused by the fashionable misuse of a few words in particular; he singled out for criticism *locality, evince, vehemently, populace, the rising generation, commence, eventuate, persuasion, sustain, experience, abnormal, æsthetic, elect, aggravate*, etc. (Alford ³1870:306–17).

Italian:	*vendetta, spaghetti, prima donna, intermezzo, scherzo, fiasco, studio, scenario*
Spanish:	*guerilla, camarilla*; through AmE: *lasso, rodeo, stampede, bonanza, vamoose*
German:	*loess, poodle, spitz, schnapps, edelweiss, kindergarten, hinterland*
Slavonic:	*mazurka, tundra, troika, polka*

6.3.5 *Languages outside Europe*
(Serjeantson 1935)

All loanwords have complex histories of transmission behind them; whereas early borrowings came through Spanish (and Portuguese, French, etc.), most items were borrowed straight into the local forms of English in the case of the US, Canada, the Caribbean, Africa, India, Australia and New Zealand. Only a few of these items became loanwords proper, most remaining designations for foreign objects, often for species of flora and fauna, food and drink, dresses and customs. Again, there is little that is systematic about all this, and the number of such words found in British texts (outside travelogues) is not large. Here are a few 19th-century loans which can serve to show how the world-view of Englishmen expanded, even if they stayed at home:

Arabic:	*alfalfa, razzia, safari*
Indian:	*cashmere, chutney, khaki, loot, nirvana, polo, pyjamas, swastika, thug*
Japanese:	*geisha, ginkgo, harakiri, tycoon*
Australian:	*boomerang, budgerigar, corroboree, koala*
North American:	*chipmunk, pemmican, toboggan*

The number of such words known outside specialist circles is small; moreover, most lexical gaps had been filled long before the 19th century, except for countries very recently discovered. The structural impact of such loans, for all their exoticness, was minimal – whether on English or on other European languages (most of these words are shared).

Ex. 54 By checking a French or German dictionary try to establish how many of the terms listed were handed on to other (European) languages through English mediation.

6.3.6 *Summary*

The impact of other languages on English was beginning to wane in the 19th century – and this is even true for French. The only exception involved words coined from Latin/Greek elements, but these are intentionally international from the moment they are created, and thus cannot be easily compared with foreign elements from living languages and national cultures. This relates not only to loanwords: calques are found almost as rarely (cf., from German, the 19th-century translations *folk etymology, folklore, folk song* and *footfolk*). Although comparative statistics are not available, it seems that from 1880 onwards the tide begins to turn: the English language, which had imported foreign words in huge quantities (which has given it one of the most 'mixed' vocabularies in the world), now started to export words, a process which reached a peak after 1945, and is still increasing.

6.4   *Word-formation*

6.4.1 *Introduction*

There are no major new patterns in 19th-century English, although a few generalizations can be made:

(1)   Marchand (1969:139–207) points out the enormous increase in prefix derivations in the 19th century, some patterns becoming notably more frequent after 1840–50. There is a smaller group of 'poetic' coinages, like those with the revived *a-* as in *ablaze* ('the 19th century was exceedingly productive'; Marchand lists forty-eight specimens). However, by far the greater portion of the new words is a consequence of technological progress and uninhibited word-coining on a neo-classical basis. The prefix types *a+symmetrical, ante+orbital, de+moralize, epi+dermis, extra+curricular, hyper+active, hypo+ basal, inter+active, intra+venous, meta+logic, micro+organism, neo+Anglican, pre+Christian, proto+Greek, re+Latinize, ultra+ radical, uni+polar* are either quite new, or their frequency increased rapidly in technical domains in the 19th century.[105] More innovative is the newly developed type *anti+war (campaign), inter+state (highway), post+war (years), pro+slavery (action)*, etc., in which the second element consists of a noun, but the derivation functions as a premodifier.

---

[105] The status of these coinages as permanent terms or as nonce-words – technical innovations or facetious new words in literary texts not intended as an addition to English lexis (cf. 6.8 below) – must be established before any judgement on frequency is possible.

(2)   Suffix derivations from NGI bases are at least as conspicuous as the combined forms. Their variety is demonstrated by a single year's neologisms: 1826 saw new words which included *cancroid*, *cerebrospinal*, *diphtheritis*, *exemplificative*, *heteromorphous*, *intermaxillary*, *invertebrate*, *mammal*, *panoptic*, *philanthropize*, *phonetic* and *reticulose*.

(3)   Individual word-formation patterns were declining (such as V+*ment* as still found in 1820 *bewilderment*, 1822 *puzzlement*, 1828 *embodiment*, 1830 *besetment*, *embranchment*, 1832 *worriment*, cf. Marchand 1969:332), others increasing: the 19th century was, amongst other things, a period of -*isms* (cf. 6.4.3.3).

(4)   Certain types notably increased in frequency, especially those of more unusual categories (often not strictly 'additive' patterns, such as verb+particle nominalizations, zero derivatives, backformations, acronyms and blends (see 6.4.4–6).

(5)   There are more idiosyncrasies in individual authors' styles in word-formation than in other fields of lexical usages; cf. the remarks on Dickens's neologisms in 6.8 below.

Also note that new types of block language (cf. 5.3.9) tend to blur the distinction between compounding and the stringing together of uninflected nouns and verbs (for instance in newspaper headlines). However, many of the items coined in the 19th century which strike us as peculiar today were specific to individual text types, such as words formed from native elements in the puristic attempts of writers like Barnes or Morris.

6.4.2 *Individual types: compounds*

No new types of compounds are attested in the 19th century. A statistical analysis is impossible because dictionaries do not list transparent compounds and it is difficult for historical periods to distinguish between compounds (forestressed, lexicalized, of frequent occurrence) and lexical strings which are combined ad hoc, often for syntactical convenience (as in block language which becomes increasingly common in the 19th century through new text types in advertising and journalism as well as the telegraph, cf. 5.3.9).[106]

The great freedom with which compounds could be formed led to many unique items in the language of individual poets (cf. Groom's analysis, 1937), but the pattern was not extensively used (as it was in German) to

---

[106] For the relatively rare cases of loan-translated compounds see 6.3.6 above; the status of *tele+phone* words as *English* compounds is questionable (cf. 6.3.3).

avoid modern NGI terminology – with a few exceptions: Barnes points to the felicitous adoption of *railway* and *steamboat* (1878:86–7).

Ex. 55 Compile a list of compounds made from native elements (e.g. with *earth-, heat-, light-, sound-, water-* as first elements) obviously coined for use in newly developed technologies and check on the dates in the *OED*. Why can the *OED*'s record not be expected to be complete?

6.4.3   *Individual types of derivation*

6.4.3.1 *-ess*

The use of the suffix to coin female agent nouns is important in so far as it tells us something about gender roles in the individual society. Most *-ess* words had been formed (or borrowed) in earlier centuries, which does not necessarily mean that these words were common: Marchand (1969:287) lists as 18th-century innovations exclusively words which look like nonce-words or at least items with a very low frequency: *citizeness, dictatress, editress, inquisitress, legislatress, manageress, presidentess* and *procuress.* Even if the evidence for the 19th century includes a few common words among the newly attested coinages (*millionairess, seductress, squiress, visitress, waitress* and *wardress*) it is quite clear that English has never been consistent in expressing feminine gender through word-formation.[107] (Contrast German where *-in* is almost universal in this function.) In English, suffragettes in the 19th century wanted to see a generic term used for both sexes as an indicator of equality – whether the term was formally marked (*teacher*) or not (*cook*). In consequence, words like *tailoress, teacheress,* etc., recorded from ME onwards, became next to obsolete from the late 19th century onward. (Note obligatory marking in *stewardess, headmistress, hostess,* etc.)

Ex. 56 Collect *-ess* formations and analyse the contribution of the 19th century to the list. What conclusions about political correctness and social history do your data permit you to draw?

---

[107] Alford's sober view appears to reflect the attitudes of his time:
Very many, indeed most names of occupations and offices, are common to both sexes, and it savours of pedantry to attempt by adding the female termination, to make a difference ... I expect we shall soon see '*groceress* and *tea-dealeress*, and licensed *vendress* of stamps'.   (³1870:122)

6.4.3.2 -*ette* and -*let*

The scarcity of suffixes for forming diminutives in St EngE led to the adoption of the French elements from the 16th century; their use increased in the 19th century. The first suffix came invariably to be spelt -*ette* and was increasingly combined with native bases: *balconette, leaderette* (in a newspaper), *novelette* and *stationette*. Many of the more recent formations are nonce-words; the pattern appears to be more frequent in AmE. (As a suffix denoting female agents, the use is 20th century.) The suffix -*let* was also infrequent before 1800; its productivity is a 19th-century innovation. The suffix was combined with native bases without any apparent restriction, as new derivatives show: *booklet, chainlet, starlet*. Many specimens listed by Marchand (1969:326) appear to be nonce-words.

6.4.3.3 -*ism*

The 19th century can be seen as a battleground of ideologies and factions; at least, such is the impression created by the frequency of derivatives ending in -*ism* (often from a personal name, and accompanied by -*ist* for the adherent, and -*istic*/-*ian* for adjectival uses). The year 1831 alone saw the new words *animism, dynamism, humorism, industrialism, narcotism, philistinism, servilism, socialism* and *spiritualism* (*CED*). Note that for 'follower of ...', -*ite* became a very frequent competitor in 19th-century innovations (*Ruskinite, Darwinite, Pre-Raphaelite*).

Ex. 57 Compile a chronological list of derivations ending in -*ism* (from the *CED*) and try to interpret the data on the basis of intellectual and political history.

6.4.3.4 -*ize*

The explosive growth of new verbs ending in -*ize* in the 19th century is certainly connected with progress in science and technology. A large number of these words came from America (although the alleged American provenance of many is not borne out by the facts); others are part of the NGI lexis and were first coined in French or German. The fact that many -*ize* verbs have become part of modern everyday lexis testifies to the spread of technical knowledge; the following 19th-century items serve to illustrate this phenomenon: *acclimatize, bowdlerize*, canalize, centralize, colonialize, emphasize, macadamize*, mobilize, nationalize, standardize, summarize, westernize** (*from native bases, a hybrid type which was still infrequent in the 19th century).

Ex. 58 Has the preferred spelling in EngE (*-ize* vs *-ise*) anything to do with the age of the words, i.e. are 19th-century coinages different from others?

6.4.3.5 *-y*

Since the dominant adjective-forming suffix is OE (*-ig*), and its productivity is unbroken over the centuries, there is little innovation to be expected. However, Marchand (1969:353) points to the notable frequency of coinages with a slangy character (*arty, beery, churchy, fishy, nosy, piggy*, etc.). What is new about these is that they cannot be paraphrased as 'full of X, characterized by X' but are derived from more complex and often idiomatic phrases. Their main interest is, however, sociolinguistic – illustrating the increasing readiness of the standard language to borrow slang terms into colloquial usage.

6.4.4 *Zero derivation*

New verbs were frequently derived from nouns and adjectives without a surface suffix in the 19th century. There is nothing new about this – even if there may be a slight loosening of the restriction that forbids us to derive a verb from a noun or an adjective clearly marked by a suffix (*to signature, to package, to referee, to reference* – all recorded in the 19th century and permitted if the meaning differs from the base verb, *sign, pack* and *refer* in the cases mentioned). Note that *to empty* and *to tidy* are unproblematic because the bases cannot be segmented, but **to guilty*, **hungry* and **mighty* are impossible.

New nouns had been derived from verbs from ME onwards, especially those of the *have a look/swim/walk* pattern (cf. Olsson 1961); there may have been a slight increase of such uses in the 19th century, but reliable statistics appear to be lacking.

6.4.5 *Verb + particle constructions and their nominalizations*
(Lindelöf 1938)

A type that had existed since the Middle Ages, but increased in due course, is the combination of verb + particle (replacing the OE type which had a movable prefix that came to be fixed in postverbal position, *ūtgān > go out*). From these verbal groups (which can be treated under word-formation or syntax) nouns were derived with increasing frequency after 1800. If we accept Lindelöf's statistics (fig. 19, p.124 based on the *OED*), then 17% of the *comeback* n. type are attested by 1800, 50% first found in the 19th century, and 33% in the 20th (the figure of 33% is certainly due to incomplete data in a dictionary finished by 1933). The following 19th-century items illustrate the productivity of the pattern: *knockout, pullover* and *takeoff*.

Whereas these zero derivations are largely transparent as to meaning, their formal analysis (according to Marchand 1969) presents problems: are we to assume *pull+over+Ø* to describe the shift from verb to noun? The analysis is theoretically sound but looks forced – in contrast to *out+come+* Ø, where the derivational Ø is in the 'correct' position. Other derivations in *-able* and *-er* are extremely rare and somewhat facetious, as the 18th-century coinage *(un)get+at+able*; the pattern varies with that in *liveable-with* and (most frequent) *reliable* in which the particle is deleted. Compare *onlooker* vs *looker-on*: only with preposed particle is the morphology undisputed (*onlooker, outspoken, outcome+Ø, outstanding*).

Lindelöf also found that the *pullover* type was more frequently attested in AmE than in BrE. A close word-study could possibly show whether some BrE formations were imported from America, or what the proportion of words is that are exclusive to either variety or shared – a problem also raised with respect to zero derivatives.

Ex. 59   Can structural concerns explain the late adoption of the *pullover* nouns? Check whether the alleged AmE preference can be confirmed in dictionaries.

6.4.6 *Backformation, blends, acronyms*

Backformation is the coining of a new word by subtraction rather than addition; analogy suggests that a word ending in *-ing* may have a verb from which the item is derived – the same applies for *-er* as an agent noun, *-(at)ion* for an action, as the case may be. New words thus created include *to sidle* (from *sidling*), *peddle* (from *pedlar*), *spectate* (from *spectator*), *backform* (vb.; from *backformation*), *laze* (vb.; from *lazy*), etc. It is obvious that the direction of the derivation is only diachronically relevant and often detectable only through etymology – although a more narrow meaning of one item of a pair may indicate that it is derived. The process is of structural significance only where it leads to new patterns, as in backderivation from synthetic compounds (*to babysit* from *babysitter/-ing*), which creates a new pattern of compound verb (N+V) formerly unknown in English.

Although the pattern is recorded for earlier periods, there was 'an upsurge in the 19th and 20th centuries' (Marchand 1969:104) which gave us words like *backpedal, bootlick, bushwhack, dryclean, handshake, housebreak, housekeep, stagemanage, thoughtread, typewrite* and *wirepull*.

It may be helpful to compare the rate of innovation in one old pattern (zero-derivation affecting various parts of speech, cf. Biese 1941) with two types which became really productive only after 1800 (the *pullover* n. type, cf. Lindelöf 1938, and backformation, cf. Pennanen 1966). Although the figures are based on the 'old' *OED*, suffer from various flaws in data and analysis, and were certainly not made with a view of being compared, a graph can bring out the diachronic difference reliably enough:

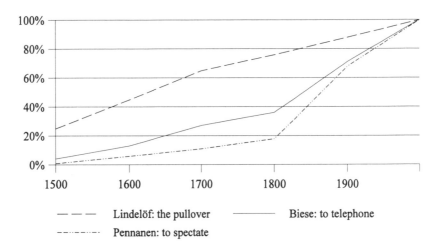

Figure 18 The increase of three types of derivations, 1500–1900

Clipping is a mechanical reduction which is not guided by morphological structures. Results of the process are the retention of the first part of a word (backclipping) as in *lab[oratory], ad[vertisement], exam[ination]* or *pram* (from *perambulator*), or preservation of the second part (foreclipping) as in *varsity* (from *university*) or *[aero]plane*, or the middle part (mid-clipping) as in *[in]flu[enza]* or *[de]tec[tive]*. As complaints by Swift in 1719 show (he criticized the use of *mob, phyzz*, etc.), the process is not quite new, but it increased in the 19th century. Most of these formations are colloquial or slangy, but many have since made their way into neutral English. The most current 19th-century coinages are probably *ad, auto, cab, exam, fan, gym, maths, pants* and *vet*.

Blends are fusions of two forms normally on the basis of a shared segment regardless of morphology. The pattern is very rare before 1800; one of the propagators was Lewis Carroll whose 'portemanteau word' *slithy* (from *slimy* and *lithe*) has become marginally current. Most of these items start as jocular and informal inventions (or are coined for advertising) – unless produced as contaminations by slips of the tongue. The few really current words are 20th-century (*smog, brunch, motel*).

Acronyms are combinations of initial letters or letter combinations which can be unpronounceable (*initialisms* such as *USSR*) or so fabricated that the sense is related to the content in a straightforward or ironic way (*CARE = Cooperative for American Remittances to Europe*). The pattern is almost exclusively 20th century, although syllable-based combinations were in use in the 19th century for artificial 'words' in chemistry, items which could also be classified as blends (Marchand 1969:453).

The types here treated as modern patterns are expressions of a desire for shortness and wit, which largely disregards morphological and etymological concerns, a combination which appears to meet modern needs of communication and which characteristically started mainly in the age of the Industrial Revolution.

6.5   Meaning and change of meaning
(Görlach 1997:119–36)

6.5.1 Introduction

Many words have changed their semantic content in the past 100 years. Since thousands of more or less conspicuous shifts are difficult to describe and to classify comprehensively, 1 will point out two types of changes in particular:

(1)   Words had new senses added by being applied to new technical developments; the result is that words became more polysemic (in due course, the old number of meanings sometimes may have been restored by the obsolescence of the sense that – metaphorically or metonymically – provided the basis for the semantic transfer). It should be noted that change in the *referent* is not normally sufficient reason for establishing change of meaning (e.g. developments in the shape of houses, ships, etc.).

(2)   The meaning of words shifted by having new evaluations attached to them (cf. 6.5.8 below).[108]

---

[108] That borrowing affects meaning (by selecting individual senses for adoption, or by giving them a different status from the one they had in the source language, cf. 6.3.2) is evident, but is not connected with semantic change within English; however, the adoption of a foreign word will restrict the meanings of the 'neighbouring' items in the semantic field.

6.5.2 *Description of meaning*

The description is here based on five assumptions:

(a)   that individual senses are relatively discrete and can be described
       synchronically as clusters of semantic components (which can be
       established by comparison) – the method of structuralist semantics;
(b)   that words have a relative semantic autonomy, at least as far as
       nouns, adjectives/adverbs and verbs are concerned;
(c)   that meaning (as an inner linguistic relation) is established for each
       language/dialect or period individually;
(d)   that the relationship between form and content is conventional
       (agreed upon by members of the speech community) and arbitrary
       (not transparent);
(e)   that linguistic signs designate (refer to) (classes of) objects and con-
       cepts but that meaning and reference are distinct.

The above assumptions make it possible for semantic change to happen;
change of meaning can also be distinguished from encyclopaedic change
occurring in *realia* (e.g. in the form of houses or ships).

Finally, the assumed discreteness of meanings permits us, in principle, to
quantify meaning (in polysemous words) and its change over time (through
extension, restriction or shift).

The assumption does not deny the fact that discreteness is a matter of
degree (it works better in semantic fields in which there are also notional
distinctions as in sets of domestic animals, etc.), that it varies with the individual users' competence[109] and that it does not capture distinctions in
register (styles, mode, formality) and connotations (evaluations).[110]

The following definitions are, then, necessary:

seme   =   the semantic component as the minimally distinctive
                 unit,
sememe   =   'sense', the minimal unit of meaning,
monosemy =   the fact that the content (*signifié*) of a word consists of
                 one sense,
polysemy =   the fact that the content of a word consists of several

---

[109] It is doubtful how far the assumption of compilers of thesauruses is justified that a user
is able to distinguish between near-synonyms and pick the one appropriate for the context; Roget (1852) firmly trusts in such competence (T12).

[110] For alternative methods see the insightful discussion by John R. Taylor (²1997) who
compares the validity of structuralist and cognitive approaches, and Geeraerts (1997) who
applies prototype semantics to diachrony.

	senses which share certain semes,
homonymy =	the fact that there are at least two senses with no semantic overlap,
synonymity =	identity of content – possible only in monosemous words, otherwise restricted to equivalence between individual sememes,
referential identity =	identity of reference expressed by different signs (which need not be synonyms).

If linguistic varieties are included in the discussion, the following terms are useful:

heteronymy =	equivalence of two terms (in meaning or reference) in two related linguistic systems (especially geographical varieties; English vs Scots, BrE vs AmE),
tautonymy =	identity of form in two related systems with differences in meaning.

In historical linguistics, a different understanding of a few terms has been established: *homonymy* here means the conflation of two formerly distinct words (through change in form as in *fair* 'beautiful' and 'trade ...' or borrowing as in *bank* 'steep hill' and 'institution dealing with money') whereas *polysemy* is used for words/meanings that have developed from a single sign (*game* 'contest' vs 'venison').

The intensional definition of meaning can be complemented by an extensional one; this applies, for instance, to legal texts in which the extension of a term is described by enumeration of its categories. In a similar way, George Eliot has Felix Holt speak about *workmen*, later on specified as 'artisans, and factory hands, and miners, and labourers of all sorts' (cf. Crowley 1989:269), which can be represented as a set of synonymous superordinates and three hyponyms, thus:

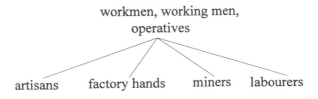

Figure 19 Superordinate terms and hyponyms

Finally, syntagmatic relations also contribute to meaning, in collocations and collocatability (cf. Görlach 1997:126).

6.5.3 *Causes of change*

Changes are prompted by changes in the material world, attitudes/evaluations and intra-linguistic conditions. Two major processes involved in extensions are metaphor and metonymy. A word can be applied to a new referent because the speaker sees a feature shared by the two (the *tertium comparationis*), as is often found in alleged characteristics of animals transferred to humans (he is a *pig*, a *sheep*, etc.) or anthropomorphic extensions (the *arm/mouth* of a river, the *head/foot* of a mountain).

Among intra-linguistic causes, the tendency to develop new semantic distinctions between former synonyms has often been noted. Trench (1851: 146–51) discussed the phenomenon with regard to the native/Romance duplicates in English; he also mentioned the active contribution of Coleridge, who coined the term 'desynonymize' for the process and applied it to his 'disentanglement' of *fanaticism* and *enthusiasm, keenness* and *subtlety, poetry* and *poesy*, and *reason* and *understanding*. (Not all of these can of course be considered proper synonyms.)

6.5.4 *The speed of change*

Semantic change can take a long time to complete. It is strange for a modern reader to discover that *traffic* did not always mean 'road traffic'; it is even stranger that although this meaning first entered the language in the 1820s, obviously filling a lexical gap, the old meaning 'trade, commerce' appears to have remained vital, or even dominant, all through the 19th century. Soule (1871) fails to indicate the 'road' sense for *traffic*: he also provides eight senses for *sport* without including the modern one. He does not give the 'phosphorous' sense of *match*, nor indeed the philatelic sense of *stamp*. While most of this is certainly due to oversight, it can also mean that the new meanings had not become dominant – as they were in the 20th century.

The number of senses which were added to polysemic words in a specific period, compared with those that became obsolete, provides a gauge to measure the expansion and reduction of the *signifié* of a word, and of the speed of change. Although the figures given in Görlach (1991:199) are not based on a properly semantic analysis but on the number of subentries in the *OED* (first edn) – which include encyclopaedic and pragmatic categories in the classification – they can here serve to illustrate the contribution of the 19th century.[111]

	–OE	–1300	–1400	–1500	–1600	–1700	–1800	–1900	Total
draught	5–2		11–6	7–2	11–5	5	2	5	46–15
form		8–3	5–1	3–1	2	2	1		21–5
sense			2–1		16–1	8–1	1	1	28–3
set			1	2–2	8–4	3–1	7	10	31–7
stock	2–1	2–1	9–2	8–3	14–4	12	6–1		53–12
trade			2–2	1–1	4–2	2	2–1	2	13–6
train			1–1	4–1	6–2	1	2	1	15–4
wit	3–1	4–1	2–2	1	2	1			13–4
Total	10–4	14–5	33–15	26–10	63–18	34–2	1–2	19	220–56

Figure 20 Increase and decrease of senses in eight lexemes (based on the *OED* and here quoted from Görlach 1991:199); first recordings minus obsolescences in individual centuries indicated

Ex. 60   Check on the number of new 19th-century senses given for the listed items in the *second* edition of the *OED*. Why is the increase notably less than in previous centuries?

6.5.5 *Types of change*

A change in the material object (referent) should not count as a semantic change. Although the forms of houses have changed a great deal from the Middle Ages onwards, the distinctive features ('building', 'for living in', 'for humans', 'man-made', 'permanent') have remained the same, as has the position of the item *house* in the semantic field (cf. Görlach 1997:125). The *signifié* must rather add (or lose) semes, or exchange the set by metonymy to qualify for 'semantic change'. This often happens without an increase or diminution in the number of senses – the respective sememe may become more specific by the addition of a distinctive feature (specification) or by its neutralization (generalization).

On the other hand, the number of sememes can increase or decrease – if

---

[111] Note, however, that the number of new senses recorded for the 19th century may be reduced by the fact that they were too new to be fully noticed by the *OED* compilers.

the old meaning survives side by side with the new: the *signifié* becomes more or less polysemic by the addition or deletion of a sense.

Frequently new senses arose by the omission of the modifying/specifying element (which came to be incorporated as a semantic component, so to speak). The process is quite clearly connected with the fact that one use becomes dominant so that the addition of the specifier comes to be considered superfluous. Note the following 19th-century developments from the railway:

> *railway station > station*
> *railway platform > platform*
> *train of carriages > train*

Occasionally the omission obscures the semantic reasons that led to the full term, as in *fall [of leaves]*. This is particularly the case where the head is deleted (uncommon in English) as in *private [soldier]* (18th century). Compare three successive processes of ellipsis which led to the homonymous nouns *capital (letter* (ME), *stock* (16th century) and *city* (17th century)) – it is open to debate whether these processes should be classified under word-formation rather than as changes of meaning.

Note that a similar explanation holds for nominalizations in which the specifying elements are deleted in the derivation process:

> a picture which is drawn => *a drawing*
> a document which is drawn up (provisionally) => *a draft*
> a document by which a man is drawn for the army => *a draft*
> a part of a cupboard which can be drawn out => *a drawer*

Ex. 61   Explain the meanings of *conductor* (of an orchestra, of a train; of heat/electricity) and *spring* as arising from the deletion of the specifying context. Were these elements, formerly present, sufficient to disambiguate the meaning?

6.5.6 *Metaphor*

Metaphors are frequent in common speech as well as being rhetorical ornaments of poetic diction; they rely on transfer of meaning to a new class of referents on the basis of a shared feature (not necessarily a semantic component). This transfer can be ad hoc, and some of the attractiveness of metaphors lies in the fact that they are not common.[112] In such cases, meaning is not affected – this happens only when the use becomes accepted and conventionalized. Such metaphoric extensions are quite common; the transfer can be initiated by the need for a new designation.

The development of modern transport led to the extension of words connected with horse carriages first to the railway and then to automobiles, as in *coach*. The word was borrowed to designate a large horse-drawn carriage (16th century), and was transferred, on the basis of many shared features, to a railway passenger or mail carriage (19th century, US) and to an overland bus (20th century). Note that words like *wheel, rim, felloe (felly)*, etc., have designated materially quite different referents in the past few centuries, but their meaning has apparently not changed.

Ex. 62 Explain the motivation that appears to be behind the retention of many pre-industrial terms for technological items in the 19th century, as in the re-use of parts of horse-drawn vehicles for parts of motorcars and railways. (*OED*)

6.5.7 *Metonymy*

The meaning of a word can be transferred to referents which are connected (locally, temporally, causally) with the original referent in a situation. The modern meaning of *bead* (from 'prayer', connecting with the telling of beads of the rosary) is a good example of the phenomenon. 19th-century specimens of this transfer (which often led to the original meaning being forgotten) include:

> *railway*: the way on which rails are laid; the system of rails on which a vehicle moves; the system/networks of public transport; the institution responsible for this. (Shortening to *rail* makes the meaning even more disconnected.)

The classic 19th-century case, which combines referential changes, is the word *match*, which had from ME onwards designated a wick (of a candle) or a fuse (of a cannon) and was then extended to 'a piece of cord … dipped in melted sulphur so as to be readily ignited with a tinder-box' and only from 1850 to 'a short slender piece of wood … tipped with a composition

---

[112] The effective use of a metaphor is thus a matter of style. Dangers that lie in inappropriate uses in journalism (which have great relevance to 19th-century practice) are summarized in *SPE Tract* (1922:1–15) under the headings of 'Live and dead m.', 'Unsustained m.', 'Overdone m.', 'Spoilt m.', 'Battles of the dead' and 'Mixed m.'.

which bursts into flame when rubbed' (*SOED*). Note that many competing designations (such as *lucifer*) were tried when modern matches came into use.

Unexplained metonymy may be the basis for enigmatic etymologies, such as *coach* 'tutor', 'trainer' (19th century, connected with *coach* 'vehicle'?). How are the PDE senses of *cockpit* (20th century) and *cocktail* (19th century) to be explained?

Ex. 63   Sketch the material history behind the new meanings of *bulb, factory, gear* and *match.*

6.5.8 *Social reasons for change*

Among the reasons that lead to new senses are social evaluations, a consequence of a changing system of morals, ethics and religious beliefs. The '*weltbild*' we stereotypically consider 'Victorian' is traceable in new interpretations given to older words in a time of changing societal values. This applies to many everyday words like *man, woman*, etc., but is most conspicuous in adjectives and abstract nouns which denote social values. Phillipps (1984) has traced the meaning of a number of such key words in 19th-century novelists, and found that adjectives and abstract nouns are the most sensitive indicators of social class and change, especially when they develop from being the expression of highly valued assets into indicators of the ambitions of social climbers. Such diagnostic words include the following adjectives:

> *agreeable, amiable, aristocratic, attractive, august, benevolent, bright, brilliant, candid, charming, civil, clever, courteous, delicate, easy, elegant, exquisite, fair, gallant, genteel, gentle, grand, handsome, illustrious, liberal, nice, polite, pretty, prudent, rational, reasonable, refined, respectable, romantic, steady, worthy,* etc.,

with their related nouns, plus words like *dignity, distinction, firmness, integrity, principle, rectitude, regard, reputation, resolution, respect, self-command* and *temper.* Many of these were inherited from the 18th century – but their meaning may have shifted considerably as a consequence of far-reaching changes in the social structure.

One of the powerful motives in the 19th century was prudery, especially with regard to sex, and the consequent use of euphemisms. This is often achieved by the use of the superordinate term, as in *undertaker* 'a special kind of undertaker' (cf. *entrepreneur, Unternehmer*) or 19th-century uses of *limb*, applied even to the legs of a piano.

Change of meaning is often signalled by the semantic unease when reading older texts. The following excerpt illustrates that the euphemistic sense predominating in PDE *intercourse* had not evolved in 1827: Esther Copley instructed her readers in the *Young Servant's Friendly Instructor ...* (originally published in the *Christian Gleaner, and Domestic Magazine*, London: Simpkin & Marshall, 1827) under 'The house-maid':

> She should be remarkably neat, quick and handy in all her movements; and not only good-tempered, but gentle and respectful in her manners, as she will have much intercourse with her employers and their friends.   (1827:34)

Different reasons are behind the deterioration of some of the terms listed above, for instance *genteel*. When the word was appropriated by upstarts with doubtful notions of what refinement and good taste meant, it was no longer usable for its neutral or positive senses. Adjectives which often include evaluations are more frequently affected by such changes. Another famous case, with quite different results, is the 19th-century development of *nice*: its 18th-century meaning had been bleached to mean anything agreeable, often in 19th-century female speech (cf. Phillipps 1984:41, who refers to statements by Bulwer-Lytton and Disraeli).

Intensifying adverbs also serve to show semantic bleaching and eventually the replacement of lexis because words become overused so that they can no longer fulfil their function properly; they also illustrate the fashionable innovations of certain parts of society. Johnson (1755) had spoken out against *abominably, horrid, mighty* and *monstrous*, all classified as 'low language, (women's) cant', etc. In the 19th century, too, the use of intensifiers is indicative of (in)formality and social class, but detailed analyses are lacking.

Ex. 64   How far does the *OED* document the social changes connected with the 'deterioration' of *genteel, nice, polite* and other words in the list above?

Ex. 65   Do the intensifiers criticized by Johnson survive into the 19th century?

6.5.9 *Application*

Change of meaning is best illustrated from semantic fields relating to the new technologies that rapidly became part of everyday experience, such as the field of vehicles/transport/traffic: *traffic* itself meant 'commerce' from 1505 on, but 'stream of vehicles' from 1825; *coach* (1556) also designated a 'railway carriage' (US) from 1832, and a 'single-decker bus' from 1923;

train (14th century) came to be employed for the railway before 1824. (For a contrast between 17th- and 20th-century structures of the field 'vehicle' cf. Görlach 1991:188, based on Wilkins's analysis in 1668:257.)

In all these cases, the change is properly semantic because the meanings remained in the field of 'transport'. For other conspicuous semantic changes caused by technological progress compare the modern meanings of *bulb* (1856), *gear* (1888) and *stamp* (1840) – electricity exhibiting some 18th-century predecessors of expanded meanings, as *circuit* (1746) and *current* (1747) show.

6.6   Obsolescence and revival

The comparative closeness of the Victorian period to our own and the effectiveness of a written tradition does not lead us to expect major lexical losses in the interim. No words appear to have been lost as a consequence of homonymic clashes or other intra-linguistic causes. Where losses are documented, they can usually be ascribed to the obsolescence of their referents (a frequent phenomenon in a world of rapid technological change) or to social stigma and changing fashions.

Entries like '272. VEHICLE' in Roget's *Thesaurus* (1852:64) contain words such as *cariole, chaise*, phaeton*, whisky, landau*, berlin, droschki*, désobligeant, diligence, calash, brougham*, clarence,* which still serve to designate the objects in a museum.[113] Similar lists could easily be compiled for dresses (Roget no. 225, 1852:55) and weapons (Roget no. 727, 1852:176).

There are fewer cases of words lost as a consequence of social stigma. This happened most frequently in colloquial usage and slang, where a quick turnover of the lexis is the rule, and can affect entire categories; rhyming slang, for instance, started off as a 19th-century lower-class phenomenon, became 'acceptable' in colloquial speech mainly through the music-hall tradition, and is obsolescent today.

Such social reasons (and loss of emphasis) are likely to account for the loss of many items listed in Roget's no. 501 – only nineteen of the seventy-nine are listed in the respective section of the 1962 edition:

> Fools, blockhead, wiseacre (ironically), simpleton, witling, ass, goose, ninny, dolt, booby, noodle, numbscull, nizy, noddy, goose-cap, half-wit, *imbecille*, ninny-hammer, *badeau*, driveller, idiot; natural, lackbrain, *niais*, child, infant, baby, innocent, greenhorn, zany, dunce, lout, loon, oaf, lown, dullard, dullhead, doodle,

---

[113] The asterisked items were still found in the *ALD* of the 1970s – all with the historical reference indicated– but only *brougham* is left in the 1995 edition.

calf, colt, buzzard, block, put, stick, stock, numps, tony, clodpoll, clotpoll, clod-hopper, clod, lubber, bull-calf, bullhead, thickscull, dunderhead, dizzard, hoddy-doddy, nonny, looby, nincompoop, a poor head, *un sot à triple étage*, loggerhead, sot, jolthead, beetlehead, jobbernowl, changeling, dotard, grasshead, mooncalf, giddyhead, *gobemouche*, rantipole, old woman, crone, April-fool.

Ex. 66 Write out the words you do not know and check whether they are included in college dictionaries; also test whether they are unknown to other (older) speakers.

Words cannot really die in a language with a written tradition; they survive in older texts (such as in the works of Chaucer, Shakespeare or Milton) from which they can be 'revived' even if they have been lost from current use. Such archaisms are a typical feature of certain styles/genres – and many *OED* quotations documenting individual words from authors in the 16th and 19th centuries (only) are misleading since they may well not be instances of survival but revivals.

A particular type of revival is connected with purist tendencies: authors may revive a Germanic word (or form a new compound from Germanic elements) to replace a foreign word. This has happened to *folk* which is used more frequently by itself and in newly formed compounds such as *folklore* (19th century), *folkwain* (for *omnibus*) and *folksong*. Authors like Barnes and Morris have a great number of such Saxonisms which were, however, not consistently entered in the *OED* (cf. 7.2.3 below and Gallasch 1979).

6.7   *Names*
(Coates 1998)

Names (whether of persons, places or products) have a marginal position in linguistics and the history of a language. The borderline with proper words can be insufficiently defined, and names can of course become 'normal' words when taken to be representative of a class of referents rather than of an individual.

There is little to record for 19th-century place-names in England. Few names were invented anew, the growing cities continuing the names of former villages where applicable. There *were* some changes in pronunciation – with increasing mobility and news-reporting, names were often first met in written form and spelling pronunciations began to replace local pronunciations, a development now completed for place-names like *Cirencester*, *Daventry*, *Southwell* or *Ruthwell* (but never begun in the case of *Gloucester*, *Leicester* and *Worcester*).

First names are remarkably stable in the English-speaking world, and were in the 19th century. Crystal (1995:151) shows that until 1925 *John* and *William* remained at the top of the male list, with *Thomas* invariably close. However, *Joseph, Richard, Henry* and *Robert*, among the top ten in 1800, had been replaced by *Frederick, Arthur, Albert* and *Ernest* in 1900 – the importance of being Earnest. However, major changes did not come until the 1960s – when none of the 19th-century favourites remained.

By contrast, the turnover of women's names was almost complete by 1900: although nearly all the top names of 1700 survived to 1800, only *Mary* and *Elizabeth* did so to 1900 – *Sarah, Jane, Hannah, Susan, Martha, Margaret* and *Charlotte* had been replaced by *Alice, Elsie, Edith, Doris, Dorothy* and *Ethel*.

(The difference from US preferences is possibly smaller than one might expect (Crystal 1995:151), but *Anna, Emma, Helen, Jean, May, Mildred* are more likely to be American girls, and *Donald, Frank, Gary, Harry* and *Samuel* to be American boys, before 1925.)

If we want to point out specific 19th-century features in name-giving, the revival of medieval names (some due to their use in Scott's novels) and those of neglected saints might be mentioned – none of these became really popular, however. Names like *Florence* and *Cecil, Victoria* and *Albert* became moderately current in imitation of Nightingale and Rhodes, and the Queen and her consort.

Ex. 68 Is there a correlation between 19th-century preferences in names and characteristic features of lexical choices?

6.8   *Idiolect*[114]

Investigations of personal diction are available only for literary writers, which limits their generalizability since the literary function of the text must

---

[114] Cf. for genres, 7.1 below. Idiolect is here understood as the total of a speaker's or writer's output, selected from the period language available to him, and is here exemplified by the 'English of Dickens' (i.e. as found in his writing, especially his novels, which must be different from the English he used in spoken and written form outside the literary productions). However, 'idiolect' can also be understood as the language of a particular (literary) character, and is so by Brook (1970:138–67), who uses the term to designate the speech of an individual in Dickens's work, such as John Browdie's Yorkshire dialect, Dick Swiveller's poetic style, or Micawber's Latinized diction. Dickens is here used as an example because analyses are available, whereas the styles of, say, Queen Victoria, Darwin or Disraeli have not been investigated (and a full range of relevant texts is not accessible outside Britain).

always be taken into account.[115] And yet the usage of writers, especially if authors of popular prose, tends to catch a great deal of the period flavour of the language. With due caution, my summary of Dickens's English (based on Brook 1970 and Sørensen 1985) can therefore also be taken as illustrative (if not representative) of 19th-century English. The title of Sørensen's book, stressing Dickens's role as a linguistic innovator, serves to warn us that an idiosyncratic penchant for effect must be distinguished from the underlying trends which allowed him to write the way he did, and to do so with the success he had. I will here summarize the evidence for a few categories:

(1) *Word-formation.* The following types of formation are particularly conspicuous and typical of the liberties Dickens took in coining new words:

(a) Agent nouns in *-er*: 'That Dickens is an innovator ... appears from the fact that some [words] antedate the *OED*, and others are not even listed' (Sørensen 1985:37, referring to the *OED*'s first edition). Since most of these are transparent *ad-hoc* formations not intended for permanent use, the *OED*'s silence is not surprising (*astonisher, crusher, hulker, rasper, quencher* and formally more experimental words like *knifer, merry-go-rounder, putter in, refreshmenter* and *town-mader*).

(b) Nouns in *-ment* and *-ness*: the first type appears to be no longer productive – Dickens has facetious coinages like *bewigment, embowerment, ramshacklement* and *reconsignment*. As regards the *-ness* words it is their unconventional character that is remarkable; cf. *coachlessness, dovetailedness, touch-me-not-ishness*, and the quote from *Boz*: 'He ... had a clean-cravatish formality of manner, and kitchen-pokerness of carriage'.

(c) Adjectives in *-ed*, formed from N+V+*ed*: *amateur-painted scenery, extinguisher-topped towers, sun-and-shadowed chequered colonade*, (cf. similar formations in *-ing*); or from N+N+*ed*: *copper-saucepaned laboratory* and *old towns, draw-bridged and walled*.

(d) Adjectives in *-y*, 'particular favourites of Dickens's perhaps because they are easily formed colloquialisms that are often of a humorous character' (1985:41): *ginger-beery, gold-dusty, hunchy, mildewy, pepper-corny, soupy*.

(2) *Latinisms.* 19th-century writers appear to have found Latinisms

---

[115] Linguists in search of sociolinguistically sound evidence will be cautioned by the speech of characters like Oliver Twist who is totally unaffected by the criminal cant around him, his language thus intimating his innocence and upper-class provenance.

expressing pompousness and often combined with malapropisms particularly funny – a kind of linguistic joke that is now somewhat stale.[116] Most specimens of such stilted diction from Dickens's works are not straightforward loanwords but rather derivatives exploiting productive word-formation patterns (cf. (1)): *acidulation, admonitorial, aquatically, auriferously, condonatory, conductorial, dilapidative, perspirational, polygamically* and *uvularly*. All of these would count as 'inkhorn terms' – had they been used seriously.[117]

(3)   *Dialect and sociolect*. Most of the effectiveness of Dickens's presentation of regional and social linguistic features lies in pronunciation, but there are also a few lexical items, used more or less stereotypically: 'Americanisms' listed by Sørensen (1985:47–9) include *hail from, chicken fixings*; 'theatre and circus terms' (1985: 49) *circuit, gag, incidental music, to mug* and *ponging*.

(4)   *Metaphor*. Dickens's most striking uses involve 'a depersonalization of human beings (and the) endow(ing of) inanimate objects with human qualities' (1985:55). Such uses are not intended to establish permanent meanings, and have not: this makes them as new as they were in the author's time.

Ex. 67   Which of the words quoted above were considered 'dictionary-worthy'? Did the fact that they were used (and popularized?) by Dickens have anything to do with the decision?

---

[116] Cf. Brook's statement: 'Much has been written about the polysyllabic humour of the Victorians. The form that it usually takes is the use of grandiloquent language to describe trivial events, thus emphasizing their triviality and causing the reader to smile at the incongruity between the language and the occasion' (1970:16).

[117] Sørensen (1985:45) notes the practice of expressing a concept first in easily intelligible language, and then taking it up in Latinized form – though not in the way that Dr Johnson is reported to have done, 'improving' his English as he was speaking. Micawber's technique is quite the contrary: 'The twins no longer derive their sustenance from Nature's founts – in short – they are weaned!' (*David Copperfield*, ch. 17, quoted from Brook 1970:161). In another context, the irony has an equivalent in existing serious texts: Mrs Wilfer's culinary advice, held up to ridicule in *Our Mutual Friend*, III, ch. 4 (cf. Brook 1970:171) sounds very much like the precepts of Mrs Beeton.

7

Text types and style

7.1   *Text types*

7.1.1   *Introduction*
(Biber & Finegan 1992, Görlach 1995c)

Text types are defined as conventional forms or formulas, the knowledge of which is shared by the writer/speaker (determining the details of production) and by the reader/listener (determining his expectations and degree of acceptance of the text produced). There are more than 2,000 text types distinguished by name in the English language; the degree of conventionalization differs widely from type to type, being largely dependent on the function of the form – legal contexts require a huge number of fossilized types, each characterized by a unique and invariable form, whereas everyday forms exhibit much more freedom and variability according to social, stylistic/functional, diachronic and idiosyncratic factors. This variability can be exploited in intentional extensions and 'misuses', particularly in literary texts or advertising. For instance, a well-known text type can be re-used for a new function, such as a cooking recipe in the form of a sonnet, or an advertisement in the form of a proclamation, or late Victorian valentines in the form of bank notes, telegrams or cooking recipes, the product thus sharing elements of the two underlying forms and the reader being expected to identify both and be attracted by the mismatch.

A particular problem connected with the concept 'text type' is the frequent instability of form, which cannot, in all cases, be interpreted teleologically, i.e. as a developmental stage on the way to present-day stable conventions. Moreover, tradition (acceptance of established rules) combines with period-specific features: conventions for texts on gravestones may be well established, but there will also be characteristics of, say, Victorian attitudes and style present which it is the linguist's job to find and describe (cf. T55). Finally, there is variation according to writer and reader/addressee, which not only depends on traditional sociolinguistic variables like sex, age, social status and education, but can be modified by expressive functions like originality, wit, irony, respect, superiority or squeamishness. Whereas all the first elements conform to the readers' expectations, derived from their 'knowledge' of what a text ought to look like, the latter often intentionally diverge in order to surprise, shock or manipulate the intended addressees. Travesties and parodies thus illustrate the intentional disregard and misuse of genre conventions (cf. T73, T86).

As the analysis of individual text types below will show, types are best classified on the basis of a list of distinctive features (which can include 'period' to account for specific developments in, say, the 19th century). The most important criteria appear to be whether:

(a)   the type is conventionalized at all, and to what degree;
(b)   the type is homogeneous or a conglomerate: a letter is defined not by the form and content of its main section, but can contain elements from various text types (cf. 7.2);
(c)   the type is independent (a free form) or by definition part of a larger (conglomerate) type, as a table of contents, foreword, dedication or index is.

A long list of sociolinguistic and stylistic components relating to form, function, topic and situation will ideally distinguish each text type from the next. Note that not all decisions are binary, but often permit gradation and the choice of a large number of options as in 'field'/'topic' or 'intention' and that components virtually form an open set determined by the distinctive functions. A provisional list includes:

(d)   the medium (written vs. spoken);
(e)   the field/topic;
(f)   the formality/officialness/publicness;
(g)   the degree of technicality;
(h)   the form (prose, verse, etc.);
(i)   obligatory accompanying elements (music, illustrations);
(k)   speech act functions;
(l)   the degree of formulaicness;
(m)   the historicity;
(n)   originality vs. intertextual dependence (translation, paraphrase, pastiche, travesty and report);
(o)   fictionality (vs truth, authenticity);
(p)   author's intention and addressee's expectation;
(q)   dialogue.

The list can be extended and the sequence is open to discussion, as is the question of whether various subcomponents should be summarized under one head.

A provisional componential analysis of selective features characterizing a few major text types produces a grid like this:

	convention.	homogen.	independent	written	topic	formal	technical	prose	accomp. el.	speech act	original	fictional	intention
letter	±	—	+	+	O	±	—	+	—	R	+	—	I
diary	—	—	+	+	O	—	—	+	—	O	+	—	R
joke	±	+	+	—	O	—	—	+	—	E	—	+	A
conversation	—	—	+	—	O	—	—	+	—	O	+	—	O
drama	—	—	+	+	O	—	—	±	—	O	+	+	A
act/bill	+	+	+	+	L	+	+	+	—	Dr	—	—	C
newsp. advert	—	—	—	+	O	—	—	+	+	C	+	—	P
sermon	—	—	+	—	R	+	—	+	—	R	+	—	T
polit.speech	—	—	+	—	P	±	—	+	—	R	+	—	T
leader	—	+	—	+	O	+	±	+	—	R	+	-	T
hymn	+	+	+	±	R	+	—	—	+	O	—	O	T
sonnet	+	+	+	+	Lt	+	—	—	—	O	+	+	A
libretto	—	—	+	+	O	—	—	±	+	O	+	+	A
oath	±	+	+	—	O	l		+	—	C	—	—	Af
proverb	+	+	+	±	O	—	—	+		O	—	O	T

Figure 21 Componential analysis of fifteen text types
topics: L = legal, Lt = literature, R = religion, P = politics; speech acts (in a general understanding): C = commissives, D = declarations, Dr = directives, E = expressives, R = representatives; intention: A = amuse, Af = affirm, C = codify, I = inform, P = publicize, R = remind, T = teach; O = indistinct or various

Ex. 68 Continue the analysis with five text types represented in the corpus (death notice T71, T75; petition T67; dedication T41; telegram T93; and directions T69, T84).

The distinction between text types is largely expressed by linguistic features which can be enumerated and applied to individual texts. Biber & Finegan (1988, 1989, 1992) have chosen this approach and arrived at convincing innovative results. Their lists of features (1989:491) constituting the cline between literate and oral styles include those expressing the purpose of the author and the conditions of the production, context-dependency and degree of concreteness, signalled by the frequencies and specific uses of pronouns, verbs, prepositions, conjuncts and adverbials (of various kinds), word-length, nominalizations, emphatics, hedges, amplifiers, discourse particles and *WH*-questions, relatives and complements (cf. the adaptation in Adamson 1998:591). Although many of their variables can be correlated with the system suggested above, I will not attempt a statistical analysis of my excerpts here since the texts are too short and the relevance of a statistical analysis is not clear for all text types. Adamson, who also decides not to use the Biber & Finegan approach, refers to the different salience of individual features, which cannot be dealt with in a convincing way by statistics. She singles out the use of the parenthesis, an accepted feature of 18th-century style aimed at conversational speech. However, late 18th-century authors placing 'a high value on unity and connectedness in discourse' came to stigmatize the pattern (Adamson 1998:595). By opposition, Cowper could use parenthesis as a 'style-marker for an opposing ideal, one which rated associationism above logic'; it could thus 'act as a standard-bearer for the oral revolution announced in Wordsworth's prefaces' (Adamson, 1998:595). It is quite obvious that no statistical analysis would be able to bring out this function.

Although Biber & Finegan's methods are not, then, applied here, their criteria can possibly be usefully employed, as being independently formulated, to serve as a control of the typology sketched above.

The formal features of individual types are conventionalized to different degrees. A cooking recipe is characterized not just by content and the general type of instruction but by a stereotypical sequence of text sections, by fixed collocations and by peculiarities of verb syntax: the use of imperatives, optional deletion of objects, etc. (cf. 7.1.7). In similar ways, weather forecasts have more or less standardized forms: deviances from the pattern will be noticed, and transfers to other functions (misuses) will be correctly interpreted by members of the speech community.

Ex. 69 Show how text type has determined the choice of features in two versions of the same story in T74 and T90. Are the genre-specific conventions changed in Barnes's translation, T35?

Ex. 70 Analyse the form of T63, pointing out the underlying formula and the implanted elements.

7.1.2 *Religion*
(Crystal & Davy 1969:147–72)

The field of religion is covered by a great variety of text types which share their content, but possibly little else, as componential analysis will bring out. Intuitively, we might wish to include here types such as prayer, sermon, holy writ (the Bible, Koran, etc.) and church hymn. The great number of text types in the religious sphere has been much reduced since the Middle Ages, when there were not only names for many specific types but also for books in which these were collected (*antiphonary, breviary, legendary, responsory*, etc.). Also, in a secularized modern world most of the surviving items have developed non-religious meanings or applications (*homily, lesson, litany, sermon*) or have become restricted to individual denominations. Here is a survey of major types which have well-marked characteristics in the 19th century:

	public	in service	stereotyped	rel. to Bible	educational	by priest	read	sung	by rote	address	dialogue
anthem	+	+	+	+	—	—	—	+	—	—	—
hymn	+	+	+	—	—	—	—	+	—	+	—
sermon	+	+	—	±	±	+	+	—	+	+	—
homily	+	+	—	±	+	+	+	—	+	+	—
lesson	+	+	+	+	—	+	+	—	—	±	—
prayer	±	±	±	—	—	—	+	—	+	+	—
litany	+	+	+	±	—	—	±	±	+	—	+

Figure 22 Analysis of seven religious genres

Anthem/hymn: features determined by 'singability' (rhythm, metre and rhyme), sung by priest and congregation, often by rote and accompanied by the organ. Textually, hymns are handed down from one generation to another, but their form is often adapted to individual denominations or specific purposes. The textual tradition of hymns is very complex so that the period contribution to the older corpus is often impossible to establish.

Sermon/homily: the two terms are usually interchangeable. The priest addresses the congregation on a specific topic (often related to the lesson). Texts may be premeditated but unscripted, although there are books of sermons produced as models to imitate, or transcripts of sermons delivered at a specific occasion; these are often edited, with the relationship between the delivered and printed forms impossible to determine. The sermon has many features in common with political speech, the homily with other forms of educational efforts – no wonder that many features of 'sermon' style are carried over into secular forms.[118]

Lesson: since the text is determined by the Bible, only the use of a specific translation, or the individual passage (both normally settled for the day and the individual denomination), is variable in principle. Biblical translation was staunchly conservative in the 19th century – textual revisions were rather minor accommodations to contemporary usage, with new translations not attempted before the 1960s.[119]

Prayer: there is a great variety of types, ranging from stereotyped (and even fossilized) forms such as texts transmitted in the *Book of Common Prayer* to individual (private, silent) forms. The latter are not normally recorded – though they may be found in literature – but a greater proportion of formal prayer in the 19th century is indicated by books intended to instruct people in how to pray.

Litany: the only major form involving priest and congregation in a question and answer pattern; it is strictly stereotypical, in order to permit speaking in chorus and to facilitate the response.

Catechism: testing, through a pupil's memorized responses to set questions, the essentials of Christian faith provided a pattern for other fields (such as grammar) in which the canonical minimal knowledge in codified form was checked.

Apart from linguistic features determined by text type we have to consider period-specific conditions which make 19th-century religious discourse appear so different from modern texts; they include the Sunday-school tradition, the high vs low church division, evangelicalism and the Oxford movement. All these traditions are worthy of detailed investigation.

---

[118] Thus Felix Holt addressing the workmen: 'You will not suspect me of wanting to preach any cant to you, or of joining in the pretence that everything is in a fine way' (quoted from Golby 1996:271).

[119] In 1770, John Worsley had translated the New Testament afresh 'according to the Present Idiom of the English Tongue'. His attempt is not, however, as radical as he pretends, and it does not seem to have been of much influence.

Ex. 71 Show the elements that a sermon and a political speech have in common (T66, T68). Was the closeness of the two genres potentially greater in the 19th century and for what reasons?

7.1.3 *Legal language*
(Cf. Crystal & Davy 1969:193–217)

Legal documents are classified under a very large number of text types; this in itself reflects one of the characteristics common to all – the specific, well-defined, unambiguous designation of such texts. The following features can be expected in all legal texts:

(a) A high degree of formulaic diction whether individual terms or complete sentences are concerned.

(b) Unambiguous meaning of terms defined in a coherent system of legal reasoning. This includes extensional definitions (by enumerating the categories) rather than intensional definitions. In syntax, repetition of terms is preferred to anaphoric pronouns (because their use might be misunderstood).

(c) Universality of application and stability of terms and arguments over time – especially in the English system of case law.

It follows that legal texts from the 19th century are as characteristic of the genre as modern ones and although they were archaic at their time, they are more or less unchanged today, being in a way outside the 'ravages of time'. It may seem strange to find that archaic elements, independently revived by poets like Morris, thus came to be shared between legal English and archaizing diction. This is the case with words like *thereinto, whenas* and *whereunder* (cf. Gallasch 1979).

Ex. 72 Analyse T59 and T87 for the formulaic features constituting legal language and the specific text type(s) in question.

7.1.4 *Philosophical exposition*

Since these texts are composed at leisure, and by educated writers, they usually fulfil the requirements set by the subject matter – careful definitions, arguments proceeding in objectively testable steps, exclusion of irrelevant or contradictory matter, and a logical structure of paragraphs and entire texts, with a very high degree of coherence and cohesion (cf. 7.1). Although much of this is timeless (and independent of the individual language and culture), 19th-century texts from England seem to be characterized by greater explicitness than today's (possibly a heritage of the 18th century – note that the writers come from the same class and are formed by the same traditions as in earlier periods).

7.1.5 *Journalism*
(Cf. Crystal & Davy 1969:173–92)

Newspapers contain a great range of text types; if considered as a super-type, it is clearly a composite one. Since advertising is dealt with in 7.1.6, I will here concentrate on newspaper reporting. The rise of the popular press in the 1830s had a number of consequences:

(a)   It made news available to unprecedented numbers of readers including the lesser-educated, for whom it became the preferred or exclusive reading matter.

(b)   Texts had to be written quickly and published without major revision.

(c)   New combinations of text, headline and illustration had to be developed.

All this was ultimately directed at easy comprehensibility, although early 19th-century texts in the daily papers (even in advertisements) tended to retain a large proportion of 18th-century ideas of good style and complex sentence structure, a style which proved inadequate and led to discrepancies between form and function. The much-decried stylistic decay in journalistic writing of the mid-century had given way to greater respectability by 1887 (cf. T98). Looking back on the 19th century, Bradley found:

> Even the much-decried 'newspaper English' has, in its better forms, some merits of its own. Writers whose work must be read rapidly if it is to be read at all have a strong motive for endeavouring not to be obscure; and the results of this endeavour may be seen in the recent development of many subtle contrivances of sentence-structure, serving to prevent the reader from feeling even a momentary hesitation in apprehending the intended construction.* We may rest assured that wherever worthy thought and feeling exist, they will somehow fashion for themselves a worthy medium of expression.
>
> *One good instance of this is afforded by the frequency with which expressions like 'the fact that,' 'the circumstance that,' are now employed where formerly a clause would have stood alone as the subject of a sentence. (Bradley 1904:239)

Ex. 73   Contrast the newspaper articles T60 and T79 to show how the forms depend on writers' intentions, the readership addressed and the topic/situation.

7.1.6 *Advertising*

Leech has sketched the history of the form commercial advertising has taken in Britain (1966:165–74). His insightful linguistic analysis suggests that diachronically there was a move from impersonal to personal, cere-monial to colloquial and discursive, and on to disjunctive style, with an in-creasing willingness to flout rules of English word-formation and syntax; all this, together with a greater variety of typefaces and the growing function of illustrations, was intended to capture the reader's attention. Whereas the history of each text type is largely determined by the history of its func-tions, it is tempting to isolate permanent text-type-specific features on the one hand (e.g. the use of evaluative adjectives, often in superlative form, in advertisements) and contrast period-specific features. Thus there is an ob-vious similarity between the new liberties of advertese and Hopkins's breaches of linguistic decorum in many of his poems; furthermore, the de-crease in both complex sentences and erudite Latinate diction is a conspicu-ous cross-stylistic development in the course of the 19th century – an ob-vious reflection of changes in readership.

Ex. 74   Analyse the advertisements (T56, T72, T96) for the features men-tioned above. What makes the style of 19th-century advertisements appear so notably different from modern texts?

7.1.7 *Cooking recipes*

My analysis of recipes has shown that, although the concept and some formal conventions remained stable over the centuries, it is very difficult to sort out the interplay between conventions and period-specific and idio-syncratic elements. The characteristic form can be analysed according to a great number of parameters, among which the following are linguistic in the narrow sense:

(a)   form of the heading;
(b)   full sentences or telegram style;
(c)   use of imperative or other verbal forms;
(d)   use of possessive pronouns with ingredients and implements;
(e)   deletion of objects;
(f)   temporal sequence, and possibly adverbs used;
(g)   complexity of sentences;
(h)   marked use of loanwords and of genteel diction.

(cf. Görlach 1995c:154–5)

Two typical cookery books of the age (Beeton (1859–61) and Francatelli (1852), cf. T78) exhibit, for all the differences in their intended audiences, clear marks of period style, such as longer distanced verbal groups replacing the traditional imperatives of the instructions, and some intrusion of genteel lexis (Görlach 1995c:160–4).

Ex. 75   Point out 19th-century features in the recipes T78 and T97. Is the addressed readership taken into account by the authors?

7.1.8 *Book dedications*

By contrast, the development of book dedications shows, after peaks of extended (sycophantic) forms in the 16th and 18th centuries (cf. T41), a final reduction to the 'to-my-wife-and-children' type after 1840, obviously a consequence of changing publishing conditions and a new type of readership (cf. Görlach 1995c:167–78). This decline is also connected with the reduction of the text on the title-pages and of the variety of typefaces used for these, although the reduction here happened for different reasons – when dust-covers were invented and blurbs were used to include information about the author and the contents of the book, the title-page could be freed of typographical clutter. The history of the dedication and title-page texts illustrate, then, various cross-connections between linguistic form and social and typographical developments.

7.1.9 *Speeches*

Speeches can serve to illustrate a type that cuts across many of the fields discussed above (sermon, political speech, etc.). It is also of interest, since the genre has a long tradition behind it, being the fountain-head of the applied art of rhetoric, the rules of which were formulated over 2,000 years ago, organized according to the five offices of the rhetor (invention, disposition, elocution, pronunciation and memorizing), with particular attention given to the 'ornaments', i.e. the formal features that attract and keep the audiences' attention and goodwill. Since the proper art is to disguise art, the features should be so carefully worked in the text that the hearer does not notice them (and does not feel manipulated). They include lexical 'flowers of speech' (mainly types of metaphor and metonymy), and clause structures and types such as rhetorical questions, anticipation of counter-arguments, and structural elements corresponding to paragraphs, headlines and enumerations of arguments in a printed text. Rhetoric also supplied useful rules on how to structure a text and arrange the arguments – the relationship with composition and the modern discipline of text syntax is obvious. Although the heyday of rhetoric in English 'liberal education' was the Renaissance, when hundreds of manuals of rhetoric appeared, there was enough of the tradition left in the 19th century to make some texts markedly more 'artificial' than modern ones – and to bring out differences in the formality of the situation and the speaker's education, as a comparison of the (fictional) speech delivered by Felix Holt and Disraeli's specimen shows (both in Golby 1996:269–74). Typical misuses of oratorical style were noticed by Karl Marx who commented on Disraeli's speech in the House of Commons, July 27, 1857 as follows:

> The three hours' speech delivered last night in "The Dead House", by Mr. Disraeli, will gain rather than lose by being read instead of being listened to. For some time, Mr. Disraeli affects an awful solemnity of speech, an elaborate slowness of utterance and a passionless method of formality, which, however consistent they may be with his peculiar notions of the dignity becoming a Minister in expectance, are really distressing to his tortured audience. Once be succeeded in giving even commonplaces the pointed appearance of epigrams. Now he contrives to bury even epigrams in the conventional dullness of respectability. An orator who, like Mr. Disraeli, excels in handling the dagger rather than in wielding the sword, should have been the last to forget Voltaire's warning, that *"Tous les genres sont bons excepté le genre ennuyeux."* (Marx 1857)

How much the formal style of a speech requires the abstractness of the standard language is neatly demonstrated by Barnes's experiment in translating the Queen's speech into dialect (1886, T35). It is quite obvious that a translation has to substitute not just the Latinate, abstract lexis but also translate much of the indirect statement into honest if blunt straight-forward diction.

Ex. 76 Contrast the rhetorical features employed in the speeches by the fictional Felix Holt and by Disraeli (in Golby 1996:269–74).

Ex. 77 What constitutes the difference between a 'note' (T3) and a 'speech' (T35) and which are the features shared between them?

7.1.10 *Letters*

Letters form a particularly interesting text type since they reflect the social and functional relations between sender and addressee to a very high degree – only spoken texts can equal this range. They also permit one in an ideal way to compare instructions provided in the vast number of letter-writing guides, which contain model letters for all occasions with linguistic realities.

Whereas certain types of formal letters are highly conventionalized (and therefore not subject to much change), private letters can contain valuable evidence on informal usage – but they rarely include dialect.[120] The Layton letter of 1816 (T26a) is therefore an exception – most letters written in dialect are literary fabrications.[121]

Compare the distinction made by Anon. (1898:23):

> For ordinary letters the conversational style is pleasantest. One hears the remark, 'So-and-So writes so exactly as he talks, it is like having a chat with him.'
>
> But for business letters the main subject should be introduced at once, and clearly, and with as much brevity as is compatible with courtesy.

Degrees of formality may, then, be indicated by a wide range of choices, including writing paper and handwriting, address (Anon. 1898:11–16), politeness features expressed by evaluative adjectives and modal verbs, sentence structure, degree of attention to conventional formulas or their intentional disregard, and the form of the conclusion.

Ex. 78   Describe the great range of letters as found in T26, T34, T57, T58, T71 and T80. How do the forms reflect the writers' and readers' social characteristics, specific intentions and genre conventions? Is there anything about them, individually or as a group, that makes them typical of the 19th century?

7.1.11 *Other nineteenth-century genres*

A few expository and literary text types which originated or were redefined in the 19th century deserve closer inspection. They include scientific style which changed from somewhat personal accounts to impersonal, objective description – compare entries for 'electricity' in various editions of the *EB* – and various minor types ranging from telegraph messages (T93) to nonsense writing and comic verse (as represented by Lewis Carroll, Edward Lear; Hood, Kipling).

---

[120] Writing is so much connected with the school and standard language that composing a letter in dialect is a breach of sociolinguistic convention – there is only one (playful) letter by Burns; and Scott making Jeanny use Scots in her letters home in *The Heart of Midlothian* is a literary solution not sanctioned by sociolinguistic reality.

[121] Many non-standard features are found in letters by emigrants, who were forced to communicate in written form although not fully qualified for this (cf. note 39 above).

7.2   *Style*

7.2.1 *Introduction*

Style can be seen as the choice among linguistic variants, its proper use being determined by:

(1)   the adequacy according to function, text type and situation – the *decorum*;
(2)   period-specific conventions;
(3)   idiosyncratic preferences.[122]

Such conventions and rules were largely in the field of rhetoric, the discipline which taught the elegant use of language (whereas grammar dealt with correctness). This tradition was extremely influential in the period when styles and registers were fixed, up to the 18th century.

Good style remained one of the objectives of writers of grammar books, many of whom still believed in the unity of grammar, rhetoric and logic (derived from the classical *trivium*), and many included sections on 'figures of speech' or even extensive sections, or second volumes, devoted to composition. Sutcliffe's statement of 1815 clearly reflects the more conservative attitudes inherited from the 18th century:

> Between grammar, logic, and rhetoric, there exists a close and happy connection, which reigns through all science, and extends itself through all the powers of eloquence.
>   Logic converses with ideas, adjusts them with propriety and truth, and gives the whole an elevation in the mind consonant to the order of nature, the flights of fancy, or the pressure of occasion.

---

[122] A terminological distinction can be made between style and mannerisms, as Breen (1857:142–3) suggests:

> Every writer has a style of his own, a mode of expressing his thoughts peculiar to himself. Style in this sense is as various as the bodily or the mental characteristics of the writers. Mannerism, on the other hand, consists in some marked peculiarity in the method of composition; being in regard to style what deformity is in regard to the human features. This peculiarity assumes different forms with different writers. With some it is mere affectation: with others, and by far the greater number, it is quite involuntary, and is as difficult to lay aside, as it is easy to take up. One writer exhibits it in the copious use of foreign words; another in the unnecessary use of parentheses; a third in a startling method of punctuation; a fourth in the repetition of certain words in close juxtaposition.

(Cf. the mannerisms listed for Pater, Macaulay, Carlyle, Bagehot, Meredith, Kipling and Wells in Fowler 1926:342–3).

> Grammar traces the operation of thought in known and received characters,
> and enables polished nations amply to confer on posterity the pleasures of intel-
> lect, the improvements of science, and the history of the world.
>
> Rhetoric, lending a spontaneous aid to the defects of language, applies her
> warm and glowing tints to the portrait, and exhibits the grandeur of the universe,
> the productions of genius, and all works of art, as enlivened copies of the fair
> original.   .
>
> The exuberance of thought, ever swelling like a river, and unfolding as the
> morning, delights to borrow the eloquence of nature to pencil her beauties, and do
> justice to her charms.   (1815:384)

Andrew (T2), like Sutcliffe a writer firmly grounded in 18th-century traditions, made the correlation of genre / subject matter with stylistic features
quite explicit. The tradition lived on throughout the 19th century, and is
reflected in grammarians' decisions whether their handbook ought to include advice on composition. Angus defines the two succinctly:

> Grammar differs from composition, as a knowledge of the rules of building differs
> from architecture. Grammar is based on material laws and on custom: compo-
> sition, on insight and taste. Grammar is largely mechanical; composition, organic.
> The one shapes sentences according to external rule; the other, according to feel-
> ing and sentiment. Grammar teaches us to speak and write accurately; composi-
> tion, clearly, impressively, efficiently. Grammar is a means; composition, the end.
>   (1862:367)

Mismatches of text type and style are often unintentional; they can betray
the user's attempts at 'refayned' diction and are then markers of genteel
aspirations or even 'vulgarity' (cf. T54, T61). Playful deviation from genre
conventions and readers' expectations are forms of parody (cf. T65, T73,
T86). Since irony is bound to intertextuality and social and stylistic
conventions of language use, it is often difficult to detect instances and
correctly interpret allusions and connotations, especially in historical
periods (where readers may also be misled by anachronistic interpretations
based on contemporary conditions).

Comment on contemporary writing was most often negative, when
writers complained about the loss of 18th-century standards of good style.
However, there were occasional statements expressing pride in stylistic progress. This is the case in an advertisement in the *Newspaper* (18 May 1844):

> *Joe Miller's Jest-book. A Reprint from the first and genuine Edition*, such omis-
> sions and alterations only having been made as were required by the greater
> delicacy observed in modern conversation

(A comprehensive documentation of such ephemeral comments would be
invaluable for a proper interpretation of 19th-century linguistic propriety.)

7.2.2 *Literary language and poetic diction*
(Adamson 1998, Bateson ³1973)

The conventions of language use have to be established for every individual writer very carefully before linguistic analysis can begin (for an insightful discussion of such questions with regard to three 19th-century poets cf. Groom 1939; for Hopkins, cf. Milroy 1977). The following variables have to be taken into account:

(1)   The genre (e.g. novel, short story; epic poem; lyrical poem; ballad; etc.); how far does the form determine linguistic choice (metre, rhyme, etc.; is the text to be delivered or to be read silently?).

(2)   The 'period style' and contemporary attitudes to language, art and culture; how far are contemporary attitudes to standard language, purism, archaism, learned words, syntactic complexity and formal correctness reflected?

(3)   The importance of the tradition (*imitatio*) and the desire to conform to expectations defined in a rhetorical-poetical framework of *decorum* (poetic diction); how far can an author hope to be understood if using norms inherited through text traditions? What means does the author see fit to use (deviances employed for foregrounding) to distance his language from everyday speech, to 'heighten current language'?

(4)   (Partly related to 1–3) The extent to which a specific author feels restricted to, or allows himself to disregard, the (standard) morphological, semantic and syntactic structures of the language used; how far is the readership willing to accept liberties?

(5)   The use of one language, in standard or non-standard form, native or non-native, or a mixture of more than one language or dialect; what kind of readership does such mono- or polyglot writing presuppose?

The Romantic manifesto which prefaced the *Lyrical Ballads* of 1798 conveniently coincides with the turn of the century. In his stress on the 'language really used by men' and his focus on rural life, Wordsworth reacted against the poetic diction of the 18th century. However, his aim was not a naturalistic depiction – this would have contradicted his sense of decorum. Instead he chose a diction which

> has been adopted (purified indeed from what appear to be its real defects, from all lasting and rational causes of dislike or disgust) because such men hourly communicate with the best objects from which the best part of language is originally derived; and because from their rank in society and the sameness and

narrow circle of their intercourse, being less under the influence of social vanity, they convey their feelings and notions in simple unelaborated expressions.
(Preface to the second edition of the *Lyrical Ballads*)

It would therefore be totally wrong to expect the local dialect of, say, the Lake District, to be used as a literary medium for the peasant's intercourse. Coleridge saw the limitations of the 'plain English' being promoted and apparently did not fully accept the creed, seeing it as inadequate for more philosophical contexts; cf. *Biographia Literaria*, ch. xvii (cf. T39):

> in that degree in which it is practicable, yet as a rule it is useless, if not injurious, and therefore either need not, or ought not to be practized.

He holds, rather, that the language of a serious poem requires 'an arrangement both of words and sentences, and a use and selection of (what are called) 'figures of speech', both as to their kind, their frequency, and their occasions, which on a subject of equal weight would be vicious and alien in correct and manly prose' (ch. xviii, cf. Bateson's discussion 1973:70–1). Bateson refers to Newman's summing up in 1829 'that attention to the language *for its own sake* evidences not the true poet but the mere artist' (1973:72). The linguistic heritage of the Romantics explains some of the problems of the poets of the Victorian age. Bateson, who provides a clear description (1973:76–86) has some insightful remarks on several of the main representatives.

The categories of description were historically determined by those of classical rhetoric (which was largely identical with poetics in the Renaissance). Although the importance of rhetorical categories decreased over the centuries (together with the relevance of Latin and classical knowledge), concepts like *decorum* (stylistic adequacy) and the terminological system of the 'figures of speech' remained largely intact. Less strictly, descriptive features of styles are often impressionistic (and mostly evaluative); here are a few terms that Victorians used:

> Vigorous, powerful, forcible, nervous, spirited, lively, glowing, racy, bold, slashing, piquant, pointed, antithetical, petulant, sententious, lofty, elevated, sublime, eloquent, full of point, poetic, &c.   – as against:
> feeble, bald, tame, meagre, jejune, vapid, cold, poor, dull, languid, prosing, prosaic   – or it could be:
> simple, unornamented, plain, unadorned, dry, unvaried, monotonous, severe, chaste, neat, &c.   – as against:
> ornamented, florid, rich, pedantic, affected, pompous, fustian, high-sounding, sententious, mouthy, inflated, bombastic, high-flowing, frothy, flowery, turgid, swelling, grandiose, grandiloquent, magniloquent, sesquipedalian
> (Roget 1852:nos. 574–7).

Ex. 79 Summarize the discussion about 'poetic diction' in statements by
   Wordsworth and Coleridge (T39).

7.2.3 *Individual authors*

Groom (1939), an active poet and critic, took up Bagehot's distinction of
1864 when he described the diction of Tennyson (1809–92), Browning
(1812–89) and Arnold (1822–88), three poets who are typical of their century and at the same time influenced it through their writings, representing
'the Traditional, the Eccentric and the Classical'. He went on to say that he
found that 'these terms are far too narrow to cover the varieties of style in
the three' (1939:93).

Tennyson's diction, quite stable over the fifty years of his writing career,
is characterized by archaisms, far-fetched expressions, periphrasis, the use
of rare forms or spellings of words – but he did not shy away from scientific
and technical words (99–106). 'Tennyson's natural style is an eclectic one,
... it is a blending of originality and conservatism, of invention and scholarship' (112); he is 'felicitous in his compound words' and notable for his use
of onomatopoeia (113) – and dialect, even outside his dialect poems (115).
In this great range of styles and their effective application, Tennyson shows
himself to be 'the skilled professional poet, and in comparison the other two
are more or less successful amateurs' (93).[123]

Browning 'was a confirmed word-collector' (118); and although words
like '*besprent, bosky, burthen, cinct, clomb, drear, dreriment*' might well be
used by other poets, 'to Browning they are more often than not the merest
makeshifts' (119). Groom notes his 'Victorian taste for compound adverbs
of the type ... *abloom, a-blush, a-bubble, a-chuckle, a-clatter*' (119), but
Browning can also 'cultivate the utmost informality of style' (121), and 'the
mood of satire, whether gay or grave, is so common that it colours [his]
whole style' (122). A morphological hallmark is his use of superlatives like
ineffablest, whimperingest, sagaciousest (128). Groom notes a number of
'faults' in Browning's diction, and sketches his influence, which is much
more limited than Tennyson's:

---

[123] Evaluations have of course changed since Victorian times; contrast Bateson:
   But the language that Tennyson found to his hands was verbose and sentimental, a flabby and submissive thing. He did what he could do with it:
   he was a natural stylist, with an inborn interest and instinct for words.
   And yet, with all his critical awareness, with all his charm and fluency,
   what a poor thing relatively Tennyson's style is! Slow, monotonous, over-
   coloured, over-musical, its essential diffuseness only emphasized by the
   niggling detail.   (1973:80)

> The pre-Raphaelites caught something of the spirit of his early style ... Certain
> features in the style of G. M. Hopkins are evidently borrowed from Browning,
> e.g. the accumulation of compound epithets. ... Browning's most profitable ex-
> ample to later poets lay in his use of colloquial English for the impassioned lyric.
>
> (Groom 1939:134)

By contrast, Arnold (like Wordsworth before him) 'dislikes any conscious attempt to widen the gap between prose and poetry. His diction is more vital than Swinburne's, which is too literary, more real than Morris's, which is too archaic' (137). His style is therefore less conspicuous and less easily imitated than that of the two others: 'the qualities which Arnold esteemed in poetry were simplicity, restraint, austerity' (138).

The three poets exemplify three different attitudes to 'poetic diction' in the Victorian age and different preferences for central words and types of coinages. Whereas the influence of Browning, and particularly that of Arnold, was quite limited, Groom saw (in 1939!) Tennyson's as comparable to that of Dryden or Wordsworth, a statement that seems dated fifty years later.

J. Milroy (1977) treated the complex problem of 19th-century literary diction with a great deal of insight in his discussion of one of the most difficult poets of the age, Hopkins. The first half of the 19th century was obviously dominated by the Romantic poets' renunciation of 18th-century poetic diction: Wordsworth and Coleridge advocated a return to plain and less clichéd expression – without advising the use of dialect. Later poets extended their diction by including archaic elements, dialect and even technical language, which would not have been acceptable to more narrowly defined concepts of what the language of poetry should be. How much of the 'continuous literary decorum' (one of Milroy's chapter titles) survives in later 19th-century poetry?

Hopkins was much more experimental and critical of many of his contemporaries; he had nothing but pity for Barnes's attempt to revive old words (letter to Bridges, 1882, quoted in Milroy 1977:77–8). Hopkins's deliberate breach of *linguistic* decorum tends to make his meaning difficult and obscure – and makes his language least useful for an analysis of period style.

Lesser poets such as Barnes and Morris illustrate 19th-century predilections in a more straightforward way (although a great deal of this is also found in Tennyson). Gallasch (1979), who analysed Morris's diction, quotes him as stating that Chaucer and Malory (and his translations from Old Norse) had a strong influence on him. No surprise, then, that his diction is marked by ME words (*hostelry, lustihead, wanhope*), 'Spenserisms' (*eld,* *rede* 'advice', *quoth, wot*), archaic word forms (*eyen, twain, foughten, spake, methinks*) and unusual derivatives of which many (*) it seems were not considered worth including in the *OED* (**ungleeful, unmerry, unrich, *unkinsome; *beblossomed, beswinked*). However, even more striking is his use of new compounds, of which the following were apparently modelled on Old Norse: *chapmen-carle, barrow-wight* 'being from the mountains', *heftsax, home-farer, speech-friend.* Eccentric as all this may seem, it serves to illustrate the fascination of much of Victorian intellectual society with Germanic history, medieval studies and dialect – topics which are of course closely related to the new developments in historical linguistics and their reflection in English grammars.[124]

However, Morris's style also reflects a tendency which is much more widespread among his contemporaries – the unwillingness to consider the language of their time a medium fit for poetic expression. In a letter to Fred Henderson, Morris wrote:

> You see things have very much changed since the early days of language: Once everybody who could express himself at all did so beautifully, was a poet for that occasion, but all language was beautiful. But now language is utterly degraded in our daily lives, and poets have to make a new tongue each for himself: before he can even begin his story he must elevate his means of expression from the daily jabber to which centuries of degradation have reduced it. And this is given to few to be able to do, since amongst other things it implies an enthusiastic appreciation of mere language, which I think few people feel now-a-days. Study early litera-ture, Homer, Beowulf, and the Anglo-Saxon fragments; the Edda and other old Norse poetry and I think you will understand what I mean, and how rare the gifts must be which make a man a poet now-a-day.
>
> (1885, quoted from Gallasch 1979:39)

This attitude was clearly interpreted by an unknown reviewer for what it was – elitism:

> The failure of the literary poets (in this case, Swinburne, Rossetti, Tennyson, Keats, Spenser, *et al.*, as well as Morris) to appreciate the active life of their times, as well as the affectations of thought and language that are such blemishes in their poetry, are due, we think ... to the exaggerated estimate which the poets have formed of their function, and the arbitrary standards of diction which they affect.
>
> (no. 132, 1872:42, quoted from Gallasch 1979:44)

---

[124] The fascination extends far beyond literature – as can be seen in the 'Gothic' style in architecture, and in other arts; that it was shared by large sections of the population is evident from books like Charles Knight's *Old England: A Pictorial Museum* (1847) which was directed at a wide audience. The trend can at least partly be seen as a backlash resulting from negative effects of the Industrial Revolution.

Ex. 80   Do you find, in the great variety of styles (and mannerisms) sketched above, a common denominator that could serve to define a diction
characteristic of the period?

7.2.4 *Plays (and dialogues in novels)*

Since we have no corpus of unpremeditated spoken English from the 19th
century, many researchers who wanted to include something of the sort
have, for better or worse, included text types that reflect the spoken voice as
closely as can be found for a period before sound recordings. Apart from
speeches (cf. 7.1.9) and court depositions (commonly in standard spelling,
and with some expected standardization in lexis and syntax) and informal
private letters (which are more formal, and less close to spoken English,
than is sometimes claimed), plays and dialogues in novels have often been
used for corpus linguistics (DeKeyser 1975, Rydén & Brorström 1987) and
for studies of sociolinguistics and attitudes (Phillipps 1984). However, the
principal differences between natural speech and literary representation
must be taken into consideration if we do not wish to be affected by a
variant form of the observer's paradox:

(1)   A writer will try to select a few features on which other characters
       comment or to which the playgoer or reader is likely to react in a way
       intended by the author. These features are stereotypical (sometimes
       learnt from predecessors) and they are distributed in a way that con-
       tradicts sociolinguistic expectations: clustered in the beginning, and
       less dense later on (when the person has been characterized).
(2)   Characters are classified in well-defined social groups, much more
       neatly than in real life, and their idiosyncratic elements/mannerisms
       are stressed.
(3)   The attention is kept by a focus of humorous, unexpected or exag-
       gerated features serving to make the character individual and memor-
       able.

Ex. 81   How far do you find expectations of lower-class characters reflected in plays claiming to illustrate scenes from the everyday life of the
lower classes (T40)?

7.2.5 *Nineteenth-century conventions in prose*

Early 19th-century writers largely built on 18th-century foundations, in
literary and expository texts, and this continuity makes many pre-1830 texts

look quite 'classical'. Gordon (1966:154) classifies three modes of (predominantly literary) prose styles inherited from the 18th century:

(1) The central speech-based prose continued to provide a norm ... But the two variants underwent vigorous development ... non-fictional prose of the time is certainly not ... of direct simplicity.

(2) ... tentative beginnings of romantic prose asserted itself and ... produced a whole range of mutations, the extremest form of which was a prose of display.

(3) ... the Johnsonian-latinized (code) continued ... as a medium for the discussion of the 'serious' topic.

Gordon points out the decisive divergence from 18th-century expectations of respectable English:

The newly literate readers of the nineteenth century had no experience of the 'polite' speech which formed the basis of the central prose of earlier years. For them simplicity and directness were suspect – education should surely produce something more ambitious than their own limited vocabulary and speech patterns. For the newly literate, the prose that descended from Johnson appeared more 'educated' than the prose that descended from Addison. The result is that much 'popular' nineteenth-century prose, even in newspapers and novels and at the 'penny magazine' level, affected an elaboration of vocabulary and sentence structure that today sounds absurdly pompous.   (1966:155)

What is characteristic of much 19th-century writing is, then, excess in the use of features that were applied with a greater degree of balance and restraint in the 18th century. Thus, Johnson's influence

is everywhere apparent. With few exceptions, the philosopher, the historian, the physical and social scientist of the last century, even in his moments of conscious popularising, tends to the vocabulary and the sentence structure of Johnsonian prose and not to the 'native easiness' and 'mathematical plainness' of his seventeenth-century predecessor.   (1966:156)

By contrast, the writer of romantic prose

is not attempting to secure the co-operation of this audience by using their normal language; nor is he trying to convince them by appealing to a shared (or ostensibly shared) intellectual background. His prose continually asserts his personal individuality, his uniqueness; and the emotionally affected audience is expected to respond not so much with comprehension as with astonished admiration.   (1966:158)

With reference to a passage of 1849 by De Quincey, Gordon writes:

Prose of this type, which has taken over the function and some of the techniques of the romantic lyric, was highly regarded in the nineteenth century. Today it seems almost an alien tongue in any serious literary context – though it continues with unabated vigour an extra-literary life in the special world of advertising.

(1966:159)

How did the Victorians see these problems? Angus summarized individual decisions as to the organization of paragraphs:

> The general arrangement and character of sentences may be easy and natural as in Dryden; or they may be rhetorical, and nicely balanced as in Hooker and Johnson. They may be plain and forcible as in Swift and Paley; or graceful and idiomatic as in Addison and Goldsmith; vehement as in Baxter, Bolingbroke, Bruke, Chalmers and Brougham; florid as in Jeremy Taylor, Cribbon, Hervey. (1862:406)

But he also took up an earlier classification into periods, adding a character-ization of his times:

> The history of English style is conveniently divided by Sir James Mackintosh into three periods: –
> The *first* period extending from Sir Thomas More to Clarendon. This was the Latin age of English composition;
> The *second* period extending from the Restoration to the middle of the 18th century. This was the age of Dryden, Pope, Addison, Goldsmith, and others; the classic age of natural, idiomatic English;
> The *third* period, from Johnson onwards, may be called the rhetorical. Its characteristics are studied antithesis and finely rounded sentences.
> Our own age may be described as the *fourth* period. The best style of this century has all the ease of Addison, with the nervous compactness of Bacon, – the sonorousness of Johnson, with the lightness of DeFoe. (1862:413–14)

Much of this is a consequence of, or determined by, the expected relation-ship between writer and reader, which underwent significant changes in the 19th century. Blake (1995) has recently attributed the instability of 19th-century style, and the extended choice of models and personal decisions, to the loss of the rhetoric-based distinction of the three styles (which was still dogma in the 18th century):

> It could be said that there had existed till this time three levels of style: the high style which relied heavily on Latin, a neutral style which was appropriate for most written works without pretensions, and a low style which drew largely on lower registers and colloquialisms. As the high style came under increasing attack it meant that writers could no longer go outside the language to create their own style. A writer had to make his own style from within the resources of his own language, and that could be done either by dipping into the pool of lower registers or simply by playing with English through wordplay, broken syntax, or whatever means presented themselves. Although this result did not become clear until the present century, its origins can be traced to the nineteenth. There is no longer an approved style so that all writers exhibit many of the same features. Each writer has to create his or her own style out of whatever material is available and this emphasizes the differences between all writers rather than their similarities.

> Individualism becomes important. Although this is true, the amount of use made
> of lower registers or of colloquial words or structures remains relatively small.
>
> (1995:19–20)

Nash (1980:120) points to the fact that 'the writer usually tries to establish a role and a tone of voice, suggesting to the reader a form of working agreement generally reflective of social conventions', and goes on to detail the author's four possible roles as *informant, instructor, disputant* and *entertainer*, and to illustrate them with variations of the same text modified so as to give prominence to one of the four functions. This relatively simple pattern is complicated, in reality, by role shifts and by the choice of a style of address ('tone' in Nash, 126–35). These intentions are signalled by indices of tone, ranging from the use of pronouns to cohesive devices, and include a battery of lexical choices (1980:135–58).

The situation is quite different for poetry. One noteworthy break, as far as literary tradition is concerned, occurred with Romantic poetry: the value of a literary work was no longer dependent on how the tradition was taken up and developed, but directly related to expressiveness (which did not necessarily affect the formal linguistic features as classified by rhetoric).

The interplay of metre, rhythm, rhyme and typography (in line arrangement) and the consequences that formal choices have for the syntax and the vocabulary are not my major concern here, but it may be useful to remember that the rejection of 18th-century poetic diction (which effectively removed a poetic norm for 19th-century writers) was paralleled in the rejection of the rigid views of metre and rhyme cultivated by Classicist authors like Pope or Gray. Coleridge felt called upon to justify his practice in 'Christabel' (1816):

> the metre of Christabel is not, properly speaking, irregular, though it may seem so
> from its being founded on a new principle: namely, that of counting in each line
> the accents, not the syllables. Though the latter may vary from seven to twelve,
> yet in each line the accents will be found to be only four
>
> (quoted from Adamson 1998:617)

The after-effects are found as late as in Hopkins's 'sprung rhythm', all in a way a return to native accentual patterns as practised in OE and ME poetry (Adamson 1998:841). This, and the adaptation of the hexameter to English stress patterns made poetry more prose-like – note the mirror-image in the rhythmical prose occasionally employed by writers like Dickens. Other attempts to get away from the five-stress line were based on the ballad tradition.

7.2.6 *Application: Dickens*
(Brook 1970, Sørensen 1985)

As in the case of lexis above, it may be useful to look at one writer's (Dickens's) work to find out how styles and text type are used to express literary functions in a particular situation – and how they are modified in the process.

(a) The speech style of a 19th-century 'cheap-jack auctioneer' is recoverable today only from a few more or less literary attestations. Dickens used the cadences and rhetoric of the profession in ch. 1 of *Doctor Marigold* (1865; Brook 1970:145). Since we have no authentic texts, we can only guess at how much Dickens selected or condensed elements of the style in his representation of it.

(b) By contrast, the epitaph is a wide-spread and sufficiently well-documented written text type (cf. T55). In his characterization of John Chivery (*Little Dorrit*, ch. 31; Brook 1970:142) Dickens could rely on his readers memorizing the original formula and its misuse, but even today we can see how closely the author adhered to the tradition. We can also see what is behind Dickens's technique if we compare the semiquote in *Dombey and Son*, ch. 39, with the original quoted by Matthew Arnold as one of the 'familiar memorial inscriptions of an English churchyard' (Brook 1970:193).

(c) Dickens modified the inquest-report format in his description of Captain Hawdon in *Bleak House*, ch. 11 (Brook 1970:45).

(d) The degree of parodying transmogrification can vary a great deal. A journalist himself, Dickens had enough experience to use the text type 'murder report in a newspaper' with hardly any modification in *Great Expectations*, ch. 18 (Brook 1970:139).

(e) The same domain supplied him with the pattern of the gossip column, again in *Great Expectations* (ch. 28, Brook 1970:92).

(f) A parody of a specific fashionable philosophy, 19th-century 'Transcendentalism', is found in *Martin Chuzzlewit*, ch. 34, which Brook juxtaposes with a quotation from the *Dial* of 1841, clearly revealing Dickens's intention to burlesque (both excerpts in Brook 1970: 147–8).

(g) Finally, the parody becomes even more apparent through the (over-) use of a particular spelling convention typical of the profession in the lawyers' letter to Esther Summerson in *Bleak House* (ch. 3; Brook 1970:73–4).

In all these cases, we cannot take the literary specimens as representative of their text types (and, since they are single tokens, certainly not as indications of the stylistic range that can be found in the individual text type). However, if interpreted with sufficient background knowledge and a great deal of caution, the skilful author's condensation of the salient features of the type, however distorted by parody, can help to reveal the features and functions of the text type in the society of the time.

Ex. 82 Compare Dickens's treatment of the 'murder case' with T74. How is the sensational news tailored to the intended readership?

8

Provisional conclusions

The above discussion does not constitute a fully convincing and coherent description of 19th-century English in England. The linguist who describes earlier periods of English is doubly privileged, since the morphological and phonological structures are more diversified than they are in PDE, and – even more conveniently – the difference between them and PDE on all levels is much more conspicuous than can ever be the case with any 19th-century text, however 'deviant'. Even when a linguist selects text types that strike him as clearly belonging to the period (as in the case of 19th-century advertising and religion), it is very difficult to describe in scholarly terms what his *Sprachgefühl* may well tell him quite unambiguously. And the concept of text type – proposed above as possibly *the* scholarly instrument suited to capturing period language in more modern times – may fail to fulfil our expectations; as my analysis of recipes (cf. ch. 7.1.7 above) has shown, the combination of a well-defined text type with 'Victorian' style produces, against all expectations, not a distinctively homogeneous and predictable diction and form, but more variation than would be expected in a teleological framework.

The analysis of a bigger sample of texts will, it is hoped, lead to a better understanding and more precise description of what makes 19th-century English distinctive, and sometimes unmistakable. However, a great deal of research and reflection is still necessary before we can feel assured that our methods of analysis are adequate.

9

Texts

The texts here selected are intended to provide as much insight into the specific character of 19th-century English, in its various text types, as possible. They were excerpted from millions of pages I have looked at; a first corpus of 660 representative texts had to be condensed to 98 specimens to be accommodated in a students' handbook published at a reasonable price. (Plans to 'publish' the full text corpus by way of CD-Rom or on a Web-site had to be given up as too labour-intensive.)

I have grouped the texts in four sections allowing the greatest space to I and II, *viz*. documents dealing with 19th-century EngE in the widest sense – since this is the topic of my book. By contrast, the section on literature and literary criticism is comparatively short: most of the relevant texts are easily accessible and, for all the linguistic importance of literary forms, I did not want to write another book in which literature predominated. Topics dealing with 19th-century conditions are, I hope, adequately represented – there is a huge variety of text types and documents of particular historical and social relevance to choose from, and a selection is especially likely to be subjective in this field. However, various collections (e.g. those by Crowley 1991, Golby 1996, Joyce 1991) will be useful to complement my corpus, and many documents relating to the social history of the period have recently been reprinted, many in facsimile. These range from Charles Knight to Mrs Beeton, and from the *Poor Man's Guardian* to a few titles from contemporary linguistics. I have referred to such titles by leading the students to the texts in some of the inserted exercises (**Ex.**).

Texts

I On language, grammar and style

T1   *Alexander Crombie, 'On sociolects' (1802)*

... to define the proper province of the grammarian, I proceed to observe, that this usage, which gives law to language, in order to establish its authority, or to entitle its suffrage to our assent, must be, in the first place, *reputable*.

5   The vulgar in this, as in every other country, are, from their want of education, necessarily illiterate. Their native language is known to them no farther, than is requisite for the most common purposes of life. Their ideas are few, and consequently their stock of words, poor and scanty. Nay, their poverty, in this respect, is not their only evil. Their narrow competence they
10 abuse, and pervert. Some words they misapply, others they corrupt; while many are employed by them, which have no sanction, but provincial, or local authority. Hence the language of the vulgar, in one province, is sometimes hardly intelligible in another. Add to this, that debarred by their occupations from study, or generally averse to literary pursuits, they are
15 necessarily strangers to the scientific improvements of a cultivated mind; and are therefore entirely unacquainted with that diction, which concerns the higher attainments of life. Ignorant of any general principles respecting language, to which they may appeal; unable to discriminate between right and wrong; every one therefore prone to adopt whatever usage casual
20 circumstances may present; it is no wonder, if the language of the vulgar be a mixture of incongruity and error, neither perfectly consistent with itself, nor universally intelligible even to them. Their usage, therefore, is not the standard, to which we must appeal for decisive authority; a usage so discordant and various, that we may justly apply to it the words of a
25 celebrated critic, *Bellua multorum es capitum*; *nam quid sequar aut quem*?

    The question then is, what is reputable usage? On this subject philologists have been divided. Dr. Campbell appears to me to decide judiciously, when he says, that the usage, to which we must appeal is, not that of the court, or of great men, nor even of authors of profound science, but of those,
30 whose works are esteemed by the public, and who may, therefore, be denominated *reputable* authors ... This usage must be, in the second place, *national*. It must be not confined to this, or that province; it must not be the usage of this, or that district, the peculiarities of which are always ridiculous, and frequently unintelligible beyond its own limits ...

35   As there is a period, beyond which precedent in language ceases to have authority; so, on the contrary, the usage of the present day is not implicitly

to be adopted. Mankind are fond of novelty; and there is a fashion in language, as there is in dress. Whim, vanity, and affectation, delight in creating new words. Of these, the far greater part soon sink into contempt.
40 They figure for little, like ephemeral productions, in tales, novels, and fugitive papers; and are shortly consigned to degradation, and oblivion. Now, to adopt every new-fangled upstart at its birth, would argue not taste, nor judgment, but childish levity, and caprice. On the contrary, if any of these should maintain its ground, and receive the sanction of reputable usage, to
45 reject it, in this case, would be to resist that authority, to which every critic and grammarian must bow with submission. ●

T2 *J. Andrew, 'Remarks on the style of prose compositions' (1817)*

STYLE denotes the quality of a literary composition as to the strength, elegance, and proportion of its parts. In prose compositions the style may be divided into historical, philosophical, rhetorical, and common, each sort being suited to its own peculiar objects, and having its own peculiar proper-
5 ties or laws. And it may be observed universally that eloquence is founded on method, that is on comprehensive views, and a regular arrangement of the several parts.

1. The historical style should be clear, simple, harmonious, and elegant; candid and impartial; neither too brief nor too diffuse; free from affected
10 arguments, and from affectations of wit and satire. Annals, memoirs, and travels, are a subordinate kind of history, of which it is sufficient if they record things with perspicuity and truth. Epitaphs and public inscriptions are amongst the shortest species of history. They should contain nothing but what is strictly true, and the words should be few and plain. Romance imi-
15 tates history in respect of style, although in respect to the fable it belongs to poetry.

2. The philosophical style belongs to mathematical, physical, and moral subjects. – In the mathematical style the utmost perspicuity and accuracy are necessary. The arrangement of propositions and arguments must be such
20 as cannot be altered but for the worse; and all tropes, figures, and other ornaments are prohibited ...

(4.) ... The style of common conversation ought to be perfectly plain and clear. Inelegant expressions, and barbarous and vulgar idioms are to be avoided. Hard words, strong figures, and studied sentences are also un-
25 seemly. To promote the happiness of those with whom we converse, to comply with their innocent humours, and not to give way to moroseness and ill nature, are principles both of politeness and virtue... ●

T3   *W. Cobbett, 'A diplomatic note corrected' (1823)*

Remarks on a Note presented by Lord Castlereagh to the Ambassadors of
the Allies, at Paris, in July 1815, relative to the Slave Trade.

    30. 'VISCOUNT Castlereagh, his Britanick Majesty's Principal Secretary
of State, &c., in reference to the communication he has made to the
conference, of the orders addressed to the Admiralty to suspend all
hostilities against the coast of France, observes, that there is *reason to*
5 *foresee* that French ship-owners *might* be induced to renew the Slave Trade,
under the supposition of the *peremptory* and *total* abolition decreed by
Napoleon Bonaparte, having *ceased* with his power; that, *nevertheless*, great
and powerful *considerations*, arising from *motives* of humanity and even of
regard for the king's authority, require, that no time should be lost *to main-*
10 *tain in France*, the entire and *immediate Abolition* of the Traffic in Slaves;
that if, at the time of the Treaty of Paris, the King's administration *could*
wish a final but gradual stop *should be put* to this Trade, in the space of five
years, for the purpose of affording the King the gratification *of having* consulted, as much as possible, the interests of the French Proprietors in the
15 Colonies, now, that the absolute *prohibition* has been ordained, the question
assumes entirely a different shape, *for* if the King were to revoke the said
prohibition, he would *give Himself the disadvantage* of *authorizing*, in the
interior of France, *the reproach* which more than once has been thrown out
against his former Government, of countenancing re-actions, and, at the
20 same time, *justifying, out of France*, and particularly in England, the belief
of a systematic *opposition* to *liberal ideas*; that *accordingly* the *time seems*
to have arrived when the Allies cannot hesitate formally to *give weight in*
France to the immediate and entire *prohibition* of the Slave Trade, a
prohibition, the necessity of which has been acknowledged, in principle, in
25 the transactions of the Congress at Vienna.'
    Now, I put this question to you: *do you understand what this great*
Statesman means? Read the Note three times over; and then say whether
you *understand what he wants*. You may *guess*; but you can go little
further. Here is a whole mass of grammatical errors; but, it is the obscurity,
30 the unintelligibleness, of the Note, that I think constitutes its greatest fault.
One way of proving the badness of this writing, is, to express the meaning
of the writer in a clear manner; thus:
    'Lord Castlereagh observes, that there is reason to apprehend that the
French ship-owners may be induced to renew the slave trade, from a
35 supposition that the total abolition, recently decreed by Napoleon, has been
nullified by the cessation of his authority; that motives of humanity as well

as a desire to promote the establishment of the king's authority, suggest that no time should be lost in taking efficient measures to maintain the decree of abolition; that, at the time of the treaty of Paris, the king's ministers wished
40 to abolish this trade, but, in order that the king might, as much as possible, consult the interests of the colonial proprietors, those ministers wished the object to be accomplished by degrees during the space of five years; that now, however, when the abolition has been actually decreed, the matter assumes an entirely different shape, seeing that it is not now an abolition,
45 but the refraining from revoking an abolition, that is proposed to be suggested to the king; that, if the king were to do this, he would warrant, amongst his own people, the injurious imputation, more than once brought against his former government, of countenancing the work of undoing and overturning, and would, at the same time, confirm foreign nations, and
50 particularly the English, in the belief, that he had adopted a systematic opposition to liberal principles and views; that, therefore, the interests of the king not less than those of humanity seem to call upon the Allies to give, formally, and without delay, the weight of their influence in favour, as far as relates to France, of an entire and immediate abolition of the Slave Trade,
55 an abolition, the necessity of which has, in principle, at least, been acknowledged in the transactions of the Congress of Vienna.' ●

T4   *C. I. Johnstone, 'Insertion test' (1828)*

RATIONAL READING

The lesson was taken from that chapter in Mrs. Herbert's books, entitled HUMANITY. Maurice was requested to read it: the blanks were afterwards to be supplied. These blanks were marked regularly by figures; and there was a key, which Mrs. Herbert kept, with corresponding figures, to which
5 the words or phrases omitted were affixed. Maurice knew quite well what a *key* meant. He had a *key* to his Grammatical Exercises, and a *key* to his questions in Arithmetic and Geography. The Hollycot children seldom now needed to refer to their key in 'Rational Reading.' George and Sophia could often fill up the blanks as they went along; but Charles needed to return to
10 them, and to take a little time for reflection. Sometimes when in doubt about a word, they were gratified to find that they had hit upon the right one, – the *true* sense and *exact* meaning of the author. Sometimes their mother said they had found even a better word than the original one. *Maurice* read as follows.
15   St. Pierre says, 'Being at Marly, I (1.) among the thickets of (2.) magnificent park to (3.) the group of children who are (4.) with vine-twigs a goat, that is represented at play with them. Near this admirable piece of

(5.) is a pavilion, where Louis the XV., on fine days, sometimes partook of
a (6.) As it was (7.) I took (8.) for a moment in this (9.,) and found (10.)
20 three children, that (11.) much more (12.) than the (13.) children. Two very
(14.) little girls were (15.) themselves, with much (16.) and (17.) from
around the pavilion bundles of dry (19.), that the (20.) had blown from the
trees, which they (21.) into a basket that (22.) upon the king's table, while
a poor boy, badly (23.) and very meagre, devoured a morsel of (24.) in a
25 corner. I (25.) the tallest of these girls, who was about eight or nine, what
she meant to do with the (26.) she was so eagerly collecting? She replied,
you see (27.) that (28.) boy there. He is very miserable. He is sent out all
day (29.) to gather (30.); when he carries none (31.) he is beaten; when he
picks up (32.) the Swiss at the (33.) of the park (34.) him of it. He is (35.)
30 with hunger; so we have given him our breakfast. After (36.) me thus, she
and her companions (37.) the little (38.) They put it on his (39.), and (40.)
before their unfortunate (41.), to see if he could pass in (42.)'

'O, mamma, such a good story,' cried little Fanny; 'I am sure I know
how to fill it up every word.'
35 'You shall have a fair trial, Fanny; and perhaps your cousin will help
you. There are 42. blank words; but a very little exercise of thought will
enable you to supply every one of them.'

Fanny began, '1. *sauntered* or *walked*.'

'Or *rambled*, ma'am,' said Maurice.
40 'I like plain *walked* best,' said Mrs. Herbert; 'we don't want fine words,
nor sounding words – but simple words, and accurate meanings.'

'2. *Its*; 3. *behold, contemplate*,' said Maurice, proud of his new talent.

'And why not *see*, plain little *see*?' said Mrs. Herbert.

'O, mamma, *see* is such a little insignificant word,' said Sophia.
45 'The less the better, Sophia, if it serve the purpose.'

'4. *Feeding*,' said Fanny; but the 5th blank was puzzling.

George at last helped the readers out with '*sculpture*.' 'Well, brother, I
believe you know almost as much as mamma herself,' and Fanny went on.
– '6. *sleep*.'
50 'And why should Louis the XV. choose a fine day to *sleep* in the
pavilion?'

Fanny paused in thought, and said '*luncheon*.'

'Or *collation*,' said Sophia.

'That is more kingly,' observed Charles.
55 '7. *Showery* or *rainy*; 8. *refuge*.'

'Think of a more appropriate word, my dear; a synonyme of *refuge*: –
from an enemy or a tempest one takes *refuge* – from a shower one takes

shelter.'

'9. *Pavilion*; 10. *there*; 11. *was* – no, *were* – three *were*; 12. *beautiful.*'

60 'We shall return to beautiful when you have finished,' said Mrs. Herbert.

'13. *Marble* or *sculptured*, which is right, mother?'

'Either, Sophia; both are good appropriate words.'

'14. *Pretty*; 15. *employing*; 16. *diligence* or *assiduity*; 17. *gathering* or *collecting*; 18. *bundles* or *fagots*; 19. *sticks*; 20. *wind*; 21. *put*; 22. *stood*; 23.

65 *dressed.*'

'Rather *clothed*,' said Mrs. Herbert; 'poor boys must not mind being badly *dressed* if they are not badly *clothed.*'

'24. *Bread*; 25. *asked*; 26. *wood*; 27. *Sir*; 28. *little* or *poor*; 29. *long*; 30. *sticks*; 31. *home*; 32. *some*; 33. *entrance*; 34. *strips.*'

70 'Think of a better word, my dear, a synonyme of *strips*. A tree is stripped of its bark, a boy stripped naked: – *strip* seems to apply to something that clings or adheres very closely.'

'Then, *bereaves*, mother, – will that word do?'

'Try again, Charles.'

75 '*Deprives*,' said Charles.

'That is better.'

'35. *faint*, 36. *answering*, 37. *filled*, 38. *bag.*'

'No – have you forgotten? Had you carefully read the story you must know this word.'

80 Charles and Maurice read again, and both together said, '*basket.*'

'39. *back* or *head*; 40. *ran*; 41. *companion.*'

'Not *companion*. The poor starved boy, the object of their compassion, could not be called the *companion* of the little girls: St. Pierre says, *friend*, and I think, Charles, you will prefer his word.'

85 'I do, mother. – And 42. *safety* or *quiet*. – Now he is past the ugly Swiss.'

'You have read your share very well, my dear Fanny; but tell me now why, in supplying the 12th blank, you used the word *beautiful*. Is there no other word more applicable to those amiable, engaging children?'

90 'Perhaps *humane*, or *tender*, or *sweet*, mother,' said Sophia.

'No, my dear, St. Pierre would scarcely use those words in comparing living children with marble figures of children, – his word is *interesting.*'

'Mamma, I said they were *beautiful*, because they were so good,' said Fanny. ●

T5   *S. Alexander, 'On the state of English' (1832)*

But now, as the English language has been brought to a state of polish, refinement and accuracy superior to any of the living languages, and also has rules formed upon analogical and rhetorical principles, and is limited and restricted by certain laws peculiar to itself, under various and systematic
5 leads, comprehending the very copious and explanatory divisions of the science, viz., Orthography, Etymology, Syntax and Prosody, and the other auxiliary idioms and observations, together with logic and rhetoric, can there be any thing more futile than to build the superstructure of such a noble edifice upon the establishment of usage, – or that improper idioms
10 should be introduced into English phraseology, and pass as if sanctioned by the rules of grammatical concord? Common sense shrinks from the idea. Our language, like others, should be founded upon just principles of construction, so far as the great variety of its derivation will permit. Every sentence should be simple, energetic, and perspicuous; laconic, yet simple
15 in explication; fertile and flowing, yet free from turgidity, pomposity and affectation, on the one hand, and sterility on the other; divested of ambiguity and vulgarity, with a strict adherence to the rules of grammar. This being granted, custom, like the hydra-monster, credulity when coupled to ignorance must be exploded and sent to seek its baneful retreat among the
20 haunts of superstition in the mountains of error, no more to make its appearance in the fruitful valleys of heaven-born science among the illuminated sons of wisdom ... In fine, no one has any right to impose arbitrary directions or laws on society; so mankind are not bound by any unfounded scientific authority to receive assumed grammatical rules
25 independent of rational principles ...

Aware that cynical malevolence plumes itself with slanderous animad-version, and is ever on the wing, the ill-natured will censure even merit itself; but the noble, generous, and good, will, like the fanning gales, separate the chaff from the wheat, and if only one grain be found, *that* shall
30 be preserved. The scientific patriot looks not to the transient moments of his own existence, nor feels the sordid selfishness that limits fame or emolument to the small circle of his own endeavours or acquirements: he acts not merely for himself, but for posterity. He views mankind emerging from ignorance into the splendour of intellectual effulgence; and laudably
35 ambitious to add another star to the bright constellation, he avails himself of every opportunity of patronising the weakest effort of genius to augment the treasury of science, convinced that knowledge is progressive, and that learning is far above rubies.   ●

T6   *W. H. Savage, 'Linguistic advice' (1833)*

... vulgarisms and inproprieties form in parlance the distinguishing features and marked deformities in our language; and our unfortunate ears are doomed not only to excruciate in the torments of bad grammar, but to agonize under the torture of a viciousness of expression and a corruption of
5   phraseology, the ridiculousness of which alone saves us from the death with which we are frequently threatened. If we find that the better portion of society be not free from these defects, we shall have less reason for astonishment, in observing that they abound with persons whose circumstances have exiled them from the path of education, and whose
10   occupations prevent them from associating study with their more immediate interests. There exist few, however, perhaps none, who do not feel a degree of conscious satisfaction in being relieved from literary error, and it is under this conviction, that the author has compiled the most notorious barbarisms, in order that the reader beholding himself as in a glass, may be enabled to
15   remove with facility the maculæ which he will find thereby to disfigure him. Many persons affect an indifference upon the subject of pronunciation; but this is the flimsy disguise of negligence and ignorance: a thousand masks would be incapable of concealing the convulsive expression of its mortification, or the blushes of its shame and confusion. Is the croaking of
20   the raven comparable to the chant of the nightingale? Is a tainted breath preferable to the odour of a rose? Is filth to be regarded before cleanliness? or pestilence to health? We hesitate not to aver, that a man whose colloquy is vitiated by barbarisms, is a nuisance which affects the nostrils of every man of taste, and of whom society desires most anxiously to be purged.
25   Against whom the 'odi profanum' is the universal watchword, and who is very properly condemned to abandon the paths of men, and to seek the haunts of that class of beings to which he has attached himself ...

     Let every young man strive to indue himself with correct language: the first step to which is to discard all mean and vulgar expressions: destitute of
30   this important advantage, however otherwise well informed, he will put his auditors to suffering: he will resemble a creaking wheel which although very useful, is also very tormenting.

     It should be recollected by all persons who have not received and who for that reason contemn education, that they carry with them a treacherous
35   associate, which in despite of the most powerful armour, the best devised disguise, and their most forcible efforts, will certainly let their secret escape. An associate that no entreaty will mitigate, no affection will soften, no faith will bind; an associate that will at each instant proclaim their vulgarity; whose voice cannot be stifled by prayer, induced by bribery, or deterred by

40 menace – that associate is the tongue. It is therefore important to ascertain
the improprieties to which we are compelled at present to succumb, in order
that expression may be the more speedily liberated from the shackles which
encumber and enfeeble it. Conversation will be thus rendered more intellectual and pleasing; and a fixity will be given to language, which will be more
45 permanent and durable in proportion to the correction of error and the diffusion of that correction. Every man of sense will spare no exertion to divest
himself of habits so hostile to a respectable position in society, and so
militative to that exalted place which a civilised being should occupy: ... To
speak without error depends upon a knowledge of the principles of
50 grammar: to pronounce words improperly is a defect of education and a
former consequence of illiterate society. The former is difficult to attain
where taste does not prevail over the feelings of habit, and where the mind
is compelled to secede to the force of brutism: the latter may be alleviated
with a small degree of attention to the incongruities that are assembled in
55 this work, and which have been concatenated for the instruction and improvement of that class who are desirous of correcting those discrepancies
of language which a want of education has imposed upon them.

To a person who is anxious of assuming a proper attitude in colloquy or
oratory, orthoepy is of grand importance; a blunder of this kind in con-
60 versation will turn the finest reasoning into laughter and ridicule, while in
oratory it will completely deprive the speaker of that respect and attention
which he should possess from his auditors. Aristophanes openly ridiculed
Æschines for a false pronunciation. Burke was laughed at for a similar
reason; and besides the great advantage produced by a propriety of
65 expression and an accurate orthoepy there is another of no unimportant
kind, which is, that when once the mind is induced to pursue one pleasure of
a higher order, it is set upon the race of greater things, and will continue to
ascend; but the mind that nothing can excite to elevate itself will not remain
stationary, but will descend in a progressive ratio until it can hardly be
70 recognized or denominated human ...

But it is not to the uneducated class that this neglect of their vernacular
tongue is alone attributable: the carelessness pervades the higher branches
of society, and we know many who would feel ashamed of a false quantity
in Greek or Latin that are absolutely incapable of reading with propriety an
75 English newspaper.   ●

T7   *R. G. Latham, 'On spelling reform' (1834)*

If I thought mey attempt destined to share the fate of mani such as have
gone before it and been similar to it, and that it was doomed to be raked up
from the pit of oblivion onli in order to be held up as a warning to others of
the futility of such leyk efforts as the present one; I should most certainli
5   withhold it from the publik, valuing, as I ought to do, their teym and mey
own: but I am enkouraged bey feynding, that of the mani who have eksprest
a wish for alterations, few have in the smallest degree *adopted* ani; and of
those who have adopted ani, few have detailed their reasons for doing so.
The publik, most naturalli, place littl releyance on a person who embodies
10   his abuse of an alfabet, in words spelt literatim, in the mode he komplains
of, and still less on one who, if he does not leave too much to their
penetration, seems to pay too littl deference to their usages.
    It is but ekwivokal advantage that the present attempt is in no weys a
parti kause, as, if it were so, men meyt be brought to think upon it, and their
15   feelings meyt be enlisted on the seyd of their judgment; but so much it is the
kommon interest of everi man who speaks English, that it is the business of
every bodi – which is nobodi; and the eydea of its being this, is what ought
especialli to be guarded against. Great as the change from wrong to reyt is,
it may be brought abowt withowt either the aid of akademis or orthografikal
20   societis, if onli a majoriti of those who read and of those who wreyt would
not so much konvince themselves of the necessiti of such a reform, but of
the power each individual has to promote it; and the eksertions necessari
thereto konsist in littl more than the konkwering of a prejudice, and the
akting upon their konviktion ...
25   I konfess I know no poetry ekwal to the kontemplation of that intuitive
and instinktive akweyrment, and that unbounded substitution of intelecktual
for fisikal power, which must and will take place when there is not in ani
one branch of ani one keynd of wisdom no other let or hindrance than those
which ley either in the nature of the subjekt itself, or in the insufficiency of
30   the meynd working thereon.   ●

T8   *G. Edmonds, '19th-century sociolinguistics' (1830s)*

Cobbett's celebrity, based on the enthusiastic cultivation of his strong but
irregular intellectual powers, was primarily founded on the accidental
discovery in early youth, that he was extremely ignorant of the language of
the country, which we are all apt to fancy we know by instinct. His rival
5   Hunt was a man possessed of great shrewdness, and entered life in circumstances of comfort, while his contemporary was driven to the ranks of the

army for subsistence; but Hunt never made the discovery that he was unacquainted with the language of the nation. Though the opinions of these men
were of a similar democratic cast, Cobbett was seldom or never refused an
10 audience, while Hunt seldom or never could obtain a hearing from the
fastidious excrescences of the august assembly. The Times' bitterest satire
on Hunt was the reporting of his speeches word for word, thereby exposing
the individual to ridicule, and holding his party up to shame as incapable of
producing advocates qualified to express their opinions with tolerable gram-
15 matical propriety ...

... Children now talk in a style of elegance that excites surprize, and often
creates horror and indignation in the retreating generation, because the
memories of the advancing generation have been familiarized with the
modes of expression used in our cheapened Press. The majority of young
20 and old read a hundredfold more than formerly. The mass of the population
have thus unconsciously gathered in the memory a store of words not
previously known or understood ...

Classification of Vulgarisms. Some blunders are considered *vulgar*; others,
very vulgar; others, *quite horrid*; and for the perpetration of which man
25 would be hanged – if tried by a jury of grammarians. *I knows I has*, for
instance, is a double mistake coming under the class of *horrid*. It is very
vulgar to utter words containing pronounceable *h*'s without sounding these
letters. But it is still more vulgar to force an *h*, or an *r*, or a *d*, into the
society of letters where the intruders have no business, as *give me a*
30 *horange*, or *shut the winder, Elizar*; or *give me a gownd*. *Vulgar* or
vulgarish blunders may be classified under the incorrect pronunciation of
foreign words, using the singular for the plural, employing *them,* when we
should say *those* &c. &c. ...

Mechanics who are masters of grammar often purposely speak ungrammati-
35 cally when in company with workmen, who are uneducated, for fear of
appearing to have a wish to play the gentleman. This too common conduct
is misapplied modesty and a bad system calculated to continue the evil we
desire to remove. I may remark that the richer men never admit the poorer
men into their society and the consequent chances of benefiting by con-
40 nexion with wealth, unless the poorer individuals have been educated to
speak with propriety. We often find *vulgar* people moving in refined circles:
but these ungrammatical personages, when not present, are considerably
ridiculed and merely tolerated through the power of the purse. ●

T9   *P. Leigh, 'The King's English and Orthography' (1840)*

'English Grammar,' according to Lindley Murray, 'is the art of speaking and writing the English language with propriety.'

The English language, written and spoken with propriety, is commonly called the King's English.

5   A monarch, who, three or four generations back, occupied the English throne, is reported to have said, 'If beebles will be boets, they must sdarve.' This was a rather curious specimen of 'King's English.' It is, however, a maxim of our law, that 'the King can do no wrong.' Whatever bad English, therefore, may proceed from the royal mouth, is not 'King's English,' but

10   'Minister's English,' for which they alone are responsible. For illustrations of this kind of 'English' we beg to refer the reader to the celebrated English Grammar which was written by the late Mr. Cobbett.

King's English (or, perhaps, under existing circumstances we should say, *Queen's* English) is the current coin of conversation, to mutilate which, and

15   unlawfully to *utter* the same, is called *clipping* the King's English; a high crime and misdemeanour.

Clipped English, or bad English, is one variety of Comic English, of which we shall adduce instances hereafter.

Slipslop, or the erroneous substitution of one word for another, as

20   'prodigy' for 'protégée,' 'derangement' for 'arrangement,' 'exasperate' for 'aspirate,' and the like, is another.

Slang, which consists in cant words and phrases, as 'dodge' for 'sly trick,' 'no go' for 'failure,' and 'carney' 'to flatter,' may be considered a third.

25   Latinised English, or Fine English, sometimes assumes the character of Comic English, especially when applied to the purposes of common discourse; as 'Extinguish the luminary,' 'Agitate the communicator,' 'Are your corporeal functions in a condition of salubrity?' 'A sable visual orb,' 'A sanguinary nasal protuberance.'

30   American English is Comic English in a '*pretty particular considerable tarnation*' degree.

Among the various kinds of Comic English it would be '*tout-a-fait*' inexcusable, were we to '*manquer*' to mention one which has, so to speak, quite '*bouleversé'd*' the old-fashioned style of conversation; French-

35   English, that is what '*nous voulons dire.*' '*Avec un poco*' of the '*Italiano,*' this forms what is also called the Mosaic dialect.

English Grammar is divided into four parts – Orthography, Etymology, Syntax, and Prosody; and as these are points that a good grammarian always stands upon, he, particularly when a pedant, and consequently somewhat

40 *flat*, may very properly be compared to a table ...

PART I. **ORTHOGRAPHY**. CHAPTER. I.

OF THE NATURE OF THE LETTERS, AND OF A COMIC ALPHABET.

ORTHOGRAPHY is like a junior usher, or instructor of youth. It teaches us the nature and powers of letters and the right method of spelling words.

45   *Note.* – In a public school, the person corresponding to an usher is called a master. As it is sometimes his duty to flog, we propose that he should henceforth be called the 'Usher of the Birch Rod.'

Comic Orthography teaches us the oddity and absurdities of *letters*, and the wrong method of spelling words. The following is an example of Comic

50 Orthography:

islinton foteenth of febuary 1840.

my Deer jemes

wen fust i sawed you doun the middle and up agin att Vite condick ouse i maid Up my Mind to skure you for my hone for i Felt at once that my

55 appiness was at Steak, and a sensashun in my Bussum I coudent no ways accompt For. And i said to mary at missis Igginses said i theres the Mann for my money o ses Shee i nose a Sweeter Yung Man than that Air Do you sez i Agin then there we Agree To Differ, and we was sittin by the window and we wos wery Neer fallin Out. my deer gemes Sins that Nite i Havent

60 slept a Wink and Wot is moor to the Porpus i Have quit Lost my Happy tight and am gettin wus and wus witch i Think yu ort to pitty Mee. i am Tolled every Day that ime Gettin Thinner and a Jipsy sed that nothin wood Cure me But a Ring ...

please to Burn this Letter when Red and excuse the scralls and Blotches

65 witch is Caused by my Teers i remain

till deth Yure on Happy Vallentine *jane you No who* ...

After this manner cockneys express themselves: – 'I sor (saw) him.' 'Dor (draw) it out.' 'Hold your jor (jaw).' 'I caun't. You shaun't. How's your Maw and Paw? Do you like taut (tart)?'

70   We have heard young ladies remark, – 'Oh, my! What a naice young man!' 'What a bee-eautiful day!' 'I'm so fond of dayncing!'

Dandies frequently exclaim, – 'I'm postively tiawed (tired.)' 'What a sweet tempaw! (temper).' 'How daughty (dirty) the streets au!' And they also call, – Literature, 'literetchah.' Perfectly, 'pawfecly.' Disgusted,

75 'disgasted.' Sky (theatrical dandies do this chiefly) 'ske-eye.' Blue, 'ble-ew.' ●

T10   *C. H. Bromby, 'How to teach English' (1848)*

2. Elementary education in England may happily be regarded as in a state of transition. The interesting class of Pupil Teachers, for whom this work is specially designed, will become the future and intelligent educators of the masses of our fellow subjects. It will be their business and privilege
5   to render the task of instruction palatable to their children. As nothing can be of greater importance in after life to the child than a knowledge of his own language, so nothing can be of greater moment to the preceptor, as a preceptor, than a complete insight into, and thorough mastery over, the philosophy and principles of his mother tongue. It has appeared to the
10 Writer that almost all school grammars have erred, as in many particulars, so especially in attempting to mould the English language upon the model of the Latin; instead of distinguishing what is common to grammar *general*, and what is peculiar to our own.

3. The present volume does not pretend to evolve in any great degree the
15 *history* of the English language; for this, the student is referred to the works of Professor Latham; but his object has been to avoid the positive errors of *principle* current in other School Grammars, and above all to point out the mode in which the subject of grammar may be pictured out to the understandings of even the youngest children ... Let a master, trained to his
20 task by such discipline as our Queen's Scholars will soon enjoy in our Normal Colleges, be conceived to address his gallery, or class, upon the subject of this work after the following, or similar method:

Master. – Children, our Grammar tell us Nouns are those things which we can *name*, or *see*, or *taste*, or *possess*. Suppose your parents took you to a shop to purchase presents
25 for you – let hands be held up of all those who would wish to receive them. *You* (pointing to one) would like to have – *an orange*. And you – *a doll*. And little Henry would like – *a watch*. Now what parts of speech are these – an orange, a doll, a watch? *They are Nouns.* You are right, because you – *see them*, and *touch them*, and *keep them*. But that little boy would not like a – *bad orange*? *No, a good one.* And what kind of doll? *A wax,*
30 *a large one.* And the watch you would like to be – *silver, pretty, gold.* Now what part of speech points out the kind of Noun? *Adjective.* And therefore *good, wax, silver*, &c. are – *adjectives*.

4. The nature of an Adjective might be further shewn by enquiring how *many* oranges the children wish for. One answers *two*, another *six*. These are
35 Adjectives because the office of an Adjective is to point out *number* as well as *kind*. Advantage might be taken to shew the different character of the boys who furnished the answers. One was a *covetous* boy – the other a *modest* boy; these remarks unfolding the parts of speech *covetous* and *modest*, and *serving* at the same time the purpose of a moral training.   ●

T11   *R. C. Trench, 'On the morality in words' (1851)*

Seeing then that language contains so faithful a record of the good and of
the evil which in time past have been working in the minds and hearts of
men, we shall not err, regarding it as a moral barometer, which indicates and
permanently marks the rise or fall of a nation's life. To study a people's
5   language will be to study *them*, and to study them at best advantage; there,
where they present themselves to us under fewest disguises, most nearly as
they are. Too many have had a hand in it, and in causing it to arrive at its
present shape, it is too entirely the collective work of the whole nation, the
result of the united contributions of all, it obeys too immutable laws, to
10   allow any successful tampering with it, any making of it to witness other
than the actual facts of the case.

Thus the frivolity of an age or nation, its mockery of itself, its inability
to comprehend the true dignity and meaning of life, the feebleness of its
moral indignation against evil, all this will find an utterance in the use of
15   solemn and earnest words in senses comparatively trivial or even ridiculous,
in the squandering of such as ought to have been reserved for the highest
mysteries of the spiritual life on slight and secular objects, in the employment almost in jest and play, it may be in honour of words implying the
deepest moral guilt – as the French 'perfide', 'malice', 'malin'; while, on
20   the contrary, the high sentiment, the scorn of everything mean or base of
another people or time, will as certainly in one way or another stamp
themselves on the words which they employ; and thus will it be with
whatever good or evil they may own ...

So too the modifications of meaning which a word has undergone, as it
25   has been transplanted from one soil to another, the way in which one nation
receiving a word from another, has yet brought into it some new force
which was foreign to it in the tongue from whence it was borrowed, has
deepened, or extenuated, or otherwise altered its meaning, – all this may
prove profoundly instructive, and may reveal to us, as perhaps nothing else
30   would, the most fundamental diversities existing between them. Observe,
for instance, how different is the word 'self-sufficient' as used by us, and by
the heathen nations of antiquity ...

How much too may be learned by noting the words which nations have
been obliged to borrow from other nations, as not having them of home-
35   growth – this in most cases, if not in all, testifying that the thing itself was
not native, was only an exotic, transplanted, like the word which indicated
it, from a foreign soil. Thus it is singularly characteristic of the social and
political life of England, as distinguished from that of the other European
nations, that to it alone the word 'club' belongs.   ●

T12   *P. M. Roget, 'Language and thought' (1852)*

It is to those who are thus painfully groping their way and struggling with the difficulties of composition, that this Work professes to hold out a helping hand. The assistance it gives is that of furnishing on every topic a copious store of words and phrases, adapted to express all the recognizable
5   shades and modifications of the general idea under which those words and phrases are arranged. The inquirer can readily select, out of the ample collection spread out before his eyes in the following pages, those expressions which are best suited to his purpose, and which might not have occurred to him without such assistance. In order to make this selection, he
10 scarcely ever need engage in any elaborate or critical study of the subtle distinctions existing between synonymous terms; for if the materials set before him be sufficiently abundant, an instinctive tact will rarely fail to lead him to the proper choice. Even while glancing over the columns of this work, his eye may chance to light upon a particular term, which may save
15 the cost of a clumsy paraphrase, or spare the labour of a tortuous circumlocution. Some felicitous turn of expression thus introduced will frequently open to the mind of the reader a whole vista of collateral ideas, which could not, without an extended and obtrusive episode, have been unfolded to his view; and often will the judicious insertion of a happy
20 epithet, like a beam of sunshine in a landscape, illumine and adorn the subject which it touches, imparting new grace, and giving life and spirit to the picture.

Every workman in the exercise of his art should be provided with proper implements. For the fabrication of complicated and curious pieces of
25 mechanism, the artisan requires a corresponding assortment of various tools and instruments ... Now the writer, as well as the orator, employs for the accomplishment of his purposes the instrumentality of words; it is in words that he clothes his thoughts; it is by means of words that he depicts his feelings ...
30 The use of language is not confined to its being the medium through which we communicate our ideas to one another; it fulfils a no less important function as an *instrument of thought*, not being merely its vehicle, but giving it wings for flight. Metaphysicians are agreed that scarcely any of our intellectual operations could be carried on to any considerable extent
35 without the agency of words. None but those who are conversant with the philosophy of mental phenomena can be aware of the immense influence that is exercised by language in promoting the development of our ideas, in fixing them in the mind, and detaining them for steady contemplation. ●

T13　　　*Encyclopædia Britannica, 'Latin vs English' (^{8}1857)*

The *second* particular by which the different methods of marking the relation of the verbal attribute can affect language, arises from the variety of expressions which either of these may admit of in uttering the same sentiment. In this respect likewise, the method of conjugation by inflection

5　seems to be deficient. Thus the present of the indicative mood in Latin can at most be expressed only in two ways, viz., SCRIBO and EGO SCRIBO, which ought, perhaps, in strictness to be admitted only as one; whereas, in English, we can vary it in four different ways, viz., – 1*st*, I WRITE; 2*dly*, I DO WRITE; 3*dly*, WRITE I DO; 4*thly*, WRITE DO I.[1] And if we consider the further

10　variation which these receive in power as well as in sound, by having the emphasis placed on the different words, instead of four we still find eleven different variations. Thus I *write*, with the emphasis upon the *I*; I WRITE, with the emphasis upon the word WRITE. Let any one pronounce these with the different emphasis necessary, and he will be immediately satisfied that

15　they are not only distinct from each other with respect to meaning, but also with regard to sound. The same must be understood of all the other parts of this example: –

| I *do write*. | I *do* WRITE. | *Write I* DO. | *Write* DO *I.* |
| I DO *write*. | *Write* I *do*. | WRITE *do I*. | *Write do* I. |

20　None of the Latin tenses admit of more variations than the two above mentioned: nor do almost any of the English admit of fewer than in the above example; and several of these phrases, which must be considered as exact translations of some of the tenses of the Latin verb, admit of many more. Thus the imperfect of the subjunctive mood, which in Latin admits of the

25　above two variations, admits in English of the following [six].　　　　●

---

[1] We are sufficiently aware that the last variation cannot in strictness be considered as good language, although many examples of this manner of using it in serious composition, both in poetry and prose, might easily be produced from the best authors in the English language. But, however unjustifiable it may be to use it in serious

30　composition, yet, when judiciously employed in works of humour, this and other forced expressions of the like nature produce a fine effect, by giving a burlesque air to the language, and beautifully contrasting it with the purer diction of solid reasoning. Shakspeare has on many occasions showed how successfully these may be employed in composition, particularly in drawing the character of Ancient Pistol in Henry V. Without

35　this liberty, Butler would have found greater difficulty in drawing the inimitable character of Hudibras. Let this apology suffice for having inserted this and other variations of the same kind, which, although they may be often improper for serious composition, have still their use in language.

T14 *H. Mayhew, 'On the language of costermongers' (1861)*

The slang language of the costermongers is not very remarkable for originality of construction; it possesses no humour: but they boast that it is known only to themselves; it is far beyond the Irish, they say, and puzzles the Jews. The *root* of the costermonger tongue, so to speak, is to give the
5 words spelt backward, or rather pronounced rudely backward, – for in my present chapter the language has, I believe, been reduced to orthography for the first time. With this backward pronunciation, which is very arbitrary, are mixed words reducible to no rule and seldom referrable to any origin, thus complicating the mystery of this unwritten tongue; while any syllable is
10 added to a proper slang word, at the discretion of the speaker.

Slang is acquired very rapidly, and some costermongers will converse in it by the hour. The women use it sparingly; the girls more than the women; the men more than the girls; and the boys most of all. The most ignorant of all these classes deal most in slang and boast of their cleverness and profi-
15 ciency in it. In their conversations among themselves, the following are invariably the terms used in money matters. A rude back-spelling may generally be traced:

Flatch	Halfpenny.	*Yenep*	Penny.
Owl-yenep	Twopence.	*Erth-yenep*	Threepence.
20 | *Rouf-yenep* | Fourpence ... | | |

Speaking of this language, a costermonger said to me: 'The Irish can't tumble to it anyhow; the Jews can tumble better, but we're *their* masters. Some of the young salesmen at Billingsgate understand us, – but only at Billingsgate; and they think they're uncommon clever, but they're not quite
25 up to the mark. The police don't understand us at all. It would be a pity if they did.' ...

The simple principle of costermonger slang – that of pronouncing backward, may cause its acquirement to be regarded by the educated as a matter of ease. But it is a curious fact that lads who become costermongers'
30 boys, without previous association with the class, acquire a very ready command of the language, and this though they are not only unable to spell, but don't 'know a letter in a book.' ...

Before I left this boy, he poured forth a minute or more's gibberish, of which, from its rapid utterance, I could distinguish nothing; but I found
35 from his after explanation, that it was a request to me to make a further purchase of his walnuts.

This slang is utterly devoid of any applicability to humour. It gives no new fact, or approach to a fact, for philologists. One superior genius among

the costers, who has invented words for them, told me that he had no system
40 for coining his term. He gave to the known words some terminating
syllable, or, as he called it, 'a new turn, just,' to use his own words, 'as if he
chorussed them, with a tol-de-rol.' The intelligence communicated in this
slang is, in a great measure, communicated, as in other slang, as much by
the inflection of the voice, the emphasis, the tone, the look, the shrug, the
45 nod, the wink, as by the words spoken.   ●

T15   *J. P. Cobbett, 'On proper pronunciation' (1866)*

The purpose of this additional chapter ... is, not to dictate any system, nor to
set down any general rules, for the right pronouncing of our whole language, but to note such faults in speech as are of the most ordinary occurrence. These faults are committed by great numbers of persons, and not
5 merely by persons in the humblest ranks of life; they are the most striking
perceptible; and they are the most offensive, because they happen to be
those which so frequently cause, with the hearer, a presumption of
'vulgarity' in the pronouncer. These, therefore, are the faults which every
teacher would first seek to prevent or correct in the speaking of young
10 people.
    If we use the word *vulgar* in the sense of *common*, it is fitly applied to
this wrong pronouncing of words. But many persons are looked upon, and
are called, vulgar people, in the sense of low-minded or low-bred people,
solely from their pronunciation being incorrect, when, in truth, there is
15 nothing about them to warrant that idea. They may, on the contrary, be, and
often are, as really high in point of thought and character as any of the most
faultless in speech. Fashion, however, or what is determined by custom to
be proper, has to be respected in this as well as in other matters of habit.
Nobody can like to be supposed ill-bred on account of a mode of speech
20 which is settled to be objectionable. Yet a good many of us, though
presumed to be generally well taught, are for such reason, and nothing
more, exposed to a mortifying ridicule. We see it pretty often with public
speakers and members of Parliament, occasionally with lawyers at the bar,
and sometimes even with preachers in the pulpit.

25   [Features discussed include omission and addition of *h-*, [ʊ] in *butter*, [əʊ] in *cloud*,
      [w = v = r], different kinds of *a*'s]   ●

T16   *H. Alford, 'The Queen's English' (1864)*

(1)   I ought to begin by explaining what I mean by the term, 'Queen's English'. It is one rather familiar and conventional, than strictly accurate. The Sovereign is of course no more the proprietor of the English language than any one of us. Nor does she, nor do the Lords and Commons in
5   Parliament assembled, possess one particle of right to make or unmake a word in the language. But we use the phrase, the Queen's English, in another sense; one not without example in some similar phrases. We speak of the *Queen's Highway*, not meaning that her Majesty is *possessed* of that portion of road, but that it is a high road of the land, as distinguished from
10   by-roads and private roads: open of common right to all, and the general property of our country. And so it is with the *Queen's English*. It is, so to speak, this land's great highway of thought and speech; and seeing that the Sovereign in this realm is the person round whom all our common interests gather, the centre of our civil duties and of our civil rights, the *Queen's*
15   *English* is not an unmeaning phrase, but one which may serve to teach us some profitable lessons with regard to our language, and to its use and abuse.

      And it may be, and is for us, a very useful phrase as conveying another meaning. That which we treat is not the grammarian's English, nor the
20   Dictionary-writers' English, but *the Queen's English*: not that English which certain individuals, more or less acquainted with their subject, have chosen to tell us we ought to speak and write, but that which the nation, in the secular unfolding of its will and habits, has agreed to speak and write. We shall have to say more of this by-and-by.

25   I called our common English tongue the highway of thought and speech; and it may not be amiss to carry on this similitude further. The Queen's Highway, now so broad and smooth, was once a mere track over an unenclosed country. It was levelled, hardened, widened, by very slow degrees. Of all this trouble, the passer-by sees no trace now. He bowls along
30   it with ease in a vehicle, which a few centuries ago would have been broken to pieces in a deep rut, or would have come to grief in a bottomless swamp.

      ... it has become for us, in our days, a level, firm, broad highway, over which all thought and all speech can travel evenly and safely. Along it the lawyer and the parliamentary agent propel their heavy waggons, clogged
35   with a thousand pieces of cumbrous antiquated machinery, – and no wonder, when they charge freightage, not by the weight of the load, combined with the distance, but by the number of impediments which they can manage to offer to the progress of their vehicle. Along it the poet and novelist drive their airy tandems, dependent for their success on the dust

40   which they raise, and through which their varnished equipages glitter. On
     the same road divines, licensed and unlicensed, ply once a week or more,
     with omnibus or carrier's cart, promising to carry their passengers into
     another land than that over which the road itself extends, just as the coaches
     out of London used to astonish our boyish eyes by the '*Havre de Grace*'
45   and '*Paris*' inscribed on them. And along this same Queen's Highway plods
     ever the great busy crowd of foot-passengers – the talkers of the market, of
     society, of the family. Words, words, words; good and bad, loud and soft,
     long and short; millions in the hour, innumerable in the day, unimaginable
     in the year: what then in the life? what in the history of a nation? what in
50   that of the world? And not one of these is ever forgotten. There is a book
     where they are all set down. What a history, it has been well said, is this
     earth's atmosphere, seeing that all words spoken, from Adam's first till
     now, are still vibrating on its sensitive and unresting medium ...

     (2)   We have before us an article from the pen of a very clever writer, and,
55   as it appears in a magazine which specially professes to represent the 'best
     society', it may be taken as a good specimen of the style. It describes a
     dancing party, and we discover for the first time how much learning is re-
     quired to describe a 'hop' properly. The reader is informed that all the
     people at the dance belong to the *beau monde*, as may be seen at a *coup*
60   *d'oeil*; the *demi-monde* is scrupulously excluded, and in fact everything
     about it bespeaks the *haut ton* of the whole affair. A lady who has been very
     happy in her hair-dresser is said to be *coiffée à ravir*. Then there is the bold
     man to describe. Having acquired the *savoir faire*, he is never afraid of
     making a *faux pas*, but no matter what kind of conversation is started
65   plunges in at once *in medias res*. Following him is the fair *debutante*, who
     is already on the look-out for *un bon parti*, but whose *nez retroussé* is a
     decided obstacle to her success. She is of course accompanied by mamma
     en grande toilette, who *entre nous*, looks rather *ridée*, even in the gaslight.
     Then, lest the writer should seem frivolous, he suddenly abandons the
70   description of the dances, *vis-à-vis* and *dos-à-dos*, to tell us that Homer
     becomes tiresome when he sings of βοῶπις πότνια ῞Ηρη twice in a page.
     The supper calls forth a corresponding amount of learning, and the writer
     concludes his article after having aired his Greek, his Latin, his French, and,
     in a subordinate way, his English.
75   Of course, this style has admirers and imitators. It is showy and preten-
     tious, and everything that is showy and pretentious has admirers. The
     admixture of foreign phrases with our plain English produces a kind of
     Brummagem sparkle which people whose appreciation is limited to the
     superficial imagine to be brilliance. Those who are deficient in taste and art

80 education not infrequently prefer a dashing picture by young Daub to a
glorious cartoon by Raphael. The bright colouring of the one far more than
counterbalances the lovely but unobtrusive grace of the other. In a similar
way, students are attracted by the false glitter of the French-paste school of
composition, and instead of forming their sentences upon the beautiful
85 models of the great English masters, they twist them into all sorts of unnatural shapes for no other end than that they may introduce a few
inappropriate French or Latin words, the use of which they have learned to
think looks smart. Of course, the penny-a-liners are amongst the most
enthusiastic followers of the masters of this style. They not only think it
90 brilliant, but they know it to be profitable, inasmuch as it adds considerably
to their ability to say a great deal about nothing. The public sees a great deal
in the newspapers about '*recherché* dinners' and 'sumptuous *déjeûners*'
(sometimes eaten at night), and about the *éclat* with which a meeting attended by the '*élite* of the county' invariably passes off; but they get but a
95 trifling specimen of the masses of similar rubbish which daily fall upon the
unhappy editors. The consequence of all this is that the public is habituated
to a vicious kind of slang utterly unworthy to be called a language. Even the
best educated people find it difficult to resist the contagion of fashion in
such a thing as conversation, and if some kind of stand is not made against
100 this invasion, pure English will soon only exist in the works of our dead
authors.
　　But it is not only on literary grounds that we think the bespanglement of
our language with French and other foreign phrases is to be deprecated.
Morality has something to say in the matter. It is a fact that things are said
105 under the flimsy veil of foreign diction which could not be very well said in
plain English. To talk in the presence of ladies about disreputable women
by the plain English names which belong to them is not considered to
display a very delicate mind, but anybody may talk about the *demi-monde*
without fearing either a blush or a frown. Yet the idea conveyed is precisely
110 the same in the one case as in the other; and inasmuch as words can only be
indelicate when they convey an indelicate idea, we should think that the
French words ought to be under the same disabilities as the English ones. In
like manner, things sacred are often made strangely familiar by the
intervention of a French dictionary. Persons whose reverence for the Deity
115 is properly shown 'in their English conversation by a becoming
unwillingness to make a light use of His holy Name, have no hesitation in
exclaiming *Mon Dieu!* in frivolous conversation. The English name for the
Father of Evil is not considered to be a very respectable noun, but its French
synonym is to be heard in 'the best society'.　　　　　　　　　　●

T17   *A. J. Ellis, 'Pronunciation and its changes' (1869)*

Without entering on the complex investigation of the idiomatic alterations of language, a slight consideration will shew that the audible forms in which these idioms are clothed will also undergo great and important changes. The habit of producing certain series of spoken sounds is acquired
5 generally by a laborious and painful process, beginning with the first dawn of intelligence, continued through long stages of imperfect powers of appreciation and imitation, and becoming at last so fixed that the speaker in most cases either does not hear or does not duly weigh any but great deviations from his own customary mode of speech, and is rendered incapable of
10 any but a rude travesty of strange sounds into the nearest of his own familiar utterances. We may apparently distinguish three laws according to which the sounds of a language change ...

At any one instant of time there are generally three generations living. Each middle generation has commenced at a different time, and has
15 modified the speech of its preceding generation in a somewhat different manner, after which it retains the modified form, while the subsequent generation proceeds to change that form once more. Consequently there will not be any approach to uniformity of speech sounds in any one place at any one time, but there will be a kind of mean, the general utterance of the more
20 thoughtful or more respected persons of mature age, round which the other sounds seem to hover, and which, like the averages of the mathematician, not agreeing precisely with any, may for the purposes of science be assumed to represent all, and be called the language of the district at the epoch assigned. Concrete reality is always too complex for science to grasp, and
25 hence she has to content herself with certain abstractions, and to leave practice to apply the necessary corrections in individual cases ...

In the present day we may, however, recognize a received pronunciation all over the country, not widely differing in any particular locality, and admitting a certain degree of variety. It may be especially considered as the
30 educated pronunciation of the metropolis, of the court, the pulpit, and the bar.[1] But in as much as all these localities and professions are recruited from the provinces, there will be a varied thread of provincial utterance running through the whole. In former times this was necessarily more marked, and the simultaneous varieties of pronunciation prevalent and acknowledged
35 much greater.   ●

---

[1] The pronunciation of the stage is inclined to be archaic, except in the modernest imitations of every day life.

T18 *H. Sweet, 'Linguistic science' (1876)*

One of the most striking features of the history of linguistic science as compared with zoology, botany and the other so-called natural sciences, is its
one-sidedly historical character. Philologists have hitherto chiefly confined
their attention to the most ancient dead languages, valuing modern
5 languages only in as far as they retain remnants of older linguistic
formations – much as if zoology were to identify itself with palæontology,
and refuse to trouble itself with the investigation of living species, except
when it promised to throw light on the structure of extinct ones.

Philologists forget, however, that the history of language is not one of
10 decay only, but also of reconstruction and regeneration. These processes are
of equal, often more importance than those by which the older languages
were formed, and, besides, often throw light on them. They have further the
great advantage of being perfectly accessible to the observer. Thus the
growth of a language like English can be observed in a series of literary
15 documents extending from the ninth century to the present day, affording
examples of almost every linguistic formation.

But before history must come a knowledge of what now exists. We must
learn to observe things as they are, without regard to their origin, just as a
zoologist must learn to describe accurately a horse, or any other animal. Nor
20 would the mere statement that the modern horse is a descendant of a three-
toed marsh quadruped be accepted as an exhaustive description. Still less
would the zoologist be allowed to ignore the existing varieties of the
Equidæ as being 'inorganic' modifications of the original type. Such, however, is the course pursued by most antiquarian philologists. When a
25 modern language discards the cumbrous and ambiguous inflexions it has
received from an earlier period, and substitutes regular and precise
inflexions and agglutinations of its own, these formations are contemptu-
ously dismissed as 'inorganic' by the philologist, who forgets that change,
decay and reconstruction are the very life of language – language is
30 'inorganic' only when it stands still in its development.

The first requisite is a knowledge of phonetics, or the form of language.
We must learn to regard language solely as consisting of groups of sounds,
independently of the written symbols, which are always associated with all
kinds of disturbing associations, chiefly historical. We must then consider
35 language in its relation to thought, which necessitates some study of the
relation of language to logic and psychology. Such investigations, if carried
out consistently, will greatly modify our views, not only of English, but of
language generally, and will bring us face to face with many of the ultimate
problems of language. ●

T19a   *J. B. Davidson, 'On punctuation' (1864)*

Punctuation, as hitherto taught, has been a difficult branch of study, while
grammarians, in order to keep pace with the march of intellect, have sought,
by every possible means, fully to develop the varied beauties of our language, they have, at all times, manifested the profoundest ignorance on the
5 subject of our present inquiry; and, while advancing, step by step, in every
other branch of grammatical science, have endeavoured to create and foster
the unhappy prejudice, that correct punctuation is known exclusively to
compositors, who have had a kind of mechanical training in the printing-
office. This unfortunate error, the succeeding pages are designed to remove.
10 ... *The Dash.* This stop has latterly assumed a position of considerable
prominence in romances and similar literature, and by many, has ascribed to
it the precision of the half and the full colon. But after every claim of the
dash, aided by the pens of its numerous recent advocates for supremacy, the
author is of opinion it is inadequate to the broad and necessary latitude of
15 application maintained by the colons.   ●

T19b   *E. A. Abbott, 'On punctuation' (³1879)*

Punctuation is the *practice** of distinguishing the constituent parts of a
sentence, and sometimes its meaning, by the use of certain marks called
'*stops*'.
       *It ought to be an *art*, but unfortunately no rules are observed. Every
5 man does that which is right in his own eyes; and one author will even
break up into separate sentences, what another combines into one ...
       It is a common mistake to suppose that stops indicate the pauses to be
made in reading aloud. No doubt a reader will usually pause at a stop; but
he will also very often find it necessary to pause where there is none; and
10 most certainly will not habitually pause longer at a semicolon than at a
comma. This notion in *rhetorical* punctuation has given birth to an insightly
object called a '*dash*' (–) which especially disfigures modern poetry, and is
for ever at the elbows of careless writers, who cannot, and will not,
construct a sentence. The student ought always to bear in mind that he can
15 neither write intelligibly without stops; nor use stops accurately without
constant reference to the principles of grammatical analysis.   ●

T20   *Anon., 'Advice on proper English pronunciation' (1880)*

It is a very general lament amongst people well educated, but upon whom Nature has not conferred any choice gifts of mind – in other words, people whom it would be idle to call clever – that they never know what to say, or 'that they could have got on so much better with So-and-so if they
5   had only known what to talk about' ... The not knowing what to talk about is the secret of why so many people in society appear to be dull, stupid, and commonplace; they probably merit neither of these uncomplimentary adjectives, and would very much object to their being applied to them ...

'Voice' and 'manner' are of paramount importance in the art of
10   Conversing. It is a very erroneous idea to suppose that men or women in 'fashionable society', or what is termed 'the best society', or 'good society', speak with a lisp or a languid drawl, or with any mannerism whatever. Well-bred people speak in natural and unaffected manner, the cadence of the voice being low and the intonation thoroughly distinct, each syllable of
15   each word being clearly pronounced, but without pedantry or exaggeration.

The modulation of the tones of the voice is also a great point with the well-educated; and this it is which gives to the voice the slow, measured ring which the uninitiated endeavour to imitate by the assuming an affected drawl, or by speaking in deep and guttural accents, as foreign to the genuine
20   voice of the well-bred man or woman as is the dialect of the Lancashire operative ... The voice is one of the best and truest indications of education and refinement, and betrays the absence of these qualities with almost painful intensity ...

The common error with the many is their rapid, or, so to say, slovenly
25   manner of speaking; the slurring over of the final syllables, the dropping the voice before the words have been but half-uttered, and the running a string of words together with hurried and ungraceful accents, too often starting with a jerk and concluding with a rush ...

Commonplace people greatly try the patience of their friends by their
30   trite commonplaces respecting the opera and the artistes, apparently oblivious of the fact that the daily newspapers contain ample criticisms on the merits and demerits of the various artistes. These observations apply solely to those mediocre people who are thoroughly incompetent to form any opinion on the matter, being wanting alike in talent, education, and intellect,
35   and these are precisely the people who step in where 'angels fear to tread', and who thrust their inane remarks upon those who are far more capable of forming a correct judgment.   ●

T21   *F. A. White, 'On changes in 19th-century English' (1882)*

Lastly, we have several dualistic forms amongst the pronouns, *viz.* either, other, neither; and even plural adjectives, *viz.* this, these, that, those.

(*b*) A multitude of verbs formerly of the strong conjugation are now either obsolete, as *slay*; or of the weak, as *reach*; or of both as *light*; and a
5 multitude formerly of the third class of the strong conjugation, as *crow*, are now of the second, *i.e.* are less inflected.

(*c*) The subjunctive is now very nearly gone. We no longer say, 'Tarry at Jericho until your beards *be* grown,' but, 'Tarry at Jericho until your beards *are* grown;' nor, 'What care I how fair she *be*,' but, 'What care I how fair
10 she *is*.' Indeed the subjunctive is now only used – except in poetry and solemn didactic prose –

(1) After *if, though, although, unless*.

(2) In the past indefinite tense of the copula (the verb *to be*); and many of the best speakers, and prose writers, too, confine it yet further to the
15 following cases: –

(3) Where it precedes its subject, as, 'Were John here.' (4) Where its subject is a personal pronoun, as, 'If I were you.' (5) Where the conjunction is emphasized as '*If* it were so, it were a grievous fault,' or, what is much the same thing, if the fact supposed is emphatically doubtful. (6) Where it is
20 used for the conditional, as in the case just given, where 'it were' is equivalent to 'it would be.'

(II.) A derivative from an alien tongue is apt at first to take its meaning from the word from which it is derived, and then by degrees to modify that meaning. Hence a great change in the meanings of many English words in
25 the course of the last two centuries; thus *animosity*, originally courage, now means passionate ill-will; *copy*, originally abundance (from 'copia'), now means the rewritten form of an original document; *miscreant*, originally meaning believing amiss, now means grossly villainous ...

(IV.) There is a tendency to convert substantives into verbs; as, *to tea*,
30 for *to drink tea* with any one.

(V.) There is an increasing tendency also to make one substantive before another do duty for a substantial adjective with or without a hyphen; as earth-works, boy-prince, Easter offering, warrior queen.

(VI.) Anomalies, whether in accidence or in syntax, tend more and more
35 to obsolescence.

(VII.) Commerce, the arts and sciences, and the profound study of our language, not only as classically written, but in its archaic, provincial, nay, even its slang and illiterate forms, daily swell the full current of modern English with fresh contributions – the latter so much so, that Spenser's

40 Pastorals are probably (spelling apart) more intelligible now than when they
were originally written.

(VIII.) Two causes have produced a change in the pronunciation of many
words (1) The tendency to carry the accent back: thus Shakespeare said
charácter, we say cháracter; Rogers said balcóny, we say bálcony; Scott said
45 Trafalgár, we say Trafálgar. (2) The more we grow a reading people the
more we pronounce words as they are spelt; hence the present pronunciation
of such words as Rome, oblige, yellow, tea, reason, Beaconsfield, St. Leger;
at one time pronounced, Room, obleege, yallow, tay, raison (as in Shakespeare's punning, 'were *raisons* as plenty as blackberries'), Běconsfield,
50 Silliger.   ●

T22 *'Examples of official letters, style, and handwriting' (1886)*

(a)   *Military Education Division, War Office, 17th March*, 1873.
                      From SECRETARY, MILITARY EDUCATION DIVISION.
                      To The Officer Commanding – BN. – REGT.
SIR,
5   In acknowledging the receipt of the School Report for February, of the
Battalion under your command, and with reference to paras. 452 and 453 of
the revised Queen's Regulations, which require that every Recruit shall
attend school at least five hours per week until he has qualified for a Fourth
Class Certificate of Education. I am desired by the Director-General of
10 Military Education to observe, that in order the Recruits may receive a full
hour's instruction at each attendance, their school should be opened for at
least one hour and a quarter on every week day except Saturday.

His Royal Highness the Field Marshal Commanding-in-Chief has
decided that the paragraphs above quoted apply to all young soldiers,
15 whether Recruits properly so called or not, and their compulsory attendance
of five hours per week is, therefore, not to be limited to the first two months
of their service, but to be continued until they obtain Fourth Class Certificates of Education.

It appears that the average attendance of Recruits in the Corps under
20 your command did not exceed 9½ hours during the month of February.

I have the honor to be, Sir, Your obedient Servant,   *Secretary.*

(b)   BUSINESS LETTERS.

Business Letters as a rule should be as short as the subject matter will allow, consistent with clearness of expression. The above noted contractions
25 are allowable between business men; but when one of the correspondents does not happen to have received a business training, it is better not to use them. Should the subject matter cause more space to be occupied than one page, it is now usual with many business men to write on the fourth and first pages in the order named, in order the more readily to copy in the letter
30 press. Should these be filled they may proceed to use the second and even third, for then the letter would be readily copied in the succeeding pages of their letter-press book.

Though the phases of business are so many and varied, still a few specimens of business letters on different subjects are here appended, not as
35 models but as guides.

(i) From a Tenant to a Landlord, concerning repairs.
                    Munster Lane, Manchester, 19th July, 1885
Sir,
        I shall be obliged by your sending some one at once to examine the
40 drains passing under this house. I suspect they are choked at or near the junction with the Main Sewer. The effluvium is very great and I dread the outbreak of disease.
                    I am, Sir, Yours, truly, W. JONES.

(ii)   From the same to the same complaining of inattention to former
45   letter.
                    Munster Lane, Manchester, 25th July, 1885.
Sir,
        My last communication to you dated the 19th inst. has as yet produced no effect. No one has come to examine the drains complained of. Owing to
50 the intense heat the danger arising from their condition is hourly increasing, and should I not hear from you in the course of three days I shall apply to the Sanitary Inspector, and whatever he advises I shall proceed to get done, charging the cost to you.   I am, Sir, Yours, Truly W. JONES.

(c)   STYLE
55   Many remarks upon this subject, which would be applicable to epistles
usual in social life, are, by the very nature of the letters under consideration
irrelevant. Such will be neglected, and attention directed solely to those
appropriate to Official Letters. It may however be pointed out, that the hints
on style now given, are applicable, not only to the species under considera-
60   tion, but also to all letters of whatsoever kind.
   No effort at polish of style should be made, as neatness and correctness
are the prime necessities. Nicety in the selection of words betrays study; and
it is as correct a remark concerning Official Letters, as any others, that the
best letters are those written without constraint. It ought, however, to be
65   remembered, that ease and simplicity should never be allowed to degenerate
into carelessness, and that almost the first requisite in correspondence is a
due attention to decorum, such as our own character and that of others de-
mands. Carelessness again may lapse into imprudence, which may be forgotten if committed in conversation, but never in correspondence, for 'The
70   written letter remains.' Though letters should not take the form of studied
compositions, *Clearness of Arrangement* should never be absent. This depends much upon the proper placing of words. All modifying words should
be placed near those with which they are connected. Words expressing
things which are connected in thought should be placed in close proximity.
75   The too frequent repetition of pronouns referring to different persons, together with the improper placing of words, often lead to doubtful meaning,
or the formation of sentences of ambiguous import. Important words should
be placed where their importance is evident, and where they can produce the
strongest effect. Each sentence should contain only one strain of thought,
80   and if it be needful to join two or more thoughts in one sentence, these
thoughts must have an intimate connection with one another. Sentences
should never be of an undue length, for force is lost by extending them
beyond their natural limit. Parenthesis should rarely be used, but, when
unavoidable, should as seldom as possible be admitted into the middle of
85   sentences ...
   Remember it is a mark of great affectation to use a foreign word when an
English equivalent exists. It is only permissible to use foreign words and
idioms in Official Letter Writing, when no English word or idiom fully
expresses the meaning desired, or for the purpose of obviating a long para-
90   graph; and even then, only when these words and idioms are well known.

(d)   CHOICE OF WORDS.

It might at first sight seem that any remarks upon this topic in connection with Official Letter Writing would be superfluous, because, from the nature of such letters, certain set forms and phrases must recur again and again.

95   This is in a certain sense true. Such phrases do occur and recur, but they are few in number, can be easily recognised, and many of them learned by a perusal of the examples of Official Letters hereto appended. It is equally true however, that these forms of phraseology do not constitute the sum total of the art; and although language be limited much more in Official,

100   than in the ordinary, social epistolary efforts, still there is variety enough, and room enough for grave errors to be made, and serious mistakes avoided. It has been truly said, that 'Language is the dress of thought;' and why should Official thought be dressed in a worse or more slovenly garb than any other? ...

105   Now coarse, vulgar or ungrammatical language detracts from, and dims in no slight degree the creditable appearance of even the best abilities; and is it not evident that the opposite would increase and enhance their lustre? How much, too, of the success or non-success of the writer might depend upon the language which flows from his pen. Every word proceeding from

110   the pen of the writer produces either the effect he wishes, or it does not, according to his skill in its use. Is not the choice of words then, worth a little consideration, looking to the ends aimed at?

Already coarse, vulgar and ungrammatical words have been alluded to, in terms which shew they, at least, ought never to be admitted. There are

115   other errors to be avoided, but none so bad as that referred to. Coarse terms shock, vulgar words disgust, and ungrammatical expressions displease.

A beginner is apt to fall into an error arising from the idea of the importance of Official Correspondence. It is, that such should always be clothed in the most pompous, high sounding and magniloquent language:

120   that because of the greater dignity, it is needful to employ as many uncommon, and what are usually termed 'hard' words as possible. This can easily be shewn to be fallacious reasoning.

'Hard' words are so, because the user of them finds them 'hard' to himself; knowing but little of them he is likely to misunderstand them;

125   misunderstanding them he is extremely likely to misuse them. Being misused they do harm, for they obscure what should be evident, and render what should be easy, plain and agreeable reading, troublesome, difficult and unpleasant. Should the words not be misused, the intelligent reader smiles to think of the useless trouble taken, when a shorter, plainer and easier set of

130   expressions might have been as effective. Long, 'hard' words may excite

surprise and admiration in the vulgar, who are most astonished by what they do not understand. Again, too, the use of 'hard' words is peculiarly open to the formation of a stiff, stilted, unnatural style, which grates upon the sensibilities of refined people. Who would not laugh at, feeling at the same
135 time a slight contempt for, one who termed a shoe 'A covering for the pedal extremities'?

(e)   HANDWRITING.

Nothing is so conducive to ill temper, grumbling, loss of time, and vexation, as the receipt of an undecipherable communication. In fact, the
140 great beauty, and much of the utility of handwriting depend upon legibility. Were the question asked, which are the best marks by which a good hand-writing can be recognised, the sole answer, many times repeated, would be legibility. Consider what is the great object to be attained by any written communication, if it be not to convey its meaning? How can this be best
145 done if not by legibility? If again the question be asked 'What is the greatest ornament of good handwriting?' The answer would again be legibility. And if once more the question be asked 'How am I to attain to a good style of handwriting?' The answer would be, strive after legibility. Legibility prevents any mistakes as to the words used; legibility prevents undue strain
150 upon the eye; legibility lessens the effort the mind requires to make in order to grasp the meaning of what the eye sees. To secure legibility is a comparatively easy matter for any painstaking person who feels the necessity of it, and resolves to attain it.

One great obstacle to the attainment of a legible hand, is the attempt to
155 cultivate what is considered a fine, dashing style of writing, ornamented with flourishes wherever and whenever these may be introduced. This habit of flourishing and dashing, sadly detracts from legibility, by withdrawing the eye from the words to the ornamentation, requiring an effort of the mind to force the eye to execute the task of reading the words presented to it.
160 Consequently flourishes should consistently be refrained from. Another obstacle to the attainment of legibility arises from an ambition to write quickly, even before the hand is properly formed. Let it be remembered that the greatest known runner had, as a child, first to crawl, then to totter on his feet, then to walk, and lastly, after years of persevering effort and training,
165 his running powers became developed as we know them. So should it be with him who is ambitious of being both a rapid and good writer; let him creep slowly but intelligently through the rudiments of the art, walk gently during the next step of progress, then having undergone a patient and persevering process of training, he will develop his writing powers into the
170 production of a free, fluent and legible running hand.   ●

T23   *Anon., 'Review of Duxbury's Grammar' (1886)*

A NEW ENGLISH GRAMMAR OF SCHOOL GRAMMARS.

With Composition, Derivation, Analysis of Sentences, and History of the Language; and also Copious Exercises and Questions for Examination. By C. DUXBURY, Author of 'John Cotton; or, the Successful Factory Lad,' 'Etymological Vocabulary,' &c.

OPINIONS OF THE PRESS.

5   'We welcome this concise and at the same time compendious little work, as an admirable school-book, and something besides. It is a student's book for wisdom, though a boy's book for simplicity; and we may say without cynicism that it is a work which we should very much wish to see made a pocket companion by most of our public speakers and many of our public
10   writers ...

'For those teachers who are regretfully conscious of the defects of Lindley Murray and Lennie, but who do not take kindly to Morell, Mason, or Bain, this is the very Book; and the student whose grammatical education has been neglected and who wishes to teach himself, cannot do better than
15   give his leisure hours to the instruction here presented. If he will work through the numerous carefully prepared Exercises (which, being mainly extracts from our best authors, are in themselves a treat to read and a culture to study), and answer the hundreds of questions here given, he will attain an enviable acquaintance with the whole subject.' – *Educational Reporter*.

20   'Mr. Duxbury has consulted a large number of works bearing on the subject of grammar, and has endeavoured to make the rules of grammar bend to the practice of our great English writers. We like his plan of giving notes on grammatical points from authorities on English grammar. It gives a special interest to the book.' – *National Schoolmaster*.

25   'We welcome this new grammar with pleasure. The fallacies which have been and are being disseminated by that over-praised 'Lindley Murray' needed upsetting. We have here a grammar suited to present wants and circumstances, and applicable to the language as spoken in the best circles in the days we live in. The author teaches his pupils in a sensible,
30   progressive, and clear manner, and there are very many individuals who fancy they know something about English grammar who will have a much clearer knowledge of the subject after the perusal of Mr. Duxbury's little book. All the difficulties are cleared away, and the study of grammar is made luminous to the dullest capacity. For public school purposes nothing
35   could be better.' – *The London Weekly Times*.   ●

T24   *H. Sweet, 'On educated Southern English' (^{3}1900)*

The object of this book is to give a faithful picture – a phonetic
photograph – of educated spoken English as distinguished from vulgar and
provincial English on the one hand, and literary English on the other hand.
At the same time I must disclaim any intention of setting up a standard of
5 spoken English. All I can do is to record those facts which are accessible to
me – to describe that variety of spoken English of which I have a personal
knowledge, that is, the educated speech of London and the district round it
– the original home of Standard English both in its spoken and literary form
...

10   The comparative purity and correctness of the different varieties of
spoken English is popularly estimated by the degree of approximation to the
written language. But these comparisons are generally carried out in a one-
sided and partial spirit. When an Englishman hears the distinct *r* and *gh* in
the Broad Scotch *farther*, *night*, etc., he is apt to assume at once that Scotch
15 English is more archaic than Southern English, but if he looks at the evidence on the other side, such forms as *ah ai oo* = *all one wool* will make
him more inclined to believe what is the truth, namely that standard spoken
English is, on the whole, quite as archaic, quite as correct and pure as any of
its dialects – a truth which before the rise of modern philological dilettante-
20 ism and dialect-sentimentality no one ever thought of disputing.

Still more caution is required in attempting to estimate the comparative
beauty and ugliness of the different varieties of spoken English. Our
impressions on this point are so entirely the result of association that it is
hardly possible to argue about them. The Cockney dialect seems very ugly
25 to an educated English man or woman because he – and still more she –
lives in perpetual terror of being taken for a Cockney, and a perpetual
struggle to preserve that *h* which has now been lost in most of the local
dialects of England, both North and South ... When the sugar-merchants of
Liverpool began to 'speak fine,' they eagerly adopted the thin Cockney *a* in
30 *ask*, which many of their descendants keep, I believe, to the present day –
long after this 'mincing' pronunciation has been discarded in the London
dialect.

Another difficulty about setting up a standard of spoken English is that
it changes from generation to generation, and is not absolutely uniform even
35 among speakers of the same generation, living in the same place, and
having the same social standing. Here, again, all I can do is to describe that
form of the London dialect with which I am sufficiently familiar to enable
me to deal with it satisfactorily. The only real familiarity we can have is
with the language we speak ourselves.   ●

T25   *[A. Heald], 'Of linguistic correctness' (1892)*

INTRODUCTION. The observant reader cannot fail to be cognisant of the
faulty grammatical construction which pervades much of the literature of
the present day, manifesting itself in forms as various as they are numerous.
We frequently find the singular number used for the plural and the plural for
5   the singular; the past, present, and future tenses of verbs employed
indiscriminately, as though they were so many interchangeable parts of a
machine; adverbs substituted for adjectives, and *vice versâ*; nouns and
pronouns in the wrong gender and case; prepositions incorrectly applied;
negatives scattered about broadcast, without any regard to the sense; words
10 diverted from their true signification; and all sorts of other improprieties too
numerous to be specified. Whether the prevailing slovenly style of literary
composition is due to neglect on the part of the instructors of youth, or to a
feeling on the part of writers that grammar is of little consequence, so long
as they make their meaning clear to their readers, or to the high pressure
15 speed at which we move in this nineteenth century, it would serve no
purpose to inquire; but that it exists is undeniable.

As might be expected, more grammatical inaccuracy is exhibited in
works of fiction than in those of a graver description; and more in the colloquial than in the descriptive portions of the former.
20   As to the Press of this country, whose superiority to that of any other is
so marked as to be beyond dispute, it is really wonderful, having regard to
the little time available for composition and printing, how small is the number of grammatical errors. When we consider that the whole of a daily
newspaper must be commenced and completed within the period of a few
25 hours, we cannot but hold it a marvel that mistakes are so rare and so
comparatively unimportant.

It may seem incredible, but there are those who regard it as immaterial
whether language is grammatical or otherwise, so long as the ideas intended
to be conveyed by one person to another are understood. But those who take
30 this utilitarian view overlook the fact that, were there no grammar, it would
be very difficult, if not impossible, to communicate ideas with exactitude;
moreover, such persons often have reason to regret their contempt for grammatical rules, as can easily be shown ...

It is well known how an author by the purity, accuracy, and perspicuity
of his style can influence the reader, even when the latter is but little in
agreement with his arguments; and how, on the other hand, the frequent
recurrence of grammatical inaccuracies detracts from the force of the
writer's arguments, diverting the reader's attention from the subject of the
book, and prompting him to search for further errors.   ●

II On dialect

T26a   *A. Layton, 'Private letter' (1816)*

For Mrs. William Layton. Ely
litle London Cambridgeshire   May 27

My Dear I have taken an oppertunity in riten to you to let you know that I
got into London on Sunday night about half past six and went to my uncle
5 James ouse amedetly and then to fishers and did sleep there but I think I
shall stop in London for awild got to sint tivs about 3 oClok and at Kisby
hut and brackfasted thar and then Came to rampton and thir I taken Coch to
London but before you doe wash my Briches look in the Wach Pocket and
thir you will find a one Pound note loose wich I for got but I think I shall
10 not wt it to moren monen I shall go to moren monen to sint Gorg Sqar for
tha aGon to bild a Grat deal thir and if not thir to Quane Chapel and if not
thir to bath on Wedinsay moren by the Coch so dont right to me tel you hear
from me agane for if I git work i Shall let you now my dearmak your Self as
easy as you Can for I shall not take any hurt thir I hope you will hear from
15 me agane in a day or two my ant and family are all well and wish to be
rembred to you all ant Fisher all well Mrs Do are well but sory to inform
you that my oncul fisher did hutry is sclf dear mother and father Give my
love to all in Quiren frinds that you dost so no more from me at this time
and God wil help me out of this trober of we pray to im for all our arts I
20 walke 39 by 11 Clok so no more from your loven husben and son at this
time Pray Clere my hoyse as sone as posibil.   ●

T26b   *Anon., 'Threatening letter from Durham' (1831)*

I was at yor hoose las neet, and myed mysel very comfortable. Ye hey nee
family, and yor just won man on the colliery, I see ye hev a greet lot of
rooms, and big cellars, and plenty wine and beer in them, which I got ma
share on. Noo I naw some at wor colliery that has three or fower lads and
5 lasses, and they live in won room not half as gude as yor cellar. I don't
pretend to naw very much, but I naw there shudnt be that much difference.
The only place we can gan to o the week ends is the yel hoose and hev a
pint. I dinna pretend to be a profit, but I naw this, and lots o ma marrows
na's te, that wer not tret as we owt to be, and a great filosopher says, to get
10 noledge is to naw wer ignerent. But weve just begun to find that oot, and ye
maisters and owners may luk oot, for yor not gan to get se much o yor awn
way, wer gan to hev some o wors now. I divent tell ye ma nyem, but I was
one o yor unwelcome visitors last neet.   ●

Anon., 'On the dialect of Craven' (1824)

I have attempted to make the second edition of the *Craven Glossary* more worthy of the reader's attention, by a large addition of words, and by numerous authorities, collected from ancient writers. Though this has been the most laborious part of my work, it has, at the same time, been the source
5 of the greatest pleasure; for whenever I found a Craven word thus sanctioned by antiquity, I was more and more convinced, that my native language is not the contemptible slang and *patois*, which the refined inhabitants of the Southern part of the kingdom are apt to account it; but that it is the language of crowned heads, of the court, and of the most
10 eminent English historians, divines, and poets, of former ages ...

Pent up in their native mountains, and principally engaged in agricultural pursuits, the inhabitants of this district had no opportunity of corrupting the purity of their language by the adoption of foreign idioms. But it has become a subject of much regret that, since the introduction of commerce,
15 and, in consequence of that, a greater intercourse, the simplicity of the language has, of late years, been much corrupted. Anxious, therefore, to hand it down to posterity unadulterated, the author has attempted to express, in a familiar dialogue, the chaste and nervous language of its unlettered natives.

20 TO'TH CONNER O' MY BOOK.

An this lile book'll gi'the onny plezer efter a hard day's wark, I sall be feaful fain on't. Bud sud onny outcumlins ivver awn this outside, staany plat, it may happen gee 'em some inseet into awyer plain mack o' talk; at they may larn, at awyer discowerse hez a meanin in't as weel as theirs; at
25 they mayn't snert an titter at huz, gin we wor hauf rocktons, but may under-cumstand, an be insensed by this book, lile as it is, at ya talk's aqual to another, seeabetide it explains yan's thoutes. Sud t'lads o' Craven yunce git a gliff o' what a seet o' words I've coud together, it'll happen mack 'em nut so keen, at iv'ry like, o'luggin into th'country a parcel of outlandish words,
30 er seea shamm'd o'talking their awn. For, o' lat years, young foak are grown seea maachy an see feeafully geen to knackin, at their parents er ill set to knaw what their barns er javverin about.

I'se at thy sarvice,   T'SETTER-OUT O'T BOOK.●

T28   *R. Forby, 'On provincial language' (1830)*

INTRODUCTION

From a writer who offers to the public a volume on a *Provincial Dialect*,
and ventures to announce his intention of confirming, by *authority* and
etymology, the strange words and phrases he is about to produce, some
introductory explanation of his design may reasonably be required. The
5   very mention of such an undertaking is likely to be received with ridicule,
contempt, or even disgust; as if little or nothing more could be expected,
than from analysing the rude jargon of some semi-barbarous tribe; as if,
being merely oral, and existing only among the unlettered rustic vulgar of a
particular district, *Provincial Language* were of little concern to general
10 readers, of still less to persons of refined education, and much below the
notice of philologists.

However justly this censure may be pronounced on a fabricated farrago
of cant, slang, or what has more recently been denominated *flash language*,
spoken by vagabonds, mendicants, and outcasts; by sharpers, swindlers, and
15 felons; for the better concealment of their illegal practices, and for their
more effectual separation from the 'good men and true' of regular and
decent society; it certainly is by no means applicable to any form
whatsoever of a *National Language*, constituting the vernacular tongue of
any province of that nation. Such forms, be they as many and as various as
20 they may, are all, in substance, remnants and derivatives of the language of
past ages, which were, at some time or other, in common use, though in
long process of time they have become only locally used and understood.

Such is the general character of *Provincial Language*, and to prove it on
behalf of a very considerable district of this country is the object of the
25 present undertaking ...

3. *Words*, which, though they may be supposed obsolete, are in fact still in
use, and likely long to continue so. These have also all been buoyant, and
have not sunk to the bottom; but, at many different times and places, have
been cast on shore; and the inhabitants of the bank, fortunate in finding so
30 valuable a sort of wreck, have duly estimated and retained the use of them.
This is the great body of Provincial Language, which, when it shall have
received the deserved attention not hitherto bestowed upon it, will yield so
ample a contribution of sound old English, as to form more than is yet imagined, of the bulk of even a large dictionary. Many of these words have
35 lurked in such profound obscurity, as never to have found their way into a
dictionary, or, indeed, into any other book.   ●

T29   *Anon., 'Dialect writing, Yorkshire' (1840)*

BAIRNSLA FOAKS' **ANNUAL,** AN ONY BODY ELS – AS AT IVE A MIND,
FOR'T YEAR OF OUR LORD 1840. BE TOM TREDDLEHOYLE.

(a)   TUT READERS AT ANNUAL.
WELL, yo see, am cumin it strong na; yo nivver egspecktad ta see owt a
5   this soat ha naw, but sea ad ment ta hed a *Annual twice a year*; but weve sa
menny yung childer at arr hause, an we am rockin't creddle so, an singing
am ta sleep, it fair daane maddles ma, do ye naw, but amsumivver al do me
gudist, ta mack wun satisfy ye, an it shall cum aght at stump end a ivvery
year, ha mean abaght Chresmas-like.
10   Well, na then, ha do ye all do? For me awn pairt, am varry well, thenk
ye; an ha hope yor all't same. If yo arn't, tak my advice, goa an liv at *Gruel-*
Thorp for a toathre daize, an yol soin mend, na mind that, an believe me
when ha say, Ha wish ye all a happy new year; so na, good by.
                                         Yors for ivver, TOM TREDDLEHOYLe.

15 (b)   MALLY MUFFINDOAF'S LETTER TUT QUEEN.
            ON HER INTENDED WEDDIN. *JENEWERRY,* 1840
Mistriss Queen, Ha Mistriss mi lass, yol think am varry brazand, am suar yo
will, at a poar wooman like me shud tak up a mesen ta write ta yo, but, mun,
ha cuddant help it, if e mud a hed all arr Taane geen ma, after at ad ead it
20 tawk't ovver at a Tea drinking, at yo wor goin ta get wed like in a toathre
weeks, to a furin chap at lives at tuther side at sea: mun yod naw me, if yo
wor to se me, becos yod rekalekt at wunce at it wor't same woman at yo laft
at soa, when yo wor e cummin up t'Owd Mill Lane like it coach ta Bairnsla;
ha wisht meny a time sin, at ad ax't boath yo an yer muther to a cumd ta ar
25 hause an hed a cup a Tea, mun yod a been az welcome az't flaars e May; av
been reight mad abaght it ivver sin yo may depend out, becos ad neidad
hauf a stoane at best flaar that mornin nobbat, so ha cud soin a thrawn a
cake intat ovan yo naw, then yod a bed a cumfatuble cup a tea, an gottan yer
sen nicely restad for anuther start like, but amsumivver yo moant think na
30 warse a me, for it slipt me memory az clean az a whisal, al asure ye. But na,
ta be reight serious, if yor goin ta get wed like, az foaks here say yo ar, ha
just want to gie ye a little bit a my advice, an that iz, doant yo gos an thraw
yer sen away, lass, same az ive dun, but befoar e goa onny farther, ha
shuddant like it ta be menshand ta that chap at's allas at yor hause heightin
35 and drinkin, at tha call Melban, wot av sed, cos if yo do, all Lunan al naw
varry soin, for eze allas slinking abaght, ...   ●

T30   *J. O. Halliwell, 'Specimens of English dialects' (1847)*

(a) Hampshire: *A Letter to the Editor of the Times, from a poor Man at Andover, on the Union Workhouse.*

Sir, – Hunger, as I've heerd say, breaks through Stone Walls; but yet I shodn't have thought of letting you know about my poor Missus's death,
5 but all my neibours say tell it out, and it can't do you no harm and may do others good, specially as Parliament is to meet soon, when the Gentlefoke will be talking about the working foke.

I be but a farmers working man, and was married to my Missus 26 years agone, and have three Childern living with me, one 10, another 7, and
10 t'other 3. I be subject to bad rumatiz, and never earns no more, as you may judge, than to pay rent and keep our bodies and souls together when we be all well. I was tended by Mr. Westlake when he was Union Doctor, but when the Guardians turned him out it was a bad job for all the Poor, and a precious bad job for me and mine.

15 Mr. Payne when he come to be our Union Doctor tended upon me up to almost the end of last April, but when I send up to the Union House as usual, Mr. Broad, the Releving Officer, send back word there was nothing for me, and Mr. Payne wodnt come no more. I was too bad to work, and had not Vittals for me, the Missus, and the young ones, so I was forced to sell
20 off the Bed, Bedstead, and furniture of the young ones, to by Vittals with, and then I and Missus and the young ones had only one bed for all of us. Missus was very bad, to, then, but as we knowd twere no use to ask the Union for nothink cept we'd all go into the Workhouse, and which Missus couldn't a bear, as she'd bin parted from the childern, she sends down to tell
25 Mr. Westlake how bad we was a doing off, and he comes to us directly, and tends upon us out of charity, and gives Missus Mutton and things, which he said, and we know'd too well, she wanted of, and he gives this out of his own Pocket.

Missus complaint growd upon her and she got so very bad, and Mr.
30 Westlake says to us, I do think the guardians wouldn't let your wife lay here and starve, but would do something for you if they knowed how bad you wanted things, and so, says he, I'll give you a Sertificate for some Mutton and things, and you take it to Mr. Broad, the releving officer. Well, I does this, and he tells me that hed give it to the guardians and let me know what
35 they said. I sees him again, and O, says he, I gived that Sertificate to the Guardians, but they chucked it a one side and said they wouldnt tend to no such thing, nor give you nothing, not even if Missus was dying, if you has anything to do with Mr. Westlake, as they had turned him off ...

(b) Lancashire: *A Letter printed and distributed in the procession that was*
40   *formed at Manchester in commemoration of free trade.*

Bury, July 15th, 1846.

TO ME LAWRD JHON RUSSELL, – Well, me Lawrd, yoan gett'n ut last up
to th' top o' th' ladthur, un th' heemust stave asnt brokk'n wi yo this time us
it did afore. Wayst see i' t'neaw wethur yo kun keep yur stonnin ur not;
45   awm rayther fyert ut yoan find it slippy un noan safe footin; but, heaw-
sumevvur, thirs nawt like thryin.

But wot'r yo fur dooin? Yo seemn to think ut o vast dyel o things wants
mendin, un yo thinkn reet, for they dun: – but kon yo mannidge um? Yur
fust job'll be a twoff un; un tho it'll be o sweet subjek, it'll ha sum seawr
50   stuff obeawt it. But seawr ur not yo mun stick like breek, un not let that
cantin, leawsy stuff obeawt 'slave-groon un free-groon' stop yo ...

(c) Suffolk: *A Letter in the Suffolk Dialect, written in the year* 1814.
DEAR FRINND,

I was axed some stounds agon by Billy P. our 'sesser at Mulladen to
55   make inquiration a' yeow if Master --- had pahd in that there money into the
Bank. Billy P. he fare kienda unasy about it, and when I see him at Church
ta day he sah timmy, says he, prah ha yeow wrot – so I kienda wef't um off
– and I sah, says I, I heent hard from Squire D --- as yit, but I dare sah, I
shall afore long – So prah write me some lines, an send me wahd, wutha the
60   money is pahd a' nae. I dont know what to make of our Malladen folks, nut
I – but somehow or another, theyre allus in dibles, an I'll be rot if I dont
begin to think some on em all tahn up scaly at last; an as to that there fulla
– he grow so big and so purdy that he want to be took down a peg – an I'm
glad to hare that yeow gint it it em properly at Wickhum ...

65   (d) Wiltshire: *The Genuine Remains of William Little, a Wiltshire man.*

I've allus bin as vlush o' money as a twoad is o' veathers; but if ever I
gets rich, I'll put it ael in Ziszeter bank, and not do as owld Smith, the
miller, did, comin' whoam vrom market one nite. Martal avraid o'thieves a
was, zo a puts his pound-bills and ael th' money a'd got about un in a hole
70   in the wall, and the next marnin' a' couldn't remember whereabouts 'twas,
and had to pull purty nigh a mile o' wall down before a' could vind it.
Stoopid owld wosbird!

Owld Jan Wilkins used to zay he allus cut's stakes, when a went a
hedgin', too lang, bekaze a' cou'd easily cut 'em sharter if a' wanted, but a'
75   cou'dnt make um langer if 'em was too shart. Zo zays I: zo I allus axes vor
more than I wants. Iv I gets that, well and good; but if I axes vor little, and
gets less, it's martal akkerd to ax a zecond time, d'ye kneow!   ●

T31 *R. W. Huntley, 'Dialect and the schools' (1868)*

Another reason, which at this present time renders dialects more worthy of remembrance, is the universal presence of the village schoolmaster. This personage usually considers that he places himself on the right point of elevation above his pupils, in proportion as he distinguishes his speech by
5 classical or semi-classical expressions; while the pastor of the parish, trained in the schools still more deeply, is very commonly unable to speak in a language fully 'understanded of the people,' and is a stranger to the vernacular tongue of those over whom he is set; so that he is daily giving an example which may bring in a latinized slip-slop. In addition to this, our
10 commercial pursuits are continually introducing American solecisms and vulgarisms. Each of these sources of change threaten deterioration. Many homely but powerful and manly words in our mother tongue appear to totter on the verge of oblivion. As long, however, as we can keep sacred our inestimable translation of the Word of God, to which let us add also our
15 Prayer-book, together with that most wonderful production of the mind of man, the works of Shakespeare, we may hope that we possess sheet-anchors, which will keep us from drifting very far into insignificance or vulgarity, and may trust that the strength of the British tongue may not be lost among the nations.
20   It has, moreover, been well observed that a knowledge of dialects is very necessary to the formation of an exact dictionary of our language. Many words are in common use only among our labouring classes, and accounted therefore vulgar, which are in fact nothing less than ancient terms, usually possessing much roundness, pathos, or power; and, what is more, found in
25 frequent use with our best writers of the Elizabethan period.
    ... The Cotswold dialect is remarkable for a change of letters in many words; for the addition or omission of letters; for frequent and usually harsh contractions and unusual idioms, with a copious use of pure Saxon words now obsolete, or nearly so. If these words were merely vulgar introductions,
30 like the pert and ever-changing slang of the London population, we should look upon them as undeserving of notice; but as they are still almost all to be drawn from undoubted and legitimate roots, as they are found in use in the works of ancient and eminent authors, and as they are in themselves so numerous as to render the dialect hard to be understood by those not ac-
35 quainted with them, they become worthy of explanation; and then they bring proof of the strength and manliness of the ancient English tongue, and they will generally compel us to acknowledge, that while our modern speech may possibly have gained in elegance and exactness from the Latin or Greek, it has lost, on the other hand, impressiveness and power. ●

T32   *Anon., 'Mock Suffolk dialect' (1869)*

TO MUSTER PUNCH, SIR, – I BAINT no skollard myself, but my bor JIM he
goo to parsons skule, and parson axed me what I thowt o'this here extrack
from a jarnal which he red to me, and as yow live in Lunnon praps you may
hev heerd on it t'sounded suffun like the *Paul Maul Gas Set*: –

5   Apart from any consideration of personal enjoyment, the ordinary subsistence of the
labourer is not sufficient to maintain him in the health and strength required for the
efficiency, and therefore for the economy, of labour, that it is impossible for him to make
any provision out of his scanty earnings for sickness and old age, and that all he has to
look forward to is a life of unintermitted toil, shut out from every hope of advancement,
10   and ending with his being pensioned as a pauper on the poor-rates.

Well say I arter person had explained all them long words I've heerd as
English folk hev paid down pretty hansom for emancipatun niggers and if
they'd ony do the same for us poor labrers we'd all sing O be joyful and
thank em for their help. Its werry bootiful to brag about how Britons never
15 never never wont be slaves but I'd like to know if slavun for a wife and
seven children upon 10 shillun a week with northun but the Workus to look
to and no Baccy, aint jist as bad a lookout as they niggers hev bin born to
and the wonder is faerm labrers dont rise up in Rebellion like them Jamaky
Blacks. And lookee here what parson read me out of the *Paul Maul*: –

20   It is a significant fact that no reformer, however advanced, has advocated the
admission of the agricultural labourer to the franchise. If use had not familiarised us to it,
we should be ashamed that this great class is decidedly in arrear of the general advance in
comfort and well-being, and is so wanting in independence and intelligence as to be
lower in the political scale than even the emancipated slaves in the United States.

25   It taint much of a complement to tell us British labrers we be Lower
down than niggers. But I dont keer for the francheese so much as for good
bread and cheese with now and then o' Sundays a crumb of good fat bacon.
Still if I wur a woter I'd arn a pint or 2 o'Beer at lection time may be and
praps my wages ud be riz for to secure my wote and influence! But as I say
30 to parson while us poor faermun labrers are treated wuss than niggers why
Gorm me! I say yar gret folk mustnt wonder at our poachun now and then to
arn a scrap o'meat. Nor yar faermurs mustnt wonder if we do em skimpun
sarvice. Fur it baint in human natur to do good work on bad feedun. And so
no moor at present from yars humbly to command,   GILES SCROGGINS.

35 P.S. Uppud o' thutty year a labrer at 10 shillun a week in the employ o'
MUSTER SKINFLINT nigh to Ipsidge Suffuk.   ●

T33a *F. H. Burnett, 'Literary Dialect (Lancashire)' (1877)*

'Let's hear,' cried a third member of the company.

'Gi' us th' tale owt an' owt, owd lad. Tha'rt th' one to do it graidely.'

Sammy applied a lucifer to the fragrant weed, and sucked at his pipe deliberately.

5 'It's noan so much of a tale,' he said, with an air of disparagement and indifference. 'Yo' chaps mak' so much out o' nowt. Th' parson's well enow i' his way, but,' in naïve self-satisfaction, 'I mun say he's a foo', and th' biggest foo' fur his size I ivver had th' pleasure o' seein'.'

They knew the right chord was touched. A laugh went round, but there
10 was no other interruption and Sammy proceeded.

'Whatten yo' lads think as th' first thing he says to me wur?' puffing vigorously. 'Why, he coos in an' sets hissen down, an' he swells hissen out loike a frog i' trouble, an' ses he, 'My friend, I hope you cling to th' rock o' ages.' An' ses I, 'No I dunnot nowt o' th' soart, an' be dom'd to yo'. It wur
15 na hos*pit*ible,' with a momentary touch of deprecation, – 'An' I dunnot say as it wur hospitible, but I wur na i' th' mood to be hospitible just at th' toime. It tuk him back too, but he gettin round after a bit, an' he tacklet me again, an' we had it back'ard and for'ard betwixt us for a good half hour. He said it wur Providence, an' I said, happen it wur, an' happen it wurn't. I wur
20 na so friendly and familiar wi' th' Lord as he seemed to be, so I could na tell foak aw he meant, and aw he did na mean. Sithee here, lads,' making a fist of his knotty old hand and laying it upon the table, 'that theer's what stirs me up wi' th' parson kind. They're allus settin down to explain what th' Lord-amoighty's up to, as if he wur a confidential friend o' theirs as they
25 wur bound to back up i' some road; an' they mun drag him in endways or sideways i' their talk whether or not, an' they wunnot be content to leave him to work fur hissen. Seems to me if I wur a disciple as they ca' it, I should be ashamed i' a manner to be allus apologisin' fur him as I believed in. I dunnot say for 'em to say *nowt*, but I *do* say for 'em not to be so dom'd
30 free an' easy about it. Now theer's th' owd parson, he's getten a lot o' Bible words as he uses, an' he brings 'em in by the scruft o' th' neck, if he canna do no better, – fur bring 'em in he mun, – an' it looks loike he's aw i' a fever till he's said 'em an' getten 'em off his moind. An' it seems to me loike, when he has said 'em, he soart o' straightens hissen out, an' feels
35 comfortable, loike a mon as has done a masterly job as conna be mended. As fur me, yo' know, I'm noan the Methody soart mysen, but I am na a foo', an' I know a foine like principle when I see it, an' this matter o' religion is a foine enow thing if yo' could get it straightforward an' plain wi'out so much trimmins. ●

T33b   *Anon., 'Parody of dialect writing' (1877)*

OUR NEW NOVEL. **THAT LASS O' TOWERY'S.**
By the Authors of Several other Things, &c. &c.
CHAPTER I. – *The Wo-Emma Mine.*

They were strange, bold, unwashed sort of people to look at. The
5 inexperienced Londoner coming among them for the first time, and asking
them, with an interested curiosity, 'how they were off for soap,' would have
received an answer that would have astonished him ...

CHAPTER IV. – *The Mill in the North Country.*
She knelt before him in the moonlight.
10   DAN BEERIE's formidable knob-stick was just about to descend on the
handsome, upturned face of his daughter – such matters were everyday
occurrence in Swiggin – when the weapon was whirled through the air, and
a strong hand was laid on the brute's shoulder.
      Shrieking a curse, DAN BEERIE turned on the man who had cared to
15 interfere with his evening's amusement.
      It was NEGUS BARCROW, The Young Engineer.
      'Yo domm'd dummer-tailed bolthead,' roared DAN BEERIE, fiercely.
'Yo yung poopy-cur snig-snagged boler! oil jewdy thee putty tupped naws,
an giv yo siccan shuv i' th' oi, as yo'll reccomember fur ivvur, domm'd av
20 oi doon't, th' oi gows t' gallus fur't!' ...
      EMMY raised a loud cry. 'A fyt! a fyt! t' owd feether's fytin an' millin
Yung Ing'neer! Coom an, av yo be coomin! tiz ar reel beet o' jam, tiz!' ...

* At present we will offer no opinion as to the *quality* of the dialect. We have sent a
Special Commissioner to the North, who, being a gentleman of considerable imitative
25 power, will give us, on his return, some idea of what the dialect may be. We don't
recollect anything exactly like it, but perhaps Mr. TAYLOR, who plays the part of '*Owd
Sammy*' in *Liz*, will step in, and give us some explanation. In the meantime we will be
cautious. – ED.
* Our Special Commissioner with a dictionary has not yet returned from the North, nor
30 has he sent us either a line or a telegram. He was sent there to inquire into the dialect and
the character of the people as represented in this story. Perhaps Miss ROSE LECLERQ,
who is now performing most admirably in *Liz*, would kindly look in one morning and
give us her opinion on the subject. Need we say we should be only too delighted to profit
by her experience. – ED.
35   *Extract from Letter of the three Co-Authors of the New Provincial Novel Company
Limited, to the Editor.* – 'We say! isn't it going on capitally? Here's your fine fresh
dialect, eh? Post the tin, sagacious *Redacteur, et croyez en nous à jamais*, as we say in
Old Gaul. Never was such local colouring, eh? Worth all the money! And then the
Curate! *that* fetches the Sunday readers.- No harm where there's a Curate. 'Yours ever,
CO-AUTHORS.'   ●

T34   *T. Hardy, 'Letter and essay on dialect' (1881–3)*

SIR, – In your last week's article on the 'Papers of the Manchester Literary Club,' there seems a slight error, which, though possibly accidental, calls for a word of correction from myself. In treating of dialect in novels, I am instanced by the writer as one of two popular novelists 'whose thorough
5 knowledge of the dialectical peculiarities of certain districts has tempted them to write whole conversations which are, to the ordinary reader, nothing but a series of linguistic puzzles.' So much has my practice been the reverse of this (as a glance at my novels will show), that I have been reproved for too freely translating dialect-English into readable English, by those of your
10 contemporaries who attach more importance to the publication of local niceties of speech than I do. The rule of scrupulously preserving the local idiom, together with the words which have no synonym among those in general use, while printing in the ordinary way most of those local expressions which are but a modified articulation of words in use elsewhere, is the
15 rule I usually follow; and it is, I believe, generally recognised as the best, where every such rule must of necessity be a compromise, more or less unsatisfactory to lovers of form. It must, of course, be always a matter for regret that, in order to be understood, writers should be obliged thus slightingly to treat varieties of English which are intrinsically as genuine,
20 grammatical, and worthy of the royal title as is the all-prevailing competitor which bears it, whose only fault was that they happened not to be central, and therefore were worsted in the struggle for existence, when a uniform tongue became a necessity among the advanced classes of the population. – I am, Sir, &c., THOMAS HARDY.

25 ... when the class lies somewhat out of the ken of ordinary society the caricature begins to be taken as truth. Moreover, the original is held to be an actual unit of the multitude signified. He ceases to be an abstract figure and becomes a sample ... As, to the eye of a diver, contrasting colours shine out by degrees from what has originally painted itself of an unrelieved earthy
30 hue, so would shine out the characters, capacities, and interests of these people to him. He would, for one thing, find that the language, instead of being a vile corruption of cultivated speech, was a tongue with grammatical inflection rarely disregarded by his entertainer, though his entertainer's children would occasionally make a sad hash of their talk. Having attended
35 the National School they would mix the printed tongue as taught therein with the unwritten, dying, Wessex English that they had learnt of their parents, the result of this transitional state of theirs being a composite language without rule or harmony. ●

T35   *W. Barnes, 'Queen's speech and dialect translation' (1886)*

In somewhat of a merry mood, I was one day minded to see how far our homely Dorset speech could give the meaning of the seemingly ministerial wording of the so-called Queen's speech on the opening of Parliament in 1884. Her Majesty's speech as written and read in Her Majesty's name.
5 Here are samples of a few clauses –

'My Lords and Gentlemen. – The satisfaction with which I ordinarily release you from discharging the duties of the Session is on the present occasion qualified by a sincere regret that an important part of your labours should have failed to result in a legislative enactment.'

10   *(1) The lightheartedness I do mwostly veel when I do let ye off vrom the business upon your hands in the Sessions, is theäse time a little bit damped, owen to a ranklen in my mind, that a goodish lot o' your work vell short o' comen into anything lik laws.*

'The most friendly intercourse continues to subsist between myself and
15 all foreign Powers.'

(2) The very best o' veelens be still a-kept up, in deälens between myzelf an' all o' the outlandish powers.

'Diplomatic relations have been resumed with Mexico, and a preliminary agreement has been signed, providing for the negotiation of a new Treaty of
20 Commerce and Navigation.'

(3) Zome deälèns have a-been a-took up ageän wi' Mexico, an' we've bwoth a-put our hands to an understanden-like that we'd meäke a new bargain about treäde and seafeärèn.

'I have to lament the failure of the efforts which were made by the
25 European Powers assembled in the recent Conference to devise means for restoring that equilibrium in the finances of Egypt which is so important an element in its well-being and good order.'

*(4) I can't but be ever so zorry that nothèn come out o' the doèns o' the Girt Powers o' Europe that put their heads together tother day in the girt
30 talking a' tryèn to vind out zome wäy o' puttèn to rights ageân the money-stock ov Egypt, a thing that do goo so vur towards the well-beèn and well-dooèn o't.*

'My Lords and Gentlemen, – I continue to view with unabated satisfaction the mitigation and diminution of agrarian crime in Ireland, and
35 the substantial improvement in the condition of its people.'

(5) I do still zee to my unlessened happiness how vield crimes be a milden'd and a lessen'd in Ireland, and in what a soundly bettered plight be the vo'k. ●

T36   *Anon., 'Appeal for* EDD *support' (1895)*

TO THE RIGHT HONOURABLE ARTHUR JAMES BALFOUR, M.P.,
FIRST LORD OF H.M.'S TREASURY
SIR,   I DESIRE to bring to your notice the case of Mr. JOSEPH WRIGHT,
M.A., Ph.D., Deputy Professor of Comparative Philology in the University
5 of Oxford, as being that of one who deserves to receive a Pension from the
Civil List, in connexion with the extraordinary efforts he has made to forward the study of modern English dialects; and I respectfully solicit your
attention to the following particulars: –
    1. In 1873, THE ENGLISH DIALECT SOCIETY was established, with
10 the express object of collecting material for the compilation of a large and
comprehensive DICTIONARY OF ENGLISH DIALECTS, on a scale
befitting the subject ... Now that this work of collection is almost finished,
the Society will be brought to an end, at the close of the present year ...
    6. In 1889, Professor JOSEPH WRIGHT prepared some specimen-pages
15 of the DIALECT DICTIONARY, mainly at my private expense; the result
being that he pronounced the material to be insufficient. But by the
extraordinary efforts that have since been made, as above described, it is
now as complete as it is ever likely to be. Practically, further delay is impossible. The dialects are dying, and the competent helpers who understand
20 them are waxing old. In a few years it will be too late. The one sole opportunity for producing a DIALECT DICTIONARY really worthy of our country will soon pass by; and the whole of the outcome of twenty-two years of
work will then remain unpublished for ever. The publication must begin
during the present year; because every year that now passes renders it
25 increasingly difficult to obtain correct information as to the exact
pronunciations in use, and as to the exact shade of meaning of the words
recorded ...
    It is our sincere hope that a similar sum [of £250 a year] may be granted
to Professor JOSEPH WRIGHT, in order that he may at last be enabled to
30 carry out to a successful issue a work upon which so many hundreds of
workers have been employed for more than twenty years, – a work of the
highest interest to many of our fellow countrymen in all parts of the Empire,
and of the very greatest importance to all students of English Literature as
well as of Teutonic Philology, – a work such as no other nation is ever
35 likely to produce, and one which cannot fail to reflect very great credit upon
the nation which it most concerns.
    I have the honour to be, Sir,
    Your obedient servant, WALTER W. SKEAT,
        Professor of Anglo-Saxon in the University of Cambridge. ●

T37   *G. B. Shaw, 'How to render dialect' (1900)*

All the same, if I were to attempt to represent current 'smart' Cockney speech as I have attempted to represent Drinkwater's, without the niceties of Mr Sweet's Romic alphabets, I am afraid I should often have to write dahn tahn and cowcow as being at least nearer to the actual sound than down
5 town and cocoa. And this would give such offence that I should have to leave the country; for nothing annoys a native speaker of English more than a faithful setting down in phonetic spelling of the sounds he utters. He imagines that a departure from conventional spelling indicates a departure from the correct standard English of good society. Alas! this correct standard
10 English of good society is unknown to phoneticians. It is only one of the many figments that bewilder our poor snobbish brains. No such thing exists; but what does that matter to people trained from infancy to make a point of honor of belief in abstractions and incredibilities? And so I am compelled to hide Lady Cicely's speech under the veil of conventional orthography.
15 I need not shield Drinkwater, because he will never read my book. So I have taken the liberty of making a special example of him, as far as that can be done without a phonetic alphabet, for the benefit of the mass of readers outside London who still form their notions of cockney dialect on Sam Weller. When I came to London in 1876, the Sam Weller dialect had passed
20 away so completely that I should have given it up as a literary fiction if I had not discovered it surviving in a Middlesex village, and heard of it from an Essex one. Some time in the eighties the late Andrew Tuer called attention in the Pall Mall Gazette to several peculiarities of modern cockney, and to the obsolescence of the Dickens dialect that was still being
25 copied from book to book by authors who never dreamt of using their ears, much less of training them to listen. Then came Mr Anstey's cockney dialogues in Punch, a great advance, and Mr Chevalier's coster songs and patter ...
In America, representations of English speech dwell too derisively on the
30 dropped or interpolated h. American writers have apparently not noticed the fact that the south English h is not the same as the never-dropped Irish and American h, and that to ridicule an Englishman for dropping it is as absurd as to ridicule the whole French and Italian nation for doing the same. The American h, helped out by a general agreement to pronounce wh as hw, is
35 tempestuously audible, and cannot be dropped without being immediately missed. The London h is so comparatively quiet at all times, and so completely inaudible in wh, that it probably fell out of use simply by escaping the ears of children learning to speak.   ●

III On literature and criticism

T38   *T. Bowdler, 'Revising Shakespeare' (1807)*

That Shakespeare is the first of dramatic writers will be denied by few, and I doubt whether it will be denied by any who have really studied his works, and compared the beauties which they contain with the very finest productions either of our own or of former ages. It must, however, be acknowl-

5   edged by his warmest admirers, that some defects are to be found in the writings of our immortal bard. The language is not always faultless. Many words and expressions occur which are of so indecent a nature as to render it highly desirable that they should be erased. Of these, the greater part were evidently introduced to gratify the bad taste of the age in which he lived,

10   and the rest may perhaps be ascribed to his own unbridled fancy. But neither the vicious taste of the age, nor the most brilliant effusions of wit, can afford an excuse for profaneness of obscenity; and if these could be obliterated, the transcendent genius of the poet would undoubtedly shine with more unclouded lustre. To banish everything of this nature from his

15   writings is the object of the present undertaking. It is the wish of the editor to render the plays of Shakespeare unsullied by any scene, by any speech, or, if possible, by any word that can give pain to the most chaste, or offence to the most religious of his readers. Of the latter kind the examples are by no means numerous, for the writings of our author are for the most part

20   favourable to religion and morality. There are, however, in some of his plays allusions to Scripture, which are introduced so unnecessarily, and on such trifling occasions, and are expressed with so much levity, as to call imperiously for their erasement. As an example of this kind, I may quote a scene in the fifth act of *Love's Labour's Lost*, respecting one of the most

25   serious and awful passages in the New Testament. I flatter myself that every reader of the *Family Shakespeare* will be pleased at perceiving that what is so manifestly improper, is not permitted to be seen in it ...

    My great objects in this undertaking are to remove from the writings of Shakespeare some defects which diminish their value, and at the same time

30   to present to the public an edition of his plays, which the parent, the guardian, and the instructor of youth may place without fear in the hands of the pupil; and from which the pupil may derive instruction as well as pleasure, may improve his moral principles while he refines his taste; and without incurring the danger of being hurt with any indelicacy of expression,

35   may learn in the fate of *Macbeth*, that even a kingdom is dearly purchased, if virtue be the price of the acquisition.   THOMAS BOWDLER ●

T39   *S. T. Coleridge, 'Criticism of Wordsworth' (1817)*

> *Examination of the tenets peculiar to Mr. Wordsworth – Rustic life*
> *(above all,* low *and* rustic life*) especially unfavourable to the formation of*
> *a human diction – The* best *parts of language the product of philosophers,*
> *not of clowns or shepherds – Poetry essentially ideal and generic – The lan-*
> 5 *guage of Milton as much the language of* real *life, yea, incomparably more*
> *so than that of the cottager.*

As far then as Mr. Wordsworth in his preface contended, and most ably
contended, for a reformation in our poetic diction, as far as he has evinced
the truth of passion, and the *dramatic* propriety of those figures and meta-
10 phors in the original poets, which, stripped of their justifying reasons, and
converted into mere artifices of connection or ornament, constitute the
characteristic falsity in the poetic style of the moderns; and as far as he has,
with equal acuteness and clearness, pointed out the process by which this
change was effected, and the resemblances between that state into which the
15 reader's mind is thrown by the pleasureable confusion of thought from an
unaccustomed train of words and images; and that state which is induced by
the natural language of impassioned feeling; he undertook a useful task, and
deserves all praise, both for the attempt and for the execution. The provoca-
tions to this remonstrance in behalf of truth and nature were still of
20 perpetual recurrence before and after the publication of this preface. I
cannot likewise but add, that the comparison of such poems of merit, as
have been given to the public within the last ten or twelve years, with the
majority of those produced previously to the appearance of that preface,
leave no doubt on my mind, that Mr. Wordsworth is fully justified in
25 believing his efforts to have been by no means ineffectual ...

My own differences from certain supposed parts of Mr. Wordsworth's
theory ground themselves on the assumption, that his words had been
rightly interpreted, as purporting that the proper diction for poetry in
general consists altogether in a language taken, with due exceptions, from
30 the mouths of men in real life, a language which actually constitutes the
natural conversation of men under the influence of natural feelings. My
objection is, first, that in *any* sense this rule is applicable only to *certain*
classes of poetry; secondly, that even to these classes it is not applicable,
except in such a sense, as hath never by any one (as far as I know or have
35 read) been denied or doubted; and lastly, that as far as, and in that degree in
which it is *practicable,* yet as a *rule* it is useless, if not injurious, and
therefore either need not, or ought not to be practised. The poet informs his
reader, that he had generally chosen *low* and *rustic* life; but not *as* low and

rustic, or in order to repeat that pleasure of doubtful moral effect, which
40 persons of elevated rank and of superior refinement oftentimes derive from
a happy *imitation* of the rude unpolished manners and discourse of their
inferiors. For the pleasure so derived may be traced to three exciting causes.
The first is the naturalness, in *fact*, of the things represented. The second is
the apparent naturalness of the *representation* as raised and qualified by an
45 imperceptible infusion of the author's own knowledge and talent, which
infusion does, indeed, constitute it an *imitation*, as distinguished from a
mere *copy*. The third cause may be found in the reader's conscious feeling
of his superiority awakened by the contrast presented to him; even as for the
same purpose the kings and great barons of yore retained sometimes *actual*
50 clowns and fools, but more frequently shrewd and witty fellows in that
character. These, however, were not Mr. Wordsworth's objects. *He* chose
low and rustic life, 'because in that condition the essential passions of the
heart find a better soil, in which they can attain their maturity, are less under
restraint, and speak a plainer and more emphatic language; because in that
55 condition of life our elementary feelings coexist in a state of greater
simplicity, and consequently may be more accurately contemplated, and
more forcibly communicated.'   ●

T40   *W. T. Moncrieff, 'Drama of low life London' (1826)*

Bob. Now, landlord, arter that 'ere drap of max, suppose we haves a
drain o' heavy wet, just by way of cooling our chaffers – mine's as dry as a
chip – and, I say, do you hear, let's have a two-penny burster (loaf), half a
quartern o' bees vax, a ha'porth o' ingens, and a dollop o' salt along vith it,
5 vill you?
Mace. Bellay! a burster and bees vax – ingens and salt here... Now then,
here you are, Muster Grimmuzzle. (*Holding out his right hand for the
money, and keeping the porter away with the other.*)
Bob. That's your sort, give us a hold on it. (*Takes Mace's empty hand.*)
10 Vy, vhere?
Mace. (*keeping the porter back*). Vy here.
Bob. Oh! you are afeard of the blunt, are you?
Mace. No, it an't that; only I'm no schollard, so I alvays takes the blunt
vith von hand, and gives the pot vith t'other – It saves chalk, and prewents
15 mistakes, you know.
Bob. You're a downey von – you'll not give a chance avay if you knows
it.   ●

T41   *A. C. Holbrook, 'Title-page and dedication' (1834)*

PATRONIZED BY HER ROYAL HIGHNESS
THE DUCHESS OF KENT.
REALITIES AND REFLECTIONS.
A *SERIES OF ORIGINAL TALES*, FOUNDED ON FACTS,
5   AND DESIGNED UNDER AN ENTERTAINING FORM
STRONGLY TO IMPRESS UPON THE YOUTHFUL MIND,
A REVERENCE FOR CHRISTIAN AND SOCIAL DUTIES.

TO HER ROYAL HIGHNESS THE DUCHESS OF KENT.
Madam, With unfeigned sentiments of gratitude, permit me to acknowledge
10   the essential service your Royal Highness's condescension has conferred, in
allowing me the use of a Name equally beloved and respected by all classes.
– While unostentatious benevolence – maternal solicitude – and propriety of
conduct – are considered *feminine* virtues – so long will your Royal
Highness retain the affections of an enlightened People. – That your Royal
15   Highness and your daughter, the Princess Victoria, may long and happily
enjoy blessings so justly merited, is the heartfelt prayer of your Royal
Highness's most grateful, and truly Devoted Servant, THE AUTHORESS.

To their Royal Highnesses the Duchesses of Cumberland, and
Gloucester, my sincerest thanks are likewise due; most feelingly and
20   amiably they honoured with their patronage an unknown individual, whose
only recommendation to their favour, was an industrious effort to relieve
sudden, and, I trust undeserved embarassment.

In appending names where rank and character are united, I hope I
indulge a justifiable propensity, and that it will be regarded by them with
25   the condescending affability I have hitherto experienced.

To these distinguished persons are added a numerous list of the Clergy
and Gentry of this, and the surrounding Counties. Were it possible that the
motives for this exertion could be rightly understood, and justly
appreciated, great indeed would be the satisfaction of my liberal
30   subscribers. Let it suffice, the humble applicant looks forward to brighter
scenes than the late dreary atmosphere presented.

To say more would be trespassing on time and patience, yet I cannot take
leave of friends so honoured, without repeating how sincerely, I must ever
feel myself their indebted, and Obliged Servant
35   Thame, September 18th, 1834.   ANN CATHARINE HOLBROOK ●

T42   *G. W. M. Reynolds, 'Gothic novel' (1840)*

PROLOGUE

It was the month of January, 1516.

The night was dark and tempestuous; – the thunder growled around; – the lightning flashed at short intervals; – and the wind swept furiously along, in sudden and fitful gusts.

5   The streams of the great Black Forest of Germany bubbled in playful melody no more, but rushed on with deafening din, mingling their torrent-roar with the wild creaking of the huge oaks, the rustling of the firs, the howling of the affrighted wolves, and the hollow voices of the storm.

The dense black clouds were driven restlessly athwart the sky; and when 10 the vivid lightning gleamed forth with rapid and eccentric glare, it seemed as if the dark jaws of some hideous monster, floating high above, opened to vomit flame.

And as the abrupt but furious gusts of wind swept through the forest they raised strange echoes – as if the impervious mazes of that mighty wood 15 were the abode of hideous fiends and evil spirits, who responded in shrieks, moans, and lamentations, to the fearful din of the tempest.

It was indeed an appalling sight!

An old – old man sat in his little cottage on the verge of the Black Forest.

He had numbered ninety years: his head was completely bald – his 20 mouth was toothless – his long beard was white as snow – and his limbs were feeble and trembling.

He was alone in the world: his wife – his children – his grand-children – all his relations, in fine, *save one* – had preceded him on that long last voyage from which no traveller returns.

25   And that *one* was a grand-daughter – a beauteous girl of sixteen, who had hitherto been his solace and his comfort, but who had suddenly disappeared – he knew not how – a few days previously to the time when we discover him seated thus lonely in his poor cottage.

But perhaps she also was dead? An accident might have snatched her 30 away from him, and sent her spirit to join those of her father and mother, her sisters, and her brothers, whom a terrible pestilence – the *Black Death* – hurried to the tomb a few years before? ...

'Oh! Agnes,' he murmured, in a tone indicative of a breaking heart, 'how couldst thou have thus abandoned me? Didst thou quit the old man to follow 35 some youthful lover, who will buoy thee up with bright hopes, and then deceive thee? O Agnes – my darling! hast thou left me to perish without a soul to close my eyes?'   ●

T43   *Anon., 'Popular prose romance' (1846)*

VARNEY, THE VAMPIRE; OR, THE FEAST OF BLOOD. A ROMANCE

MIDNIGHT. – THE HAIL-STORM. – THE DREADFUL VISITOR. – THE VAMPYRE.

The solemn tones of an old cathedral clock have announced midnight – the air is thick and heavy – a strange, death-like stillness pervades all nature.
5 Like the ominous calm which precedes some more than usually terrific outbreak of the elements, they seem to have paused even in their ordinary fluctuations, to gather a terrific strength for the great effort. A faint peal of thunder now comes from far off. Like a signal gun for the battle of the winds to begin, it appeared to awaken them from their lethargy, and one
10 awful, warring hurricane swept over a whole city ...

    Oh, how the storm raged! Hail – rain – wind. It was, in very truth, an awful night.

    There is an antique chamber in an ancient house. Curious and quaint carvings adorn the walls, and the large chimney-piece is a curiosity of itself.
15 The ceiling is low, and a large bay window, from roof to floor, looks to the west. The window is latticed, and filled with curiously painted glass and rich stained pieces, which send in a strange, yet beautiful light, when sun or moon shines into the apartment. There is but one portrait in that room, although the walls seem panelled for the express purpose of containing a
20 series of pictures. That portrait is of a young man, with a pale face, a stately brow, and a strange expression about the eyes, which no one cared to look on twice. There is a stately bed in that chamber, of carved walnut-wood is it made, rich in design and elaborate in execution; one of those works of art which owe their existence to the Elizabethan era. It is hung with heavy
25 silken and damask furnishing; nodding feathers are at its corners – covered with dust are they, and they lend a funereal aspect to the room. The floor is of polished oak.

    God! how the hail dashes on the old bay window! Like an occasional discharge of mimic musketry, it comes clashing, beating, and cracking upon
30 the small panes; but they resist it – their small size saves them; the wind, the hail, the rain, expend their fury in vain ...

    She has endured much fatigue, and the storm does not awaken her; but it can disturb the slumbers it does not possess the power to destroy entirely. The turmoil of the elements wakes the senses, although it cannot entirely
35 break the repose they have lapsed into.

    Oh, what a world of witchery was in that mouth, slightly parted, and exhibiting within the pearly teeth that glistened even in the faint light that

came from that bay window. How sweetly the long silken eyelashes lay
upon the cheek. Now she moves, and one shoulder is entirely visible –
40   whiter, fairer than the spotless clothing of the bed on which she lies, is the
smooth skin of that fair creature, just budding into womanhood, and in that
transition state which presents to us all the charms of the girl – almost of the
child, with the more matured beauty and gentleness of advancing years.

Was that lightning? Yes – an awful, vivid, terrifying flash – then a
45   roaring peal of thunder, as if a thousand mountains were rolling one over
the other in the blue vault of Heaven! Who sleeps now in that ancient city?
Not one living soul. The dread trumpet of eternity could not more
effectually have awakened any one.

The hail continues. The wind continues. The uproar of the elements
50   seems at its height. Now she wakens – that beautiful girl on the antique bed;
she opens those eyes of celestial blue, and a faint cry of alarm bursts from
her lips. ...

(2) Undated playbill:

The Sleeping Chamber of Flora Bannerworth.
55   MIDNIGHT. THE HAIL STORM. THE FEARFUL VISITOR.
THE VAMPIRE! How the Graves give up their dead, and how the night
hideously groans with shrieks. **'It was in truth an awful Night.'** She
Weeps! – She Prays! – the door is burst open – The Conflict – My Sister –
My Sister – the hideous form leaves its Victim – 'T'is most awful – **The
60   Pursuit. The Pistol Shot.** Despair and Terror of Flora – A New Enterprise
– Hark it comes again – fear not, her hand is upon the Pistol – The Window
opens Oh! horrible it is there again – She Fires – He is wounded – THE
STORM! THE MILL IN FLAMES. The Madness of Flora – the Lover –
Fearful Disclosure – the Pursuit – Disappearance of the Body. A VISIT TO
65   THE VAULTS. **THE MYSTERY, The COFFIN & ABSENCE of the
DEAD**. The Terrified Servant – the Letter. **The Study of Sir FRANCIS
VARNEY**. The announcement – the Resemblance – the Visit –
YES! A VISIT FROM THE TOMB! What shall I do? Kill him! Destroy
him! – Scattered to the Winds of Heaven! **Chamber** of **FLORA BANNER-
70   WORTH**. The Meeting of Charles and Flora – Revolution of Charles – I
will hurl his fiendish soul to perdition – Flora's reflection – Those sounds –
It comes again – the door opens 'T'is **VARNEY THE VAMPYRE!**   ●

Edith, my child, thou hast not forgotten my lessons, I trow; thou singest the hymns I gave thee, and neglectest not to wear the relic round thy neck ...'

'If thou beest Saxon, shame us not with thy ceorlish manners; crave pardon of this Norman thegn, who will doubtless yield it to thee in pity. Uncover
5 thy face – and – ...'
When Harold leaves London, I trow well towards that house will his road wend; for there lives Edith the swan's-neck, with her awful grandam the Wicca. If thou art there a little after noon, depend on it thou wilt see Harold riding that way.

10 Methought I saw death writ on his countenance, and I bribed the German leach ... the Atheling knows it not, but he bears within him the seeds of a mortal complaint. Thou wottest well what cause I have to hate Earl Harold.

●

(a) Northern dialect from *Hard Times* (1854)
Every line in his face deepened as he said it, and put in its affecting evidence of the suffering he had undergone.
'From bad to worse, from worse to worsen. She left me. She disgraced
5 herseln everyways, bitter and bad. She coom back, she coom back, she coom back. What could I do t' hinder her? I ha' walked the streets nights long, ere ever I'd go home. I ha' gone t' th' brigg, minded to fling myseln ower, and ha' no more on't. I ha' bore that much, that I were owd when I were young.'
10 Mrs. Sparsit, easily ambling along with her netting-needles, raised the Coriolanian eyebrows and shook her head, as much as to say, 'The great know trouble as well as the small. Please to turn your humble eye in my direction.'
'I ha' paid her to keep awa' fra' me. These five year I ha' paid her. I ha'
15 gotten decent fewtrils about me agen. I ha' lived hard and sad, but not ashamed and fearfo' a' the minnits o' my life. Last night, I went home. There she lay upon my har-stone! There it IS!'

(b) Parody of turgid rhetoric from *Nicholas Nickleby* (1838-9)
'My conduct, Pugstyles,' said Mr Gregsbury, looking round upon the
20 deputation with gracious magnanimity – 'My conduct has been, and ever will be, regulated by a sincere regard for the true and real interests of this

great and happy country. Whether I look at home, or abroad; whether I behold the peaceful industrious communities of our island home: her rivers covered with steamboats, her roads with locomotives, her streets with cabs,
25 her skies with balloons of a power and magnitude hitherto unknown in the history of aeronautics in this or any other nation − I say, whether I look merely at home, or, stretching my eyes farther, contemplate the boundless prospect of conquest and possession − achieved by British perseverance and British valour − which is outspread before me, I clasp my hands, and turn-
30 ing my eyes to the broad expanse above my head, exclaim, "Thank Heaven, I am a Briton!".'

(c) Parody of 'genteel' Latinate diction from *Our Mutual Friend* (1864-5)
  'First,' returned Mrs Wilfer solemnly, 'if you persist in what I cannot but regard as conduct utterly incompatible with the equipage in which you
35 arrive −'
  ('Which I do, Ma.')
  'First, then, you put the fowls down to the fire.'
  'To − be − sure!' cried Bella; 'and flour them, and twirl them round, and there they go!' sending them spinning at a great rate. 'What's next, Ma?'
40   'Next,' said Mrs Wilfer with a wave of her gloves, expressive of abdication under protest from the culinary throne, 'I would recommend examination of the bacon in the sauce-pan on the fire, and also of the pota- toes by the application of a fork. Preparation of the greens will further be- come necessary, if you persist in this unseemly demeanour.'
45   'As of course I do, Ma.'

(d) Rhapsodical prose from the beginning of *Bleak House* (1853)
  Fog everywhere. Fog up the river, where it flows among great aits and meadows; fog down the river, where it rolls defiled among the tiers of ship- ping, and the water-side pollutions of a great (and dirty) city. Fog on the
50 Essex marshes, fog on the Kentish heights ... Fog in the eyes and throats of ancient Greenwich pensioners, wheezing by the fireside of their wards; fog in the stem and bowl of the afternoon pipe of the wrathful skipper, down in his close cabin; fog cruelly pinching the toes and fingers of his shivering little 'prentice boy on deck. Chance people on the bridges peeping over the
55 parapets into a nether sky of fog, with fog all round them, as if they were up in a balloon and hanging in the misty clouds.   ●

G. Eliot, 'Literary criticism' (1856)

ART. VI. – SILLY NOVELS BY LADY NOVELISTS.

SILLY Novels by Lady Novelists are a genus with many species, determined by the particular quality of silliness that predominates in them – the frothy, the prosy, the pious, or the pedantic. But it is a mixture of all these – a composite order of feminine fatuity, that produces the largest class
5 of such novels, which we shall distinguish as the *mind-and-millinery* species. The heroine is usually an heiress, probably a peeress in her own right, with perhaps a vicious baronet, an amiable duke, and an irresistible younger son of a marquis as lovers in the foreground, a clergyman and a poet sighing for her in the middle distance, and a crowd of undefined
10 adorers dimly indicated beyond. Her eyes and her wit are both dazzling; her nose and her morals are alike free from any tendency to irregularity; she has a superb *contralto* and a superb intellect; she is perfectly well-dressed and perfectly religious; she dances like a sylph, and reads the Bible in the original tongues. Or it may be that the heroine is not an heiress – that rank
15 and wealth are the only things in which she is deficient; but she infallibly gets into high society, she has the triumph of refusing many matches and securing the best, and she wears some family jewels or other as a sort of crown of righteousness at the end. Rakish men either bite their lips in impotent confusion at her repartees, or are touched to penitence by her
20 reproofs, which, on appropriate occasions, rise to a lofty strain of rhetoric; indeed, there is a general propensity in her to make speeches, and to rhapsodize at some length when she retires to her bedroom. In her recorded conversations she is amazingly eloquent, and in her unrecorded conversations, amazingly witty. She is understood to have a depth of insight
25 that looks through and through the shallow theories of philosophers, and her superior instincts are a sort of dial by which men have only to set their clocks and watches, and all will go well. The men play a very subordinate part by her side. You are consoled now and then by a hint that they have affairs, which keeps you in mind that the working-day business of the world
30 is somehow being carried on, but ostensibly the final cause of their existence is that they may accompany the heroine on her 'starring' expedition through life. They see her at a ball, and are dazzled; at a flower-show, and they are fascinated; on a riding excursion, and they are witched by her noble horsemanship; at church, and they are awed by the sweet
35 solemnity of her demeanour. She is the ideal woman in feelings, faculties, and flounces.   ●

T47 *Anon., 'Criticism of popular novels' (^{8}1859)*

Fashionable novels. The public taste having been attracted to prose works of fiction as the most agreeable form of light reading, a whole host of labourers offered themselves as candidates for employment in the vineyard. The immense circulation of the novels of Scott, and the high remunerative
5 price which he was known to have received from the publishers, proved as irresistible a temptation to literary adventurers as is the discovery of a new gold-field to the unemployed population of a continent. Ingenuity was racked for subjects. Fashionable life was supposed, not without reason, to have some interest for those of the middle classes, always furnishing a large
10 number of readers, who lived beyond its pale; and accordingly the market was inundated with novels, each in three volumes, purporting to give glimpses of the serene existence of the arbiters of Almack's, and containing revelations of the mysteries of the boudoir and the ball-room. It is no exaggeration to say, that neither before nor since has there ever been such a
15 deluge of absolute inanity. The few debutants in print who really had the means of describing such society from actual knowledge, were for the most part needy dowagers, illiterate danglers, or very impudent pretenders; yet such was the rage, at one time, for anything which savoured of high life, that large sums were given by a certain class of publishers for novels of the
20 most trashy description, provided the author or authoress had a name recognisable in the *Court Guide* or in the *Peerage*. Such exclusiveness, however, in dealing with an exclusive subject, could not be maintained; and novels purporting to depict the etherealization of fashion, the sayings and doings of the earthly Olympus, were fabricated by clever rogues, who drew
25 their inspiration from the pothouse. We are bound to say that, in point of talent, the mere imitators excelled those who professed to draw from reality. Both were most ludicrous caricaturists; but while we yawned over the platitudes of the one class of writers, mirth was actively excited by the preposterous misconceptions of the other.
30 A few brilliant exceptions, however, redeemed the fashionable novel from the charge of utter inanity ...

Newgate novelists. After a time, that portion of the reading public which is the mainstay of circulating-libraries became wearied with the fashionable frivolities and tiresome iteration of scenes pertaining to the *beau monde*.
35 The demand for such literary syllabubs declined, and the value of copyrights dwindled. Then arose a new school of novelists, who sought to win the public ear, disgusted with drawing-room prattle, by converse of another kind. They selected their heroes, not from the frequenters of the saloon or boudoir, but from the denizens of the haunts of vice. ●

T48   *Anon., 'Popular ballad' (c. 1860)*

SHOCKING MURDER OF A WIFE AND SIX CHILDREN.

Attend you feeling parents dear,
While I relate a sad affair;
Which has filled all around with grief
    and pain,
5 It did occur in Hosier Lane.

On Monday, June the 28th,
These crimes were done as I now state,
How horrible it is to tell,
Eight human persons by poison fell.

10 In London city it does appear,
Walter James Duggin lived we hear,
And seemed to live most happily,
With his dear wife and family.

They happy lived, until of late,
15 He appear'd in a sad desponding state,
At something he seem'd much annoy'd,
At his master's, where he was employ'd

He was discharged, and that we find,
It preyed upon his anxious mind,
20 Lest they should want – that fatal day
His wife and children he did slay.

Last Sunday evening as we hear,
To the Wheatsheaf he did repair,
Then homewards went as we may read,
25 For to commit this horrid deed.

To the police he did a letter send,
That he was about this life to end,
And that he had poisoned, he did declare
His wife, and his six children dear.

30 To Hosier Lane in haste they flew,
And found it was alas, too true,
They found him stretched upon the bed
His tro[u]bles o'er – was cold and dead.

They searched the premises around,
35 And they the deadly poison found;
And the shocking sight, as you may hear
Caused in many an eye a tear.

They found upon another bed,
The ill-fated mother, she was dead,
40 While two pretty children we are told,
In her outstretched arms she did enfold.

It is supposed this wretched pair,
First poisoned their six children dear.
Then took the fatal draught themselves,
45 Their state of mind no tongue can tell.

Of such an heartrending affair,
I trust we never more may hear,
Such deeds they make the blood run cold
May God forgive their sinful souls

50 This wholesale poisoning has caused
    much pain,
   It did take place in Hosier Lane.

●

T49   *[Dean of Canterbury], 'Church hymns' (1867)*

I. – FIRST SUNDAY AFTER CHRISTMAS.

'Set thine house in order:
For thou shalt die, and not live.'

'SET thine house in order,
    Thou shalt die, not live.'
5 May the voice to each one
    Solemn warning give:
Pilgrims here and strangers,
    Weak and frail alike,
Who can tell among us
10   Where the blow may strike?

Set thine house in order,
    All its bulwarks tell;
Try the ground beneath thee,
    Stir and delve it well:
15 Soon shall break the tempest:
    Wouldst thou bide the shock?
Hearer be and doer,
    Founded on the rock.

Set thine house in order,
20   Search and sweep it clean,
That God's Spirit loathe not
    To abide therein.
Thoughts and plans unholy,
    Schemes that shun the day,
25 Pride, and greed, and rancour,
    Purge them all away.

Set thine house in order,
    Gather up thy stores,
Every weapon brighten
30   For thy Captain's wars:
Sort out all thy treasures,
    Earthly dross remove:
Three alone are lasting –
    Faith, and Hope, and Love.

III. – SEXAGESIMA SUNDAY.

'Who seest that we put not our trust
In anything which we do.' – *Collect*.

NOT in anything we do,
Thought that's pure, or word that's true,
Saviour, would we put our trust:
Frail as vapour, vile as dust,
5 All that flatters, we disown:
Righteousness in Thine alone.

Though we underwent for Thee
Perils of the land and sea,
Though we cast our lives away,
10 Dying for Thee day by day,
Boast we never of our own:
Grace and strength are Thine alone.

Native cumberers of the ground,
All our fruit from Thee is found:
15 Grafted in Thine olive, Lord,
New begotten by Thy word,
All we have is Thine alone:
Life and power are not our own.

And when Thy returning voice
20 Calls Thy faithful to rejoice,
When the countless throng to Thee
Cast their crowns of victory,
We will sing before the throne,
'Thine the glory, not our own!'

T50   *L. Carroll, 'Nonsense and nonsense explained' (1872)*

... she turned over the leaves, to find some part that she could read, '- for it's all in some language I don't know,' she said to herself.

It was like this.

ykcowrebbaJ

5   sevot yhtils eht dna ,gillirb sawT'
         :ebaw eht ni elbmig dna eryg diD
         ,sevogorob eht erew ysmim llA
         .ebargtuo shtar emom eht dnA

She puzzled over this for some time, but at last a bright thought struck
10   her. 'Why, it's a Looking-glass book, of course! And if I hold it up to a glass, the words will all go the right way again.'

This was the poem that Alice read: *Jabberwocky* ...

'You seem very clever at explaining words, Sir,' said Alice. 'Would you kindly tell me the meaning of the poem called 'Jabberwocky'?

15   'Let's hear it,' said Humpty Dumpty. 'I can explain all the poems that were ever invented – and a good many that haven't been invented just yet.'

This sounded very hopeful, so Alice repeated the first verse: ...

'That's enough to begin with,' Humpty Dumpty interrupted: 'there are plenty of hard words there. '*Brillig*' means four o'clock in the afternoon –
20   the time when you being *broiling* things for dinner.'

'That'll do very well,' said Alice: 'and '*slithy*'?

'Well, '*slithy*' means 'lithe and slimy'. 'Lithe' is the same as 'active'. You see it's like a portmanteau – there are two meanings packed up into one word.'

25   'I see it now,' Alice remarked thoughtfully: 'and what are '*toves*'?'

'Well, '*toves*' are something like badgers – they're something like lizards – and they're something like corkscrews.'

'They must be very curious-looking creatures.'

'They are that,' said Humpty Dumpty; 'also they make their nests under
30   sun-dials – also they live on cheese.'

'And what's to '*gyre*' and to '*gimble*'?''

'To '*gyre*' is to go round and round like a gyroscope. To '*gimble*' is to make holes like a gimlet.'

'And '*the wabe*' is the grass-plot round a sun-dial, I suppose?' said
35   Alice, surprised at her own ingenuity.

'Of course it is. It's called '*wabe*' you know, because it goes a long way before it, and a long way behind it –'

'And a long way beyond it on each side,' Alice added.

'Exactly so, Well then, '*mimsy*' is 'flimsy' and 'miserable' ...   ●

T51   *W. Morris, 'Translation of the Aeneid' (1875)*

Juno then took up the word and said:
'That shall be my very work, how that which presseth now
May be encompassed, hearken ye, in few words will I show:
Æneas and the hapless queen are minded forth to fare
5 For hunting to the thicket-side, when Titan first shall bear
Tomorrow's light aloft, and all the glittering world unveil:
On them a darkening cloud of rain, blended with drift of hail,
Will I pour down, while for the hunt the feathered snare-lines shake,
And toils about the thicket go: all heaven will I awake
10 With thunder, and their scattered folk the mid-mirk shall enwrap:
Then Dido and the Trojan lord on one same cave shall hap;
I will be there, and if to me thy heart be stable grown,
In wedlock will I join the two and deem her all his own:
And there shall be their bridal God.' ...
15 Meanwhile Aurora risen up had left the ocean stream,
And gateward throng the chosen youth in first of morning's beam,
And wide-meshed nets, and cordage toils & broad-steeled spears abound,
Massylian riders go their ways with many a scenting hound.
The lords of Carthage by the door bide till the tarrying queen
20 Shall leave her chamber: there, with gold and purple well beseen,
The mettled courser stands, and champs the bit that bids him bide.
And last she cometh forth to them with many a man beside:
A cloak of Sidon wrapped her round with pictured border wrought,
Her quiver was of fashioned gold, and gold her tresses caught;
25 The gathering of her purple gown a golden buckle had ...
'O Jupiter, almighty lord, to whom from painted bed
The banqueting Maurusian folk Lenæan joy pours forth,
Dost thou behold? O Father, is our dread of nothing worth
When thou art thundering? Yea, forsooth, a blind fire of the clouds,
30 An idle hubbub of the sky, our souls with terror loads!
A woman wandering on our shore, who set her up e'en now
A little money-cheapened town, to whom a field to plough
And lordship of the place we gave, hath thrust away my word
Of wedlock, and hath taken in Æneas for her lord:
35 And now this Paris, hedged around with all his gelding rout,
Mæonian mitre tied to chin, and wet hair done about,
Sits on the prey while to thine house a many gifts we bear,
Still cherishing an idle tale who our begetters were.' ...

IV On history and culture

T52   *D. Wordsworth, 'Diary' (Nov./Dec. 1801)*

Wednesday 11th. Baked bread and giblet pie − put books in order − mended stockings. Put aside dearest C.'s letters, and now at about 7 o'clock we are all sitting by a nice fire − W. with his book and a candle and Mary writing to Sara.

5   *Friday 27th.* Snow upon the ground thinly scattered. It snowed after we got up & then the sun shone & it was very warm though frosty − now the Sun shines sweetly. A woman came who was travelling with her husband he had been wounded and was going with her to live at Whitehaven. She had been at Ambleside the night before, offered 4d at the Cock for a bed − they
10   sent her to one Harrison's where she & her husband had slept upon the hearth & bought a pennyworth of Chips for a fire. Her husband was gone before very lame − 'Aye' says she 'I was once an officer's wife I, as you see me now. My first Husband married me at Appleby. I had 18£ a year for teaching a school and because I had no fortune his father turned him out of
15   doors. I have been in the West Indies − I lost the use of this Finger just before he died he came to me & said he must bid farewell to his dear children & me − I had a Muslin gown on like yours − I seized hold of his coat as he went from me & slipped the joint of my finger − He was shot directly. I came to London & married this man. He was clerk to Judge
20   Chambray, *that man* that man that's going on the Road now. If he, Judge Chambray, had been at Kendal he would [have] given us a guinea or two & made nought of it, for he is very generous.'...

       Tuesday 22nd Still thaw. I washed my head. Wm & I went to Rydale for letters, the road was covered with dirty snow, rough & rather slippery. We
25   had a melancholy letter from C, for he had been very ill, th' he was better when he wrote. We walked home almost without speaking − Wm composed a few lines of the Pedlar. We talked about Lamb's Tragedy as we went down the White Moss. We stopped a long time in going to watch a little bird with a salmon coloured breast − a white cross or T upon its wings, & a
30   brownish back with faint stripes. It was pecking the scattered Dung upon the road − it began to peck at the distance of 4 yards from us & advanced nearer and nearer till it came within the length of Wm's stick without any apparent fear of us. As we came up the White Moss we met an old man, who I saw was a beggar by his two bags hanging over his shoulder, but
35   from a half laziness, half indifference & a wanting to *try* him if he would speak I let him pass. He said nothing, and my heart smote me. I turned back & said You are begging?   ●

T53   *Anon., 'Proclamation against Luddite Rioters' (1812)*

Second Letter.   **Fellow Weavers!**

Since I last wrote to you, I have been considering within myself what class of persons amongst you is injured by Machinery? I shall therefore ask each of them separately, and desire them to put the question to their own breast.

5   Who is injured by Machinery? As I understand that the *Colliers* were particularly active in the late wicked outrages, I shall address myself first to them:

Colliers! Are *ye* injured by the demand for Coals to work the Steam-Engines, that set in motion the Machinery? Do the Steam-Engines or
10 Machinery consume food?

No, – but they save that which must otherwise be consumed by *Horses*. They are even named from this, as the *ten-horse power* saves the food of ten horses, for the use of man.

Canal-Diggers! Are *ye* injured? Have not the canals been dug to carry
15 our goods and our coals to other markets, and to bring us food? – At those markets we could not undersel other persons, unless the goods were made cheap by machinery; and both the goods and the coals cheaper by canals. If we could not sell our goods, how are we to pay for our food'?

Spinners and Weavers, are *ye* injured? Least of all persons are ye entitled
20 to complain. For four times your number are employed since the invention of machinery: – and why? because your little children, by the help of machinery, can earn their own livelihood, and it is easy to rear a family.

Smiths, Carpenters, Engine makers, in short tradesmen of all kinds, which of you is injured by having clothes made cheap, and employment
25 more plentiful? But if here and there one man has less employment because another makes goods cheaper by improvements in machinery, must it not be so in all trades?

Which of us will not go to the cheap baker, the cheap carpenter, and why not to the cheap manufacturer? – When all but a few receive benefit, what
30 right have those few to complain? What right has any man to prevent thousands from buying their goods cheap? ...

They were not more unreasonable than those who now provoke a riot, because some weavers have contrived to make goods cheaper by improvements in machinery, and have thus found a *New Bridge* for sending our
35 GOODS OVER THE WORLD.

I am, as before, Your Well-Wisher, *AN OLD WEAVER* ●

T54   *W. Hazlitt, 'On vulgarity and affectation' (1821)*

Few subjects are more nearly allied than these two – vulgarity and affectation. It may be said of them truly that 'thin partitions do their bounds
divide.' There cannot be a surer proof of a low origin or of an innate
meanness of disposition, than to be always talking and thinking of being
5   genteel. We must have a strong tendency to that which we are always trying
to avoid: whenever we pretend, on all occasions, a mighty contempt for any
thing, it is a pretty clear sign that we feel ourselves very nearly on a level
with it. Of the two classes of people, I hardly know which is to be regarded
with most distaste, the vulgar aping the genteel, or the genteel constantly
10   sneering at and endeavouring to distinguish themselves from the vulgar ...
     Gentility is only a more select and artificial kind of vulgarity. It cannot
exist but by a sort of borrowed distinction. It plumes itself up and revels in
the homely pretensions of the mass of mankind. It judges of the worth of
everything by name, fashion, opinion; and hence, from the conscious ab-
15   sence of real qualities or sincere satisfaction in itself, it builds its
supercilious and fantastic conceit on the wretchedness and wants of others.
Violent antipathies are always suspicious, and betray a secret affinity. The
difference between the 'Great Vulgar and the Small' is mostly in outward
circumstances. The coxcomb criticises the dress of the clown, as the pedant
20   cavils at the bad grammar of the illiterate, or the prude is shocked at the
backslidings of her frail acquaintance. Those who have the fewest resources
in themselves, naturally seek the food of their self-love elsewhere. The most
ignorant people find most to laugh at in strangers: scandal and satire prevail
most in country-places; and a propensity to ridicule ever the slightest or
25   most palpable deviation from what we happen to approve, ceases with the
progress of common sense and decency. True worth does not exult in the
faults and deficiencies of others; as true refinement turns away from
grossness and deformity, instead of being tempted to indulge in an unmanly
triumph over it. Raphael would not faint away at the daubing of a sign-post,
30   nor Homer hold his head the higher for being in the company of a Grub-
street bard. Real power, real excellence, does not seek for a foil in
imperfection; nor fear contamination from coming in contact with that
which is coarse and homely. It reposes on itself, and is equally free from
spleen and affectation. But the spirit of gentility is the mere essence of
35   spleen and affectation; – of affected delight in its own *would-be* qualifications, and of ineffable disdain poured out upon the involuntary blunders or
accidental disadvantages of those whom it chooses to treat as its inferiors.

T55   *'Epitaphs' (1819-1875)*

(a)   As a Warning/ to the Young of both Sexes.
This Stone is erected by public/ Subscription over the remains of MARY
ANN WEEMS,/ who at an early age became acquainted/ with THOMAS
WEEMS formerly of this Parish,/ this connexion terminating in a com-
5   pulsory/ Marriage occasioned him soon to desert her/ and wishing to be
Married to another Woman/ he filled up the measure of his iniquity/ by
resolving to murder his Wife,/ which he barbarously perpetrated at Wendy/
on their Journey to London toward which place/ he had induced her to go
under the mask/ of reconciliation May the 7ᵗʰ 1819./ He was taken within a
10   few hours after/ the crime was committed, tried and/ subsequently executed
at Cambridge/ on the 7ᵗʰ of August in the same Year./

> Ere Crime you perpetrate survey this Stone.
> Learn hence the God of justice sleeps not on his Throne.
> But marks the Sinner with unerring Eye.
15   The suffering Victim hears and makes the Guilty die.

(b) In Memory of/ William Pickering,/ who died Decᴿ 24. 1845/ aged 30
years/ Also Richard Edger/ who died Decᴿ 24. 1845/ aged 24 years./

The Spiritual Railway

The Line to heaven by Christ was made
20   With heavenly truth the Rails are laid,
From Earth to Heaven the Line extends,
To Life Eternal where it ends
Repentance is the Station then
Where Passengers are taken in.
25   No Fee for them is there to pay
For Jesus is himself the way
God's Word is the first Engineer
It points the way to Heaven so dear.
Through tunnels dark and dreary here
30   It does the way to Glory steer.

God's Love the Fire, his Truth the Steam,
Which drives the Engine and the Train,
All you who would to Glory ride,
Must come to Christ, in him abide
35 In First and Second, and Third Class,
Repentance, Faith and Holiness.
You must the way to Glory gain
Or you with Christ will not remain
Come then poor Sinners, now's the time
40 At any Station on the Line.
If you'll repent and turn from sin
The Train will stop and take you in.

(c) 1828.
A tender mother sleepeth here,
45   A loving wife, a friend sincere;
In love she lived, in peace she died,
Her life was craved, but God denied.

(d) 1857.
Death little warning to me gave,
50   but quickly sent me to my grave;
Then haste to Christ, make no delay,
For no one knows their dying day.

(e) 1837.
In this cold, dark, and solitary bed,
55 The roses of her countenance all fled,
Faded like flowers on the coffin spread –
My loving Mary's numbered with the dead.

(f) 1851.
To thee, O silent grave, I trust
60 The sleeping remnant of his dust;
Keep it, O keep it, sacred tomb,
Until a wife shall ask for room.

(g) 1833.
Affliction sore long time I bore,
65 Physician's skill was vain,
Till God did please death should me
 seize,
And ease me of my pain.

(h) 1836.
70 While on the earth I did remain
I was afflicted with much pain,

But when the Lord He thought it best,
He took me to a place of rest.

(i) 1833.
75 Life is uncertain, death is sure,
Sin is the wound, and Christ the cure.

(k) 1836.
My children Ten, pray now agree;
Strive to be fit to follow me.

80 (l) Tanridge Churchyard, Surrey. 1826
Sacred to the Memory of Margaret, daughter of James and Mary Grum-
bridge, of the parish of St. James, London, who departed this life Nov. 17,
1826, aged seven years and eleven months.

 Adieu, sweet innocent! a flower too fair
85 To bless thy anxious parents' tender care;
 Too bright thy bloom for us on earth to view,
 We gaz'd, admir'd, or wept and bade adieu.
 Return'd thee back to heaven's illumin'd sphere,
 To bloom for ever as an angel there.

90 (m) In St. Andrew's Churchyard, Holborn. 1824.
Beneath this stone are interred the mortal remains of Samuel John Neale,
late of Henrietta Street, Brunswick Square, who departed this life on May
13, 1824, aged 66.

 Good night, good night, sweet Spirit! thou hast cast
95 The bonds of clay away from thee at last,
 Broke the vile earthly fetters which alone
 Held thee at distance from thy Maker's throne.
 But, oh! those fetters to the immortal mind
 Were links of love to those thou hast left behind;
100 For thee we mourn not: as the Apostle press'd
 His dungeon pillow till the Angel guest
 Drew nigh, and when the light around him shone,
 Beam'd on the Prisoner, his bonds were gone,
 So wert thou captive to disease and pain
105 Till Death, the brightest of the angel train,
 Pour'd Heaven's own radiance to divine decree
 Around thy suffering soul, and it was free.

(n) In Sutton Churchyard. 1817.
As a warning to female virtue, and a humble monument of female Chastity,
110 this stone marks the grave of Mary Ashford, who, in the 20th year of her
age, having incautiously repaired to a scene of public amusement without
proper protection, was brutally murdered on the 27th May, 1817.

Lovely and chaste as is the primrose pale,
Rifled of virgin sweetness by the gale:
115　Mary, the wretch who thee remorseless slew,
Avenging wrath, which sleeps not, will pursue:
For though the deed of blood be veiled in night,
Will not the Judge of all the earth do right?
Fair, blighted flower, the muse that weeps thy doom
120　Rais'd o'er thy murdered form this warning tomb.

(o) On Peers Naylor, a railway engineman, in Newton-le-Willows Churchyard, Lancashire (also Bromsgrove Churchyard?) n.d.

My engine is now cold and still,
No water does my boiler fill;
125　My coke affords its flame no more,
My days of usefulness are o'er;
My wheels deny their noted speed,
No more my guiding hand they need;
My whistle, too, has lost its tune,
130　Its shrill and thrilling sounds are gone;
My valves are now thrown open wide;
My flanges all refuse to guide;
My clacks also, though once so strong,
Refuse to aid the busy throng;
135　No more I feel each urging breath,
My steam is now condensed in death;
Life's railway's o'er, each station's past,
In death I'm stopt, and rest at last.
Farewell, dear friends, and cease to weep,
140　In Christ I'm safe, in Him I sleep.
He sleeps among the sleepers, and thousands shall follow in his train.

(p) In Harrow-on-the-Hill Churchyard. 1838.
To the memory of Thomas Port, son of John Port of Burton-upon-Trent, in the County of Stafford, Hat Manufacturer, who near this town had both his
145　legs Severed from his body by the Railway Train. With the greatest fortitude he bore a second amputation by the surgeons, and died from loss of blood, August 7th, 1838, aged 33 years.

Bright rose the morn, and vigorous rose poor Port,
Gay on the train he used his wonted sport.
150　E'er noon arrived his mangled form they bore,
With pain distorted, and o'erwhelmed with gore;
When evening came to close the fatal day,
A mutilated corps the sufferer lay.

T56   *[Manchester Guardian], 'Notices and advertisements' (1821)*

(a)   MISSING, Since Mid-Lent Sunday, the 1st of April instant, and
supposed by his Friends to be Drowned or Murdered;
A GENTLEMAN, about the age of Forty-six, of middle Stature, about five
feet five inches of height, moderately stout, and fresh complexioned, scarce
5   of hair, inclining to grey, and bald on the forehead and the back of the
crown. He had on, when he left his friends after dinner on Sunday the 1st
instant as aforesaid, a black coat and waistcoat, blue trowsers, and Welling-
ton boots, with a green silk umbrella in his hand. It is believed he was seen
walking about two miles from Manchester, on the Cheetham Hill Road, a
10   little after two o'clock on the above day.
    Any person who can give information of any one answering this descrip-
tion, to ... or at the POLICE OFFICE, Manchester, shall be liberally re-
warded for their trouble.   Manchester, April 30th, 1821.

(b)   MICHAEL PEACOCK begs most respectfully to apprize his Friends and
15   the Public, that he has REMOVED from his old Shop, to his new
Establishment, No.270, on the opposite side of Deansgate, where he solicits
a continuance of past favours. – His present stock consists of a very capital
selection of every description of HOSIERY, which (if equalled) will not be
surpassed, in point of cheapness, by any House in the kingdom. – Also,
20   Poplins, Bombazines, Stuffs, Manchester & Scotch Muslins, Silk Shawls
and Scarfs, Cotton Shawls and Scarfs, Irish Linens, Dowlas Linens and
Sheetings, Fancy Prints, Printed and Dimity Furnitures, Cassimere Shawls
and Scarfs, Linen Checks, all kinds of Silk and Cotton Handkerchiefs,
Lancashire and Welsh Flannels, &c. &c.; – the whole of which he is now
25   selling most astonishingly cheap.
                     Wellington House, 270, Deansgate, Manchester.

(c)   WHEREAS a commission of bankrupt is awarded and issued against
JOHN GOODAIR, late of Chorley, in the county of Lancaster, Cotton spin-
ner, dealer and chapman, and he being declared a bankrupt, is hereby re-
30   quired to surrender himself to the commissioners in the said commission
named, or the major part of them, on the ninth and tenth days of May next,
and on the second day of June following, at the Mosley Arms Inn, in Manchester, in the said county of Lancaster, at eleven o'clock in the forenoon,
and make a full discovery and disclosure of his estate and effects; when and
35   where the creditors are to come prepared to prove their debts, and at the
second sitting to choose assignees, and at the last sitting the said bankrupt
is required to finish his examination, and the creditors are to assent to or
dissent from the allowance of his certificate ...   ●

T57 *W. Wordsworth, 'Private letter' (1822)*

My Lord, Rydal Mount, July 18th, 1822

Mr Monkhouse who is now in London, begs that if I were writing to your Lordship, I would request leave for two or three days shooting on some of the Moors for himself and Mr Horrocks jun[r] of Preston, from the
5   12th of August. Though aware of the embarrassments which these numerous applications some times occasion, I do not scruple to make this request, more especially as it furnishes me with an opportunity of congratulating your Lordship, directly, as I have previously done through others, upon the happy issue of the operation upon your eyes, and likewise
10 upon the recovery from the effects of the severe accident which befel you in the Park. In these heart-felt congratulations all my family unite, with wishes and prayers for the blessing of heaven upon you and yours.

From various causes this last spring and the present summer have been melancholy to my Family. Our heaviest trouble was caused by my younger
15 Son who nearly three weeks ago returned from School suffering under dropsy, without our having heard a word of anything ailing him. Mr Harrison was called from Kendal; he had I believe little hope of his recovery; but I am happy to say that within these last three days a most favorable change has taken place; so that we are full of hope. The anxiety I
20 have suffered on his account has made me feel that my head is not so strong as before my late accident.

We hear nothing of Sir George and Lady Beaumont. Sir Richard le Fleming is our present Rector; he has done duty in the Church and is said to read agreeably.

25 Mr Dawes the clergyman of Ambleside a few days ago was struck with apoplexy; his recovery was despaired of; but there are expressed hopes of his getting better.

With respectful remembrances to Lady Lonsdale, in which Mrs Wordsworth and My Sister unite I have the honor to be my Lord ever faithfully
30 your Lordship's friend and Ser[vnt] Wm Wordsworth ●

T58 *'Business letters' (1826)*

(a) Aberdeen, James Duguid, Thomas Greig 5 October (1826)

Altho' we wrote to you only two days ago yet such is the situation of the times here that we are induced again to address you. We cannot on any account accept of an order from new people, nor from those that are long
5 winded, or do not without waiting for your going around conform to the terms of remitting us in 5 months – It will be of no use talking, it is totally

out of our Power to execute orders for such people. When the writer looks
at our Order Book he is quite astounded. We cannot get the orders executed
& our only wish is not to get into disgrace with our old friends – With them
10 we will do our best but stocks are much exhausted & every article is getting
up – We do not think it will last, but we must be careful. As to money
matters nothing is to be done here but for cash & you must send us as much
as you can. You know we never feel quite easy about H Hall & Co. – their
last Bill is not due until the 10th of this month. We have an order in work
15 for them of 12 Pieces. We have heard it said that they sell to people who are
not very respectable – in these times it is necessary to be very particular &
pay attention to all points – we shall be glad to receive all the information
you can send us about them & all our other customers.

We have just received your letter from Dundee with a Bill of £124 – and
20 two orders which shall have every attention, but we must again repeat our
wish that you should not, this Journey take an order from any new people,
or any old customer that has not paid up, nor push even the best of men to
order largely – for if they do, we see disappointment & dissatisfaction either
as to time o[r] quality as likely to ensue. With such people as Duguid we
25 will do everything that is possible: we have still many goods to send him
that have been much lower in preparation than we feel comfortable at
referring to *Robert Greeg* of Anstruther has sent us an order that will
amount to £40 you never gave us a very high opinion of him: do you think
we should now execute it? Let us know as soon as possible, as we shall do
30 nothing until we get your reply. James *Anderson & Son* Peterhead have sent
us an order that will amount to £40 which we have executed – who do they
succeed? You will recollect we already have several Andersons at that
place.
We wish you a good Journey & are &c.

35 (b) Edinburgh, John & Wm Luke,   7th October 1826

We are this day in receipt of your favour of the 4th & should be happy to
send you the Cloth therein mentioned, but the present state of the times
compels us to adhere closely to the terms stated in our Invoices since the
commencement of this year. In this quarter every article of our manufacture
40 must be furnished with Cash, that we have it not in our power to deviate
from the rule we have adopted of not giving more than 5 months credit, at
which period we allow 5 perCent discount. We shall be glad to receive your
answer & remain   ●

T59   *'Reform Act' (1831)*

XXVII. And be it enacted, that in every city or borough which shall
return a member or members to serve in any future Parliament, every male
person of full age, and not subject to any legal incapacity, who shall occupy,
within such city or borough, or within any place sharing in the election for
5   such city or borough, as owner or tenant, any house, warehouse, counting-
house, shop, or other building, being either separately or jointly with any
land within such city, borough, or place occupied therewith by him as
owner, or occupied therewith by him as tenant under the same landlord, of
the clear yearly value of not less than ten pounds, shall, if duly registered
10 according to the provisions herein-after contained, be entitled to vote in the
election of a member or members to serve in any future Parliament for such
city or borough: Provided always, that no such person shall be so registered
in any year unless he shall have occupied such premises as aforesaid for
twelve calendar months next previous to the last day of July in such year,
15 nor unless, such person, where such premises are situate in any parish or
township in which there shall be a rate for the relief of the poor, shall have
been rated in respect of such premises to all rates for the relief of the poor in
such parish or township made during the time of such his occupation so
required as aforesaid, nor unless such person shall have paid, on or before
20 the twentieth day of July in such year, all the poor's rates and assessed taxes
which shall have become payable from him in respect of such premises
previously to the sixth day of July in such year, all the poor rates and
assessed taxes which shall have become payable from him in respect of
such premises previously to the sixth day of April then next preceding:
25 Provided also, that no such person shall be so registered in any year unless
he shall have resided for six calendar months next previous to the last day of
July in such year within the city or borough, or within the place sharing in
the election for the city or borough, in respect of which city, borough, or
place respectively he shall be entitled to vote, or within seven statute miles
30 thereof or of any part thereof.   ●

T60   *'Travesty of the Catechism' (1832)*

THE RADICAL REFORMER'S CATECHISM.
Q. What is your name? – A. Radical Reformer.
Q. Who gave you that name?
A. The National Union of the Working Classes on my baptism; wherein
5   I was made a true Republican, a child of the better sort; and an inheritor of

equal rights and equal laws of the Commonwealth of England.

Q. What did the National Union then for you?

A. They did promise and vow three things in my name: first, that I
should for ever renounce the Boroughmongers, and all their works;
10   secondly, that none should be disfranchised except those flagrantly guilty of
political crimes, and that I should strenuously assert, and valiantly maintain,
'Universal Suffrage, Annual Parliaments, and Vote by Ballot;' thirdly, and
more especially, that the wholesome doctrine of our Champion of Reform,
H. Hetherington, be invariably recognized, namely – that upon no pretence
15   whatever shall *property* form any part of the qualification of a Candidate for
a seat in the People's House of Parliament.

Q. Dost thou not think that thou art bound to believe and do as they have
promised for thee?

A. Yes, verily; and by the People's help so I will; and I heartily thank my
20   fellow citizens of the National Union for bringing me to a sense of my
rights and wrongs through Citizen Hetherington of the *Poor Man's Guard-*
ian, and Citizen Hunt of the Den of Thieves; and I earnestly beseech the
Class Leaders of our Union to continue me steadfast and immovable to my
life's end.

25   Q. Rehearse the Articles of thy belief?

A. I believe the National Union of the Working Classes is the Corinthian
Pillar of an enlightened society; and that KINGS, TORIES; AND WHIGS,
whether Guelph with his million – or the bloodhound of Waterloo, the
murderer of the brave Ney, with his sixty thousand annually, besides many
30   thousands from foreign despots – or Peel and Lyndhurst, with their empty
professions of retrenchment, ought to be exiled for life to the mines of
Siberia; I believe in the greedy rapacity of the tithe-gorging Bishops – that
the Working Classes are the only useful classes – the working bees, the
honey makers; most properly speaking, the better sort of folk; while those
35   so called are the pests of society, the worse than useless classes, and the
consumers of the honey, the drones of the Hive. And I look for the
appellation of 'House of Lords,' and the epithet 'Lord,' as applied to a
mortal, to become obsolete; also I look for the total extinction of all unjust
monopolies, whether of law, physic, or divinity; the Whig and Tory bank;
40   the East and West Indian monopolies; the repeal of the Aristocrats' corn
laws; the speedy passing of the 'Short-time Bill,' &c. &c.; the restoration of
the glebelands, falsely called Church-lands, to the People; likewise the
crown-lands, so called, that they may be cultivated by the People for their
own special use; for the application of the Sponge to the figures of the debt
45   falsely called National, with a whole train of *et ceteras*   ●

T61   *Anon. 'The stamped and the unstamped' (1833)*

And if the *Weekly Dispatch*, which is decidedly one of the honestest and most justly popular journals of the legitimate press, will thus seek to degrade us because we write for the poor man, what can we expect from its more aristocratic compeers? Need we wonder at being so often stigmatized
5   by the morning papers under vague descriptions, or altogether Burked in those occasional Parliamentary debates which refer to the newspaper stamp-duties, when even the *Weekly Dispatch*, the honestest of the dishonest, will thus disingenuously vent its spleen? No matter, my friends, we shall have our revenge – we will go on opposing our penny and two-penny truth to
10 their seven-penny humbug and twaddle, until the people will stomach nothing else, and (our life for it!) we will soon make the *Times* and *Chronicle* as honest as the *Weekly Dispatch*, and the *Dispatch* itself a great deal honester than it can as yet afford to be.

And now for a glorious specimen of the 'legitimate' press! that press to
15 which we are constantly referred for instruction and for antidotes against the 'poison' and 'ignorance' of the Unstamped. Read it my friends, for God's sake, and for our sake, and for your own. It is from a no less orthodox source than the pious *Standard* itself, and comes recommended to you by all the holiness of Mother Church, of whom Dr. Gifford is the devoted para-
20 mour and champion. Read it, we say, and then listen to us while we expose its ignorance, its vulgarity, and its falsehood ...

Every body is aware of the miscellaneous multitude of cheap publications which the last two or three years have called into existence. Some of these have had a very considerable sale; but we have it in evidence that all,
25 without any exception, of an innocent and respectable kind, have been sold, *not* as cheap publications, but in collected numbers, at prices such as the upper and middle classes are accustomed to purchase. We need not hesitate to say, therefore, that those classes which have been the objects of eleemosynary education, have not availed themselves of the cheapness of
30 innocent and respectable reading. But perhaps they have been reading – doubtless they have, and we are enabled, from an authentic source, to give some account of their reading. We give it upon evidence wholly above exception – evidence which the conductor of the *Morning Chronicle* or the *Examiner* shall be cheerfully furnished with at our office. It is a list of the
35 unstamped political publications published in defiance of law, with the late average sales of each: Average Circulation.
Poor Man's Guardian   16,000
This is printed by Hetherington, an Irish Papist,
and ex-student of Maynooth.

40 *Destructive*   8,000
    Printed by the same. It is scarcely necessary to mention the principles of
    these publications; they are Jacobinical of the deepest, bloodiest dye. It
    will be remembered that Hetherington has preached the use of the dagger
    as an instrument of rebellion. The *Poor Man's Guardian* and *Destructive*
45 circulate in Lancashire.
    Gauntlet   22,000
    The conductor of this is the notorious Carlile – his name is enough.
    Cosmopolite   5,000
    Working Man's Friend   7,000
50 *Crisis*   5,000
    The Man   7,000
    Reformer   5,000
    These are the principal unstamped publications of London – the reading,
    with the *Times*, *Weekly Dispatch*, of the educated democracy of the
55 metropolis. Are men to be turned loose upon such garbage as this? In the
    country, there are also several unstamped newspapers – particularly at
    Leeds, Bradford, Manchester, &c., all taking their tone from the *Poor Man's
    Guardian*, and the others, which we have described as the penny press of
    London. These are the *primitiæ*, the first fruits of the late active exertions in
60 behalf of indiscriminate education.
    Glorious news! With all their trickery and subscribing, it seems the Whig
    doctrinnaires can obtain no readers! '*Those classes which have been the
    objects of eleemosynary education have not availed themselves of the
    cheapness of innocent and respectable reading.*' A thousand thanks, Dr.
65 Gifford – not for the *information*, for we knew it before – but for your
    manly avowal of the truth. So the people will not buy literature in the Whig
    market! Alas! for the firm of Brougham and Co.! Though cheap as dirt, (and
    God knows it ought) the radicals will have nothing to do with '*innocent and
    respectable reading.*' Nay, the naughty 'full-grown babes,' with the fear of
70 God and Lord Brougham's birch before their eyes, will still '*inflame their
    minds with the Poor Man's Guardian, and make themselves nasty by
    dabbling in the Times.*' Naughty, naughty, 'full-grown babes!'
    But zounds! what company we are in! The *Poor Man's Guardian* and the
    Times 'cheek by jowl!' – Marry, we never dreamt of such promotion. And
75 how respectably we come off, too! Mark! The *Guardian* is '*fire,*' the *Times*
    a '*house-pail*' – the *Guardian* '*burns,*' the *Times* '*stinks.*' The *Guardian* is
    what Prometheus stole from heaven to animate the sons of earth – the *Times*
    a fetid mass of ordure, to be presented to Cloaca by the nightman. The devil
    is in it if we be not the more respectable of the two.   ●

T62   *Mrs. C. Cecil, 'Educational prose' (c. 1835?)*

USES OF WATER

How common, and yet how beautiful and how pure, is a drop of water!
See it, as it issues from the rock to supply the spring and the stream below.
See how its meanderings through the plains, and its torrents over the cliffs,
add to the richness and the beauty of the landscape. Look into a factory
5 standing by a waterfall, in which every drop is faithful to perform its part,
and hear the groaning and rustling of the wheels, the clattering of shuttles,
and the buzz of spindles, which, under the direction of their *fair* attendants,
are supplying myriads of fair purchasers with fabrics from the cotton-plant,
the sheep, and the silk-worm ...

10   The majestic river, and the boundless ocean, what are they? Are they not
made of drops of water? How the river steadily pursues its course from the
mountain's top, down the declivity, over the cliff, and through the plain,
taking with it every thing in its course! How many mighty ships does the
ocean float upon its bosom! How many fishes sport in its waters! How does
15 it form a lodging-place for the Amazon, the Mississipi, the Danube, the
Rhine, the Ganges, the Lena, and the Hoang Ho!

How piercing are these pure limpid drops! How do they find their way
into the depths of the earth, and even the solid rock! How many thousand
streams, hidden from our view by mountain masses, are steadily pursuing
20 their courses, deep from the surface which forms our standing-place for a
few short days! In the air, too, how it diffuses itself! Where can a particle of
air be found which does not contain [a]n atom of water?

How much would a famishing man give for a few of these pure, limpid
drops of water? And where do we use it in our daily sustenance? or rather,
25 where do we not use it? Which portion of the food that we have taken
during our lives did not contain it? What part of our body, which limb,
which organ, is not moistened with this same faithful servant? How is our
blood, that free liquid, to circulate through our veins without it?

How gladly does the faithful horse, or the patient ox, in his toilsome
30 journey, arrive at the water's brink! And the faithful dog, patiently
following his master's track – how eagerly does he lap the water from the
clear fountain he meets in his way!

The feathered tribe, also – how far and how quick their flight, that they
may exchange the northern ice for the same common comfort rendered
35 liquid and limpid by a southern sun!

Whose heart ought not to overflow with gratitude to the abundant Giver
of this pure liquid, which his own hand has deposited in the deep, and
diffused through the floating air and the solid earth? ...   ●

T63   *'Agogos', 'Introduction to book on etiquette' ([15]1837)*

It would be absurd to suppose those persons who constitute the upper ranks
of the middle classes in LONDON are ignorant of the regulations here laid
down; – but in the country (especially in the mercantile districts), where the
tone of society is altogether lower, it is far otherwise, although country
5 people may not feel inclined to *acknowledge* what is, nevertheless, strictly
true ...

ETIQUETTE is the barrier which society draws around itself as a protection
against offences the '*law*' cannot touch, – it is a shield against the intrusion
of the impertinent, the improper, and the vulgar, – a guard against those
10 obtuse persons who, having neither talent nor delicacy, would be
continually thrusting themselves into the society of men to whom their
presence might (from the difference of feeling and habit) be offensive, and
even insupportable.

Many unthinking persons consider the observance of Etiquette to be
15 nonsensical and unfriendly, as consisting of unmeaning forms, practised
only by the *silly* and the idle; an opinion which arises from their not having
reflected on the *reasons* that have caused certain rules to be established,
indispensable to the well-being of society, and without which, indeed, it
would inevitably fall to pieces, and be destroyed.
20   Much misconstruction and unpleasant feeling arises, especially in
country towns, from not knowing what is '*expected*,' or necessary to be
done on certain occasions, resulting sometimes from the prevalence of local
customs, with which the world in general are not supposed to be acquainted.

Besides, in a mercantile country like England, people are continually
25 rising in the world. Shopkeepers become merchants, and mechanics manufacturers; with the possession of wealth they acquire a taste for the luxuries
of life, expensive furniture, and gorgeous plate; also numberless super-
fluities, with the use of which they are only imperfectly acquainted. But
although their capacities for enjoyment increase, it rarely occurs that the
30 polish of their manners keeps pace with the rapidity of their advancement:
Such persons are often painfully reminded that wealth alone is insufficient
to protect them from the mortifications a limited acquaintance with society
will entail upon the ambitious.   ●

T64 *Anon., 'Public announcement' (1838)*

CAMBRIDGE CORONATION FESTIVAL.
RUSTIC SPORTS,

In Celebration of the CORONATION of Her Most Gracious Majesty
QUEEN VICTORIA, *On THURSDAY the 28th day of JUNE, 1838.*
5 The Committee appointed for conducting the **RUSTIC SPORTS** on the
approaching Festival announce to the Public, that the following
Amusements will commence precisely at Four o'clock in the afternoon,
ON MIDSUMMER GREEN.
THE **NEWMARKET BAULK** *OR, HOW TO RISE IN LIFE!*
10 Well-Soaped Scaffold Poles, stuck up indifferently out of the perpendicular – will be
climed for, by youthful and unsophisticated Cantabs, for **BREECHES, LEGS OF
MUTTON, &c. &c.** If any competitor obtains an elevation two yards higher than the top
of the pole – it is no go!
Jumping in Sacks.
15 A distance of 50 yards by Six Men. Each man to jump in a 4-bushel Sack (to be provided
by himself for the occasion.) The winner to receive a **New Pair of Boots.** – Second best,
a New Hat, warranted to fit. – The Third a **Pair of Shoes.**
BISCUIT BOLTING.
Twelve Boys to eat a Pennyworth of **Biscuits** each. The First shall have a **Victoria
20 Waistcoat.** Second a **New White Beaver Tile.** Third, a regular out-and-out **Wide-
awake.**
A JINGLING MATCH,
Or, Blind Buff and the Bellman.
This Match will take place in a 24ft roped ring, between 12 young Men, (not less than 18
25 years of age) for a **New pair of Cord Trowsers.** The time allowed for this Match is 16
Minutes; and the Bellman will not be allowed to silence his Bell longer than 30 seconds
at one time.
WHEELBARROW RACE,
By Ten Men, Blindfolded. The winner in this Match to receive a pair of **High Shoes.**
30 Second best a pair of **Low Shoes.** Third best, a **Melton Mowbray Cravat,** or **Coronation Stock!**
Bobbing for Oranges in Wash Troughs
By Twelve Youngsters with hands tied behind them, to be approved of by the Committee
at the time. No one need apply whose mouth is more than twelve inches wide – or who
35 can drink a bucket of water at one draught!
ROYAL PIG RACES.
By 10 Men. The tail to be soaped. The First Man who twice catches it by the tail, and
fairly suspends it over his shoulder, to receive the **Pig** as a Prize.
An Elegant Pie-bald Short-legged Well-fed Curley-tailed PIG,
40 To be run for and caught in same manner as first Pig, for the same prize. – Also, 2 other
Royal Pig Races – on same terms.
GRINNING MATCH.
OR, WHICH IS THE UGLIEST PHIZ!! ...

BY COMMAND OF THE KING OF KINGS,[*]
And at the *Desire* of all who *love* HIS *Appearing.*[*]
At the Theatre of the Universe,[*] On the EVE of TIME,[*] will be performed,
THE GREAT ASSIZE;[*] or, **DAY of JUDGEMENT.**

5   THE SCENERY, which is now *actually* preparing, will not only surpass
every thing that has yet been seen, but will infinitely exceed the utmost
stretch of human Conception.[*] There will be a just Representation of ALL
THE INHABITANTS OF THE WORLD, in their *various* and *proper*
Colours; and their *Customs* and *Manners* will be so exactly and minutely
10   delineated, that *the most secret* THOUGHT will be discovered.[*]
   For God shall bring every Work into JUDGMENT, *with every secret*
   Thing, whether it be Good, or whether it be Evil.
   This THEATRE will be laid out after a new Plan, and will consist of PIT
and GALLERY only; and, contrary to all others, the GALLERY is fitted up
15   for the Reception of the People of high (or *heavenly*) Birth;[*] and the PIT for
all those of low (or *earthly*) Rank.[*] – N.B. The GALLERY is very
spacious,[*] And the PIT *without Bottom.*[*]
   To prevent Inconvenience, there are *seperate Doors* for admitting the
Company; and they are so different, that none can mistake that are not wil-
20   fully BLIND. The Door which opens into the GALLERY is very *narrow*,
and the Steps up to it are somehow difficult; for which reason there are
seldom many People about it.[*] But the Door that gives Entrance into the PIT
is very *wide*, and very commodious; which causes such numbers to flock to
it, that it is generally crowded. – N.B. The *strait* Door leads towards the
25   Right Hand, and the *broad* one to the left.[*]
   IT will be in vain for one in a tinselled Coat and borrowed Language, to
personate one of high Birth, in order to get Admittance into the upper
Places;[*] for there is One of wonderful and deep Penetration, who will search
and examine every Individual;[*] and all who cannot pronounce *Shibboleth*[*]
30   in the Language of *Canaan*[*], or have not received a *white Stone* or *New*
Name,[*] or cannot prove a clear Title to a certain Portion of the Land of
Promise,[*] must be turned in at the Left-Hand-Door.[*]
                   The PRINCIPAL PERFORMERS
   Are described in 1 *Thess.* iv. 16. 2 *Thess.* i. 7, 8, 9. *Matt.* xxiv. 30, 31.
35   xxv. 31, 32. *Daniel* vii. 9, 10. *Jude*, 14, 15. *Rev.* xx. 12 to 15, &c. But as
there are some People much better acquainted with the Contents of a *Play-*
Bill than the Word of God, it may not be amiss to transcribe a verse or two
for their Perusal.   ●

T66   *Anon., 'Sermon' (1839)*

THE THEATRE. FROM this we may proceed at once to the second
principle, viz. that we must do nothing to endanger the soul of any man. The
single fact, that the soul is to live for ever, in heaven or in hell, should be
enough to lead any man of common benevolence to tremble when he sees a
5 soul in danger. The same spirit which would lead a man to relieve bodily
sufferings, and to shudder when witnessing the pain of his brother, should
lead him, in a tenfold degree, to labour for the salvation of the soul, and to
watch with the most pressing anxiety against any evil influence that may
lead that soul to ruin. But here there is another and yet more powerful
10 motive brought to bear. We are directed not merely to the value of the soul,
but to the loved Christ; 'through thy knowledge shall the weak brother
perish for whom Christ died?' And, again; 'when ye sin so against the
brethren, ye sin against Christ.' ...
   But, perhaps, it may be said, that there is not this dangerous tendency in
15 the stage. Let us, then, pause for a few moments to consider the influence of
a theatre; and take, first, its influence on the spectators. In order to make the
pieces popular, they are compelled to pander to the worst passions of men.
The plays that are acted may be arranged under two classes. The first, which
is the larger, consists of those which represent scenes of the grossest
20 profligacy. Read the list of the works of the flesh, in Galatians, v. 19,
'Adultery, fornication, uncleanness, lasciviousness, ... hatred, variance,
emulations, wrath, strife, ... envyings, murders, drunkenness, revellings, and
such like:' and you see the chief subject of these low plays. It was not long
ago that I observed a scene of adultery advertised as an amusement for a
25 Christian people. The faults of the other class are of a more refined
character; they are not so profligate and lascivious, but yet they appeal to
some of the worst passions of our nature. There is a total absence of
Christian principle; and inordinate love, pride, jealousy, and revenge, are
the chief elements which form their interest. Now what must be the effect of
30 such performances? 'I speak as to reasonable men, judge ye what I say.' Are
they likely to fit men for glory? Are they likely to prepare the heart for the
work of the Spirit? When men have the vilest sins set before them for their
entertainment, is it likely to lead to an abhorrence of sin? Is it likely to
corrupt or to purify the heart? What must be the tendency of such
35 exhibitions? what their probable influence? What can we expect, but that
they should lead men from God; that they should harden the heart against
the truth; that they should bring men to the very character described by
Scripture, where it says, 'Fools make a mock at sin?'.   ●

T67   *E. W. Binney, 'Petition on child labour' (c. 1840)*

Female Slavery in England, or Truth stranger than Fiction.
YOUNG GIRLS EMPLOYED IN COAL MINES INSTEAD OF BEASTS!
Copy of a Petition Presented Lately to Parliament by Mr. Brotherton.
THE HUMBLE PETITION OF EDWARD WILLIAM BINNEY, OF MAN-
5   CHESTER, IN THE COUNTY OF LANCASTER, GENTLEMAN,
Sheweth, – That your petitioner, in the course of his geological pursuits, has
had occasion to visit many of the coal-mines of Lancashire, where he has
often been astonished to find *great numbers of females employed, of ages
varying from eight years and upwards*. Their occupation is chiefly in
10   pushing and drawing tubs or small waggons full of coal, from the places
where it is hewn down to the waggon ways. The coals are generally drawn
along the waggon ways to the pit-mouth by ponies; but down the bays or
boards (the passages running on the rise and dip of the seam) which are
often at considerable inclinations, sometimes as much as two feet in five,
15   and very low, *these animals cannot be employed, so women are made use of
in their stead*. At first view it is difficult to distinguish the sexes employed
in a mine, since both, when dressed, are clothed in miners' rough frocks and
trousers, and it was only by the exposure of the upper part of their persons,
and their voices, that your petitioner first noticed the women, blacked and
20   dressed as they were ...

Your petitioner entered into conversation with the elder man, who was
an intelligent person for his class, and remarked that the bay was very wide
to be worked without props or punches being used. He replied, that it was
perfectly safe, as the roof was good, and falls in the mine were not common.
25   While engaged in this conversation, a child, not four years of age, crept out
of a hole. The old man said that he was his son, and that he would not be fit
for work for a year. On your petitioner asking the father why he brought
such an infant down into the pit, he replied that his wife and daughters all
worked in the mine, and there was nobody at home to take care of the child,
30   so he brought him there to be out of harm's way ...

The disgusting nature of the employment of these poor creatures was bad
enough in itself, but to hear the awful swearing, obscene conversation, and
filthy songs, would lead any person to believe that he was in a land of
savages, rather than in civilized England ...

35   Your petitioner, therefore, prays that your Honourable House will be
pleased to adopt such measures for preventing the employment of females
in coal-mines as to your Honourable House shall seem meet.
And your petitioner will ever pray &c.
February 26, 1842.   EDW. WM. BINNEY ●

T68   *Anon., 'Political speech' (1841-4)*

THE 'TOO-IMMORAL-TO-BE-INTRUSTED-WITH-THE-FRANCHISE' CANT.

I hurl back the foul imputation which is so often cast upon the character of
Working men – that they are too ignorant and too immoral to be intrusted
with the franchise, and I tell their proud and haughty calumniators, that it is
a base and unprincipled falsehood, and a miserable plea for the injustice
5 they have so long practised upon honest industry. (Immense Cheering.)
True it is that there exists in society at present a lamentable prevalence of
vice and immorality; but at the same time it is equally true that that frightful
mass of moral degradation and ruined virtue which pollutes the bosom of
society, is the result of those unjust and disgraceful enactments which class
10 legislation has stamped upon the statute book of these realms. (Hear hear.)
But gentlemen, can it be reasonably supposed that the people of any nation
would be strictly moral and virtuous, when the very Government itself of
that nation depends in a great measure, for its support upon the vice and
immorality of the people: – true it is that we have jails and prisons erected
15 in every town and city throughout the land for the punishment of moral
delinquents; but it is equally true, that we have taverns, beerhouses and gin
palaces, directly licensed from the Government, to hold out every gilded
allurement and every pleasing temptation to seduce the young and innocent
from the paths of virtue, to the practice of vice and prepare them as proper
20 inmates of those gloomy monuments of national disgrace which our sapient
legislators have established for the promotion of virtue: – (Loud Cheers.)
Can it, gentlemen, be expected that immorality will decrease, and virtue
become more generally practised so long as the younger branches of the
aristocratic families possess their present undue influence in the making of
25 the laws; men who are trained up from their youth to impose upon the
credulity of the ignorant, and mislead the judgment of the unsophisticated
mind, who are expensively educated to dress out Falsehood in the garb of
Truth, and with the mantle of virtue, to conceal the hideous deformity of
disgusting vice, – to convert a Court of Justice into a Temple of Mammon,
30 where truth, where virtue, where honesty and justice are sacrificed at the
shrine of gold – accursed gold – the God 'which rules in scorn all earthly
things but virtue.' (Loud cheers.)   ●

PLAN. I advise that a committee should be chosen in every locality, who should make arrangements for the use of the Chartist meeting place for the purpose of establishing sunday schools, both for children and adults, in which all kinds of useful knowledge should be taught, so far as the abilities
5 of those engaged as teachers might enable them to proceed. The plan acted upon should be that of co-operative unity; the scholars in the higher classes acting in relation, and in such a manner as not to impede their own progress, as teachers of the lower classes; and if a plot of ground could be procured to be cultivated by the scholars, and the produce applied to their own advant-
10 age, so much the better; but in this the local circumstances of each school must decide the course to be pursued. In order to facilitate the cause, and secure unity both of plan and objects, I advise that a society, to be called the 'National Charter Association Sunday School Union,' should be framed under the sanction of the Executive Council; and I beg to lay before you the
15 following rules to be, if approved, generally adopted: –

1. That each school shall be called the Chartist Sunday School, in connection with the National Charter Association Sunday School Union, for diffusing sound and practical education amongst the working classes.

2. That each school shall be open for the reception of both children and
20 adults, of both sexes, and without reference to any sectarian religious creed.

3. That the superintendents, teachers, and other officers of each school shall be members of the National Charter Association, and that, should any of them withdraw from the said Association, such withdrawal shall be considered a resignation of the office held in connection with any Chartist
25 school.

4. That each school shall be opened by singing a suitable hymn, and the offering up of prayer, and shall be closed also by singing.

5. That the Holy Scriptures shall in all the schools be used as a school book, the superintendents and teachers having a discretionary power in the
30 choice of their particular portions they deem advisable to teach in the respective classes.

6. That no sectarian creed or catechism shall in any case be introduced, but that, instead thereof, every scholar shall be required to learn the Lord's prayer, the Ten Commandments, and the Christian Chartist Creed, as
35 prepared by the Rev. W. Hill, and published in the Northern Star of April 3rd, 1841. ●

T70   *Anon., 'Death report' (1843)*

Borough of Cambridge in the County of Cambridge to wit.

An Inquisition indented taken for our Sovereign Lady the Queen, at the *Cambridge Union Workhouse* in the Parish of *Saint Andrew the Less* ... in the *sixth* year of the reign of our Sovereign Lady VICTORIA, by the

5   grace of God of the United Kingdom of Great Britain and Ireland Queen, Defender of the Faith, and in the year of our Lord, one thousand eight hundred and *forty three* Before CHARLES HENRY COOPER, gentleman, Coroner of the said Lady the Queen for the said Borough, on view of the body of *Sarah Layton* then and there lying dead, upon the oath of [12

10   names] good and Lawful men of the said Borough duly chosen, and who being then and there duly sworn and charged to enquire for our Sovereign Lady the Queen, when, how, and by what means the said *Sarah Layton* came to *her* death, do upon their oath say That *the said Sarah Layton on the fourth day of January in the year aforesaid at the Parish aforesaid in*

15   *the Borough aforesaid being then in bed in a certain room in the Cambridge Union Workhouse situate in the Parish aforesaid in the Borough aforesaid it so happened that accidentally, casually and by misfortune she then and there fell out of the said bed to and against the ground by means whereof she then and there received one mortal contusion.*

20   *The said Sarah Layton ... until the fourteenth day of January ... did languish and languishing did live on which [14 January] the said Sarah Layton of the mortal contusion did die. And so the Jurors aforesaid upon their oath aforesaid do say that the said Sarah Layton in manner and by means aforesaid accidentally casually and by misfortune came to her death*

25   *and not otherwise.*

In witness whereof, as well the said Coroner of our said Lady the Queen as the Jurors aforesaid, have hereunto set and subscribed their hands and seals, the day and year first above written.

[Coroner and 12 signatures]. ●

T71   *C. Pemberton, 'Private letter' (1844) and 'Advert' (1843)*

a) My dear Sir,   Cambridge, 2nd September, 1844

I saw Mr. Lieving's Son who brought you Note, & there fixed *Wednesday* to see his Father; I understood from the Son that his Father was ready to take a long lease of it – In times like the present I feel myself quite

5   incompetent to fix the annual value of this Mill – the Depreciation in the Value of Mills at this time, is so great that I fear there is no chance of letting it for any thing like the value it would have been 10 or 15 year ago. At that

time I should have fixed the Rent at £120 per ann at the least, & I doubt
much whether it will now let it for more than 2/3rd of this Sum – I cannot
10 advise your letting it for a long Term now, – the value of Mill Property
cannot I think fall lower, & the Rail Road or other Circumstances may
increase the value of your Mill. I state this as a reason against your granting
a Long Lease at this time. – Let me know by return of Post whether any of
the Cottages about the Mill can be let with it – the adjoining Meadow must
15 of course go with the Mill – The Miller will expect the privilege of catching
Eels at the Mill, & of course that adds to the value of what he hires – Let me
know whether you will take £80 a year rather than not let it; but of course
the Land could ... to be ... for, at a Rent say of 40/ per acre, exclusive of the
Rest of the Mill.
20   Yours very sincerely. Christopher Pemberton
P.S. Understand that I know nothing of Mr Lieving, as regards either his
Character or his property. Perhaps you can gain some Information & Let
[me] have it, in your letter which is to answer this.
[added] Terms agreed upon between R^{d} H Esq. & Living for the latters
25 occupation of Dernford Mill.
In consideration of Living putting the above Mill in working order he is to
occupy it Rent free from the 29th of Sepr 1844 to the 29th of Sepr 1845; from
the latter period to Sepr 1846 he is to pay a Rent of £50. With the above
Mill the Land & Cottages lately occupied by Miller are included. – A New
30 Arch to the Back water is to be built & two serviceable Gates placed by R^{d}.
Hud^{n} Esq on the Premises. Should Living put an additional Pair of French
Stones for Grinding or add any other conveniences for his business, he shall
have the liberty of removing them at the termination of the [2nd ?] year
unless Mr Hud^{n} choses to take them at a valuation which valuation is to be
35 agreed upon by two persons one named by Mr Living the other by R^{d} Hud.

b) DERNFORD MILLS, *SAWSTON, Cambridgeshire. To Be Let,* – All that
First-rate *Watercorn, Oil,* and *Trefoil Mill,* situate on an excellent Stream of
Water, having a Fall of great power, with two Water-Wheels.
    The above Mill comprises a spacious and substantial Brick *Building,*
40 which has recently undergone a thorough repair, and New Waste-Water-
Gates have been attached to the Mill. – The Corn and Oil Mill is fitten up
with two pair of four-feet-two-inch French Stones, and there was lately
another pair of Stones, the Machinery for which is upon the premises, and
if required by a tenant will be replaced ... The Chambers to this Mill are
45 capable of containing five hundred quarters. There are *Four Cottages*
contiguous to the Mill, with Gardens, which can be let with the Mill. Also
Seven Acres of Excellent *Pasture Ground.*   ●

T72 *Anon., 'Newspaper advertising' (1844)*

(a) DESTRUCTIVE ANIMALCUÆ. – As Spring approaches, the larvæ of DESTRUCTIVE INSECTS are propagated in infinite multitudes, and impregnate with millions of insects the very air we breathe. J. READ begs to inform every person interested in the practice of Horticulture, that he has made
5 considerable improvements in his ENGINES AND MACHINES for the purpose of destroying those Animalculæ which make such deadly havoc on all choice Fruit-trees and Plants at this season of the year. The above are fitted with tubes that will bear any degree of pressure required, and are water, air, and steam proof. From 31 years' practice in Horticulture, and 21 years in
10 manufacturing and improving Engines, J.R. can warrant them the best adapted for the above purposes of any hitherto made; the valves being solid spherical metal are never liable to be out of repair, even in the hottest climates. Manufactured only by the Patentee, 35, Regent Circus, Piccadilly, where they may be seen and proved. N.B. – None are genuine except
15 stamped with the words, 'READ's Patent.'
(b) ROWLAND'S ODONTO, or Pearl Dentifrice, patronised by 'Her Majesty,' H.R.H. Prince Albert, the Royal Family, and the several Courts of Europe. A FRAGRANT WHITE POWDER, prepared from Oriental Herbs of inestimable virtue, for strengthening, preserving, and cleansing the teeth. It eradicates
20 the factitious formation of tartar, and by the removal of that extraneous substance lends a salutary growth and freshness to the gums. It removes from the surface of the teeth the spots of incipient decay, polishes and preserves the enamel, substituting for discolour and the aspect of impurity, the most pure and pear-like whiteness; while, from its salubrious and
25 disinfecting qualities, it gives sweetness and perfume to the breath, bestowing at once cleanliness, and the appearance and reality of health. Price 2s. 9d. per box, duty included. CAUTION. – To protect the public from fraud, the Hon. Commissioners of Her Majesty's Stamps have authorised the Proprietors' Signature to be engraved on the Government Stamp thus, –
30 A. ROWLAND and SON, 20, Hatton Garden, which is affixed to each Box. Ask for ROWLAND'S ODONTO. Sold by them, and by Perfumers and Chemists. All others are SPURIOUS IMITATIONS.
(c) THE HAIR. – Of the numerous compounds constantly announced for promoting the growth, or reproduction of the Hair, few survive, even in
35 name, beyond a very limited period; whilst ROWLAND'S MACASSAR OIL, with a reputation unparalleled, is still on the increase in public estimation. The singular virtues of this successful invention for *restoring, preserving*, and *beautifying* the *Human Hair*, are too well known and appreciated to need comment. ●

T73   *Anon., 'Travesties of various instructions' (mid 19th century)*

(a) **CURE FOR LOVE.** *Presented gratis to* _____

Procure 4 scruples of mortal antipathy, 3 drachms of the strongest
aversion, 2 penny-weights of the opium of jealousy, 15 ounces of the aquae
of oblivion,

5   DISTIL BY THE FIRE OF CONQUERED PASSION

Render the mixture palatable with time's sure balm, use the funnel of
firmness, the filter of disgust, and the phials of contempt,

SEAL WITH THE WAX OF ANOTHER ATTACHMENT,

Destroy the prescription and have faith in the remedy, and your hollow eyes

10   will resume their former lustre.

*The above drugs are to be had of Careaway Comfort, Heart's Ease
Valley, in the County of Resignation.*

(b) **CURE FOR DECEIT.** Procure of the Essence of Seeclear sufficient to
blend with the greatest Weight of CANDOUR AND DIS-INTERESTEDNESS,

15   Mingle with them a fair proportion of Love your Brethren, and a Few Drops
of Self Humility, participate often. Effervescing with the acid of

CLEAR CONSCIENCE AND THE SUGAR OF LOVE

For the Human Race – Clarify with the Isinglass of Experience ...

(c) **HOW TO COOK A HUSBAND.** As Mr. Glass said of the hare you must

20   first *catch him*. Having done so, the mode of cooking him, so as to make a
good dish of him is as follows: – Many good husbands are spoiled in the
cooking; some women go about it as if their husbands were bladders, and
blow them up. Others keep them constantly in hot water, while others freeze
them by conjugal coldness. Some smother them with hatred, contention and

25   variance, and some keep them in pickle all their lives.

These women always serve them up with tongue sauce. Now it cannot be
supposed that husbands will be tender and good if managed in this way. But
they are on the contrary, very delicious when managed as follows: – Get a
large jar called the jar of carefulness, (which all good wives have on hand,)

30   place your husband in it, and set him near the fire of conjugal love; let the
fire be pretty hot, but especially let it be clear – above all, let the heat be
constant. Cover him over with affection, kindness, and subjection. Garnish
with modest becoming familiarity and the spice of pleasantry: and if you
add kisses and other confectionaries let them be accompanied with a

35   sufficient portion of secrecy, mixed with prudence and moderation. We
would advise all good wives to try this receipt and realize how admirable a
dish a husband is when properly cooked.   ●

T74   *Anon., 'Broadsheet – prose and verse' (mid 19th century)*

EXECUTION OF **JOHN GLEESON WILSON,**

At Kirkdale Gaol, on Saturday, September 15th, 1849, the Murderer of Mrs. Hinrichson, her Two Children, and Female Servant.

One of the most appalling murders which has for years startled and
5   disgusted society took place on the morning of Wednesday, March 28th, 1849, at No. 20, Leveson Street, Liverpool, at mid-day. A miscreant in the most brutal manner murdered two unprotected women and two helpless children.

In due course Wilson was committed for trial, which took place before
10   Mr Justice Patteson and a respectable jury, who, in less than five minutes, returned a verdict of GUILTY.

On Saturday morning, a few minutes before twelve o'clock, the iron gate leading to the drop was opened, and the prisoner appeared between two priests – the Rev. Mr. Duggan and the Rev. Mr Marshall. A general feeling
15   of horror seemed to pervade all present, which found expression in the most distant part of the assemblage by bursts of execration.

Calcraft, the London executioner, was unable to be present from illness, and the office was performed by Howard, from York, who was especially brought to Liverpool by the Under Sheriff. The priests read in English, the
20   service of the Catholic Church for a departing soul until the bolt was drawn, and the wretched culprit was launched into eternity.

Thus terminated the life of one of the greatest criminals that ever disgraced the human family. Upwards of 100,000 persons were present, the railway company running cheap trains from all available parts.

25   **THE LIVERPOOL TRAGEDIES**.

Come all you feeling christians and listen unto me,
The like was not recorded in British history,
It's of three dreadful murders committed, I am told,
By one John Gleeson Wilson, for the sake of cursed gold.

30   On Wednesday the 28th, consternation did prevail,
In Leveson Street in Liverpool, where thousands did bewail,
The fate of this poor family, who we're left to deplore,
Snatched from a father's fond embraces, who ne'er will see them more.

This monster in human shape did go there to dwell,
35   And that he went for plunder to all it is known full well,

And when this callous villain saw their defenceless state,
He did resolve them all to kill and rob them of the plate.

His bloody work he did commence all in the open day,
By striking at the children while their mother was away,
40   The servant girl did interfere, said, 'should not do so,'
Then with a poker in his hand he gave her a severe blow.

Numberless times he did her strike till she could no longer stand,
The blood did flow profusely from her wounds, and did him brand,
Then the eldest boy of five years old, in supplication said,
45   'Oh master, spare our precious lives, don't serve us like the maid.'

This darling child of five years old he brutally did kill,
Regardless of its tender cries, its precious blood did spill,
The youngest child to the kitchen ran, to shun the awful knife,
This villain followed after and took its precious life.

50   The surgeon thus describes the scene presented to his view,
A more appalling case than this he says he never knew,
Four human beings on the floor all weltering in their gore,
The sight was sickening to behold on entering the door.

The mother's wounds three inches deep upon her head and face,
55   And pools of blood as thick as mud, from all of them could trace,
None could identify the boy, his head was like a jelly;
This tragedy is worse by far than Greenacre or Kelly.

To the hospital in this sad state they quickly were conveyed,
The mother with her infant dear, and faithful servant maid,
60   Thousands did besiege the gates, their fate for to enquire,
But in three days from incise wounds, both of them did expire.

'Twill cause the captain many a pang to know their awful doom,
His loving wife and children sent to an untimely tomb,
'Twill make his hair turn grey with grief, no skill their lives could save,
65   And he did go, borne down with woe, in sorrow to the grave.

But now he's taken for this deed, bound down in irons strong,
In Kirkdale Jail he now does lie, till his trial it comes on,
May God above receive the souls of those whom he has slain,
And may they all in heavenly bliss for ever with him reign.

T75   *Anon., 'Death notice' (1850)*

FRANCES MOOR OF HARTLEPOOL, IN THE STOCKTON CIRCUIT
Was born in October, 1819; And on May 7th, 1850,

She went to the blood-washed throng in Heaven. Seven years since an
illness befell her, and, reminded by one of our members of her unfitness for
5 Heaven, seriousness took hold of her, and penitently she sought the Lord,
and obtained a 'new heart.' Her subsequent course was onward, though she
sometimes moved tremblingly. Last year, when the cholera was raging in
the town, she rendered me efficient help in my open-air meetings.
Consumption seized her three months ago, and in about a month afterwards
10 her mental depression was such as to inspire all her friends with sorrowful
sympathy on her behalf. My soul was much bowed down on her account;
but, to my surprise and joy, when I entered her room about a fortnight
before her death, she exclaimed, 'Heaven's my home!' Her future
experience was quite satisfactory. As she neared the eternal world she said,
15 'I see my way clearly. Come, Jesus! I am ready;' and with that assurance
she departed.   ●

T76   *Anon., 'Fashion report' (1851)*

FASHIONS FOR AUGUST. (From '*Le Follet.*')
     Independent of the mania for locomotion which prevails in all quarters of
the world, and covers the ocean with vessels bearing the anxious travellers
to the Crystal Palace, the moment has now arrived when the fashionable
5 watering-places, with their sea baths, are completing the migration of all
that was left amongst us of elegant society.
     Boulogne, Dieppe, and Trouville, have the privilege of attracting the
greater number of Parisiennes, who would unite, with the benefit of sea air
and bathing, the charm of society and fashionable amusements. It is for
10 these destinations that the present charming variety of elegant toilettes are
being prepared.
     Morning *negligés* are composed of peignoirs with their vestes, or
pelerines *châles* of jean, quilting, valencia of toile cashemire, in shades,
grey, dust-coloured, and pale brown; the greater part are trimmed with
15 broad braids, and lined with pink or blue taffetas. A second sleeve is worn
under the pagode of the redingotes of the same material, but tight, with a
small turn-up cuff trimmed with braid; the same trimming in two or three
rows forms a ruche around the throat; a small plaid cravat, fixed with a large
enamel or frosted silver brooch; and an embroidered muslin cap, richly
20 trimmed with strings of the same, or ribbon to match the coques, which

takes the place of the bandeaux until the hour of dressing. *Capelines* of taffetas, embroidered muslin, or coloured jaconot, with large curtain, protecting the face most successfully from the sun or wind, are much worn in morning promenades. Large scarf shawls of plain cashemire in blue,
25 green, or grey, trimmed with a deep fringe, surmounted by a very broad velvet, with two or three rows of narrow on each side, either black or of the same color as the shawl, but of a much deeper shade, completes this toilette. As it is often cold at the sea-side, the mantelet scarfs are slightly wadded.

At the hour of promenade, the sea-side nearly resembles the grand walk
30 of the Tuilleries, ladies and children displaying all the richness and grace of the Parisienne toilette. Robes of *chiné, pékin pompadour, taffetas d'Italie, grenadine,* or barege, have flounces printed in designs of wreaths of roses, honeysuckle, lilac – indeed all kinds of graceful flowers, whose colours harmonise so well on grounds of grey, white, or sea-green. With this style
35 of robe is worn the mantelet. *Maintenon,* with its triple *garniture* of black lace upon dark coloured taffetas, or white lace upon lighter shades; the *Mathilde* mantelet, with its drawn ribbons mixed with guipure of the same shade as the mantelet, the cut of which so gracefully delineates the waist, that it appears an attribute of all young and elegant ladies. The mantelet
40 *Valerie,* of white taffetas, or grenadine, with its beautiful embroideries in silk, or mixed *soutaches,* with deep headings which float as light as lace; or the *mantille andalouse* of black lace, with a wide trimming. This *mantille,* both for shape and elegant *negligée,* is suitable for all toilettes. We must not forget the large square shawl of black lace, or rounded in front, forming a
45 shawl behind and mantelet in front, being equally fashionable this season.

Most of the dresses are now made with two bodies, in order to form double dresses, yet not to greatly increase the luggage.

The low body has a berthe descending *en cœur,* the front trimmed with bows of ribbon, passementerie and *bouillonnés,* matching the trimming on
50 the short sleeves and skirt. The high bodies are often made with basquines, cut in indentations; the sleeves match, and are sometimes open the whole length of the arm, and fastened at intervals with bows of ribbon or buttons. This kind of Spanish sleeve is a very pretty novelty, and an agreeable change to the uniformity of the *pagodes,* which, however, are still *the*
55 fashion.

When the basquines bodies are open in front, a small embroidered waistcoat is added, the buttons of which are of pearl, amethyst, turquoise, or emeralds. These waistcoats, which appear at first rather venturesome, derive all their distinction from the happy manner in which they are combined. ●

T77   *J. W. Hudson, 'On mechanics' institutions' (1851)*

Prospectus. THE work contains an exact comprehensive register of the principal changes which have occurred in the management of the Mechanics' and Literary Institutions in the large towns in Great Britain. The history of each Institution is given at length, accompanied with tabular
5 annual returns.

The history of the Educational Societies of the middle classes, and the Adult Poor Schools in an unbroken chain, for upwards of a century, exhibited by statistical details and annual returns, and proving by existing societies, that Mechanics' Institutions were established long prior to their exten-
10 sion and developement by the late Dr. Birkbeck.

The operations of Adult and Benevolent Evening Schools, Village and Farmers' Clubs, Young Men's Reformation and Mental Improvement Societies, &c. The failure of Public and Itinerating Libraries, as tested and demonstrated after an experience of fifty years in Great Britain. – Decline of
15 Philosophical Institutions in England.

The rise, progress, and present state of Literary and Institutional Unions, Schools of Design, Museums, Factory News Rooms, and Libraries, &c. On the management of Athenæums, Literary, and Mechanics' Institutions – their extension and present tendency – new features – the necessity for
20 internal improvement and general developement. The Mechanics' Institutions in all quarters of the world.

A Tabular return of all the Institutions in Great Britain, Ireland, &c. The present number of Members, extent of Library, and their educational operations. Name of the Secretary, &c., &c.

25 PREFACE. THE unexampled efforts now making in every part of the kingdom for the intellectual and physical improvement of the lower classes of the community, distinguish the present, as the age of philanthropy and good-will to all men. The middle classes vie with the rich in promoting the great and good-work of education. The brightest minds in literature and
30 science direct their talents to its developement; preparing the ignorant by addresses, by lectures, and by their writings, to receive and understand the great and interesting truths which the Creator unfolds before them. The beloved Sovereign of these realms lends her fair and royal name in behalf of Bazaars, to increase the stores of Institution Libraries. The lawned Divine,
35 and the ermined Duke feel a pleasure in presiding over the festivals of the artizan and the day labourer. The press is prolific with carefully collated proofs of the connection between offences and ignorance, as they appear in the calendar of crime; civic magistrates begin to hold it a duty to take part in

all meetings which have for their object, the dissemination of useful know-
40 ledge amongst the multitude; the agriculturist is alive to the importance of
the allotment system, and institutes Farmers' Clubs; while the manufacturer
finds it *profitable* to form schools and factory libraries, to rear amateur
bands of musicians amongst his workmen, to encourage frugality by sav-
ings' banks, benefit societies, sick clubs, clothes clubs, burial associations,
45 and by occasional tea meetings, at which, he and his family partake, to
destroy that barrier between men, which pride and wealth sometimes un-
graciously erects ...

    ... The universal complaint that Mechanics' Institutions are attended by
persons of a higher rank than those for whom they were designed, applies
50 with equal force to the Athenæums and Literary Institutions of the country.
It will be found on investigation, that Athenæums have ceased to be the
societies of young men, not only the roll of members, but a glance round the
news-room will show an assemblage of men of middle age, principals of
firms, professional men, managing and confidential clerks, factors, brokers,
55 agents, and wholesale shopkeepers, who form both the directory and the
majority of the association. Hence it has been assumed, that the employer
and the employed are to be seen side by side perusing alike the newspaper
and the review, drawing knowledge from the same fount; but such is not the
fact, the clerk turns aside from his employer, either from respect or
60 humility, and when he joins his companions he generally gives utterance to
his discontent by an intimation that he shall join the Mechanics', for he will
not subscribe to an Institution where 'the governor' is present. The same
influences are produced in the other Institution, the warehouseman, the
packer, the carter, and the mill-hand shun the society of the clerk and the
65 foreman, and they in turn quit the Institution which was established
expressly for them. The result is made manifest in the classification of the
occupation of members of these societies, but wherefore should the
educationist complain, since it only demonstrates the necessity for creating
another class of societies, to which the working operative shall alone be
70 admissable. With the increase of population, society has extended and
developed itself in new circles, and the requirements of the age, demand for
the labouring classes, not only free public libraries, free public news-rooms,
free public lectures, but evening classes, free to the half-educated shopboy,
and the unlettered apprentice. Mechanics' Institutions, and Literary
75 Societies must be immediately rendered self-supporting; for the donations
of the wealthy and benevolent are demanded for higher services.   ●

T78   *C. E. Francatelli, 'Cooking recipe' (1852)*

No. 3. ECONOMICAL POT LIQUOR SOUP.

A thrifty housewife will not require that I should tell her to save the liquor in which the beef has been boiled; I will therefore take it for granted that the next day she carefully removes the grease, which will have become set firm on the top of the broth, into her fat pot; this must be kept to make a pie-
5 crust, or to fry potatoes, or any remains of vegetables, onions, or fish. The liquor must be tasted, and if it is found to be too salt, some water must be added to lessen its saltness, and render it palatable. The pot containing the liquor must then be placed on the fire to boil, and when the scum rises to the surface it should be removed with a spoon. While the broth is boiling, put as
10 many piled-up table-spoonfuls of oatmeal as you have pints of liquor into a basin; mix this with cold water into a smooth liquid batter, and then stir it into the boiling soup; season with some pepper and a good pinch of allspice, and continue stirring the soup with a stick or spoon on the fire for about twenty minutes; you will then be able to serve out a plentiful and nourishing
15 meal to a large family at a cost of not more than the price of the oatmeal.●

T79   *Anon., 'War despatches (the Crimean War)' (1854)*

In the stagnant water which ripples almost imperceptibly on the shore there floated all forms of nastiness and corruption which the prowling dogs, standing leg-deep as they wade about in search of offal, cannot destroy. The smell from the shore was noisome, but a few yards out from the fringe of
5 buoyant cats, dogs, birds, straw, sticks – in fact, of all sorts of abominable flotsam and jetsam, which bob about on the pebbles unceasingly – the water became exquisitely clear and pure. The slaughter-house for the troops, erected by the sea-side, did not contribute, as may readily be imagined, to the cleanliness of this filthy beach, or the wholesomeness of the
10 atmosphere.
... Horrors occurred here every day which were shocking to think of. Walking by the beach one might see some straw sticking up through the sand, and on scraping it away with his stick, be horrified at bringing to light the face of a corpse which had been deposited there with a wisp of straw
15 around it, a prey to dogs and vultures. Dead bodies rose up from the bottom in the harbour and bobbed grimly around in the water or floated in from sea and drifted past the sickened gazers on board the ships – all buoyant, bolt upright, and hideous in the sun.
It was a vast armada. No pen could describe its effect upon the eye. Ere
20 an hour had elapsed it had extended itself over half the circumference of the

horizon. Possibly no expedition so complex and so terrible in its means of destruction, with such enormous power in engines of war and such capabili-ties of locomotion, was ever yet sent forth by any worldly power. The fleet, in five irregular and straggling lines, flanked by men-of-war and war
25 steamers, advanced slowly filling the atmosphere with innumerable columns of smoke, which gradually flattened out into streaks and joined the clouds, adding to the sombre appearance of this well-named 'Black' Sea. The land was lost to view very speedily beneath the coal clouds and the steam clouds of the fleet, and as we advanced not an object was visible in
30 the half of the great circle which lay before us, save the dark waves and the cold sky ...

The dark French columns on our right looked very small compared to our battalions, though we knew they were quite as strong; but the marching of our allies, laden as they were with all their packs, etc., was wonderful –
35 the pace at which they went was really 'killing'. It was observable, too, that our staff was showy and more numerous than that of the French. Nothing in the shape of head-dress strikes the eye so much as a cocked hat and bunch of white cock's feathers, and several of our best officers very wisely doffed the latter adornment, thinking that they were quite conspicuous enough by
40 their advanced positions on horseback and by the number of their staff around them. At this time I was riding in front, and when the regiments halted I went through the Light Division, part of the 2nd Division, the Guards and the Highlanders. I found all my friends, save one or two, in high spirits. Some had received letters from wives and children by the mail,
45 which made them look grave and think seriously on the struggle to come. Others were joking and laughing in the best possible spirits. Many a laugh did I hear from lips which in two hours more were closed for ever. The officers and men made the most of this delay and ate whatever they had with them; but there was a great want of water, and the salt pork made them
50 so thirsty that in the subsequent passage of the Alma, under the heaviest fire, the men stopped to drink and to fill their water canteens ...

As we advanced, we could see the enemy very distinctly – their great-coated masses resembling patches of wood on the hill sides. The line of the river below the heights they occupied was indicated by patches of the
55 richest verdure and by belts of fine fruit trees and vineyards.   ●

T80   *'Royal letters' (1855-6)*

(a) *Queen Victoria to the King of the Belgians.*

BALMORAL CASTLE, 11th September 1855.

MY DEAREST UNCLE. – The great event has at length taken place – *Sebastopol has fallen!* We received the news here last night when we were
5   sitting quietly round our table after dinner. We did what we could to celebrate it; but what was but little, for to my grief we have not *one* soldier, no band, nothing here to make any sort of demonstration. What we did do was in Highland fashion to light a *bonfire* on the top of a hill opposite the house, which had been built last year when the premature news of the fall of
10   Sebastopol deceived every one, and which we had to leave *unlit*, and found here on our return!

On Saturday evening we heard of one Russian vessel having been destroyed, on Sunday morning of the destruction of another, yesterday morning of the fall of the Malakhoff Tower – and *then* of *Sebastopol!* We
15   were not successful against the Redan on the 8th, and I fear our loss was considerable. Still the *daily* loss in the trenches was becoming so serious that no loss in achieving such a result is to be compared to that. This event will delight my brother and faithful ally – and *friend*, Napoleon III. – I may add, for we really are *great friends*; this attempt, though that of a madman,
20   is very distressing and makes one *tremble* ...

We expect the young Prince Fritz Wilhelm of Prussia on a little visit here on Friday.

I must now conclude. With Albert's love, ever your devoted Niece,

VICTORIA R.

25   (b) *Lord Panmure to General Simpson.*

[*Telegram.*]   12th September 1855.

The Queen has received, with deep emotion, the welcome intelligence of the fall of Sebastopol.

Penetrated with profound gratitude to the Almighty, who has vouchsafed
30   this triumph to the Allied Armies, Her Majesty has commanded me to express to yourself, and through you to the Army, the pride with which she regards this fresh instance of its heroism.

The Queen congratulates her Troops on the triumphant issue of this protracted siege, and thanks them for the cheerfulness and fortitude with
35   which they have encountered its toils, and the valour which has led to its termination.

The Queen deeply laments that this success is not without its alloy in the heavy losses which have been sustained; and while she rejoices in the

victory, Her Majesty deeply sympathises with the noble sufferers in their
40   country's cause.

You will be pleased to congratulate General Pélissier in Her Majesty's
name upon the brilliant result of the assault on the Malakhoff, which proves
the irresistible force as well as indomitable courage of her brave Allies.

(c) *Queen Victoria to General Simpson*
45   BALMORAL, 14th September 1855
With a heart full of gratitude and pride, as well as of sorrow for the many
valuable lives that have been lost, the Queen writes to General Simpson to
congratulate him, as well on her own part as on that of the Prince, on the
glorious news of the *Fall of Sebastopol*! General Simpson must indeed *feel*
50   *proud* to have commanded the Queen's noble Army on *such* an occasion.

She wishes him to express to that gallant Army her high sense of their
gallantry, and her joy and satisfaction at their labours, anxieties, and cruel
sufferings, for nearly a year, having *at length* been crowned with such
success ...

55   (d) *Queen Victoria to Miss Florence Nightingale.*
                                    WINDSOR CASTLE, [January] 1856.
DEAR MISS NIGHTINGALE, – You are, I know, well aware of the
high sense I entertain of the Christian devotion which you have displayed
during this great and bloody war, and I need hardly repeat to you how warm
60   my admiration is for your services, which are fully equal to those of my
dear and brave soldiers, whose suffering you have had the *privilege* of
alleviating in so merciful a manner. I am, however, anxious of marking my
feelings in a manner which I trust will be agreeable to you, and therefore
send you with this letter a brooch, the form and emblems of which
65   commemorate your great and blessed work, and which, I hope, you will
wear as a mark of the high approbation of your Sovereign!

It will be a very great satisfaction to me, when you return at last to these
shores, to make the acquaintance of one who has set so bright an example to
our sex. And with every prayer for the preservation of your valuable health,
70   believe me, always, yours sincerely,   VICTORIA R.

T81   *'Student unrest (various excerpts)' (1856)*

The Vice-Chancellor appoints *Thursday*, February 7, for the ELECTION of a Burgess to serve in Parliament for the university, in the room of the late Right Honourable HENRY GOULBURN. The Poll will be taken in the Senate-House on ... and in the evenings ... in the Public Schools.

5   WE, the undersigned, having been engaged with the VICE-CHANCELLOR in receiving and recording the Votes in the Senate-House on *Thursday* the 7th, the First Day of the Election, offer to Members of the Senate our testimony, that in consequence of the noise made by the persons in the galleries, it was impossible for us to hear the VICE-CHANCELLOR when he read the names
10   and designations of the Voters; and that, in our opinion, the VICE-CHANCELLOR could not do otherwise, in the discharge of his duty, than take effectual means for the prevention of his inconvenience.

The Master trusts to the good feeling of the Gentlemen in College, that they will carefully refrain from continuing (?) or taking any part in a
15   *repetition of the annoyance caused to the Vice-Chancellor yesterday Evening. He entreats them most urgently to attend to this request. May Lodge Feb 8/56*

The VICE-CHANCELLOR begs leave to offer his respectful thanks to those Members of the Senate who yesterday assisted in repressing the attempts of
20   certain Undergraduates to enter the Senate-House and the Public Schools by force. At the same time he takes the liberty of observing that such attempts, and cries intended to be offensive to the University Officers, ought not only to be repressed, but punished; and that Members of the Senate will be rendering a service to the University, by learning, for that purpose, the
25   names of offenders.   TRINITY LODGE FEB. 9, 1856

Floreat Cantabrigia! TO THE UNDERGRADUATES OF CAMBRIDGE
GENTLEMEN,   The outrage publicly offered to our University in the person of its VICE-CHANCELLOR so intimately concerns us all, that you will excuse an independent observer addressing you at this time. I do this without
30   concert with anyone here. I came up to Cambridge to exercise my right of voting. I am living on hereditary property, and in no way connected with the University except as a Member of its Senate ...

   If it may be said, as I could testify from personal observation (of the name of any individual member I am happy to be ignorant), that Cambridge
35   men can, under cover of night, suborn a vile rabble of the lowest people to offer insult and violence to their chief authorities, the reputation of our undergraduates, of one generation at least, for the highest qualities of

English gentlemen, is forfeited. The name of a Member of the University is
no longer a proud distinction among men. Hasten, I charge you, for the
40   honour of your University and for your own, to remove the stain!

That your high and honourable minds will feel indignant at the very
imputation, and are utterly ignorant and innocent of the charge, I can well
believe; and yet it is true of some wearing the University dress, and
members of our body; and you can only clear yourselves individually by an
45   individual protest, and a renunciation as public as the conduct which has
given occasion to the scandal. Such a disclaimer will reflect credit on
yourselves, and will, no doubt, lead to a restoration of your privileges ...

I have the honour to be, Gentlemen, Your sincere Friend,
Cambridge, FEB. 9, 1856   A JUNIOR MEMBER OF THE SENATE.

50   The Election being over, I wish to make a few remarks, suggested by what
has occurred on the occasion.

It was with great regret that I found myself, as Vice-Chancellor, under
the necessity of directing that the Undergraduates should be excluded from
the Galleries in the Senate-House ... Of the necessity of this exclusion, no
55   one who attached any importance to the business which was then and there
transacted, could doubt. While the Galleries were occupied, the noise was,
for a great part of the time, so great and incessant, that the Vice-Chancellor,
his Assessors, and the Scrutineers, who sat at the Voting Table close to each
other, could not hear each other's voices, and were compelled to try to
60   transact the business of the Election in dumb show ...

The University has to regard its public proceedings as they bear upon the
Education of the young men in England. To allow an habitual and prominent part of such proceedings to be irrational and uncontrolled outcries on
the part of our Students, would be to disregard that object; because such
65   conduct, permitted on their part, degrades and brutalizes them. It tends to
extinguish all respect for others, and all self-respect; and to reduce them to
the level, in manners and conduct, of the lowest street mob at a borough
election of the worst kind ...

I the more confidently believe that the majority of the Undergraduates
70   have a due self-respect, and a due respect for just authority temperately exercised, because I have ever found it so, both as Master of a College, and as
Vice-Chancellor. One of the happiest recollections of my life is that of a great
occasion in my former Vice-Chancellorship, when I had need to ask for great
orderliness and considerable self-denial on the part of the Undergraduates.
75   This demand they responded to with a dignified and sweet-tempered obe-
dience which endeared them to me then, as many good qualities which I have
seen in successive generations of Students have endeared them to me since ●

T82   *Anon., 'Election campaigning' (1857)*

ELECTORS OF HARTLEPOOL.

To the Rescue. Deliver your Borough from the hands of a Drunken and
incompetent Council.

Think of at least three Honourable Gentlemen who had gone in with
5 cringing promises of Economy, Diligence, &c., &c., being drunk at one
time, and another filled to repletion, and oblivious of the external world.

Think of men pandering to the cry of a false Economy, till the Corporation is struck fast for funds; and when you are run upwards of £1,000 in
Debt, and your Credit damaged, a deputation is sent off to beg the loan of
10 £150 to pay Interest; it is for you to say when the misrule of the Borough
shall cease, when drunken rows in the Town HALL shall end, when the
paltry dribbling expenditure of your money, which gives you almost
nothing in return, shall give place to an enlightened and comprehensive
Economy, which, while careful of the true Interests of the Borough, shall
15 give you Value for the Money you contribute to the Taxes of the Town.

In the approaching Election, beware of Men who come to you with the
Address of a mean hireling, full of empty and unmeaning promises.

Value and support manly Independence; look carefully to the previous
character of the Candidates, for Honesty, Truth, Sobriety, and Intelligence.
20 Good character is the best guarantee, that you will be faithfully served,
and well Represented in the Council of the Borough.

True Men are now before you, Among such are STEPHEN ROBINSON,
and WILLIAM GRAY. Rally round them, give them your support on the
day of Election, Return them as your Representatives.

25 Slumbering Electors, 'Awake, arise, or be for ever fallen.'
                  I am, Gentlemen, Yours faithfully, ANGLO-SAXON ●

T83   *H. Mayhew, 'The life of a coster lad' (1861)*

'On a Sunday I goes out selling, and all I yarns I keeps. As for going to
church, why, I can't afford it, – besides, to tell the truth, I don't like it well
enough. Plays, too, ain't in my line much; I'd sooner go to a dance – its
more livelier. The 'penny gaffs' is rather more in my style; the songs are out
5 and out, and makes our gals laugh. The smuttier the better, I thinks; bless
you! the gals likes it as much as we do. If we lads ever has a quarrel, why
we fights for it. If I was to let a cove off once, he'd do it again; but I never
give a lad a chance, so long as I can get anigh him. I never heard about
Christianity; but if a cove was to fetch me a lick of the head, I'd give it him
10 again, whether he was a big 'un or a little 'un. I'd precious soon see a

henemy of mine shot afore I'd forgive him, – where's the use? Do I
understand what behaving to your neighbour is? – In coorse I do. If a feller
as lives next me wanted a basket of mine as I wasn't using, why, he might
have it; if I was working it though, I'd see him further! I can understand that
15   all as lives in a court is neighbours; but as for policemen, they're nothing to
me, and I should like to pay 'em all off well. No; I never heerd about this
here creation you speaks about. In coorse God Almighty made the world,
and the poor bricklayers' labourers built the houses arterwards – that's *my*
opinion; but I can't say, for I've never been in no schools, only always hard
20   at work, and knows nothing about it. I have heerd a little about our Saviour,
– they seem to say he were a goodish kind of a man; but if he says as how a
cove's to forgive a feller as hits you, I should say he know'd nothing about
it. In coorse the gals the lads goes and lives with thinks our walloping 'em
wery cruel of us, but we don't. Why don't we? – why, because we don't.
25   Before father died, I used sometimes to say my prayers, but after that
mother was too busy getting a living to mind about my praying. Yes, I
knows! – in the Lord's prayer they says, 'Forgive us our trespasses, as we
forgives them as trespasses agin us.' It's a very good thing, in coorse, but no
costers can't do it.' ...
30   There are but five tailors in London who make the garb proper to
costermongers; one of these is considered somewhat 'slop,' or as a coster
called him, a 'springer-up.'
     This springer-up is blamed by some of the costermongers, who condemn
him for employing women at reduced wages. A whole court of coster-
35   mongers, I was assured, would withdraw their custom from a tradesman, if
one of their body, who had influence among them, showed that the tradesman was unjust to his workpeople. The tailor in question issues bills after
the following fashion. I give one verbatim, merely withholding the address
for obvious reasons:
40   'ONCE TRY YOU'LL COME AGAIN.
Slap-up Tog and out-and-out Kicksies Builder. Mr. – nabs the chance of
putting his customers awake, that he has just made his escape from Russia,
not forgetting to clap his mawleys upon some of the right sort of Ducks, to
make single and double backed Slops for gentlemen in black, when on his
45   return home he was stunned to find one of the top manufacturers of Manchester had cut his lucky and stepped off to the Swan Stream, leaving
behind him a valuable stock of Moleskins, Cords, Velveteens, Plushes,
Swandowns, &c., and I having some ready in my kick, grabbed the chance,
and stepped home with my swag, and am now safe landed at my crib.' ●

T84 *'Rules and regulations of the Cambridge Free Library.' (1862)*

1. THE Lending Department is open daily (except Sunday, Good Friday, Christmas Day, and any day appointed by public authority as a day of General Fast or Thanksgiving) for the issue and return of Books to persons above the age of 14 years, between the hours of *Eleven* A.M. and *Two* P.M.

5 and *Six* and *Nine*, in the evening.

2. No person shall be entitled to borrow a book without having first obtained the signatures of two Burgesses of the Borough to a voucher, which may be had on application; this voucher must have been delivered to the Librarian three clear days before the first issue of books to the person

10 recommended, and if found satisfactory a card will be issued. In case of the Librarian refusing a card, the applicant may appeal to the Committee. When either of the persons who may have signed the voucher shall desire to withdraw from his engagement, he must give notice in writing to the Librarian, who will give a release as soon as he shall have ascertained that

15 no liability has been incurred, or remains undischarged.

3. The borrower shall produce his card on every application for a book and no card shall be transferable. When a card is renewed, the sum of one penny shall be paid for the same.

4. The Librarian shall carefully examine, or cause to be examined, each

20 book returned; and if the same be found, to have sustained any damage or injury, or to have been rendered of less value by being soiled or written in, the borrower or his sureties shall pay the amount of the damage or injury done, or otherwise procure a new copy of equal value; in the latter case such person shall be entitled to the damaged copy on depositing the new one.

25 5. No person shall have more than one volume, except works of Fiction, out at the same time; and each book must be returned to the Library within the time specified on its cover, under the penalty of one penny for each day over the time allowed, but no fine shall exceed the value of the book borrowed. If not returned within four weeks from the day of issue, the book

30 shall be considered lost, and the borrower's sureties applied to for a new copy, or its value.

6. No book shall be issued to any person in arrear for fines, or who has not replaced any book lost or damaged by him.

7. No borrower shall be at liberty to lend or part with the possession of any

35 book obtained by him from the Library.

8. Each borrower shall deposit his card with the Librarian for the space of three clear days during the month of January in each year, for the purpose of examination and renewal. ●

T85   *Anon., 'Public notices' (1862-88)*

(a) ORDER REGULATING THE USE OF LOCOMOTIVES
WITHIN THE BOROUGH OF CAMBRIDGE

Whereas it appears to me, the Right Honourable Sir George Grey, Bart., one
of Her Majesty's Principal Secretaries of State, that the use of Locomotives
5   unless restricted, as hereinafter mentioned, on any highway within the limits
of the borough of Cambridge, is dangerous and inconvenient to the public:
I hereby do, by virtue of the provisions of 'The Locomotive Act, 1861,'
by this Order, under my hand, prohibit the use of any kind of Locomotive
whatever propelled by steam or any other than animal power on the
10 highways within the limits of the borough of Cambridge, at any time except
between the hours of nine at night and seven in the morning.
Given under my hand at Whitehall, this 24th day of December, 1862.

(b) *Borough of Cambridge.* CAUTION.

Every person who within any street, road, square, court, alley, thoroughfare,
15 or public passage within this borough, shall wantonly discharge any fire
arms to the obstruction, annoyance, or danger of residents or passengers, is
by the Town Police Clauses Act (incorporated with the Cambridge
Corporation Act, 1850) liable to a penalty not exceeding forty shillings, or
in the discretion of the convicting justice, may be committed to prison for a
20 period not exceeding fourteen days.
By Order, C.H. COOPER, TOWN CLERK. *Guildhall, 21 December, 1864.*

(c) BOROUGH OF CAMBRIDGE.

BY the Locomotives Act 1865 (28 & 29 Vict. c. 83) and the Order made by
the Council under the said Act, 10 Oct. 1865, any Locomotive propelled by
25 steam or any other than animal power on any turnpike road or public highway within this Borough, must be worked according to the following rules
and regulations:

1. At least three persons shall be employed to drive or conduct such Locomotive, and if more than two waggons or carriages be attached thereto,
30   an additional person shall be employed, who shall take charge of such
   waggons or carriages.
2. One of such persons, while any Locomotive is in motion, shall precede
   such Locomotive on foot by not less than sixty yards, and shall carry a
   red flag constantly displayed, and shall warn the riders and drivers of
35   horses of the approach of such Locomotive, and shall signal the driver
   thereof when it shall be necessary to stop, and shall assist horses, and
   carriages drawn by horses, passing the same.

3. The driver of such Locomotive shall give as much space as possible for the passing of other traffic.

40 4. The whistle of such Locomotive shall not be sounded for any purpose whatever; nor shall the cylinder taps be opened within sight of any persons riding, driving, leading, or in charge of a horse upon the road; nor shall the steam be allowed to attain a pressure such as to exceed the limit fixed by the safety valve, so that no steam shall blow off when the

45 Locomotive is upon the road.

5. Every such Locomotive shall be instantly stopped, on the person preceding the same, or any other person with a horse, or carriage drawn by a horse, putting up his hand as a signal to require such Locomotive to be stopped.

50 6. Any person in charge of any such Locomotive shall provide two efficient lights to be affixed conspicuously, one on each side on the front of the same, until one hour before sunrise.

7. No Locomotive shall pass through between seven in the morning and twelve at night.

55 8. No Locomotive shall be driven at a greater speed than two miles an hour.

A penalty of not exceeding £10 is incurred by non-compliance with any of these rules and regulations. GUILDHALL, 10 *Oct.* 1865.

(d) FOOT PAVEMENTS.

THE attention of the Inhabitants is directed to Section LXXXII. of the
60 above Acts, by which it is enacted That if any person or persons shall run, drive, or draw, or cause to be run, driven, or drawn on any foot pavements within the Town any Wheel or Wheels, Sledge, Wheelbarrow, or Carriage whatever, or roll any Cask, or drive or lead, or cause to be driven or led any Horse or Cattle on any foot pavement, other than in cases of absolute neces-
65 sity, such person or persons shall forfeit and pay 5s. for the first offence, 10s. for the second, and for the third and every other offence 20s., to be recovered as in the said Acts directed, no person being however liable to such penalties for rolling any Cask for a less distance than 20 yards.

And NOTICE IS HEREBY GIVEN, that all persons found so offending
70 will be at once proceeded against in manner by the said Acts directed.

By Order, FRED. BARLOW, *Clerk to the Commissioners.*

St. Andrew's Street, Cambridge, October 10, 1868.

●

T86   *Anon., 'Mock valentines' (mid 19th century)*

(a) CUPID'S OFFICIAL TELEGRAPHS.
                    Dated Stamp of Sᵗ Valentines Delivering Office, Feb 14.
If the sincerity of the sentiments conveyed in this Telegram be doubted,
they will be repeated, but double the number of kisses anticipated will be
5   required in payment. If too many are given by mistake, the sender of this
will gladly repay such excess on the ruby lips of the fair recipient of this
Telegram. When the cost of a reply to a Lover's Telegram has been prepaid,
and the number of words in such reply are in excess of 'Well I'm sure,' 'Be
quiet do,' garnished by a few blushes, the sender of such reply is bound to
10 pay extra for such excess, by an extra number of endearments. Fractions of
kisses do not count, and when Telegrams are taken in by a third party the
same must not open them and kiss by proxy.
              N.B. – This Form should occupy a lady's thoughts on the Festival of St.
Valentine.

15 (b) **Bank of Love.** *I promise to pay to you on Demand*
              the entire **Love** *of the suppliant who sends this.*
              1861. Febʸ 14 Temple of Hymen, 14 Feb.ʸ 1861.
              For the Gov.ʳ and Comp.ᵃ of the **BANK of LOVE.**
                          Cupid.

20 (c) **V. R. Summons to a Person Charged with an Indictable Offence**
    Court of Hymen,   To   *George Pegg*
    to Wit.   of   *Tomlins Grove*

Whereas you have this day been charged before the undersigned, one of His
Majesty's Cupid's Justices of the Peace in and for the said Court of Hymen,
25 for that you *willfully, feloniously and designedly, waylaid, entrapped, and
stole from the Plaintif in this cause A Heart, the whole sole and real
property of the said Plaintif – Mary Anne Sophia Tomlin*
These are therefore to command you in his Majesty's name to be and appear
on *next the 14th, day of February at Ten o'clock* in the Forenoon, or at
30 such other day and hour as I the undersigned, may think proper to appoint,
at the said Court of Hymen to answer to the said Charge, and to be dealt
with, according to Law.
              HEREIN FAIL NOT AT YOUR PERIL,-
          GIVEN under my Hand and seal, this *14ᵗʰ* day of *February* in the Year
35 of our Lord, One Thousand, Eight Hundred, and SIXTY *nine*
    I Love Well   Justice of the Peace in the Court of Hymen ●

T87 *Anon. 'Commission' (1867)*

*VICTORIA R. **Victoria**,* by the Grace of God, of the United Kingdom of Great Britain and Ireland, Queen, Defender of the Faith. ***To Our*** right trusty and well-beloved Councillor Sir William Erle, Knight; ... Barristers at Law; and Our trusty and well-beloved William Mathews, Esquire, greeting.

5 ***Whereas*** it has been represented unto Us that it is expedient that inquiry should be made into the several matters herein-after mentioned.

Now Know Ye, that We, reposing great trust and confidence in your ability and discretion, have nominated, constituted, and appointed, and do by these Presents nominate, constitute, and appoint, you, the Said Sir
10 William Erle, Thomas George Earl of Lichfield, Francis Charteris, Esquire (commonly called Lord Elcho), ..., to be Our Commissioners for the purposes of the said inquiry.

And We do hereby enjoin you, or any Four of you, to inquire into and report on the Organisation and Rules of Trades Unions and other Associa-
15 tions, whether of Workmen or Employers, and to inquire into and report on the effect produced by such Trades Unions and Associations on the Workmen and Employers respectively, and on the Relations between Workmen and Employers, and on the Trade and Industry of the Country; with power to investigate any recent acts of intimidation, outrage, or wrong alleged to
20 have been promoted, encouraged, or connived at by such Trades Unions or other Associations, and also to suggest any improvements to be made in the law with respect to the matters aforesaid, or with respect to the relations between Workmen and their Employers, for the mutual benefit of both parties.

25 ***And*** for the better discovery, of the truth in the premises, We do by these Presents give and grant unto you, or any Four of you, full power and authority to call before you, or any Four of you, such persons as you shall judge necessary, by whom you may be better informed of the truth in the premises, and to inquire of the premises and every part thereof by all other
30 lawful ways and means whatsoever.

And Our further Will and Pleasure is that you, Our said Commissioners, do, with as little delay as may be consistent with a due discharge of the duties hereby imposed upon you, certify unto Us from time to time, under your hands and seals, your several proceedings in the premises ...

35 ***And*** for your assistance in the execution of these Presents We do hereby authorize and empower you to appoint a Secretary to this Our Commission, to attend you, whose services and assistance We require you to use from time to time as occasion may require. ●

T88   *Anon. 'Matrimonial advertisements' (1869)*

When will our fair friends cease to trust not so much in 'deceitful man,' as in advertising man? Two cases have lately been reported in which degradation, misery, and ruin have been brought on young girls, mainly through the influence of the pernicious penny journals of the period. One
5 was the victim of the *soi-disant* Major-General Haynes, whose case we alluded to lately, and who, we are thankful to say, is now undergoing a five years' penal servitude for bigamy. In this rascal's case, letters were produced to show that the prisoner carried on a regular system of swindling over too credulous ladies anxious for matrimony, and that he had a
10 confederate to whom he paid a percentage upon his illgotten receipts! The other was the case of a villain, who, by inserting and answering advertisements, had married several women and seduced more. Luckily his career has likewise been cut short. But when will young girls learn common sense, and give over corresponding with the trashy periodicals of the day?
15 Nothing can really in these days be more horrible than the facilities that are offered to such, and we may say the temptations, by the flagrant yet supposed-to-be virtuous advertisements which the *London Journal* and the *London Reader* and similar productions weekly present to their hundreds of thousands of readers. At one time we fancied they were mere inventions,
20 but the sad cases that occasionally crop up in our courts prove they are terrible realities. Read the following from the last numbers of the journals we have mentioned, and imagine the mischief that is being done among the girlhood of the nation.

From the *London Journal*: – T.D. has been asked for his *carte de visite*
25 by T.L., who is twenty-one; Lola, middle-aged, a widow, tall, and dark; M.G.T., granddaughter of a colonel in the army; Emilie L., nineteen and beautiful – her hair is dark brown; Amy Grey, good-tempered and domestic.

Happy Joe would be delighted if he could find a wife who was from eighteen to twenty-one, dark, well-educated, and knew music. He is twenty-
30 two, and occupying a good farm with a comfortable homestead in the west of England. It is his own property, and he has other means.

Horace H., a tall, dark, well-educated mechanic, about to set up on his own account, wishes to receive the *carte de visite* of a respectable young lady about his own age.
35 M.P., twenty-one, and a pretty blonde of the medium height, well-educated and connected, would like to marry a gentleman in at least a comfortable position.   ●

T89 *J. Ruskin, 'Inaugural lecture' (1870)*

There is a destiny now possible to us – the highest ever set before a nation to be accepted or refused. We are still undegenerate in race; a race mingled of the best northern blood. We are not yet dissolute in temper, but still have the firmness to govern, and the grace to obey. We have taught a religion of

5 pure mercy, which we must either now betray, or learn to defend by fulfilling. And we are rich in an inheritance of honour, bequeathed to us through a thousand years of noble history, which it should be our daily thirst to increase with splendid avarice, so that English men, if it be a sin to covet honour, should be the most offending souls alive. Within the last few

10 years we have had the laws of natural science opened to us with a rapidity which has been blinding by its brightness; and means of transit and communication given to us, which have made but one kingdom of the habitable globe. One kingdom; – but who is to be its king? Is there to be no king in it, think you, and every man to do that which is right in his own

15 eyes? Or only kings of terror, and the obscene empires of Mammon and Belial? Or will you, youths of England, make your country again a royal throne of kings; a sceptred isle, for all the world a source of light, a centre of peace; mistress of Learning and of the Arts; – faithful guardian of great memories in the midst of irreverent and ephemeral visions; – faithful

20 servant to time-tried principles, under temptation from fond experiments and licentious desires; and amidst the cruel and clamorous jealousies of the nations, worshipped in her strange valour of goodwill towards men?

  29 'Vexilla regis prodeunt.' Yes, but of which king? There are the two oriflammes; which shall we plant on the farthest island, – the one that floats

25 in heavenly fire, or that hangs heavy with foul tissue of terrestrial gold? There is indeed a course of beneficent glory open to us, such as never was yet offered to any poor groups of mortal souls. But it must be – it *is* with us, now 'Reign or Die'. And it shall be said of this country, 'Fece per viltate, il gran rifiuto', that refusal of the crown will be, of all yet recorded in history,

30 the shamefullest and most untimely. And this is what she must either do, or perish: she must found colonies as fast and as far as she is able, formed of her most energetic and worthiest men; – seizing every piece of fruitful waste ground she can set her foot on, and there teaching these her colonists that their chief virtue is to be fidelity to their country, and that their first aim

35 is to be to advance the power of England by land and sea: and that, though they live off a distant plot of ground, they are no more to consider themselves therefore disfranchised from their native land, than the sailors of her fleets do, because they float on distant waves. So that literally, these colonies must be fastened fleets. ●

T90 *Anon., 'Fabricated non-standard love letter' (mid 19th century)*

PRETTY MAIDENS BEWARE! A LOVE LETTER FROM SARAH TO CHARLES.

    The following epistle was written by a girl at Deal to her sweetheart, a
sailor on board a man of war in the Downs. The lieutenant of the ship found
it on board, twisted up with tobacco in it, by which it seems our seafaring
5 spark had as little regard for his mistress, after enjoyment, as if he had been
of a more illustrious rank.
Lovin Der Charls,
    This mi kind love to yow is to tell yow, after all owr sport and fon, I am
lik to pay fort, for I am with child; and wors of al, my sister *Nan* knos it, and
10 cals me hore and bech, and is redy to ter my sol owt, and curs *Jack Peny* lies
with her evry tim he cums ashor; and the saci dog wold have lade with me
to, but I wold not let him, for I wil be always honest to yow; therfor der
Charls com ashor, and let us be mared to safe my vartu; and if yow have no
munni, I will paun my new stais and sel mi to new smoks yow gave me, and
15 that will pay the parsen and find us a diner; and pray der lovin *Charls* cum
ashor, and der *Charls* dont be frad for wont of a ring, for I have stole mi
sister *Nans*, and the nasty tod shall never have it no mor; for she tels abot
that I am goin to have a bastard, and God bles yowr lovin sol cum sune, for
I longs to be mared accordin to yowr promis, and I will be yowr der vartus
20 wife tel deth,   SARAH JOHNSON.   Feb 19th

P.S. – Pray dont let yowr mesmat Jack se this, if yow do hel tel owr *Nan*,
and shel ter mi hart owt then, for shes a devil at me now.

A Poetical Version of the foregoing.
    Dear object of my love, whose manly charms
25   With bliss extatic fill'd my circling arms;
    That bliss is past, and nought for me remains
    But dire reproach, and sharp unpitied pains:
    For (Death to me, and food to others pride)
    My sister has my growing shame descry'd,
30   Ev'n she assails me with opprobious name,
    When the prude's conscious she deserves the same
    Her loose associate, sated, from her flies,
    And vainly to seduce my virtue tries:
    True, as a wife, I only want the name;
35   O! haste and wed me, and preserve my fame.
    Unlike most modern matches ours shall be,
    From settlement, the lawyers fetters free;
    I'll quit my All, and be content with thee ...

T91   *'Report on schools' (1871)*

The Catechism and the ordinary services of the church are better taught. Children, however, still know very little about the special offices of the church. Surely it would profit them greatly in after life to have been in their youth well instructed in the Communion service, in the Office for the Rite
5   of Confirmation, the Visitation of the Sick, &c. A knowledge of these would be useful to them in all the various situations they might hereafter occupy in the world ...

Reading. Reading still continues below the mark. Only in a few schools children read with ease and enjoyment, and in fewer still is poetry read with
10 proper emphasis. Still some schools have mastered this difficulty, and I have been surprised to hear even very small children in such schools read fluently with proper emphasis and accent. Infant-school teachers can greatly assist reading. When a child reads well in an infant school such reading is seldom afterwards lost. *Loud* reading is advisable in beginners. In good
15 infant schools reading is generally so taught. The child who begins is persuaded almost to hollow, and then, its reading being eulogized, by degrees the rest follow its example, and thus loud reading becomes the habit of the whole class ...

Review of the 24 years of reports. It may not be considered out of
20 place here, and at this time, when the system to which I have now for 24 years been attached, has ceased to exist, to introduce a summary of each year's work performed, with the improvements and results as they successively occurred, a total change having recently taken place in the Education Department of the State.
25 In 1840 almost similar expectations were excited as in this present 1871. It was hoped that great progress would be made in 20 years in the general education of the people, and that the pious wish of the pious King would be accomplished, and every child of 8 years of age would be able to read his Bible. The wish and hope have proved fallacious. Doubtless much has been
30 advanced, much more than even many persons interested in education are acquainted with, but how much remains behind. In the changes that have been introduced, it may be of advantage to show that 30 years have effected, and how the recommendations of the Inspectors have been embodied in recent legislative Acts. It may also help to further more and more vast
35 improvements, as well as check all ridiculous expectations by showing what can, and, of much more consequence, what cannot, be performed, confining the idea to what is really practicable, not visionary or sentimental.

●

T92   *Anon., 'Obituary' (1878)*

England is the poorer by what she can ill-spare – a man of genius. Good, kind, genial, honest, and enthusiastic GEORGE CRUIKSHANK, whose frame appeared to have lost so little of its wiry strength and activity, whose brain seemed as full of fire and vitality at four-score as at forty, has passed away
5   quietly and painlessly after a few days' struggle. He never worked for *Punch*, but he always worked with him, putting his unresting brain, his skill – in some forms of Art unrivalled – and his ever productive fancy, at the service of humanity and progress, good works, and good will to man. His object, like our own, was always to drive home truth and urge on improve-
10 ment by the powerful forces of fun and humour, clothed in forms sometimes fanciful, sometimes grotesque, but never sullied by a foul thought, and ever dignified by a wholesome purpose.

His four-score and six years of life have been years of unintermitting labour, that was yet, always, labour of love. There never was a purer,
15 simpler, more straightforward, or altogether more blameless man. His nature had something childlike in its transparency. You saw through him completely. There was neither wish nor effort to disguise his self-complacency, his high appreciation of himself, his delight in the appreciation of others, any more than there was to make himself out better,
20 or cleverer, or more unselfish than his neighbours.

In him England has lost one who was, in every sense, as true a man as he was a rare and original genius, and a pioneer in the arts of illustration. It is gratifying to see the tributes of hearty recognition his death has called forth. It is a duty on *Punch's* part, as a soldier in the same army in which GEORGE
25 CRUIKSHANK held such high rank so long, to add his wreath to the number already laid upon this brave old captain's grave.   ●

T93   *Anon. 'Telegrams' (1882)*

1) Professor Palmer, passenger for Brindisi, has been instructed to go to you. He speaks Arabic and knows Bedouins, keep him at your disposal.

2) In anticipation of arrival of troops, hire all available camel transport in vicinity of Suez Canal. This will be a good opportunity of enlisting
5   services of Bedouins ...

3) MR. PALMER has arrived from Gaza. All well. Reports Jehad being preached at Gaza. Saw Turkish soldiers there. Bedouins loyal. Camels procurable in quantities, but no place to bring them to until Suez is occupied.

10 4) ARRANGE with Mr. Palmer for his employment under Government as principal interpreter on staff of Admiral on such terms as he suggests and you approve. Congratulate him from me on safe arrival.

5) PROFESSOR Palmer confident that in four days he will have 500 camels, and within 10 or 15 days 5,000 more. He waits return of messenger sent
15 for 500, so he cannot start for Desert before Monday.

6) Gill, who is in Desert to cut Syrian wire, has not yet been heard of. If no news of him tomorrow will send to Jaffa.

7) Have you heard anything of Gill? What orders did you give him? ...

8) Returned from Akabah, unfavourable reports of safety of Palmer's party;
20 am prosecuting search. Bedouin tribes still much disturbed.

9) A reasonable reward for recovery of either or all of the missing gentle-men may be offered.

10) REMAINS of Gill and Charrington found and identified. Of Palmer nothing certain, but small truss possibly his. Bedouins are very hostile;
25 those compromised threatening to attack search party.

11) FOLLOWING just received from Colonel Warren: – 'Visited place where party were murdered. Found remains to identify W. Gill and H. Charrington, and a truss for small man, but nothing of Palmer that I can be certain of. Am bringing in remains.

30 12) REACHED Alexandria last night. Not satisfied with news of deaths. Want permission to visit Suez. Letter follows.

13) MET Warren. Cairo to-morrow to meet Moore from Gaza.

14) REPORT what Moore, after consultation with Burton, advises as to steps for arresting culprits implicated in attack on Palmer Expedition.

35 15) WANT gunboat to Gaza, Jaffa, and back.

16) PROVIDE small vessel of war to convey Captain Burton from Alexandria to Gaza, Jaffa, and back, on receiving requisition from him.

17) DELIVER at once to Captain Burton following message: – Latest advices respecting Palmer Expedition render it undesirable that you should
40 proceed to Gaza. You are instructed, therefore, to return at once to Trieste. ●

T94   *Anon., 'Letters of consolation' (1886)*

(1) Dear J.   The news that reached us this morning (in a telegram to
Franks) has completely knocked me out of myself. I cannot express my
sorrow in words. The loss of one of the best & kindest of friends
enhances the sorrow I should feel at the loss sustained by King's and the
5 University. I am so thankful I saw him well & cheerful last Sunday. I am
very anxious about Jenkinson; it will be such a crushing blow to him. I
have telegraphed to him to offer to come up to be with him if he wished.
Perhaps you will let me know how he is. Why is it that the most precious
are always taken first.   [signature]

10 (2) My dear J.   I was much chocked to see in the Papers this morning
that Bradshaw of Kings after dining with you on Wednesday evening
died suddenly in his own rooms. I am afraid that it will upset your wife.
He was a good fellow, and always claimed relationship with me, and the
last time I spent a Sunday in Cambridge you and I were in his rooms. By
15 his death I see the office of University librarian becomes vacant. Do you
by any chance intend to try for it? Let me have a line when you have
time. Believe me, y^r ever   H.P. Powells

(3) Dearest J.   I had seen this grievous news in the 'Globe' last night,
and it has scarcely been out of my mind ever since. What a dreadful loss
20 it is to all the Cambridge people – and more especially to those like
yourself who had had more than ordinary opportunities of understanding
the scope of his abilities and the charm of his unselfishness. It is to me as
if a great fire had suddenly gone out, leaving us all cold and cheerless
and in the dark: he was such a centre of all that was best and brightest in
25 the university, and one always felt the happier for coming within range
of his comfortable presence. I sympathize with you in your particular
disappointment, as you know, from the bottom of my heart. It seems
cruelly hard that the one person who was thoroughly qualified to
appreciate your work should be snatched away like this just before it was
30 completed. But it is some satisfaction to feel that he *had already*
appreciated it, & it will always make it sacred in your eyes to think that
the very night he died you had rejoiced over it together.
    I am sending a few flowers ... I heard tonight that the funeral was
fined (?) for Monday, but I cannot possibly get away I fear.
35   I am wondering whether you will still go to Oxford. I hope so, and
that you stay over Thursday night, as I want to have a talk with you. Ever
dearest J., with fullest sympathy, your affectionate   Hal ●

T95   *Anon., 'Church service' (1887)*

A FORM OF THANKSGIVING AND PRAYER TO ALMIGHTY GOD, UPON THE
COMPLETION OF FIFTY YEARS OF HER MAJESTY'S REIGN; TO BE USED On
Tuesday the 21st day of June next, and certain other days as herein ap-
pointed, IN ALL CHURCHES AND CHAPELS OF ENGLAND AND WALES, AND IN
5 THE TOWN OF BERWICK-UPON-TWEED. *By Authority.* LONDON: Printed by
EYRE AND SPOTTISWOODE, Printers to the Queen's most Excellent Majesty. 1887.

ALMIGHTY God, we humbly offer unto Thy Divine Majesty our
prayers and hearty thanksgivings for our gracious Sovereign Lady Queen
VICTORIA, unto whom Thou hast accomplished full fifty years of
10 Sovereignty. We praise Thee that through Thy grace She hath kept the
charge Thou gavest Her in the day when Thou didst set the Crown upon Her
head, bidding Her 'to do Justice, stay the growth of iniquity, and protect the
Holy Church of God; to help and defend widows and orphans; to restore the
things gone to decay, maintain the things that are restored; punish and
15 reform what is amiss, and confirm what is in good order; to keep the Royal
Law and Lively Oracles of God.' We bless Thee that Thou hast heard,
through sorrow and through joy, our prayer that She should alway possess
the hearts of Her people. And we humbly pray Thee that for the years to
come She may rejoice in Thy strength, and at the Resurrection of the Just
20 enter into Thine immortal kingdom; through Jesus Christ our Lord. *Amen.*

ALMIGHTY God, who didst call Thy servant VICTORIA, our Queen, as
at this time to the Throne of Her Ancestors in the governance of this Realm;
we yield Thee humble thanks for the abundance of Dominion wherewith
Thou hast exalted and enlarged Her Empire, and for the Love of Her in
25 which Thou hast knit together in one the hearts of many nations: we praise
Thee for the swift increase of knowledge with power, for the spreading of
Truth and Faith in Her times, and gifts above all that we could ask or think.
And humbly we beseech Thee that overmastering both sinful passion and
selfish interest, and being protected from temptations, and delivered from
30 all evil, the unnumbered peoples of Her heritage may serve Thee, bearing
one another's burdens and advancing continually in Thy perfect Law of
Liberty; through Jesus Christ our Lord. *Amen.*

O LORD our God, Who upholdest and governest all things in heaven
and earth; receive our humble prayers with our hearty thanksgivings, for our
35 Sovereign Lady VICTORIA, as on this day set over us by Thy grace and
providence to be our Queen; and so together with Her bless *Albert Edward*
Prince of Wales, the Princess of Wales, and all the Royal Family, that they
all, ever trusting in Thy goodness, protected by Thy power, and crowned
with Thy grace and endless favour, may continue before Thee in health ●

FREEMAN'S SYRUP OF PHOSPHORUS,

NATURE'S GREAT BRAIN AND NERVE TONIC,

SUPPLIES NEW AND RICH PURE BLOOD.

PHOSPHORUS is now acknowledged by the highest medical authorities to be the only cure for Consumption, Wasting Diseases, Mental Depression, Loss of Energy, Stomach and Liver Complaints, and many other dreadful MALADIES AT ONE TIME THOUGHT INCURABLE.

The climax of Chemical Discovery, supplying the long-felt want of a perfect cure and reliable Solution of Phosphorus. It is very pleasant to the taste, and may be taken by the most delicately-constituted female or infant. It thoroughly re-vitalizes the human frame, and BUILDS UP A NEW AND HEALTHY CONSTITUTION.

INDIGESTION, CONSTIPATION, LOSS OF ENERGY, MENTAL DEPRESSION, especially when caused by excessive brain-work in general, are quickly and permanently relieved by a few doses of FREEMAN'S SYRUP OF PHOSPHORUS. Highly and confidently recommended TO ALL WHO ARE ENGAGED IN EXCESSIVE BRAIN-WORK.

CONSUMPTION and WASTING DISEASES *can be cured or alleviated by* FREEMAN'S SYRUP OF PHOSPHORUS. Quickly supplies *new, rich,* and *pure blood, restoring the failing functions of life*; the Appetite returns; the long-lost colour once more gives a healthful sparkle to the eye, the true sign of a return of *Health, Strength and Vitality. No more Cod-Liver Oil.* ONE DOSE IS EQUAL TO TEN DOSES OF COD-LIVER OIL.

NONE NOW NEED DESPAIR OF LIFE—With FREEMAN'S SYRUP OF PHOSPHORUS a man may easily *add twenty years to his life.* Thousands have been snatched from the brink of the grave by an early use of FREEMAN'S SYRUP OF PHOSPHORUS. THE MOST EXTREME CASES NEED NOT DESPAIR.

Order it of any Chemist. Should there be any difficulty in procuring it from your Chemist, the undersigned will, upon receipt of Stamps or Post Office Order for the amount, forward it to any address, packed securely.

Sold in Bottles, at 2/9, 4/6, 11/- *and* 33/- *each,*

BY CHEMISTS AND PATENT MEDICINE DEALERS.

Proprietors—GOODALL, BACKHOUSE & Co., Leeds.

6,000,000 BOTTLES SOLD ANNUALLY!

Largest Sale of any Sauce in the World!

A TRIAL SOLICITED.

YORKSHIRE RELISH,

THE MOST DELICIOUS AND CHEAPEST SAUCE IN THE WORLD.

Warranted Pure, and Free from any Injurious Ingredient.

This cheap and excellent Sauce makes the plainest viands palatable, and the daintiest dishes more delicious. The most cultivated culinary connoisseurs have awarded the palm to YORKSHIRE RELISH, on the ground that neither its strength nor its piquancy is overpowering, and that its invigorating zest by no means impairs the normal flavour of the dishes to which it is added. Employed either *au naturel* as a fillip to Chops, Steaks, Game, or Cold Meats, or used in combination by a skilful cook in concocting Soups, Stews, Ragouts, Curries, or Gravies for Fish and made dishes, it is

THE ONLY CHEAP AND GOOD SAUCE! BEWARE OF IMITATIONS!

H. R. H. the Prince of Wales has recently expressed himself as highly pleased with the "Yorkshire Relish" and requests his grocer to supply him with some in each parcel.

151, Bramhall Lane, Stockport.

Dear Sirs,—I have used your "Yorkshire Relish" for many years, and think it is the best Sauce in existence, and recommend it to all my friends.—Yours respectfully,   J. P.

New Bond Street, London.

Gentlemen.—I know of one good thing, and that is, one large tablespoonful of "Yorkshire Relish," added to a salad mixture, makes it as near perfection as anything you can get in this world.—Faithfully yours, E. P.

Sold in Bottles at 6d., 1s., and 2s. each,

BY GROCERS, OILMEN AND ITALIAN WAREHOUSEMEN
All over the World.

SOLE PROPRIETORS:

GOODALL, BACKHOUSE & CO.,
White Horse Street, LEEDS.

T97   *Anon., 'Cooking recipes' (1887)*

STRIKE THE IRON WHILE IT IS HOT.

A WILLING HELPER DOES NOT WAIT TILL ASKED.

TEA-CAKES.

MATERIALS.—Quarter of a pound of butter; two ounces of sifted sugar; one pint of milk; two pounds of flour; six teaspoonfuls of GOODALL'S BAKING POWDER; half a teaspoonful of salt.

PROCESS.—Melt the butter in the milk as directed in the preceding recipe, and the sugar also; mix the flour, baking powder, and salt, and here add the milk, &c., incorporating the whole well together. Knead it well, and make it into round cakes, which should be left on a greased tin before the fire, in order to rise. When the cakes appear to be sufficiently risen, put them into a hot oven and bake for half-an-hour.

TEA-CAKES.

☞ *For making Tea Cakes, and all kinds of bread, cakes, pies, puddings, pastry, &c., GOODALL's BAKING POWDER, made by Messrs. Goodall, Backhouse, and Co., of Leeds, is unequalled.*

Is bread made with baking powder digestible?

Far more so than bread made with yeast, which is *fermented* bread, while bread made with baking power is unfermented, and therefore far more wholesome. It may be eaten as soon as it is cold without any fear of indigestion, which is almost sure to follow, with most people, when new fermented bread is eaten. The great secret of success in making bread with baking powder is to thoroughly incorporate the baking powder, flour, and other ingredients, mixing them well together and putting the dough, when ready, into a very hot oven to bake.

GOLDEN RULE.—*In making unfermented bread with* GOODALL'S BAKING POWDER, *never deal with more than from two pounds to four pounds of flour at a time. The bread is better made in small quantities.*

ALWAYS USE TIME AS THOUGH YOU KNEW ITS VALUE.

RUNNING HARES NEED NO SPURS.

73

EXAMPLE TEACHES MORE THAN PRECEPT.

IT IS PRIDE AND NOT NATURE THAT CRAVES MUCH.

POT-AU-FEU.

MATERIALS.—Four pounds of leg of beef, or of pieces of meat—beef, mutton, veal, &c., which may be bought of the butcher at a reduced rate; three onions; three carrots; three turnips; some tops of celery; three cloves; pepper and salt to taste; quarter of a pound of dripping; four quarts of water.

PROCESS.—Wash the meat and vegetables, cutting the latter into small pieces, and, with the dripping, fry the whole for about ten minutes. Then put the meat and vegetables thus prepared into an earthen pot, with a cover, which will hold about five quarts, and add the water. Put the pot into the oven, or by the side of the fire—the former is preferable—and let the whole stew or simmer gently for about four hours; remove the pot, and when the contents are cold take off the fat that has risen to the top. Next day put the pot into the oven again for an hour, adding the celery and cloves, and pepper and salt to taste. Put some pieces of bread, plain, toasted, or cut into dice and fried, into a tureen, and pour the liquor over them; the meat must be served in a hash-dish with the vegetables round it.

☞ *When in the tureen the soup should be perfected by adding two tablespoonfuls of* YORKSHIRE RELISH, *which is made by Messrs. Goodall, Backhouse, and Co., of Leeds, and may be bought of any grocer or oilman.*

Every one who partakes of the meat should flavour it with YORKSHIRE RELISH.

Is it absolutely necessary to make this soup and stewed meat in an earthern pot or jar?

No; a stew-pan may be used, but the stoneware jar is better for the purpose, as the process of stewing is effected more slowly and completely than in an ordinary metal stew-pan. An earthern jar can be put in the oven, but a stew-pan must stand on the fire or hot plate.

IF THINGS WERE TO BE DONE TWICE, ALL WOULD BE WISE.

ALL IS FINE THAT IS FITTING.

11

T98   *Anon., 'On freedom of the press' (1887)*

... Sedition, blasphemy, scurrility, and immorality, if they have not been quite kept out of newspapers, have dwindled down and have lost all their force now that enlightened public opinion has substituted a new censorship for that of the old benighted tyranny. Such unwholesome journalism as once
5   flourished in spite of arbitrary laws and vicious restraints has been rendered insignificant by the freedom that has enabled wholesome journalism to grow so plentifully as almost to cover the field. Unwholesome growths remain, however, and some unhealthy influences are apparent in nearly all newspapers. Stray murmurs are still heard against the liberty under which
10   the journalism the murmurers object to is allowed to exist; and where, as in Ireland even now, their views are shared by the authorities, the attempts to enforce them have most cruel and mischievous effects. Louder complaint, moreover, is made by others who, without going so far as to call upon the legislature to suppress the journalism that is obnoxious to them, hold the
15   journalists and the newspaper proprietors responsible for it. These complainers may be reminded that, with no more exceptions than serve to prove the rule, only such journalism is provided as there is a market for. If it is unpleasant to many that there should be survivals of the old Monmouth Street and Holywell street literature, that the betting-ring and other adjuncts
20   of 'sport' should have organs of their own in the press, that loathsome police cases and law cases should be detailed by respectable newspapers for family reading, and so forth, these things are only as they are because so many newspaper readers require journalism of the obnoxious sort that the journalists are encouraged or compelled to satisfy the demand. All that can
25   be fairly said against the newspapers in this respect is that, they being business concerns, and the competition among them being as keen as it is, their conductors are not self-sacrificing enough to withhold such information as the readers seek.

        Not only have we now almost complete freedom of the press, but
30   journalism is, as it always has been, one of the freest of all trades; and here also what may be disadvantages are mixed with the advantages. No apprenticeship is needed for entering it, and no preliminaries are required for participation in its highest rewards. As a matter of fact, indeed, those rewards are often assigned to men sufficiently qualified for them by native
35   wit or training in other ways, without any previous newspaper drudgery, and therefore, inevitably, to the detriment of the drudges who, fully entitled to promotion, may have been vainly hoping for it through many years. A smart member of parliament, a successful barrister, a versatile clergyman, a retired schoolmaster, a popular novelist, or any one else with enough

40 influence or intellect, or with a name likely to prove useful, may slip into an
editorship or be made a principal leader writer in preference to men of long
standing in the office, who perhaps have to teach him his duties and correct
his blunders. These latter also suffer because, in most cases, the work they
continue doing is of a kind that almost any one with aptitude for it can do.
45 Such moderate skill in writing as every schoolboy should possess, with a
knowledge of shorthand in some cases, and a fair amount of general
intelligence in all, enables a novice quickly to become a proficient in some
of the largest departments of newspaper work, and the newly imported
novices, by reason of the freshness they bring to the business, are
50 sometimes more acceptable than the jaded proficients. This state of things
may be inevitable, but it causes some harm to journalism as a whole, or
much of it, as well as to many journalists. Unhappily for them, and perhaps
also for the public, their calling is one that is more easily taken up than
abandoned. It would not be more unfair to say, with Lord Beaconsfield, that
55 'critics are men who have failed in literature or in art,' than to say that
journalists are men who are unfit for any other occupation; but the
temperaments that incline them to journalism are apt to render other
pursuits distasteful to them, and distaste or inaptitude is encouraged by the
habits or the necessities incident to the pursuit they have chosen. One who
60 by accident or of set purpose has become a journalist may before long see
reason to regret his position, may soon discover that his chances of
advancement in it are small, and may grow callous or desperate, but he
seldom migrates to another line of life, and when he does he seldom
succeeds in it. Hence, though the Fleet Street of to-day is in may ways an
65 improvement on the Grub Street of the last century, the traditions and
infirmities of Grub Street are not extinct.   ●

Information on texts and authors

The following notes include information on the selected 19th-century texts, the sources of the excerpts, information on authors (taken from the *Dictionary of National Biography* and introductions to the individual works) and a few remarks on the relevance of the texts. References to scholarly discussions of the works are provided where available; 'Görlach *ABib*' with accompanying number refers to my annotated bibliography of 19th-century grammars (= Görlach 1998a).

I On language, grammar and style

T1: From: Revd. Alexander Crombie, LL.D. *The Etymology and Syntax of the English Language, Explained and Illustrated*. London: for J. Johnson, 1802:235–8. The passage is reprinted without changes in later editions, as in [9]1865:256–7. (Görlach *ABib* 390)

A conservative account of the diversity and poor expressiveness of the vernacular as spoken by the illiterate 'vulgar', contrasted with written norms as defined by the usage of reputable authors.

T2: From: James Andrew. *Institutes of Grammar*. London: Black, Parbury & Allen, 1817:91–8. (Görlach *ABib* 43)

Extensive advice geared to functionally defined text types and literary genres endebted to the classical idea of decorum (without using the categories developed by traditional rhetoric).

T3: From: William Cobbett. *A Grammar of the English Language, in a Series of Letters. Intended for the use of schools and of young persons in general; but more especially for the use of soldiers, sailors, apprentices and plough-boys. To which are added, six lessons to prevent statesmen from using false grammar, and from writing in an awkward manner.* [[1]1818.] London: for John M. Cobbett, rev. and new edn 1823; ed. and intro. R. W. Burchfield, Oxford: Oxford University Press, 1984:167–8. (Görlach *ABib* 336)

Cobbett expanded the first edition of 1818 with the lessons of which no.5 is here printed; correcting the usage of 'the best authors' he attacks the style of one of the leading statesmen of his time – and supplies a better, clearer version of the criticized passage, which allows us to contrast two early 19th-century expository styles. (Cobbett's analysis of the mistakes which is appended should be carefully read.) There is a vast literature on Cobbett, who was one of the most influential grammarians (and radicals) of the early 19th century; cf. Burchfield's 'Introduction' (1984:v–xii), Bailey (1996:253–60), Mugglestone (1995:71–2, 82–3, 88–9) and T15.

T4: From: [Christian Isabel Johnstone]. *Diversions of Hollycot, or the Mother's Art of Thinking*. Edinburgh: Oliver & Boyd, 1828:31–7.
The passage provides an excellent idea of how the search for the appropriate expressions could be taught in a lively manner, adapted to the capacities of smaller children. The use of conversational style was frequently tried to reduce the widespread disgust with turgid grammar style.

T5: From: Samuel Alexander. *A practical and logical Grammar of the English Language*. [¹1822.] London: Longman, etc., enl. and amended ⁴1832:vi, ix. (Görlach *ABib* 25)
A spirited pleading for reason as the guiding principle of linguistic correctness, directed against the dominant schools of linguists who believed in (or paid lip-service to) usage.

T6: From: W. H. Savage. *The Vulgarisms and Improprieties of the English Language; containing also Grammatical Errors, Orthoepical Readings, Tautological Phrases, Aspiration of H, together with a critical preface on stage pronunciation*. London: T. S. Porter for T. Bumpus, 1833:i–vi.
The author's verdict on grammatical blunders is among the strongest-voiced specimens of prescriptivism of the 19th century, as is evident from expressions like *arbitrary caprice* (reminiscent of Dr Johnson), *ignorant, barbarism, vulgarity, deformities, viciousness*, etc., which appear to equate linguistic impropriety with deficiencies of character, morals and social standing. The book was singled out by Phillipps (1984:82-3, 128–31) as illustrating sociolinguistic prejudice in its most outspoken form. Also cf. Bailey (1996:119–21, 128-9, 219-20).

T7: From: R. G. Latham. *An Address to the Authors of England and America, on the necessity and practicability of permanently remodelling their alphabet and orthography*. Cambridge: for J & J J. Peighton, 1834:47–9.
Latham was one of the best-known writers on grammar in the 19th century. In this early passage he showed concern for a systematic revision of English spelling, the forms of which he wished to keep to a minimum to make it more easily acceptable.

T8: From: George Edmonds. *Complete English Grammar, with a supplemental grammar of etiquette*. London: for the author, ⁵1837:3–6. (Görlach *ABib* 484)
The author reflects on how the expansion of literacy has affected the standards of English since the publication of Cobbett's *Grammar* (T3).

T9: From: Percival Leigh. *The Comic English Grammar; a New and Facetious Introduction to the English Tongue*. London: Richard Bentley, 1840:13–17, 25–7. Facs. London: Bracken Books, 1989. (Görlach *ABib* 1073)
Leigh's successful attempt to treat grammatical problems in a light-hearted way was enhanced by humorous illustrations by J. Leech. The excerpts show his awareness of various improper varieties and of deviant spelling which he illustrated with a fabricated letter written by a semiliterate Londoner – a pattern widely used in literature and in *Punch*.

T10: From: Charles Henry Bromby. *The Pupil-teacher's English Grammar, and Etymology of the English Language, adapted to the use of normal schools*. London: Simpkin, Marshall, 1848:8–11. (Görlach *ABib* 209)
Bromby's reflections on practical problems of English language teaching are specially relevant because they came at a time when the system was drastically extended and new methods (such as the employment of pupil teachers) were called for.

T11: From: Richard Chenevix Trench. *On the Study of Words*. London: Parker, 1851:3–8.
Trench (1807–86), Archbishop of Dublin, was, among many other things, one of the leading linguists of the mid 19th century, chiefly remembered for his leading role in instigating the *OED*. The passage shows him aware of the connection between proper language use and moral standards and the dangers of a decline in both. A fuller excerpt is included in Crowley (1991:136–49); also cf. Aarsleff (1967:234–46) and Bailey (1996:147–9).

T12: From: Peter Mark Roget. *Roget's Thesaurus of English Words and Phrases*, London: Longman, etc., 1852:vii–xiii. Facs. London: Bloomsbury Books, 1992.
Roget (1779–1869) was a physician also active in the establishment of the University of London. His *Thesaurus* is related to John Wilkins's pioneering *Essay towards a real character...* (1668, EL 119); it established a tradition of 'Rogets' although modern editions retain little more than his name. Roget's introduction presents interesting reflections on the interrelationship of the conceptual and linguistic structures of the world: he sets out the onomasiological competence of native speakers and the interrelationship of language and thought, and he does so in a type of expository prose which has many features of the mid-century and in which abstract reasoning is combined with unexpected metaphors.

T13: From: Anon. 'Latin and English compared'. *Encyclopædia Britannica*. Vol.XIII, [8]1857:190–1.
Most writers, from the Renaissance onwards, felt called upon to excuse English for its lack of grammar, i.e. scarcity of inflection. The *EB* author by contrast points to the great advantages of analytical languages such as English.

T14: From: Mayhew 1861, I:23
This metalinguistic passage ranks among the most informative on mid 19th-century cant; the style is purely descriptive, there is no explicit or implicit evaluation: Mayhew acts as the descriptive sociolinguist, and it is now impossible to say how much he may have been misled by the 'observer's paradox'. Cf. T83 below and Matthews 1938.

T15: From: James Paul Cobbett. New edn of William Cobbett's *A Grammar of the English Language, in a Series of Letters* with an additional chapter by J. P. Cobbett. London: G. Routledge & Son, 1866:241. (Görlach *ABib* 336)
Whereas his father still believed that a standardization of English pronunciation was both unnecessary and impracticable, societal pressures to conform with linguistic norms had increased to such an extent in the course of the 19th century that the son included a detailed discussion of the most stigmatized features.

T16: From: Henry Alford. *The Queen's English: A Manual of Idiom and Usage*. [[1]1864.] London: Longman & Green, [3]1870.

Alford (1810–71), Dean of Canterbury, translator of the *Odyssey* and revisor of the New Testament, was one of the most dedicated authors defending the correctness of the written standard. His extended metaphor comparing the state of the language with the road traffic of his times is here complemented by sarcastic remarks on fashionable adoptions from French. A more extensive excerpt is printed in Crowley 1991:173–80.

T17: From: Alexander John Ellis. *On Early English Pronunciation*. Vol. I (EETS 2). London: Asher, 1869:18–23.

A. J. Ellis (1814–90) was one of the most noteworthy polymaths of the period. His philological interests included phonetics and spelling reform (in cooperation with Pitman) and historical phonology to which his monumental *EEP* in five volumes is devoted. The excerpt includes his observations of developments on spoken English in the Victorian era. Cf. Bailey (1996:72–7, 102-3, 120–2) and Mugglestone (1995:196–9, 231–4, 316–21).

T18: From: Henry Sweet. 'Introduction'. *Transactions of the Philological Society*. 1875/6:470–1. Repr. H. C. Wyld, ed. *Collected Papers of Henry Sweet*. Oxford: Clarendon, 1913:1–33.

The excerpt is significant on two levels: in terms of its contents, it is a creed of the new age of grammarians, pleading for a stronger concentration on phonetics and the grammar of the living language. Stylistically, it is a carefully structured exposition in plain style: short sentences prevail, and technical terms are not used excessively. Cf. Bailey (1996:97-8, 245-6) and Mugglestone (1995:157-8, 319–21).

T19a: From: John Best Davidson. *Punctuation Made Easy*. Leeds: Hamer / London: Simpkin, Marshall & Co., 1864:7.

T19b: From: Edwin A. Abbott. *A Handbook of English Grammar*. Rev. by William Moore. London: James Martin, [3]1879:70–1. (Görlach *ABib* 3)

Most 19th-century grammars include a section devoted to punctuation, although its position and relation to other sections such as those devoted to spelling and syntax remained largely unsettled.

T20: From: Anon. *Society Small Talk*. London: Fred. Warne, 1880:1–2, 7.

The selected passage on enunciation is obviously highly relevant for the 'good tone' in society; the topic is largely neglected by grammar books proper (no longer felt relevant after the obvious decline of 'rhetorical' grammars).

T21: From: Frederick Averne White. *An Unconventional English Grammar*. [[1]1882.] London: W. Swan Sonnenschein, [2]1883:18–19, 22–3. (Görlach *ABib* 1843)

The changes that have occurred in 19th-century English are carefully recorded by a contemporary grammarian: if usage is the major gauge of correctness, linguistic change must obviously be taken into account – a rule neglected by most prescriptive grammarians who prefer to see – and to describe – stability.

T22: From: Anon. *Guide to Official Letter Writing*. London, 1886:6, 39–48, 90–1.

The formal letter is printed as a pattern to use in military communication – one of the areas in which conventions are strictly prescribed and followed. Similarly, the forms of business letters and the half-legal types illustrated by specimens are largely formulaic. By contrast, the author's advice on style and the choice of words is not related to text types, nor is it even very typically Victorian. Advice on handwriting was, of course, relevant in an age without typewriters and computers.

T23: From: Anon. 'Reviews of C. Duxbury, *A New English Grammar of School Grammars.*' Quoted in C. Duxbury, *A New English Grammar of School Grammars.* London: W. Stewart, [3]1886. (Görlach *ABib* 473) From *Educational Reporter, National Schoolmaster, The London Weekly Times.*

The texts here printed represent a Victorian blend of review and advertisement; the type is often appended to books as unpaged front or end-leaves, and commonly stresses information on, combined with sometimes excessive praise of, the work described.

T24: From: Henry Sweet. *A Primer of Spoken English.* [[1]1890.] Oxford: Clarendon, [3]1900: 'Preface' v–x. (Görlach *ABib* 1708)

Sweet (1845–1912) matriculated in Heidelberg in 1864; he became one of the major representatives of the philological method in Britain, combining an interest in Old and Middle English, phonetics and language teaching. His classic accounts are still stimulating to read – not just as historical documents. It is significant that the *Primer* was first published in German (Oxford 1886), reflecting the strong continental influence on English philology at the time. His publications culminated in *A New English Grammar, Logical and Historical,* 1892–8. The present excerpt discusses evaluations of English varieties of his time.

T25: From: [A. Heald]. Pseud.: 'Anglophil'. *The Queen's English (?) Up to Date: An Exposition of the Prevailing Grammatical Errors of the Day, with Numerous Examples.* London: Economic Pr. & Publ. Co., 1892/[2]1898. (Görlach *ABib* 826)

The text (which takes up Alford's considerations of 1864, cf. T16) is one of the numerous complaints about increasing grammatical incorrectness as a consequence of sloppiness – and the speed of the times. The function of the press, as the most important gauge for the common reader, is duly stressed. Note the elevated diction throughout, which was obviously considered suitable for a text advising on linguistic propriety.

II On dialect

T26a: From: Aaron Layton. *Riot and Be Hanged.* Cambridge: Isle of Ely Education Committee, n.d.

The letter, written in 1816 by one of the 'rioters' of Ely and Littleport, illustrates many features of a semi-educated dialect speaker of the region: note phonetic spellings, variable capitalization and virtually no punctuation, and *-en* for *-ing, h*-dropping, and the mixed construction in *you dost.*

T26b: Anon. 'Letters'. From: H. G. Klaus. *The Literature of Labour.* Brighton: Harvester Press, 1985:66.

This anonymous threatening letter of 1831 represents 'a characteristic form of social protest in any society which has crossed a certain threshold of literacy, in which forms of collective organised defence are weak, and in which individuals who can be identified as the organisers of protest are liable to immediate victimisation' (quoted from Klaus 1985:65). The letter derives special interest from the fact that it is written in the 'natural' dialect of County Durham, long before general education came to mean that reading and writing indicate the standard language.

T27: From: Anon. *The Dialect of Craven ... with a Copious Glossary ... and*

Exemplified by Two Familiar Dialogues. [¹1824.] By a native of Craven. London: W. M. Crofts, ⁷1828: 'Preface', 'Dedication'.

The text is a typical account of a gentleman dialectologist, who gives an objective account of the qualities of the rural dialect of his region, accompanied by various textual excerpts.

T28: From: Robert Forby. *The Vocabulary of East Anglia*, vol I. London: J. B. Nichols & Son, 1830. Repr. Newton Abbot: David & Charles, 1970:1–2, 54.

Forby stresses the value of East Anglian dialect for the reconstruction of the history of English, contrasting the 'flash' language of the conurbations.

T29: From: *Bairnsla Foaks' Annual.* Barnsley, 1840.

The specimens here selected represent typical genres of dialect writing: a short preface and a mock address to the Queen. The texts, among the first of the almanac tradition, were written for a readership who – at least in their spoken English – were firmly grounded in the dialect. So the text does not compromise with St E, not even in spelling (where it might have been argued that a version closer to standard conventions would have been easier to read).

T30: From: James Orchard Halliwell. *Dictionary of Archaic Words*. London: John Russell Smith, 1850:xviii–xxxv.

Halliwell's collection of archaic and dialect words of 1847 (printed 1850) is the largest before the *EDD*. His main interest was clearly in *old* words – dialect items were valuable for the evidence they provided on the history of the English language. As a consequence, Halliwell does not properly distinguish between 'old' and 'dialectal' and is not interested in the currency (or even authenticity?) of his dialect words which he collected from all available printed sources and from informants living in various parts of the country. In the dialect texts, arranged according to counties and printed in his introduction, historical texts (from ME) again predominate; specimens from modern dialect writing are given without sources. Their authenticity can, therefore, not be established – but they include some counties, and text types, otherwise only poorly recorded. Halliwell's important position is described by Ihalainen (1994:210–12).

T31: From: Revd. Richard Webster Huntley. *A Glossary of the Cotswold (Gloucestershire) Dialect*. London: John Russell, 1868.

Huntley describes with great insight the position of Cotswold dialect just before general education came to provide the final blow to the continuance of broad rural varieties.

T32: From: *Cambridge Chronicle*. 2 Oct. 1869:4. Quoting from 'Slavery in Suffolk' in *Punch*.

The miserable position of agricultural labourers in Suffolk is highlighted by the contrast of the objective description of their plight in St E and the paraphrase in local dialect which claims that their condition is in fact worse than that of black slaves (an argument sometimes also used with regard to working conditions in mining and in factories in the Midlands; cf. T67).

T33a: From: Frances Hodgson Burnett. *That Lass o' Lowrie's*. New York: Armstrong / London: F. Warne, 1877. Repr. Woodbridge: Boydell Press, 1985:91–3.

Burnett (1849–1924) was born in Manchester, wrote various popular stories and is best known as the author of *Little Lord Fauntleroy* (1886). Her first novel, *That Lass*, was written after her emigration to the US in 1865, where it was published in Boston in 1877. It proved a great success – in spite of the dialect. The novel, set in the Lancashire mining village of Riggan, comes from an area in which dialect was particularly strong in both rural and industrial surroundings. The author (who was certainly influenced by Mrs Gaskell's *Mary Barton* of 1848) sticks to Scott's pattern in confining dialect to direct speech, but the use is remarkable for both its extent and its (dialectological and socio-linguistic) authenticity. (The passage chosen illustrates the well-known device of introducing large amounts of dialect by letting a dialect speaker narrate a story.)

T33b: From: *Punch*, 20 Oct. – 17 Nov. 1877.

The text parodies the fashion of dialect novels, illustrated by the huge success of Burnett. The parodist's technique is to caricature the personae and use them as mouthpieces for somewhat unintelligible gibberish masquerading as northern dialect (commented on in footnotes) and other linguistic stereotypes, such as the curate's 'Oxford' student's slang.

T34: From: Thomas Hardy. Letter to the *Spectator*, 15 October 1881, and 'The Dorsetshire Labourer', *Longman's Magazine*, July 1883:252–69; quoted from: H. Orel, ed. *Thomas Hardy's Personal Writings*. Lawrence: University of Kansas Press, 1966:92–3, 168–71.

The two statements are significant for Hardy's use of dialect in his novels, but also for the discussion about the use of dialect in literature that peaked in the late 1870s and the 1880s (cf. Orel's annotations). Hardy's attitude is very carefully expressed, and the compromise he favours the only possible one for an audience used to reading St E, but nostalgically interested in the disappearing rural dialect. In the essay, dialect is shown to be only one facet of rural life, and the initial misconception cleverly put right. Cf. Blake (1981:166–71).

T35: From: William Barnes. *A Glossary of the Dorset Dialect with a Grammar*. Dorchester: Case, 1886. Repr. St Peter Port, Guernsey: Toucan Press, 1970:vi–vii.

The original passages and Barnes's translation are beautiful illustrations of 19th-century English: the formal character of the Queen's speech is brought out by the Latinate lexis and nominal style of the statements, which can be said to disguise more than they disclose (not unexpectedly in political language; the text was of course formulated by an anonymous ghostwriter). The Dorset version brings out the contents much more bluntly, the dialect lacking a formal register. Note the differences in syntax and lexis – part of this may in fact be owing to Barnes's puristic attempts to stick to Germanic vocabulary and to coin new words where St E – or the dialect – had no equivalent to offer.

T36: From: Cambridge Papers, 1895. BP 721–880.

The appeal is here included for the text type it represents and for the factual information it provides on the stage when publication of Wright's *EDD* was far from certain.

T37: From: George Bernard Shaw. *Captain Brassbound's Conversion* (Notes), 1900. In *Three Plays for Puritans*. London: A. Constable, 1906:306–7.

Shaw (1856–1950) had moved to London in 1876. By the time he wrote the notes here printed he had had ample time to study the dialects he heard around him and to look critically at conventions used to portray them in literary writings. His major attempt at dramatizing London speech was not before *Pygmalion* in 1913, which can be compared with his statements of 1900.

III On literature and criticism

T38: From: Thomas Bowdler. *Family Shakespeare*. London: for J. Hatchard, 1807: 'Introduction'.

Bowdler's (1754–1825) attempts at expurgating Shakespeare and Gibbons gave the eponymic *to bowdlerize* (1836) to the English language. Rather than finding fault with Shakespeare's language for grammatical correctness (as Dryden and Johnson had done), he omitted 'whatever is unfit to be read aloud by a gentleman to a company of ladies', objecting in particular to religious as well as sexual improprieties.

T39: From: Samuel Taylor Coleridge. *Biographia Literaria*. 1817, ch. 17, ed. John Shawcross. Oxford: Clarendon, 1907, II:28–30.

Coleridge (1772–1834) was one of the major poets of the Romantic period. Though he shared many interests with Wordsworth (with whom he co-published the *Lyrical Ballads* in 1798) his intentions were more philosophical, as shown in his criticism of his friend's diction. He at once conceded that Wordsworth was basically right, but felt called upon to define his own tenets more precisely. This position of correction, qualification and re-interpretation, with many allusions to, and quotations from, the 1802 text results in highly complex sentence patterns – much more complex than an original composition would have been. Note the repeated *as far...* structures, the imbalance in the opening sentence culminating in 'I cannot likewise but add'. Statements like 'he undertook a useful task', 'W. is fully justified in believing his efforts to have been by no means ineffectual' show the distancing function of Coleridge's understatement. Cf. Blake (1981:127-8).

T40: From: W. T. Moncrieff. *Tom and Jerry*. 1826. Quoted from: William Matthews. *Cockney Past and Present*. 4 vols. London: Routledge & Kegan Paul, 1938:47–8.

Moncrieff's dramatization of low life in London was based on Pierce Egan's prose work of 1821; it continued a tradition started in the 18th century, when Cockney came to be typical of the 'vulgar language of novels' (Blake 1981:118, cf. 131–3). In the 19th century, the tradition was enhanced by a great variety of uses ranging from Dickens to the music-hall, and from *Punch* to Shaw (cf. T37). Cf. Matthews (1938) and Blake (1981:131–3).

T41: From: Ann Catharine Holbrook. *Realities and Reflections*. Thame: H. Bradford, 1834.

Both title-page and dedication bear the hallmarks of 18th-century style: the first being too explicit for 1834, and the latter cultivating the fawning humility so widespread in 18th-century books. The *humble applicant* is in stark contrast to the addressee graced by every conceivable virtue (of course *unostentatious*). The text is stereotypical, stuffed with rhetorical figures, a fact now disguised by the type having gone out of use.

T42: From: G. W. M. Reynolds. *Wagner, the Wehr-Wolf*. London, 1840; facs. New York: Dover, 1975:1–2.

Some late imitators of the Gothic novel pushed the improbable contents and the weird diction to the extreme; Reynolds's style is a repository of such stereotypes, which cannot be exaggerated any further. Note the descriptive and emotional adjectives and the verbal apparatus of horror, used for its own sake, and often quite redundantly, rather than serving any structural function.

T43: From: Anon. Popular prose romance and undated playbill, 1846.

Quoted from James 1976:215, 226.

The text of this vampire story in the 'Gothic' tradition aims at suspense combined with genteel diction ('elaborate in execution' could also serve to define the author's style). The narrative is studded with exclamations, rhetorical questions, dashes, frequent inversions and verbose periphrasis all adding to the pompous expression. By contrast, the playbill reduces the melodramatic horror to effective snippets, mostly noun phrases or exclamations and questions.

T44: From: Edward Bulwer-Lytton. *Harold*. [[1]1848.] London & Glasgow: Collins, 3rd edn, n.d.:213–15.

Bulwer-Lytton (1803–73) was one of the most prolific and versatile writers of his times. His works include twenty-four novels – historical romances (such as *Harold*), tales of magic, Newgate novels and philosophical novels – as well as ten plays. The fairly short excerpts here printed are in the tradition of Sir Walter Scott's *Ivanhoe* (cf. Tulloch 1980). Bulwer-Lytton explained in detail why and how he turned 'history into flagrant romance', but did not comment on the artificial language he used in the dialogues. This must be an obvious compromise between authenticity and readability but the resulting archaic speech sounds more like quasi-EModE, with a few OE words, than language evoking early 11th-century West Saxon.

T45: From: Charles Dickens, various works. 1838–65. (*Hard Times* 1854, ch. 11; *Nicholas Nickleby* 1838–9, ch. 16; *Our Mutual Friend* 1864–5, III. ch. 4; *Bleak House* 1853, I. ch. 1). (Items (b) and (c) quoted from Brook 1970: 170–1.)

Dickens, all critics will admit, had a good ear for the English he heard around him; accordingly, his rendering of lower (middle)-class London speech is more convincing than his portrayal of northern (Lancashire) dialect in *Hard Times*. Critics are also divided about his attempts at 'fine' writing. For more detailed information see Brook (1970), Blake (1981:157–60), Mugglestone (1995:141–53, 218–22, 237–43), Phillipps (1984: 34f.) and Sørensen (1985).

T46: From: George Eliot. 'Silly Novels By Lady Novelists'. *Westminster Review*, 1856:442–61. Quoted from: Ira B. Nadel, ed. *Victorian Fiction*. New York: Garland, 1986.

This caustic review demolishes a popular brand of novel and their authoresses in a most sophisticated way: George Eliot writes up a devastating piece of criticism by using the genre's stereotypes, linguistic, literary and social, in her characterization, and often quoting passages verbatim. A linguistic analysis would have to interpret the semantics of irony, with its value system turned upside-down, very carefully. The syntax is carefully constructed to convey the niceties of the irony.

T47: From: Anon. 'Romance'. *Encyclopædia Britannica*. Vol. XIX, [8]1859: 283.

The excerpt from the article 'Romance'(!) deals with the flood of ephemeral novels in a language that would be considered inappropriate for a reference book today, and is now more likely to be found in a newspaper review.

T48: From: Anon. 'Shocking murder...', c. 1860. Quoted from: Peter W. Carnell, ed. *Ballads in the Charles Harding Firth Collection of the University of Sheffield*. 1979, no. 47.

The text of this street ballad was obviously made straight after the horrid deed it reports. Ballad-makers could fall back on traditional patterns, including set phrases, which they would apply more or less skilfully to spectacular criminal cases (cf. prose reports of similar gruesome instances). Syntactical features which are quite conspicuous in this hackneyed piece include: overuse of empty *do*, postponed adjectives, forced transpositions (esp. sentence-initial objects); the lexicon is conspicuous for the naive adjectives (*dear, sad, horrid, fell, cold, dead*, etc.). Assonances must serve for rhymes where even transpositions and use of *do/did* were unable to provide them.

T49: From: Anon. *Good Words for 1867*. London, 1867:194–7.

The two hymns come from a collection of sixteen items, newly composed in 1867 but apparently never accepted into regular hymn-books. The wording, made up from biblical allusions and recollections of earlier hymns, is stilted and the syntax sometimes distorted for reasons of metre and rhyme. Aware of the common practice of adapting hymns to particular purposes, without any concern for textual faithfulness or copyright, the Dean adds a footnote: 'These Hymns, and all others by the same Author, are at the disposal of any who may be desirous to use them. One condition only is imposed: that no alterations be made without the Author's consent.'

T50: From: Lewis Carroll. *Through the Looking-Glass*. 1872. Chicago: McNally, 1916.

Lewis Carroll (= Charles Lutwidge Dodgson, 1832–98), lecturer of mathematics at Christ Church, Oxford, is best known for his contributions to children's literature (*Alice in Wonderland* (1865), etc.). The *Jabberwocky* poem has become a classic to illustrate portmanteau words (e.g. *slithy* from *lithe + slimy*) and other unconventional forms of coinage; of course the principle is here carried to an absurd extreme, or extreme absurdity, in the concentration of such 'words' and in their exaggerated forms. The 'explanations' parody textual annotations as found in the apparatus of editions of classical authors.

T51: From: William Morris. *The Aeneid of Virgil*. 1875. In *The Collected Works of William Morris*, ed. May Morris. Vol. XI, London: Longmans Green & Co., 1911:70–3.

Morris (1834–96) was a writer, artisan and socialist, and a leading member of the Pre-Raphaelites. He was deeply influenced by ME Arthurian literature and Old Norse sagas; his archaizing language is found in many prose works and translations such as his *Beowulf* and *Aeneid*. (Compare translations of the passages here included in Görlach (1991:285–92)).

IV On history and culture

T52: From: Dorothy Wordsworth. *The Grasmere Journals*. Ed. Pamela Woolf. Oxford: Clarendon, 1991:37, 42, 50.

The diary exhibits alternately full and elliptical sentences of plain language (and often contents) and, as a conglomerate, can include other text types and styles, as in the woman's report and the conversation with the beggar.

T53: From: Anon. 'Letter'. 1812. Quoted from: John Lewis. *Printed Ephemera*. London: Faber & Faber, 1969.

The proclamation, possibly promoted by the industrialists, answers questions and slogans of Luddite rioters protesting against mechanization, which they feared would put them out of work. The persuasiveness of the text comes from the combination of logical argument and rhetorical questions, formulating self-evident truths which it would be foolish to contradict.

T54: From: William Hazlitt. 'Essay xvi'. In: *Table-Talk*. London, 1821. Ed. P. P. Howe. London: Dent, 1931, VIII:156–7.

The language of this essay is modelled on the classical 18th-century tradition of good writing, as practised by writers from Addison to Johnson; in fact, the readership addressed by Hazlitt is very much the same as the educated 'upper-crust' of the 18th century – as are their social, aesthetic and linguistic concepts and prejudices. Note in particular his sociolinguistic comment on fashionable speech.

T55: From: Pseud. 'Old Mortality, Jr.'. *Epitaphs, or, Church-Yard Gleanings*. London [[1]1874].

The texts here chosen are exceptional: where the majority of tombstones carry 'NN departed this life' and dates of birth and death, the first two present an educational exemplum and the rhymed admonition on behalf of two early railway enthusiasts couched in an extended metaphor.

T56: From: *Manchester Guardian*. No.1, Saturday, 5 May 1821.

The three complete texts, chosen from the forty-one items printed on the front page of the first issue, illustrate the variety of matter assembled in this prominent position. Note the respectful tone of tradespeople offering their foods.

T57: William Wordsworth. 'Letter to Lord Lonsdale'. 1822. In: Alan G. Hill, ed. *The Letters of William and Dorothy Wordsworth*. Oxford: Oxford University Press, [2]1978:142.

Contrary to the informal style expected in a private letter (and one written by Wordsworth), the syntax and diction is quite formal throughout, probably as a reflex of the social distance from the addressee and the request made, a neat illustration of style as a marker of 19th-century social-class differences.

T58: From: Leeds Business Archives. Lupton 4–26, 1826:132–4.

The specimens, selected from a vast corpus of letters documenting the correspondence of the Lupton firm, illustrate 19th-century conventions of formal business letters (and 'informal' ones sent to salesmen in other parts of Britain); they contain the expected formulas, but in the letter to Greig also a very personal and confidential style.

T59: From: *Poor Man's Guardian*. London. 1831. Repr. London: Merlin Press, 1969.

The clause here selected illustrates the hallmarks of legal English (not confined to the 19th century, so that only the contents serve to date the text): endless sentences, with conditional clauses inserted; formulas (*be it enacted, provided always, herein-after*, etc.); definition by enumeration; a high ratio of participles and other infinite verb forms, often forming part of passive constructions.

T60: From: *Poor Man's Guardian*. London. 25 Aug. 1832. Repr. London: Merlin Press, 1969.

The use of religious texts, like the Lord's Prayer or the Catechism, for Radical propaganda was a well-known feature of 19th-century political prose. Such texts draw their effectiveness from the readers' knowledge of the original and the authors' clever substitutions which deliberately 'distort' the meaning. Note the pathetic tone which is partly mock-quotation, but also a reflex of the opponents' diction.

T61: From: 'The stamped and the unstamped. Calumnies of the Standard, etc.' in *Poor Man's Guardian*. London. 21 Sept. 1833, 302–3. Repr. London: Merlin Press, 1969.

The excerpt illustrates the vitriolic war of words waged between the establishment and the unstamped *Guardian*. It shows the range of styles possible in early 19th-century journalism.

T62: From: Mrs Charles Cecil. *New Juvenile Scrap Book*. London: Benshaw & Kirkman, [c. 1835]:88–9.

The sickly sweet diction of this piece combines a description of natural phenomena with explanations relating to utility and beauty. The wheels groan (and not the *fair* attendants = female workers who live in poverty and squalor). The choice of adjectives (*fair, gentle, elegant, limpid*), verbs (*bedeck*) and noun phrases (*the feathered tribe* – straight from 18th-century poetic diction) all combine in this passage crammed with the worst clichés – linguistic and social.

T63: From: 'Agogos'. *Hints on Etiquette and the Usages of Society: With a Glance at Bad Habits*. London: Longman, etc., [15]1837:6, 9, 35, 37, 55, 75.

The 'sociological' analysis relates to etiquette in general but includes advice on proper speech and grammar, the most sensitive fields of conduct which are likely to give upstarts away. Such dangers are especially obvious for people who have risen to wealth outside London – who are likely to exhibit genteel features betraying 'provincial lag'.

T64: From: *Cambridgeshire Collections*. 1838. Cambridge University Library.

The excerpt is of both folkloristic and linguistic interest, comprising a large set of words of everyday use rarely recorded elsewhere.

T65: From: Anon. 'Announcements', c. 1840s. Quoted from James 1976: 153.

This broadsheet takes the form of a playbill authorized by the king of kings to combine as many biblical quotations and allusions as can be crammed into a text travestying the theatrical announcement for a higher purpose. The resulting patchwork is linguistically interesting because of its play with the well-known text forms, and the tension between 17th-century diction lifted from the Authorized Version and contemporary conditions. The readers are asked to 'Search the scriptures', more than 100 references to sources being provided in the margins and within the text (here asterisked).

T66: From: *Church of England Magazine*. No. 7. 1839:285–6.

The excerpt is in a long tradition of preaching against the liberty and immorality of the stage. Note the use of biblical quotations, but also of key terms like *benevolence, pure, reasonable*. The writer obviously knows how to build his arguments, with clever use of rhetorical figures, into effective climaxes, which end in a persuasive appeal underlined by the use of anaphora.

T67: From: *The English Chartist Circular*; 1968:2.

The text combines personal narrative ('your petitioner') reporting on abuses in British coal-mines with the traditional formulas expected in a petition, here confined to the introductory phrases containing the eye-witness proof of the allegations and the end-formula. The description is restrained, but a certain degree of emotion is visible in the use of adjectives.

T68: From: *The English Chartist Circular* 1842; 1968:2.

This specimen of a political (Chartist) speech serves to illustrate both the continuity of rhetoric and typically 19th-century features. The function of evaluative adjectives is again prominent (*foul, immoral, haughty, base, unprincipled, lamentable, frightful*, and many nouns referring to negative qualities contrasted with *honest, moral, virtuous*, etc.). As a piece of political agitation, the text depends on responses to claims made by the opponents, to the denigration of their position, and – obviously – carefully planned climaxes followed by pauses to allow the audience to utter their applause. Note the clichés, partly biblical, in the metaphors (*garb of Truth, Temple of Mammon, shrine of gold*) and the use of quotations. An analysis of rhetorical devices employed is rewarding; they are obviously determined by the use of the text in spoken campaigning.

T69: From: *The English Chartist Circular*. 1842; 1968:46.

The plan detailed in the following text explicitly describes the steps to be taken to set up a system of Sunday schools; the rules specify all the measures necessary, in a formulaic way, with certain qualifications. These formulas are, of course, not typically 19th-century, whereas the contents of the passage are. The end-piece, couched in religious diction, is a persuasive appeal to the 'respected friends' to support the project.

T70: From: Cambridge Record Office. 1843.

The text combines the printed form with handwritten data added in the empty spaces. The text was written by a professional scribe and does not exhibit any 19th-century peculiarities.

T71: From: Christopher Pemberton. 'To Richard Huddleston, re lease of Dernford Mill, with a note on the terms of the agreement'. 1844. Cambridge Record Office 488/P20. The newspaper advertisement is from: *Cambridge Chronicle*, 3 June, 1843.

The handwritten letter provides evidence of the spelling conventions of a Cambridgeshire gentleman in mid-century. The description of Dernford Mills in the advertisement contrasts with the information that can be gathered from the private correspondence of the following year.

T72: From: *Newspaper*, 11 and 18 May 1844.

The advertisements are meant for leisurely reading; their diction is refined, stressing the Latinate element, and the syntax characterized by long sentences, including a great number of dependent clauses, participles and gerundial constructions. The array of linguistic sophistication is, of course, employed to impress the reader with authoritative language and divert his attention from the spurious (and often dangerous) remedies advertised.

T73: From: *John Johnson Collection*, Bodleian Library, Oxford.

These short items play on well-known text types which are reused for different functions (especially love matters), namely medical receipts (a, b) and a cooking recipe (c); cf. mock valentines (T86). The linguistic interest is in the tension between the expectation arising from the close connection between form and function of the texts, and the playful distortion.

T74: From: Charles Hindley. *Curiosities of Street Literature*. London: Reeves & Turner, 1871:196. Repr. London: Broadsheet King, 1966.

The anonymous author patched up his horror story with verbal clichés; in particular the adjectives used show his black-and-white manner of 'characterization'. The appended 'poem' is worse, because it adds unusual word order, empty *did* and forced syntax for the sake of rhyme and metre, and the sensational diction used is even more brutal than that of the prose.

T75: From: Wood 1967:243.

The report of a young woman's death is written by an anonymous preacher of a free church (Methodist?). It is drenched with religious language that sounds slightly sickening today but was quite common in the 19th century. Religious metaphors abound and are not always easy to interpret fully: *the blood-washed throng* sounds like a phrase from an 18th-century hymnbook. The educational element is strong (*unfitness for Heaven*); the girl's progress is keenly observed (*seriousness*, '*new heart*', *course was onward*) with increasing sympathy during her illness, to lead to the bathetic 'Her future experience was quite satisfactory.'

T76: From: *Cambridgeshire Chronicle*. 2 August 1851:3.

The report makes lavish use of decorative adjectives (*fashionable, charming, elegant, graceful, pretty,* etc.) and an impressive array of French words designating dresses or clothes (partly explained by the fact that the report is obviously a translation). Note the absence of imperatives – the directions are suggested in an indirect way rather than given as orders.

T77: From: J. W. Hudson. *The History of Adult Education*. London: Longman, etc., 1851:iv–vii.

The excerpt summarizes the state of the art of adult education in a period of change, in a language that is remarkable for its biblical and metaphoric elements.

T78: From: Charles Elmé Francatelli. *A Plain Cookery Book for the Working Classes*. London: Routledge, etc., 1852:14. Facs. London: Scolar, 1977.

Francatelli, *maître d'hôtel* to Queen Victoria, who won himself a mention in the *DNB*, here stooped to address the working classes; the 'plainness' he aims at takes the form of a condescending chattiness quite unlike the style found in a normal cookery book. Note the frequency of modal verbs where imperatives are expected, and the stress on *thrifty*; *plentiful and nourishing meal*; *cost*.

T79: From: Caroline Chapman. *Russell of the Times. War Despatches and Diaries*. London: Bell & Hyman, 1984:19–25.

The excerpts reflect the unbroken enthusiasm of imperial Britain; Russell, the best-known correspondent of the time, writes in a style expressing the gruesome beauty of the scene in which even corpses have a certain aesthetic appeal, occasionally heightened by lexis evoking a kind of poetic diction. Typical of the genre, sentences are short and arranged according to descriptive detail or the time sequence of events.

T80: From: *The Letters of Queen Victoria*. 1854–61. Vol. III. London: John Murray, 1908:142–4, 170, 186–7.

The set of letters, written by the Queen and addressed to her, all relate to the end of the Crimean War. Their special linguistic interest is the difference in style, varying with the situation and the relationship of the correspondents, which ranges from almost informal ('My dearest uncle') to very formal, from full accounts to a précis as found in the telegram.

T81: From: Anon. Cambridge Pamphlets, b4, 1856:28–34.

The six texts here printed illustrate the range of stylistic variation in commenting on the same event (the students' view is, alas, not represented – neither that of the 'rioters' nor the 'faithfuls'). The quasi-legal official prose of the university authorities contrasts with the enraged expressions of the letter (*suborn a vile rabble* nicely contrasts erudite lexis with maledictory terms). Note the complex patterns of nominalizations and word order in the 'official' statements.

T82: From: Wood 1967:231.

The very personal style of this text, charging the former council with incompetence and drunkenness, and offsetting the enlightened character of the competitors, is peculiarly 19th-century. Note the black-and-white contrast throughout.

T83: From: Mayhew 1861, I:39–40, 51–2, 162–3.

Mayhew, it is generally conceded, comes closer to actual Cockney spoken at his time than literary accounts do. The life-story here recorded sounds authentic: this is the type of text a sociolinguist would try to elicit when documenting spontaneous speech. It is of course impossible to say how much Mayhew may have smoothed the language, not necessarily bringing it closer to standard, but possibly generalizing features such as 'present-tense' -*s*. Note the extremely short sentences which would seem to be appropriate to the speaker and the genre. Cf. T14 above.

The tailor's bill, which was allegedly quoted verbatim by Mayhew, is crammed with cant lexis; whether the claim is true, or the text a cleverly contrived concoction, it is impossible to say: it reminds one of Harman's 16th-century texts, and a long tradition of such documents collected by later compilers. The lexis here recorded agrees with that found in cant dictionaries, like Grose's *Dictionary of the Vulgar Tongue* (most contemporary edition of 1811).

T84: From: Anon. *Catalogue of the Cambridge Free Library Lending Department*. Cambridge: J. Webb, 1862.

The excerpt illustrates the text type 'regulation', characterized by its conventional sentence patterns and semi-legal language; it comes from a context which is of particular relevance for mid 19th-century literacy.

T85: From: Cambridge Collections. Cambridge University Library.

The notices here printed are of obvious relevance for Victorian culture, but they also illustrate text types close to legal language, since they must be both unambiguous and binding.

T86: From: *Strand Magazine*. 1895.

The traditional valentine was becoming dated by the end of the 19th century. Fitzgerald's article 'Vanishing valentines' (from which the specimens are quoted) starts:

> At the present day, when ladies in bifurcated nether garments may be seen awheel in Piccadilly, or enjoying a cigarette in the smoking-room of their own club, it is no wonder that the pretty custom of sending valentines is fast falling into desuetude ... in 1832, comic valentines were unknown; people took their love affairs somewhat seriously.

Playful distortions of existing text types (or anti-valentines) came to be common after 1850; the three here included are of linguistic interest because of the tension between the expected wording of the text forms and their playful re-use: a telegram (a), a bank note (b) and a summons (c).

T87: From: Anon. *Report Presented to the Trade Unions Commissioners by the Examiners Appointed to Inquire into Acts of Intimidation, Outrage, or Wrong Alleged to Have Been Promoted, Encouraged, or Connived at by*

Trade Unions in the Town of Sheffield. London: HMSO, 1867.

The formulaic text provides little opportunity for variation. Note the opening of the first text in the form of a letter following Latin conventions (*Victoria ... greeting*), capital *We/Us* and legal style in *herein-after*, etc., and in serial verbs. Paragraphs are introduced by stereotypical words (*whereas, and, now know ye*).

T88: From: 'Talk of the week'. *Cambridge Chronicle.* 24 July 1869:4.

The style of 'flagrant yet supposed-to-be virtuous advertisements' is very modest by modern standards – the greater is the information on popular attitudes reflected in the anonymous correspondent's criticism.

T89: From: *The Works of John Ruskin.* Vol. XX. Ed. E.T. Cook & Alexander Weddenburn. London: George Allen, 1905:41–3. Also quoted in Edward W. Said. *Culture and Imperialism.* London: Vintage, 1994:123–5.

The excerpt shows Ruskin as a representative of the heyday of imperialism of the late 19th century. Linguistically, the passage is characterized by a carefully constructed series of long sentences exhibiting all the aesthetic and rhetorical features of a deliberate stylist. Note the archaisms in his syntax and the quotations in foreign languages, both enhancing the effect.

T90: From: Charles Hindley, *Curiosities of Street Literature.* London: Reeves & Turner, 1871:34. Repr. London: Broadsheet King, 1966.

The two fabricated texts bring out the stereotypes of what was thought sub-standard speech (and spelling) contrasted with high-falutin' genteel diction, surviving in a *petit bourgeois* milieu as a heritage from 18th-century classical poetry.

T91: From: 'Church of England schools; Mr. Graham's General Report for 1870'. *Report of the Committee of the Council of Education.* London: HMSO, 1871:92–3.

The report is one of the numerous accounts of the state of education in Britain at the time when General Education was introduced. The description of conditions summarizes the achievements made since a previous report, the review also being, explicitly or implicitly, intended as advice on how to proceed in the future. Sentences are short; the tone is remarkably detached.

T92: From: 'George Cruikshank, born 1792, died February 1, 1878'. *Punch*, 9 February 1878:53.

The genre conventions of the obituary are followed, including formal diction (*passed away*), but – as would be expected in *Punch* – the language is more vivid, and the praise and sense of loss expressed in more convincing, honest terms than in the outworn diction normally used for such occasions.

T93: From: Cambridge Pamphlets. Vol. III, 26, a. 500. Cambridge University Library.

The newly invented telegraph brought with it a new style of reduced sentences; the specimens here printed in chronological order – but with longer letters, other documents and a few telegrams omitted – come from a Blue Book on a spectacular and somewhat mysterious mission in Egypt which ended disastrously. Note that not all telegrams make use of the reduced style; more than in texts employing full sentences, some background and intertextual knowledge is needed for complete understanding – but few vital problems arise. The syntactic curtailment is effected almost exclusively by the omission of articles, the personal pronoun *I* or *he*, and the copula.

T94: From: Anon. 'Henry Bradshaw, University Librarian, died February 1886'. Quoted from: Cambridge Pamphlets. Vol. III, 26, a. 500 V [165–75].
The handwritten letters illustrate the stylistic range of expression for the same sad event, the formality largely depending (obviously) on the closeness of personal relations. Note the synonyms used for *loss, shocked, (good/old) Bradshaw* and the wavering between straightforward, sometimes colloquial words and extended metaphor (*fire*).

T95: From: J. W. Clark's Cambridge Collection. Cambridge University Library.
The regulations distributed in all parishes of England modify and complement the church service to provide a special form of thanksgiving to commemorate Queen Victoria's jubilee. The religious language is characterized by the expected features in lexis and syntax: special meanings, archaic uses of pronouns and verb inflections, paratactic structure with a great deal of parallelism and repetition, 'empty' *do/didst*, all of which are genre-specific and archaic/formal.

T96: From: Anon. *Good Things Made, Said & Done for Every Home & Household*. Leeds: Goodall, Backhouse & Co., White-Horse Sweet, 1887: front and end-pages.
Although the advertisements here reproduced use exaggerated language, they are modest in comparison with what other Victorian specimens offered by way of texts and illustrations.

T97: From: *Anon. Good Things Made, Said & Done for Every Home & Household*. Leeds: Goodall, Backhouse & Co., White-Horse Sweet, 1887:66–7, 77, 82–3.
In this simple cookery-book, the producer of Yorkshire relish, baking-powder and many related kitchen aids poses as a publisher. The unassuming text is clearly meant for wide distribution, easily understood in language and instruction: the latter including useful hints as to how to improve dishes by the use of Goodall's products. The text is made more lively by a fictitious user asking questions, which are then answered by the manu-facturer, who often uses this method to draw attention to his products.

T98: From: H. R. Fox Bourne. *English Newspapers. Chapters in the History of Journalism*. 2 vols. London: Chatto & Windus, 1887:370–2.
The text is largely descriptive, a case of expository prose striking a compromise between formal and technical explanation and 'narrative' (note the long sentences composed of short clauses).

References

The list includes a few important studies not quoted in my book, but does not normally list primary literature quoted second-hand. References to individual titles used are in square brackets. Sources, indicated by T plus number, are listed on pp. 286–302. References quoted underneath chapter headings indicate major sources also useful for further reading.

Aarsleff, Hans. 1967. *The Study of Language in England 1780–1860*. Princeton: Princeton University Press ([2]1983). [8, 19, 20, 25]

Aarts, F. G. A. M. 1986. 'William Cobbett: radical reactionary and poor man's grammarian'. *Neophilologus* 70:603–14.

Abbott, Revd Edwin Abbott. [3]1879. *A Handbook of English Grammar*. Rev. by William Moore, London: James Martin. [52, 289; T19b]

Adamson, John William. 1930. *English Education, 1789–1902*. Cambridge: Cambridge University Press.

Adamson, Sylvia. 1998. 'Literary language'. In Romaine 1998: 589–692. [81–2, 89, 142, 153, 161]

ALD. [2]1963. A.S. Hornby *et al.*, *The Advanced Learner's Dictionary of Current English*. London: Oxford University Press (the edition used in *CED* and in Finkenstaedt *et al.* 1973). [93–4, 96, 134]

Alford, Henry. 1864, [3]1870. *The Queen's English: A Manual of Idiom and Usage*. London: Longman & Green. Excerpt in Crowley 1991:171–80. [22, 23, 27, 50, 57–8, 84, 116, 120, 288–9; T16]

Algeo, John. 1998. 'Vocabulary'. In Romaine 1998: 57–91.

Allison, M. A. 1825. *First Lessons in English Grammar; for the Nursery and for Junior Classes*. London: Longman. ([8]1851). [108]

Alston, Robin Carfrae. 1965–72. *A Bibliography of the English Language from the Invention of Printing to the Year 1800*. Leeds: Arnold. (Corrected re-issue 1974). [1, 10]

ed. 1967–70. *English Linguistics 1500–1800* (A Collection of Facsimile Reprints). Menston: Scolar Press (= EL). [15]

1992. *Linguistics. The Nineteenth Century*. A collection of over 1,200 19th-century texts for the historical study of language. Cambridge: Chadwick-Healey (Microfiche edition). [15]

Altick, Richard Daniel. 1957. *The English Common Reader: A Social History of the Mass Reading Public, 1800–1900*. Chicago: Chicago

University Press. [21]

Angus, Joseph. [2]1862. *Hand-book of the English Tongue*. London: Religious Tract Society ([1]1861). [52, 152, 160]

Anon. 1797. *A Vocabulary of Such Words in the English Language as are of Dubious or Unsettled Pronunciation*. London: for F. & C. Rivington. (EL 46, 1967). [44, 56, 62]

Anon. [n.d.]. *Riot and Be Hanged*. Cambridge: Isle of Ely Education Committee.

Anon. 1898. '*What Shall I Say?*' *A Guide to Letter Writing for Ladies*. London: James Bowden. (Repr. Whitstable: Pryor, 1994). [41, 46, 150]

Arnaud, R. 1983. 'On the progress of the progressive in the private correspondence of famous British people (1800–1880)'. In S. Jacobson, ed. *Papers from the Second Scandinavian Symposium on Syntactic Variation*. Stockholm: Almqvist & Wiksell, 83–94. [82]

1998. 'The development of the progressive in 19th century England'. *Language Variation and Change* 10:123–52.

Atkinson, Dwight. 1992. 'The evolution of medical research writing from 1735 to 1985: the case of the Edinburgh Medical Journal'. *Applied Linguistics* 13.4.

Bailey, Richard W. 1991. *Images of English. A Cultural History of the Language*. Cambridge: Cambridge University Press.

1996. *Nineteenth-Century English*. Ann Arbor: The University of Michigan Press. [iv, 8, 11, 21, 38, 44–6, 56, 58, 59, 287, 289]

Bain, Alexander. 1872. *A First English Grammar*. London: Longmans. [109]

Barnes, William. 1863. *A Grammar and Glossary of the Dorset Dialect with the History, Outspreading and Bearings of South-Western English*. Berlin: Asher. [105]

1878. *An Outline of English Speech-Craft*. London: Kegan Paul. [105, 116, 120]

1886. *A Glossary of the Dorset Dialect with a Grammar*. Dorchester: Case. (Repr. St Peter Port, Guernsey, 1970). [292; T35]

Barnhart, Robert K. 1988. *The Barnhart Dictionary of Etymology*. New York: H.W. Wilson. [102]

Batchelor, Thomas. 1809. *An Orthoëpical Analysis of the English Language* ... to which is added, a minute and copious analysis of the dialect of Bedfordshire. London: for Didier & Tebbett. (Facs. edn Arne Zettersten, Lund: Gleerup, 1974.) [30, 47]

Bateson, F. W. [3]1973. *English Poetry and the English Language*. Oxford: Clarendon ([1]1934). [153–5]

Baugh, Albert C. and Thomas Cable. [4]1993. *A History of the English Language*. London: Routledge. [6, 7]

Beaugrande, Robert de & Wolfgang Dressler. 1981. *Introduction to Text Linguistics*. London: Longman. [91]

Bédarida, F. 1975. *A Social History of England 1851–1975*. London: Methuen. [3]

Biber, Douglas. 1988. *Variation Across Speech and Writing*. Cambridge: Cambridge University Press. [141]

Biber, Douglas & Edward Finegan. 1989. 'Drift and the evolution of English style: a history of three genres'. *Language* 65:487–517. [141–2]

1992. 'The linguistic evolution of five written and speech-based English genres from the 17th to the 20th centuries'. In Matti Rissanen *et al.*, eds. *History of Englishes*. Berlin: Mouton de Gruyter, 688–704. [139, 141]

Biese, Y.M. 1941. *Origin and Development of Conversions in English*. Helsinki: Suomalainen Tiedeakatemia. [124]

Blake, Norman Francis. 1981. *Non-Standard Language in English Literature*. London: Deutsch. [34–5, 46, 292–4]

1995. 'Speech and writing: an historical overview'. *Year's Work in English Studies* 25:6–21. [160–1]

Bradley, Henry. 1904. *The Making of English*. London: Macmillan. [24, 71, 146]

Breen, Henry H. 1857. *Modern English Literature: its Blemishes and Defects*. London: Longman. [8, 52, 86, 108, 110, 151]

Bridges, Robert. 1913. *A Tract on the Present State of English Pronunciation*. (SPE Tract). Oxford: Clarendon.

Brook, George Leslie. 1970. *The Language of Dickens*. London: Deutsch. [15, 37, 45, 52, 75, 92, 96, 104, 136–8, 162, 294; T45bc]

Brunner, Karl. 1950. *Die englische Sprache*. Halle: Niemeyer. [2]1960–2, Tübingen: Niemeyer. [6]

Buchanan. 1757. *Linguae Britannicae vera pronunciatio*, or a New English Dictionary. repr. EL 39. [63]

Buchmann, E. 1940. *Der Einfluß des Schriftbildes auf die Aussprache im Neuenglischen*. Würzburg: K. Triltsch. [56]

Burton, John R. 1870. *Roots and Derivations*. London: Educational Trading Co. [101]

CED. 1970. Thomas Finkenstaedt *et al*. *A Chronological English Dictionary*. Heidelberg: Winter. [vi, 92–4, 96, 111, 121]

'Censor' c. 1880. *Don't: A Manual of Mistakes & Improprieties More or*

Less Prevalent in Conduct & Speech. London: Field & Tuer. (Repr. Whitstable: Pryor, 1982). [1, 37, 62, 80]

Chapman, Raymond. 1973. *Linguistics and Literature. An Introduction to Literary Stylistics.* London: Arnold.

1994. *Forms of Speech in Victorian Fiction.* London: Longman. [33]

Cherubim, Dieter & Klaus J. Mattheier, eds. 1989. *Voraussetzungen und Grundlagen der Gegenwartssprache.* Berlin & New York: De Gruyter.

[Clarke, Hewson]. 1811. *Lexicon Balatronicum. A Dictionary of the Vulgar Tongue.* A dictionary of buckish slang, university wit, and pickpocket eloquence. London: for C. Chappel. (Repr. Northfield, Ill.: Digest Books, 1971). [39, 99]

Coates, Richard. 1998. 'Onomastics'. In Romaine 1998: 330–72. [135]

Cobbett, William. 1818. *A Grammar of the English Language, in a Series of Letters.* New York/London: Clayton & Kingsland, for the author, sold by T. Dolby. Revised edn 1823, London. (Repr., with an introduction by Robert Burchfield, Oxford: Oxford University Press, 1984). [10, 11, 20, 22, 45, 55, 67–8, 90, 108, 287–8; T3, T8/1,9, T9/12, T15]

Colls, R. 1977. *The Colliers' Rant: Song and Culture in the Industrial Village.* London: Croom Helm.

Craigie, W. A. 1927. *English Spelling, Its Rules and Reasons.* New York: F.S. Crofts. [104]

1937. *Northern Words in Modern English.* (SPE Tract 50:327–60). Oxford: Clarendon. [102]

1946. *The Critique of Pure English.* (SPE Tract). Oxford: Clarendon.

Crowley, Tony. 1989. *The Politics of Discourse: the Standard Language Question in British Cultural Debates.* London: Macmillan. [8, 127]

1991. *Proper English? Readings in Language History and Cultural Identity.* London: Routledge. [98, 165, 289]

Crystal, David. 1995. *The Cambridge Encyclopedia of the English Language.* Cambridge: Cambridge University Press. [136]

Crystal, David & Derek Davy. 1969. *Investigating English Style.* London: Longman. [143, 145–6]

Danielson, Bror. 1948. *Studies on the Accentuation of Polysyllabic Latin, Greek, and Romance Loan-Words in English.* Stockholm: Almqvist & Wiksell. [64]

Darby, H. C., ed. 1973. *A New Historical Geography of England.* Cambridge: Cambridge University Press. [2]

DeKeyser, Xavier. 1975. *Number and Case Relations in 19th Century British English. A Comparative Study of Grammar and Usage.* Antwerp & Amsterdam: Uitgeverij De Nederlandsche Boekhandel. [5,

67, 69–70, 78–9, 158]

Denison, David. 1993. *English Historical Syntax*. London: Longman. [69]
 1998. 'Syntax'. In Romaine 1998: 92–329. [38, 53, 67, 69–71, 73–5, 78–9, 81–5, 87]

Dennis, R. 1984. *English Industrial Cities in the Nineteenth Century: A Social Geography*. Cambridge: Cambridge University Press.

De Quincey, Thomas. 1839. 'The English language'. *Blackwoods Magazine* 45 (April). (Repr. in Harris 1995, I:78–89). [108]

Dobson, E.J. ²1968. *English Pronunciation 1500–1700*. 2 vols. Oxford: Clarendon.

Donaldson, William. 1986. *Popular Literature in Victorian Scotland*. Language, Fiction and the Press. Aberdeen: Aberdeen University Press. [33]

Earle, John. 1892. *A Simple Grammar of English Now in Use*. New York: Putnam's Sons. (Anr. edn 1898, New York: G. P. Putnam's Sons / London: Smith, Elder & Co.). [75, 80]

Earnshaw, Christopher. 1817. *The Grammatical Remembrancer: a Short but Comprehensive English Grammar for the Use of Young Students*. Huddersfield. [73, 88]

Eastlake. 1902. 'Changes in the pronunciation of English' *Nineteenth Century* 52:992–1001. [42]

Ellis, Alexander J. 1845. *A Plea for Phonotopy and Phonography*. Bath/London: Pitman. (²1848, as *A Plea for Phonetic Spelling*. London: Pitman). [47]
 1869–74. *On Early English Pronunciation*. London: Asher. [7, 28, 49, 54, 57, 61, 98, 289; T17]

Elphinston, John. 1786–87. *Propriety Ascertained in Her Picture*. 2 vols. London: J. Walter. [46, 59]

Elworthy, Frederick. 1886. *The West Somerset Work-Book*. (English Dialect Society 50). London: Trübner. [31]

Encyclopædia Britannica. ⁸1853–60. [11–14, 22, 115, 150, 288, 294; T13, T47]

Engels, Friedrich. 1845. *Die Lage der arbeitenden Klasse in England*. Leipzig. (Repr. Munich: dtv, 1973). English translation: 1993. *The Condition of the Working Class in England*. Oxford: Oxford University Press. [10]

The English Chartist Circular and Temperance Record for England and Wales. London: Cleave, 1841–4. (Repr. New York: Kelley, 1968).

Fairman, Tony. 1986. 'Prestige, purity, and power'. *English Today* 7:13–16. [20]

Finegan, Edward. 1992. 'Style and standardization in England: 1700–1900'. In Tim William Machan & Charles T. Scott, eds., *English in Its Social Contexts. Essays in Historical Sociolinguistics*. New York & Oxford: Oxford University Press, 102–30.

　　1998. 'English grammar and usage'. In Romaine 1998: 536–88. [21]

Finkenstaedt, Thomas *et al.* **see** *CED*.

　　1973. *Ordered Profusion. Studies in Dictionaries and the English Lexicon*. Heidelberg: Winter.

Foster, Alexander F. & Margaret E. Foster. 1869. 'English, literary and vernacular'. *London Review*. 15 Oct. (Repr. in Harris 1995: I, 312–38.). [34]

Foster, John. ³1977. *Class Struggle and the Industrial Revolution. Early Industrial Capitalism in Three English Towns*. London: Methuen. [3, 29]

Fowler, Henry W. 1925. ''s incongruous'. *SPE Tract* 20:39–40. [80]

　　1926. *A Dictionary of Modern English Usage*. Oxford: Clarendon. (²1965, ed. E. Gowers; ³1997, ed. R. W. Burchfield). [8, 38, 61, 65–6, 73–6, 85–6, 110, 151]

Fowler, Henry W. & F. G. Fowler. 1906. *The King's English*. Oxford: Clarendon. (²1907, ³1930). [5, 53, 66, 82, 84, 87, 89–90, 110]

Gallasch, Linda. 1979. *The Use of Compounds and Archaic Diction in the Works of William Morris*. Bern, Frankfurt/Main etc.: Lang. [106, 109, 135, 145, 156–7]

Garcia-Bermejo Giner, Maria F. & Michael Montgomery. 1997. 'British regional English in the 19th century: the evidence from emigrant letters'. In Alan R. Thomas, ed. *Issues and Methods in Dialectology*. Bangor: University of Wales, 167–83. [36]

Gaskell, Elizabeth C. 1857/1919. *The Life of Charlotte Brontë*. Oxford: Oxford University Press. [109]

Geeraerts, Dirk. 1997. *Diachronic Prototype Semantics. A Contribution to Historical Lexicology*. Oxford: Oxford University Press. [126]

Ghadessy, Mohsen, ed. 1988. *Registers of Written English: Situational Factors and Linguistic Features*. New York: Pinter.

Golby, J.M., ed. 1996. *Culture and Society in Britain 1850–1890*. A Source Book of Contemporary Writings. Oxford: Oxford University Press in association with The Open University. [31, 144, 149, 165]

Gordon, Ian A. 1966. *The Movement of English Prose*. London: Longman. [20–1, 159–60]

Görlach, Manfred. 1989. 'Zur englischen Sprachgeschichte des 19. Jahrhunderts'. In Cherubim & Mattheier 1989: 303–13. [1]

1990a. *Studies in the History of the English Language.* Heidelberg: Winter.

1990b. 'The development of Standard Englishes'. In Görlach 1990a:9–64. [1, 9]

1990c. 'Corpus problems of text collections: linguistic aspects of the canon'. In Görlach 1990a:163–78. [iv]

1991. *Introduction to Early Modern English.* Cambridge: Cambridge University Press. [iv, 9, 39, 47, 49, 56, 87, 105, 107, 115, 128-9, 134, 295]

1992. 'Sociolinguistic determinants for literature in dialects and minority languages'. In J. J. Simon & Alain Sinner, eds. *Proceedings of the Third Conference on the Literature of Region and Nation.* Part 2. Luxembourg: University, 130–60. [32, 34–5]

1995a. *New Studies in the History of English.* Heidelberg: Winter. [1]

1995b. 'Dialect lexis in Early Modern English dictionaries'. In Görlach 1995a:82–127. [iv]

1995c. 'Text types and language history'. In Görlach 1995a:141–78. [139, 147–8]

1997. *The Linguistic History of English.* London: Macmillan. [iv, 111, 125, 128–9]

1998a. *Aspects of the History of English.* Heidelberg: Winter. [87]

1998b. 'French in 19th-century Britain'. In Görlach 1998a, 179-99. [92, 107, 111]

1998c. *An Annotated Bibliography of 19th-century Grammars of English.* Amsterdam: Benjamins. [iv, 15, 16]

fc. 'Regional and social variation in Early Modern English (1450–1800)'. In Roger Lass, ed. *The Cambridge History of the English Language: 1476–1776.* (Vol. IV.). Cambridge: Cambridge University Press.

Gourvich, T. R. & Alan O'Day. 1988. *Later Victorian Britain.* London: Macmillan.

Graham, G. F. 1869. *A Book About Words.* London: Longman & Green. (Excerpt in Crowley 1991:159–70.) [99, 104, 109]

Groom, Bernard. 1937. *The Formation and Use of Compound Epithets in English Poetry from 1579.* (SPE Tract 49). Oxford: Clarendon. [119]

1939. *On the Diction of Tennyson, Browning and Arnold.* (SPE Tract 53). Oxford: Clarendon. [153, 155–6]

Grose, Francis. 1785. *A Classical Dictionary of the Vulgar Tongue.* London: Hooper. (Repr. Menston: Scolar (EL 80)). [39, 300]

Hancock, Ian. 1984. 'Romani and Angloromani'. In Peter Trudgill, ed. *Language in the British Isles.* Cambridge: Cambridge University Press, 367–83.

Harris, Roy, ed. 1993. *British Linguistics in the 19th Century*. 7 vols. London: Routledge/Thoemmes. [8]

ed. 1995. *Language and Linguistics*. Key 19th Century Journal Sources in Linguistics. 4 vols. London: Routledge/Thoemmes. [8, 18, 29, 41, 47, 96]

Hartley, Charles. 1879. *Frequent Faults in Speaking and Writing Explained and Corrected*. Brighton: the author. [14]

Hazlitt, William. 1810. *A New and Improved Grammar of the English Tongue...* London: for Richard Taylor. [19]

[Heald, A.] [2]1898. *The Queen's English (?) Up to Date: an Exposition of the Prevailing Grammatical Errors of the Day, with Numerous Examples*. [Publ. anonymously by 'Anglophil'.] London: Literary Revision and Translation Office. ([1]1892). [23, 43, 290; T25]

Hindley, Diana & Geoffrey Hindley 1972. *Advertising in Victorian England*. London: Wayland.

Hollingworth, Brian, ed. 1977. *Songs of the People. Lancashire Dialect Poetry of the Industrial Revolution*. Manchester: Manchester University Press. [28, 32–3]

Holmberg, Börje. 1964. *On the Concept of Standard English and the History of Modern English Pronunciation*. Lund: Gleerup. [55]

Honey, John. 1988. '"Talking proper": schooling and the establishment of English "Received Pronunciation"'. In Graham Nixon & John Honey, eds. *An Historic Tongue. Studies in English Linguistics in Memory of Barbara Strang*. London & New York: Routledge, 209–27. [21, 22, 26, 28, 42]

1989. *Does Accent Matter? The Pygmalion Factor*. London and Boston: Faber & Faber. [26, 28, 60–2]

Horn, Wilhelm & Martin Lehnert. 1954. *Laut und Leben. Englische Lautgeschichte der neueren Zeit (1400–1950)*. Berlin: Deutscher Verlag der Wissenschaften. [58–9]

Hotton, John Camden. 1874. *The Slang Dictionary: Etymological, Historical and Anecdotal*. London: Chatto & Windus. (New edn 1882). [39]

Howatt, Anthony P.R. 1984. *A History of English Language Teaching*. Oxford: Oxford University Press. [13, 20, 110]

Ihalainen, Ossi. 1994. 'The dialects of England since 1776'. In Robert Burchfield, ed. *English in Britain and Overseas: Origins and Development*. (*The Cambridge History of the English Language*, vol. V.) Cambridge: Cambridge University Press, 197–274. [28, 30, 32, 35, 40, 291]

Isbister, Alexander K. 1865. *Outlines of the English Language*. London: Longmans, Green & Co. [77]

Jacobs, Willis D. 1952. *William Barnes Linguist*. Albuquerque: University of New Mexico Press. [31, 105–6]

Jacobsson, U. 1962. *Phonological Dialect Constituents in the Vocabulary of Standard English*. Lund: Gleerup.

James, Louis, ed. 1976. *English Popular Literature, 1819–1851*. Columbia: University Press. (Published in Britain as *Print and the People*. London: Allen Lane, 1986.) [Specimens mainly from the John Johnson Collection in the Bodleian Library, Oxford.] [T43, T65]

Jespersen, Otto. 1905. *Growth and Structure of the English Language*. Leipzig: Teubner. (^{9}1946, Oxford: Blackwell).

1909–49. *A Modern English Grammar on Historical Principles*. 7 vols. Heidelberg: Winter / Copenhagen: Munksgaard. (Repr. London: Allen & Unwin, 1961). [79–81]

Johnson, Samuel. 1755. *A Dictionary of the English Language*. London: for J. & P. Knapton, etc. (Repr. London: Times Books, 1983; revised edn by Todd, London: for Longman, etc., 1818). [9, 10, 19, 24–5, 63, 67, 98, 100, 133]

Jones, Charles, ed. 1997. *A History of the Scots Language*. Edinburgh: Edinburgh University Press. [102]

Joyce, Patrick. 1991. *Visions of the People. Industrial England and the Question of Class, 1848–1914*. Cambridge: Cambridge University Press. [165]

Kay-Shuttleworth, James. 1973. *Four Periods of Public Education as Reviewed in 1832, 1839, 1846, 1862*. Brighton: Harvester Press. [115]

Kelly, Edith & Thomas Kelly 1977. *Books for the People*. Harmondsworth: Penguin.

Kennedy, Arthur Garfield. 1927. *A Bibliography of Writings on the English Language from the Beginning of Printing to the End of 1922*. Cambridge, Mass.: Harvard University Press. (Repr. New York: Hafner, 1961).

Kirk, John, *et al*., eds. 1985. *Studies in Linguistic Geography*. London: Croom Helm.

Knight, Charles. 1847. *Old English: a Pictorial Museum of Regal, Ecclesiastical, Municipal, Baronial, and Popular Antiquities*. London: Sangster. (Facs. repr: New York: Crown Press, 1987). [157, 165]

Kroeber, Karl. 1971. *Styles in Fictional Structure: the Art of Jane Austen, Ch. Brontë, George Eliot*. Princeton: Princeton University Press

Kruisinga, Etsko. 1932. *Handbook of Present-Day English*. 3 vols. Groningen: Noordhoff.

Lambe, J. 1849. *The Westminster Handbook to the Study of the Science of*

Universal Grammar, Exemplified in its Application to the English Language. London: H. Hurst. [22]

Laqueur, Thomas Walter. 1976. *Religion and Respectability: Sunday Schools and Working Class Culture, 1780–1850.* New Haven: Yale University Press.

Lass, Roger, fc. 'Phonology and Morphology'. In Roger Lass, ed. *1476–1776* (CHEL, 3). Cambridge: Cambridge University Press. [62]

Latham, Robert G. 1841. *The English Language.* London: Taylor & Walton. [23, 69]

Leech, Geoffrey N. 1966. *English in Advertising. A Linguistic Study of Advertising in Britain.* London: Longman. [147]

Leech, Geoffrey N. & Michael H. Short. 1981. *Style in Fiction. A Linguistic Introduction to English Fictional Prose.* London: Longman.

Legg, Rev. J.P. 1890–1. 'Cape English and its future'. *Cape Illustrated Magazine* 1:94–6 (repr. in *English World-Wide* 18:271–4). [57]

Leigh, Percival. 1840. *The Comic English Grammar. An Introduction to the English Tongue.* London: R. Bentley. (Repr. London: Bracken 1989).

Leith, Dick. 1983. *A Social History of English.* London: Routledge & Kegan Paul. (²1997). [6, 7]

Leitner, Gerhard. 1986. 'English traditional grammars in the 19th century'. In Dieter Kastovsky & Aleksander Szwedek, eds. *Linguistics Across Historical and Geographical Boundaries. In Honour of Jacek Fisiak.* Berlin: Mouton de Gruyter, 1333–55. [19]

— ed. 1991. *English Traditional Grammars. An International Perspective.* Amsterdam: Benjamins.

Lennie, William. ²1816. *A Key to Lennie's Principles of English Grammar.* Edinburgh: Guthrie & Tait, Oliver & Boyd. [16]

Leonard, Sterling Andrus. 1929. *The Doctrine of Correctness in English Usage 1700–1800.* Madison: University of Wisconsin. [1]

Lindelöf, Uno Lorenz. 1938. *English Verb-Adverb Groups Converted Into Nouns.* Helsinki: Societas Scientiarum Fennica. [122–4]

Lloyd, R. J. 1897. 'Can the English tongue be preserved?' *Westminster Review* 147 (March 1897), quoted from Harris 1995:II, 374. [23]

— 1899. *Northern English.* Leipzig: Teubner. (²1908). [9]

Lowth, Robert. 1762. *A Short Introduction to English Grammar, With Critical Notes.* London: for A. Millar and R. & J. Dodsley. (Repr. Menston: Scolar (EL 18)). [10, 15, 20, 22, 24, 25]

Macaulay, Ronald K. S. 1997. 'RP R.I.P.'. In R. K. S. Macaulay. *Standards and Variation in Urban Speech. Examples from Lowland Scots.* (VEAW G20). Amsterdam: Benjamins, 35–44. [62]

McClure, J. Derrick. 1994 'English in Scotland'. In R. W. Burchfield, ed. *English in Britain and Overseas: Origins and Development.* (CHEL 5). Cambridge: Cambridge University Press, 23–93. [102]

MacMahon, Michael K. C. 1998. 'Phonology'. In Romaine, 373–535. [42, 44, 54, 57]

Marchand, Hans. [2]1969. *The Categories and Types of English Word-Formation.* Munich: Beck. [93, 112, 118–23, 125]

Marshall, William. 1788. *Provincialisms of East Yorkshire*; repr. English Dialect Society 1 (1873), 15–43. [40]

Martin, Thomas. 1824. *A Philological Grammar of the English Language.* London: Rivingtons. [76–7, 108]

Marx, Karl. 1857. 'The Indian question'. *New York Daily Tribune*, August 14, 5091. [149]

Matthews, William. 1938. *Cockney Past and Present. A Short History of the Dialect of London.* 4 vols. London: Routledge & Kegan Paul. [35, 100]

Mayhew, Henry. 1861–2. *London Labour and the London Poor.* 4 vols. London: Griffin, Bohn & Co. (Repr. London, New York: 1967). [25, 35, 36, 39, 100, 288, 300; T14, T38]

Michael, Ian. 1970. *English Grammatical Categories and the Tradition to 1800.* Cambridge: Cambridge University Press. [1, 10, 76, 78]

1987. *The Teaching of English from the Sixteenth Century to 1870.* Cambridge: Cambridge University Press. [10, 14, 15, 18, 20, 29, 37, 76]

1991. 'More than enough English grammars'. In Gerhard Leitner, ed. *English Traditional Grammars.* Amsterdam: Benjamins, 11–26. [10, 15, 19, 43]

1993. *Early Textbooks of English.* Reading: The Textbook Colloquium. [15]

1997. 'The hyperactive production of English grammars in the nineteenth century: a speculative bibliography'. *Publishing History* 41:23–61. [10, 14–7]

Milroy, James. 1977. *The Language of Gerard Manley Hopkins.* London: Deutsch. [153, 156]

Mitch, David F. 1992. *The Rise of Popular Literacy in Victorian England. The Influence of Private Choice and Public Policy.* Philadelphia: University of Pennsylvania Press.

Mitchell, Brian Redman & Phyllis Deane. 1962. *Abstract of British Historical Statistics.* Cambridge: Cambridge University Press. [4]

Mitchell, Sally, ed. 1988. *Victorian Britain. An Encyclopedia.* New York & London: Garland.

Mitford, Nancy. 1956. *Noblesse Oblige*. London: Hamilton. [37]

Morpurgo Davies, Anna. 1998. *History of Linguistics, IV.* Nineteenth-Century Linguistics. London: Longman

Mudie, George. [1841]. *The Grammar of the English Language Truly Made Easy and Amusing, by the invention of three hundred moveable parts of speech* (with cards). London: John Cleave. [18]

Mugglestone, Lynda. 1995. *'Talking Proper': The Rise of Accent as Social Symbol.* Oxford: Clarendon. [iv, 8, 36, 37, 39–40, 56–7, 59, 61, 289, 294]

  1997. 'Cobbett's *Grammar*: William, James Paul, and the politics of prescriptivism'. *RES* NS, 48, No. 192:471–88.

  ed. fc. *Lexicography and the OED*. Oxford: Oxford University Press. [8, 97]

Müller, Friedrich Max. 1861/3. *Lectures on the Science of Language.* I (1861), II (1863). London: Longman, etc. (Facs. edn by Roy Harris, London: Routledge/Thoemmes Press, 1994.) [29, 48]

  1876. 'On spelling'. *Fortnightly Review* n. s. 19, April. (Repr. in Harris 1995: II, 205–29). [48]

Murray, James A. H. 1888. 'Preface to volume I'. *A New English Dictionary*. Oxford: Clarendon. (Repr. in Raymond 1987). [44, 61–2, 102]

  1900. *The Evolution of English Lexicography*. (The Romanes Lecture.) Oxford: Clarendon. [98]

  1905. 'Preface to volume VII'. *A New English Dictionary*. Oxford: Clarendon. (Repr. in Raymond 1987). [96]

Murray, K. M. Elizabeth. 1977. *Caught in the Web of Words: James Murray and the* Oxford English Dictionary. New Haven & London: Yale University Press. [98]

Murray, Lindley. 1795. *English Grammar, Adapted to the Different Classes of Learners*. York: Wilson, Spence, and Mawman. (Repr. Menston: Scolar (EL 106)). [5, 10, 15, 16, 22, 24, 25]

Nash, Walter. 1980. *Designs in Prose*. London: Longman. [161]

Nesfield, John C. 1898. *English Grammar, Past and Present*. 3 vols. London: Macmillan. [70]

Olsson, Yngve. 1961. *On the Syntax of the English Verb with Special Reference to 'Have a Look' and Similar Complex Structures.* (Gothenburg Studies 12). Göteburg: Almqvist & Wiksell. [122]

Ousby, Ian. 1988. *Companion to Literature in English*. Cambridge: Cambridge University Press; re-ed. *The Wordsworth Companion to English Literature*. Ware: Wordsworth Editions, 1992. [38]

Outis, Gaspar (pseud.). 1868. *Remarks on Some Errors in Grammar and Syntax; as also in the Pronunciation and Meaning of Certain Words.* London: David Nutt. [16, 21, 42]

Page, Norman. 1973. *Speech in the English Novel.* London: Longman.

Partridge, Eric. 1933. *Slang To-day and Yesterday.* London: Routledge & Kegan Paul. (⁴1970). [99–100]

1940. *Slang.* (SPE Tract 55). Oxford: Clarendon. [95]

Paz, D. G. 1980. *The Politics of Working-Class Education in Britain.* Manchester: Manchester University Press.

Pearson, William. 1865. *The Self-help Grammar of the English Language.* London: Hamilton. [40]

Pennanen, E.V. 1966. *Contributions to the Study of Back-Formation in English.* Tampere: JYK. [124]

Petyt, K. Malcolm. 1985. *Dialect and Accent in Industrial West Yorkshire.* Amsterdam: Benjamins. [31]

Phillipps, Kenneth C. 1970. *Jane Austen's English.* London: Deutsch. [80]
1984. *Language and Class in Victorian England.* Oxford: Blackwell. [14, 26–8, 31–2, 37, 40, 46, 60, 71, 83, 100, 110, 115, 132–3, 158, 287, 294]

Pickering, John. 1816. *A Vocabulary or Collection of Words and Phrases which have been supposed to be peculiar to the United States of America.* Boston: Cummings & Hilliard. [71]

Piozzi, Hester Lynch Thrale. 1794. *British Synonymy.* 2 vols. (Facs. edn Menston: Scolar (EL 113)).

Poutsma, H. 1926. *A Grammar of Late Modern English.* Groningen: Noordhoff.

Priestley, Joseph. 1761. *The Rudiments of English Grammar.* London: R. Grifiths. (Repr. Menston: Scolar (EL 210)). [10]

Puttenham, George. 1589. *The Arte of English Poesie.* London: R. Field. (EL 110, 1968). [9]

Quirk, Randolph *et al.* 1972. *A Grammar of Contemporary English.* London: Longman. [79]

Ramson, William Stanley. 1966. *Australian English. A Historical Study of the Vocabulary.* Canberra: Australian National University Press.

Raudnitzky, H. 1911. *Die Bell-Sweetsche Schule: Ein Beitrag zur Geschichte der englischen Phonetik.* (Marburger Studien, 13). Marburg: N. G. Elwert. [48]

Raymond, Darrell R. 1987. *Dispatches from the Front: The Prefaces to the Oxford English Dictionary.* Waterloo, Ont.: UW Centre for the New Oxford English Dictionary.

Redford, Arthur. 1926. *Labour Migration in England. 1800–1850.* Manchester: University Press.

Richardson, Charles. 1835–7. *A New Dictionary of the English Language.* London: William Pickering. [97–8, 101]

Robbins, Keith. 1988. *Nineteenth-Century Britain: Integration and Diversity.* Oxford: Clarendon.

Roberts, Paul. 1953. 'Sir Walter Scott's contribution to the English vocabulary'. *PMLA* 67:189–210.

Rogers, R. R. 1855. *Poor Letter R, Its Use and Abuse.* London. [59]

Roget, Peter Mark. 1852. *Thesaurus of English Words and Phrases,* classified and arranged so as to facilitate the expression of ideas and assist in literary composition. London: Longman, etc. (Facs. edn London: Bloomsbury Books, 1992). [92, 107, 110, 112, 126, 134, 154, 288; T12]

Romaine, Suzanne, ed. 1998. *The Cambridge History of the English Language: 1776–Present-day* (Vol. IV). Cambridge: Cambridge University Press. [iv, v, 7, 8]

Ross, A. S. C. 1954. 'Linguistic class-indicators in present-day English'. *Neuphilologische Mitteilungen* 55:20–56. [37]

Rydén, Mats & Sverker Brorström. 1987. *The Be/Have Variation with Intransitives in English.* (Stockholm Studies in English, 70). Stockholm: Almqvist & Wiksell. [69–72, 158]

Savage, W. H. 1833. *The Vulgarisms and Improprieties of the English Language.* London: T. S. Porter. [26, 37, 55, 60, 63, 66, 68, 72, 78, 83, 86, 287; T6]

Schlauch, Margaret. 1959. *The English Language in Modern Times.* Warsaw: Polish Scientific Publishers.

Scragg, D.G. 1974. *A History of English Spelling.* Manchester: Manchester University Press. [46–9, 52]

Serjeantson, Mary S. 1935. *A History of Foreign Words in English.* London: Routledge & Kegan Paul. [110, 116–7]

Sheldon, E. K. 1947. 'Walker's influence on the pronunciation of English'. *PMLA* 62:130–46.

Shelley, Edward. [2]1848. *The People's Grammar; or English Grammar Without Difficulties for 'the Million'.* Huddersfield: Bond & Hardy. [13]

Shorrocks, Graham. 1996. 'Non-standard dialect literature and popular culture'. In Juhani Klemola *et al.*, eds. *Speech Past and Present. Studies in English Dialectology in Memory of Ossi Ihalainen.* Frankfurt/Main: Peter Lang, 385–411.

fc. 'The dialectology of English in the British Isles'. In Sylvain Auroux, *et al.* eds. *Geschichte der Sprachwissenschaften / History of the Language Sciences*. Berlin: De Gruyter.

Simpson, John A. 1990. 'English lexicology after Johnson to 1945'. In F. J. Hausmann *et al.*, eds. *Wörterbücher. Dictionaries. Dictionnaires.* Berlin: De Gruyter, II:1953–67. [96–7]

Smart, B. H. 1812. *A Grammar of English Sounds*. London: Richardson. [54]

1836. *Walker Remodelled: A New Critical Pronouncing Dictionary of the English Language*. London: T. Cadell. [59]

Smith, Olivia. 1984. *The Politics of Language 1791–1819*. Oxford: Oxford University Press. [20]

Sørensen, Knud. 1985. *Charles Dickens: Linguistic Innovator*. Aarhus: Arkona. [70, 93, 96, 137–8, 162, 294]

Soule, Richard. 1871. *A Dictionary of English Synonymes Designed as a Practical Guide to Aptness and Variety of Phraseology*. New edn revised and enlarged by G. H. Howison. London: F. Warne, 1891. [128]

Stone, Lawrence. 1969. 'Literacy and education in England, 1640–1900'. In *Past and Present* 42:69–139.

Strang, Barbara M. H. 1970. *A History of English*. London: Methuen. [38, 56, 62, 77, 80–2, 104]

1982. 'Some aspects of the history of the *be+ing* construction'. In J. Anderson, ed. *Language Form and Linguistic Variation: Papers Dedicated to Angus McIntosh*. Amsterdam: Benjamins, 427–74. [82]

Sundby, Bertil *et al.* 1991. *A Dictionary of English Normative Grammar 1700–1800*. (SHLS 63). Amsterdam: Benjamins. [1, 38, 70, 78–9]

Sutcliffe, Joseph. 1815. *A Grammar of the English Language. To which is Added, a Series of Classical Examples of the Structure of Sentences, and Three Important Systems of the Time of Verbs*. London: T. Cadell & W. Davis. [151–2]

Sweet, Henry. 1877. *A Handbook of Phonetics*. Oxford: Clarendon.

1884. 'On the practical study of language' *Transactions of the Philological Society*:577–84. [49]

1890. *A Primer of Spoken English*. Oxford: Clarendon. (^{3}1900 (based on his *Elementarbuch des gesprochenen Englisch*. Oxford: Clarendon, 1886).) [27, 50–2, 57, 62–4, 82, 87, 290; T24]

1891–8. *A New English Grammar, Logical and Historical*. Oxford: Clarendon. [18, 22–3, 24, 83, 290]

Taylor, Dennis. 1993. *Hardy's Literary Language and Victorian Philology*. Oxford: Clarendon.

Taylor, John R. [2]1997. *Linguistic Categorization. Prototypes in Linguistic Theory*. Oxford: Oxford University Press. [126]

Taylor, Watt. 1939. *Doughty's English*. (SPE Tract 51). Oxford: Clarendon. [95]

Tieken-Boon van Ostade, Ingrid, ed. 1996. *Two Hundred Years of Lindley Murray*. Münster: Nodus.

Tooke, John Horne. 1798. *The Diversions of Purley*. 2 vols. London. (Repr. Menston: Scolar (EL 127)). [76, 101]

Trench, Richard Chenevix. 1851. *On the Study of Words*. London: John W. Parker. (Facs. edn by Roy Harris, 1993). [22, 29, 47, 95, 97, 100–1, 105, 128]

   1857. *On Some Deficiencies in our English Dictionaries*. London: John W. Parker.

Trudgill, Peter. 1986. *Dialects in Contact*. Oxford: Blackwell.

Tulloch, Graham. 1980. *The Language of Walter Scott*. London: Deutsch. [103, 294]

Vicinus, Martha. 1973. 'Literary voices of an industrial town'. In Harold James Dyos/Michael Wolff, eds. *The Victorian City. Images and Realities*. Vol. VII. London: Routledge & Kegan Paul, 739–61.

   1974. *The Industrial Muse. A Study of Nineteenth-Century British Working-Class Literature*. New York: Croom Helm.

Vincent, D. 1989. *Literacy and Popular Culture in England 1750–1914*. Cambridge: Cambridge University Press.

Visser, Fr. T. 1963–73. *An Historical Syntax of the English Language*. 3 parts. Leiden: Brill. [82]

Wakelin, Martyn F. 1972. *English Dialects: an Introduction*. London: Athlone. ([2]1977).

   1988. *The Archaeology of English*. London: Batsford.

Walker, John. 1785. *A Rhetorical Grammar*. London: for the Author; facs. EL 266, 1971.

   1791. *A Critical Pronouncing Dictionary and Expositor of the English Language*. London: G. G. J. & J. Robinson and T. Cadell. (Facs. edn: Menston: Scolar, 1968 (EL 117)). [25, 54, 56–59, 63, 97, 101]

Walmesley, John. 1999. 'English grammatical terminology from the 16th century to the present' Art. 261 in Lothar Hofmann, *et al.* eds. *Fachsprachen. Languages for Special Purposes*. Berlin: de Gruyter, 2: 2494–2502.

Webb, Robert K. 1955. *The British Working-Class Reader. 1790–1848: Literacy and Social Tension*. London: Allen & Unwin. [21]

Webster, Noah. 1789. *Dissertations on the English Language*. Boston:

Isaiah Thomas. (Repr. Menston: Scolar, 1969).

1828. *American Dictionary of the English Language*. New York: Converse. [97, 103]

White, Richard Grant. 1880. 'English in England'. *Atlantic* 45:374–86, 669–79; 47:697–707.

Wilkins, John. 1668. *An Essay Towards a Real Character, and a Philosophical Language*. London; Facs. EL 151. [134, 288]

Wood, Robert, ed. 1967. *Victorian Delights*. London: Evans.

Wright, G.T. 1974. 'The lyric present: simple present verbs in English poems'. *PMLA* 89:563–79. [82]

Wright, Joseph. 1892. *A Grammar of the Dialect of Windhill, in the West Riding of Yorkshire*. London: Kegan Paul, Trübner.

1898–1905. *The English Dialect Dictionary*. 6 vols. London: Kegan Paul for the English Dialect Society. [vi, 7, 28, 98]

Wright, T. 1857. *Dictionary of Obsolete and Provincial English*. London: Bohn.

Wrigley, Edward Anthony. 1966. *An Introduction to English Historical Demography*. London: Weidenfeld & Nicolson.

1972. *Nineteenth-Century Society*. Cambridge: Cambridge University Press.

Wyld, Henry Cecil. 1921. *A History of Modern Colloquial English*. Oxford: Blackwell. (^{3}1936). [21, 58]

1934. *The Best English*. (SPE Tract). Oxford: Clarendon.

X [1819]. *A Critical Examination of Cobbett's English Grammar, in a Letter to a Friend*. n.p.

Zachrisson, R. E. 1914. 'Northern English or London English as the standard pronunciation'. *Anglia* 38:405–32.

1931/2. 'Four hundred years of English spelling reform'. *Studia Neophil.* 4:1–69. [46, 48–50]

Index of names

(for authors also check References)

Index of topics and titles

Index of selected words and pronunciations